Sugar and the Origins of Modern Philippine Society

Sugar and the Origins of Modern Philippine Society

JOHN A. LARKIN

University of California Press
BERKELEY LOS ANGELES LONDON

University of California Press
Berkeley and Los Angeles, California

University of California Press, Ltd.
London, England

Library of Congress Cataloging-in-Publication Data

Larkin, John A.
Sugar and the origins of modern Philippine society / John A. Larkin.
p. cm.
Includes bibliographical references and index.
ISBN 0-520-07956-6 (alk. paper)
1. Sugar trade—Philippines—History. 2. Philippines—Economic conditions. 3. Philippines—Social conditions. 4. Philippines—History.
HD9116.P61L37 1993
338.1'7361'09599—dc20 92-6325

Printed in the United States of America
9 8 7 6 5 4 3 2 1

The paper used in this publication meets the minimum requirements of American National Standard for Information Sciences—Permanence of Paper for Printed Library Materials, ANSI Z39.48-1984. ∞

To my many Filipino hosts
and to the late Donn V. Hart,
without whom . . .

There is no event in Philippine history which can be properly examined without constant reference to agriculture.

Harlan R. Crippen,
"Philippine Agrarian Unrest,"
Science and Society (1946)

Contents

Illustrations

Figures

Maps

Plates

Tables

Preface

Recently, the Philippine people have endured a series of harsh blows—from nature in the form of earthquakes, volcanic eruptions, killer typhoons, and floods and from the government through its mismanagement, abuse, neglect, and corruption. Such events have saddened me considerably, for during my many years of study in and about this country I have developed a great affection and admiration for its citizens. They have been open and hospitable to me, and I can only offer this book as a token of my appreciation. Here I try to explain in what I think is a sympathetic fashion how colonialism and the international export economy shaped their lives. Hopefully, with the ebbing of neocolonialism, Filipinos can put the larger control of their own destiny more to the service of the many. They deserve a better fate.

A book of this dimension could not exist but for the assistance of many friends and organizations. As always, the late Adelina Ventura and her children, now scattered to the winds, supplied a roof, encouragement, or a quick translation whenever I appealed to them. Norman Owen, Ben Kerkvliet, Yoshiko Nagano, and Ronald R. Edgerton read portions of the manuscript and gave me the benefit of their valuable comments. Sheila Levine eased the process of moving the manuscript along to publication, and Doug Perrelli patiently created meaningful maps from my imperfect directions. Dore Brown and Joanne Sandstrom did an excellent job preparing the manuscript for publication. Serafin Quiason, my *kabalen*, offered me special access to Pampanga and loaned me the services of the able Roland Bayhon to lighten the burden of archival work. Lina Concepcion not only opened the Philippine National Archives to me, she also listened sympathetically to the problems of a struggling researcher. And Janet

Baglier, my wife, did the major hand holding that saw this book to completion. It is customary to absolve the above for any errors in the text, and I do so; as well, there are certainly fewer mistakes because of them.

Others who supplied either materials, expertise, or moral support include the late Domingo Abella, John and Myrna Adkins, Marysol Aizpuro, Dorothy Baglier, Charles Bryant, Nita and Jim Burris, Linda Casper, Amado Castro, Rosendo Coruña (of SPCMA), Nicholas Cushner, Marina Dayrit, Noel de Paula, Eden Divinagracia, Evelyn Dizon, the late Fred Eggan, Oscar and Susan Evangelista, Doreen Fernandez, the late Frank Golay, Mitchell Harwitz, Namnama Hidalgo, Karl Hutterer, Natividad Jardiel, the residents of Jesuit House in Chicago, Carl Landé, Emma Larkin, Judith Larkin, Sarah Larkin, Sean Larkin, La Salle Brothers of Bacolod, Violeta Lopez Gonzaga, Stephen Moscov, Barbara Nowak, Mario Nuñez, Akil Pawaki, Kathleen Revelle, the J. B. L. Reyes family, Norman Schul, the Smith, Bell & Co. staff, Wilhelm Solheim, the late Tony Tan, and Pedro Tison.

Grants for time away from teaching came from the American Council of Learned Societies, the Center for Asian and Pacific Studies at the University of Hawaii, the U.S. Department of Education (Fulbright Office), and the State University of New York at Buffalo. The School of Economics at the University of the Philippines, Diliman, loaned me an office for a year and facilitated my interaction with its knowledgeable staff.

Unfailingly the staffs at the following repositories assisted me in my search for obscure materials: Newberry Library, Lilly Library, Lockwood Library (SUNY/Buffalo), Colgate-Rochester Divinity School Library, Harvard Library, Yale Library, Library of Congress, New York Public Library, University of Michigan Library, University of Hawaii Library, Cornell Library, Hawaiian Sugar Planters Association Library, University of the Philippines Library, Ateneo de Manila University Library, Philippine National Library, U.S. National Archives, and Philippine National Archives.

Finally, at a time when my spirits were especially low, Donn V. Hart gave me a much needed boost in morale that put me back on the track to finish. In his own ebullient manner he kept me on that track until the time of his death. For his caring ways and his contributions to keeping Philippine studies alive, I include him in my dedication.

One note on names and sources: with Spanish proper names and references I have used Spanish accents, but with Philippine names I have adopted the local practice that drops those accents.

Quezon City, January 1992

ONE

Introduction

Fortunes have been made in this Colony in cane-sugar.
John Foreman, *The Philippine Islands* (1906)

Sugar is chronically in oversupply, because it is one of the few products that can be produced in almost any country in the world.
Philippine Sugar Handbook (1972)

This book examines the influence of an export sugar economy upon the people of the Philippines through a study of its two most important sugar-producing areas. Although natives of the archipelago cultivated and chewed sugar cane before the coming of the Spaniards, the milling, consumption, and shipping abroad of brown sugar followed in the wake of the sixteenth-century Iberian conquest, when Catholic friars and Chinese entrepreneurs introduced the technology and created the first middlemen networks. Commercial sugar thus became intricately associated with the colonial experience. Eventually, the exporting of sugar brought the Philippines into direct contact with the outside world and provided a chief means for the introduction of new and foreign ideas into native society and culture. To a great degree, then, "sugarmen" shaped Philippine social and economic life. The main contention here is that the sugar industry had adverse effects on economic development, that it led to wide, harsh social and economic cleavages among the Filipino people, and that it skewed political power in the archipelago, in colonial times and later.

Social historians have commonly accepted the tenet that modern Philippine society and culture derived from the interaction between native traditions and Western ideas introduced through colonialism. They have acknowledged as chief vehicles of occidental penetration the Catholic religion and the American educational system, as well as the forms of government introduced by the two powers. Less well recognized, however, is the role of economic enterprise in the molding process, even though commerce has long been a staple of archipelago activity.[1]

Scholars, for example, have taken it for granted that commerce had minimal influence upon social life during the first two and a half centuries of Spanish occupation, when the tripartite galleon trade operated between China, Manila, and Acapulco.[2] This notion, however, is only partially correct, for, even in this early era, a pattern of foreign domination of export enterprise was already emerging. At this time, too, began the collaboration between members of the native elite and foreign merchants that has remained a characteristic of Philippine business ever since. This pattern of cooperation strongly informed the native socioeconomic structure and, subsequently, nationalist attitudes toward international and domestic affairs. The early choice, too, of sugar as a primary cash crop has played an important part in Philippine social development, for sugar production carries with it certain social ramifications that derive from its particular technology and from the nature of world market conditions.

Recent studies of the sugar cane industry in diverse regional and national settings have affirmed its role as a social determinant.[3] The methods of crystallizing sugar from cane syrup originated in India during the first millennium B.C.E., and Arabs subsequently introduced this technology to the Mediterranean world in the seventh and eighth centuries. The beginnings of the modern mass production–mass consumption market, however, date back to the seventeenth century, to the time of the formation of estates in the French and English colonies of the Caribbean. Here European planters used African slaves to grow cane and operate mills.

Slavery proved an expeditious system because of the peculiar labor needs of planting and harvesting cane. The two activities follow closely upon one another: the growing period for cane is about one year, and the new crop must go into the ground as soon as the old one leaves. Moreover, because cane begins to deteriorate immediately upon being cut, it must be delivered rapidly and in proper amounts to keep mills operating efficiently. The harvest season, therefore, is very busy, and only a large, well-disciplined labor force capable of toiling in the tropical heat can meet its demands. During nonpeak periods, just a fraction of those workers are required to weed and maintain the fields. Thus, unpaid chattels best fulfilled the requisites of this sector of the industry.[4]

Milling—a capital-intensive activity that utilizes machinery to grind the cane, boil the extracted syrup, and crystallize it into brown sugar—is the other component of sugar production. In various eras owners have employed animal power, windmills, waterwheels, and steam and electricity to run their factories. Mechanical advances have gradually reduced labor costs, enlarged grinding capacity, speeded up manufacturing, and improved the purity of the end product, thus yielding ever greater profits to mill owners. At the same time, because of the general availability of an abundant, cheap work force in tropical and semitropical climes, the invention of laborsaving field machinery has not kept pace with the technological improvements in milling. Only recently in places like Australia and Hawaii has sophisticated mechanical harvesting equipment come into use.[5]

During the eighteenth century, slave-produced sugar became a staple in the diet of Europe's expanding industrial labor pool. In the Caribbean world, sugar created a society of rich landowners and millers living with poor field hands in closed agricultural communities known as plantations. Over time the West Indian living pattern changed somewhat as more planters became absentee, but the socioeconomic dichotomy persisted in the manufacture of sugar. When the sugar industry spread to Africa, Asia, and Oceania, the legacy of slavery lingered on in the bifurcated income distribution of sugar societies. Sugar farming tended to find a niche in regions where the labor force could be turned to or coerced into doing field work for low wages. Henceforth, production became associated with extremes in social structure: the very poor who cultivated and cut the cane, and estate owners and millers who controlled the conversion of cane to sugar.

Sugar's status in the modern world economy helped perpetuate this social division. The sugar market faces two givens: first, sugar, which can be produced in numerous settings, is a taste additive rather than an essential food, and second, world sugar supplies have usually exceeded demand. Sugar is a sweetener and preservative, the carbohydrate sucrose extracted chiefly from sugar cane in the tropics and from sugar beets in more temperate climates. It enhances flavor in food but has little nutritional value. Sugar contributes much less to human food requirements than, say, cereal staples, so it can be sacrificed from the diet more readily than the latter in times of privation and high prices.[6]

Because so many countries historically have fulfilled their own need for sweeteners, only a few areas, chiefly North America, northern Asia, and Western Europe, have had to import large quantities of sugar during the past two centuries. From the early nineteenth century on, the expansion of European and American beet sugar cultivation has somewhat reduced the dependence of even those markets on cane sugar. As a result, world sugar supply, except during wartime, has matched or surpassed demand, and sugar has usually remained a buyers' market; moreover, attempts to form international sugar cartels have consistently failed. To stay competitive under such conditions, sugar exporters have faced two options: to seek privileged access to specific markets, the quantity of export sometimes adjusted downward by some kind of quota limitation, and/or to reduce production costs through investments in milling technology and minimal wages and thus eke out higher profits. Whether in capitalist areas like Hawaii and Louisiana, in colonies such as the Philippines and Java, or in the socialist milieu of Cuba, market forces have reinforced the old pattern of powerful mill owners and grossly underpaid field hands.[7]

Those who adhere to Immanuel Wallerstein's theoretical division of the "capitalist world-economy" into core industrial, semiperipheral, and raw material producing peripheral areas will identify the Philippines as a typical peripheral region given over to sugar production. Certainly that characterization aptly applies; however, visualizing insular society as structured like other peripheral areas offers only a partial view of its nature. Wallerstein's analysis refers mainly to political-economic formations and leaves out the social and cultural dimensions that specifically identify a human community; hence, such an approach will scarcely satisfy the concerns of social historians.[8]

The very diversity of the Filipino population makes it difficult to portray clearly the impact of the sugar industry. The early Philippines where sugar manufacture first took hold was not a unified society, but rather, several communities separated along ethnolinguistic lines. The great cultural traditions of India and China that had provided central organization and a common identity to other parts of Southeast Asia had not reached the sparsely settled archipelago, save for the southernmost islands, where Islam held sway. Spain managed to establish a uniform colonial government and to convert most denizens to Catholicism, but, because of the island nature of the country, regional variation—linguistic, ethnic and economic—has persisted ever since. How sugar affected such a heterogeneous population poses a problem for investigators.

A useful means of assessing the influence of the sugar industry upon Philippine society and culture resides in cultural ecology, a branch of anthropology that seeks to comprehend the creative way humans interact with their environment and the culture that results from those interactions.[9] Julian Steward points out that, as a means of understanding, cultural ecology rejects the contentions of human ecologists that the environment determines human adaptation, as well as those of anthropologists who regard the physical environment as far less important than cultural diffusion in shaping human adaptation. He maintains, rather, that "cultural ecology pays primary attention to those features which empirical analysis shows to be most closely involved in the utilization of environment in culturally prescribed ways."[10]

According to Steward, to understand the interplay between environmental exploitation and society, it is necessary to consider its "culture core," which he defines as "the constellation of features which are most closely related to subsistence activities and economic arrangements. The core includes such social, political, and religious patterns as are empirically determined to be closely connected with these arrangements."[11] He then describes the method to uncover the interaction between culture core and society:

> First, the interrelationship of exploitative or productive technology and environment must be analyzed. . . .
>
> Second, the behavior patterns involved in the exploitation of a particular area by means of a particular technology must be analyzed. . . .
>
> The third procedure is to ascertain the extent to which the behavior patterns entailed in exploiting the environment affect other aspects of culture.[12]

In the Philippine case cultural ecologists would conclude that the methods by which Filipinos produced sugar shaped to a large degree their cultural and social behavior, especially those aspects closely associated with the industry. In regard to millers and landowners, their capitalist outlook and extravagant behavior sprang from their control over and ownership of land and energy-efficient equipment. As for field hands, the way they cultivated cane as tenant farmers or plantation workers molded their social behavior and attitudes. Where tenancy and barrio communal living prevailed, a cooperative outlook developed that expressed itself not only in mutual assistance, but also in joint resistance to oppression. On isolated haciendas where wage labor dominated, social anomie and a sense of helplessness became the behavioral norm. Moreover, because the industry grew to such importance, in terms of political power, economic prestige, and the great number of people who participated in it, the attitudes of both rich and poor sugarmen spread throughout the archipelago. Hence, to understand the values and attitudes of Philippine society, one needs to understand something about the manner in which the sugar industry functioned.

Large-scale sugar production eventually spread to regions possessing diverse social and labor systems; therefore, the resultant sugar society exhibited considerable variation in structure, norms, and behavior. To describe change in all these places in any meaningful fashion would require a work of massive proportions; instead, I have opted to focus upon just two areas, northern Pampanga and western Negros. Besides encompassing the two largest sugar-growing regions in the country, they also had very different histories and social circumstances. Long-settled Pampanga benefited from its proximity to the colonial capital of Manila and began making sugar in the seventeenth century; Negros, more isolated, remained a wilderness until the opportunity to grow sugar led to its nineteenth-century transformation into a plantation economy. Landholders in the former area built their sugar agriculture upon a traditional patron-client relationship with their tenants; in contrast, newly arrived Negrense entrepreneurs exuding a frontier spirit established and operated haciendas through the more efficient, economical, and flexible use of paid labor. The determinants of the sugar market were common to both.

The sugar industry and Philippine society interacted in complex ways, and concentrating on two disparate local regions as well as upon the insularwide and international levels enhances comprehension of three dimensions of that interaction. First, examining what happened to Pampanga and Negros reveals the regularities in sugar's impact upon local farming areas. The development in both places of the classic pattern of very rich and very poor, millers and field hands, argues persuasively for the universal determinism of sugar in societal development.

Second, observing the contrasts between the two regions, even under the impact of sugar, indicates just how the original culture of each endured and continued to shape local society. Farmers could and did grow cane under differing systems of labor organization, and the degree of sugar's sway varied from place to place. Especially in Pampanga old traditions proved persistent. Moreover, ideas about society and social organization formed in the provinces sometimes affected the way people thought and acted at the insular level. In brief, the influence of the sugar industry did not move just one way.[13]

Finally, portraying broad changes in the industry focuses attention upon the emerging supraregional sugar elite, a small number of powerful and influential individuals and families, many of them from Negros and Pampanga. Because of their political clout and extravagance, derived from their ownership of vast lands and mills, they heavily influenced Philippine society, government, and economic life. On one hand, elite leadership at the local level encouraged the kind of regional identity and loyalty that has operated to the detriment of national political unity; on the other hand, their business and lobbying activities at home and abroad led to the acceptance of a national economic purpose on behalf of their industry. They forged social links in every sugar-growing area, and, through their interactions and business contacts with Europeans and Americans, they became internationalists. At the same time, their need to secure overseas markets strengthened the ties of dependency and neocolonialism that have characterized modern Philippine-American relations.

This book is not exclusively about millers and planters, however, but also about those who toiled physically in sugar factories and fields. They too contributed to the development of both regional and insular culture, for, although their individual voices were seldom heard, they expressed themselves collectively through their work and through figures who represented them in various ways. Sugar hands contributed ideas about social and labor organization, about cooperation in the accomplishment of tasks, and about resistance to oppression and exploitation. Those who articulated their laments and aspirations ranged from rural rebels and messiahs to labor bosses, intellectuals, and politicians. Sugar's contribution to Philippine society and culture, then, includes the thinking and acts of its poor.

I use the term "sugarmen" throughout the book because others in the Philippines have and do employ it to refer to those who participate in the industry. I do not mean to imply that sugar was exclusively a male preserve, however, for it was decidedly not so. Women, young and old, labored in the fields, especially during planting and weeding season, and they participated in family decision making on economic matters. Some women owned sugar lands in their own right, supervised work on their holdings, and made all kinds of investments from sugar profits. The sources, however, proved somewhat stingy in yielding specific information on the activities of women and children, for in the Philippines the tendency is for men to receive much of the public attention in all economic and political endeavors, even when others deserve a goodly share of the credit. So, while I have not been able to describe the particular impact women may have had upon the industry, let it be recognized that they played a substantial role.

Broadly speaking, modern historians of the Philippines have pursued their subject by adopting either a general or a local approach. With the first they have sought to form an overview of the progress of the Philippine state from its origins in the prehispanic, protohistorical past to its more integrated national present. This approach has chiefly emphasized political evolution, especially in the Manila capital complex and the surrounding Tagalog-speaking region. The other avenue has focused upon change in circumscribed, variously defined subregions within the archipelago. Theory has it that such studies, when available in sufficient number and then integrated, will provide a more comprehensive vision of the Philippine experience. So far, local historians have adopted mainly a socioeconomic perspective, paying some attention to geographic, demographic, and political detail.[14]

Each approach has served an important role in illuminating Philippine history, but both have their shortcomings. The first concentrates too narrowly on Manila-based happenings and assumes, as those who study national centers usually—and sometimes incorrectly—do, that capital events and politics serve as an accurate measure of the country's general development, mood, and sense of unity. The local studies, while concerned with occurrences in rural areas of a vastly agricultural country, have tended to be too region-specific and have merely provided samples of one. Furthermore, because each local history has stressed the unique aspects of its particular region, broad comparisons with other areas have proved awkward. The Philippines, in other words, is more than a nation in the making or the sum of its diverse regional experiences. A need exists for consideration of the ways the insular center and outlying regions have interacted and how and what influences have passed between them. A history of the sugar industry can offer a view of the linkages between the two spheres.

This book, then, is neither regional nor national history as heretofore done, but, rather, comparative and integrative history. Comparative history works best when the areas contrasted share common experiences. During the early centuries of Spanish occupation, Pampanga and western Negros bore little resemblance to one another; thus, I have treated the two regions during this time as distinct. However, in modern times, as their histories converged under the impact of sugar, I have intermingled the two accounts more. By looking at ways each area responded to insularwide forces, I have tried to add new insight into colonialism, the frontier, the Philippine Revolution, the independence struggles, and rural unrest, to understand better the diverse response of Filipinos to economic crises, political events, and social differentiation.

In the end, sugar created a native elite, prestigious and powerful who, despite their disparate provincial origins, acted together with the collusion of foreigners to shape the course of Philippine modernization. For more than a century and a half, sugar represented the most important and influential sector of an insular commercial life that this elite, with rare exception, exploited almost exclusively for their personal advancement. Their conspicuous consumption contributed not so much to the progress of the islands as to the outflow of cash and to the inequitable colonial economy. Among sugar workers the maldistribution of profits created not a consuming public but permanent pockets of poverty, and attempts to ameliorate their circumstances came mostly to naught.

In 1982, Philippine newspaper columnist Arlene Babst wrote the following about the contemporary elite, whom she called "eternal":

> I have been charged with belonging to this elite group myself. . . . The charge, to be fair, should be modified to the peripheries of such an elite group. At the risk of "treason" to this group, I must say that even one who has ties to it recognizes it

> as an enormous obstacle in the process of building a kinder society.
>
> This elite group has had more power than it should; more wealth than it has fairly worked for; more privileges than it deserves.
>
> It has failed as a social institution because it has not used its leadership to better the lot of the majority; sadly, it has consistently bettered mainly its own lot, not caring enough about that majority which sustains the elite.[15]

Sugar no longer steers the Philippine economy, but its legacy endures in a native elite largely insensitive to the needs of the underprivileged.

Pampanga and Western Negros

Since the mid-nineteenth century numerous regions of the Philippines have yielded export sugar, among them Batangas and Laguna provinces on Luzon, southern Negros Oriental, and the islands of Panay and Cebu. More recently, the Cagayan Valley of far northern Luzon, and Davao Province on Mindanao have become significant sources. The fields of Pampanga and Negros Occidental, however, have remained the two most consistently productive areas in the archipelago (see map 1).

The sugar lands of Pampanga and western Negros do not conform to any provincial boundaries; rather, they follow certain edaphic and terrain features of the Central Luzon Plain and Negros Island, respectively. In both places, where the soil is a sandy, friable loam and the grade not too steep, farmers have regularly planted cane for a century or longer. The Negros lowlands and Pampanga plain where sugar predominates comprise some of the finest and most extensive stretches of flat alluvial farmland in the archipelago.[16]

Pampanga's sugar area forms a rough triangle with its southern apex at a point where Lubao and Floridablanca, Pampanga, meet Dinalupihan, Bataan (see map 2). The western leg of the triangle follows the slope of the Zambales foothills as far as Barrio San Miguel in the capital of the province of Tarlac. The eastern line skirts the edge of the delta of the Pampanga River, follows the San Fernando River, bends toward the slopes of Mount Arayat (1,026 meters), then slants toward Tarlac. The northern cap encompasses the lands of Hacienda Luisita in Barrio San Miguel. Southern Tarlac was one of the last parcels of the Central Plain settled, and it still has the lowest population density in the area. Alongside the southeastern flank of sugar lands rise the Pampangan towns of the Pampanga River and the Candaba Swamp, very old communities where rice cultivation and fishing have long flourished. Even within the sugar area, because the lowest land has a hardpan suitable for growing rice, farmers possess a degree of

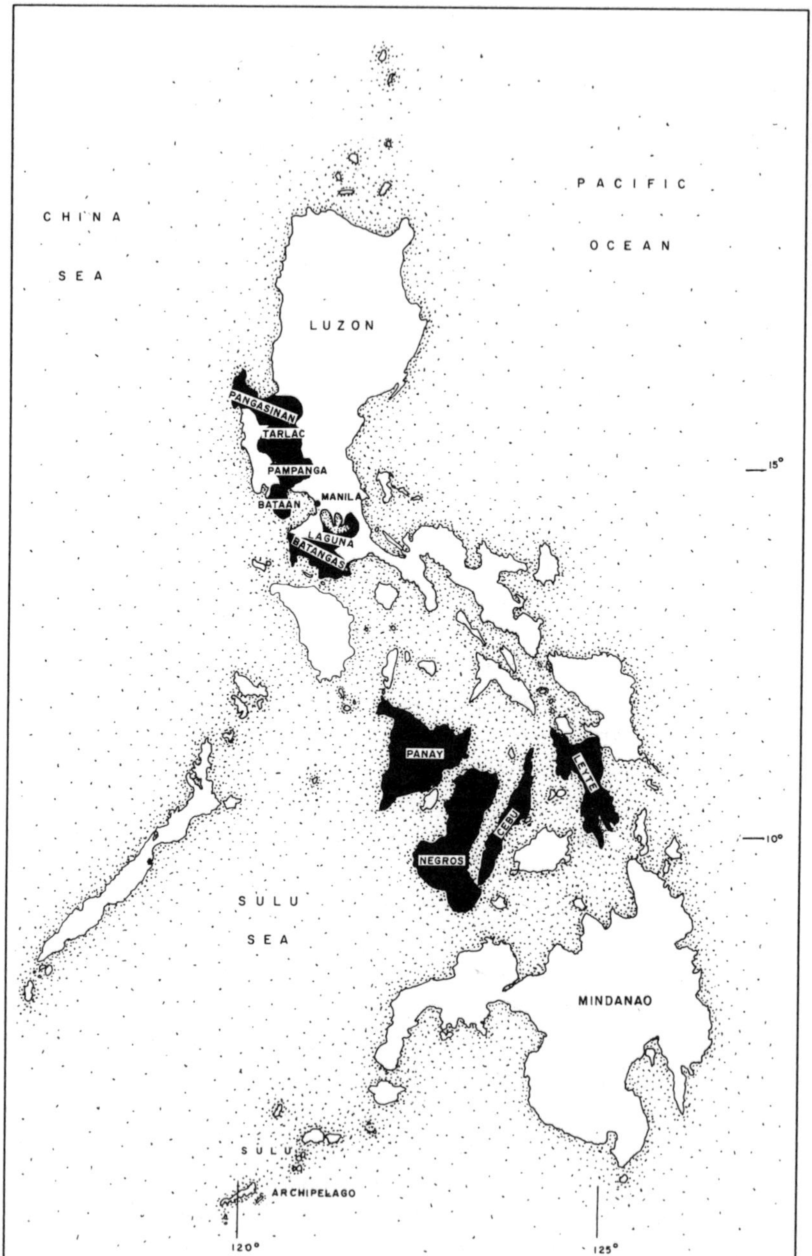

Map 1. Philippines, Major Sugar-Producing Areas, 1939

flexibility in what they plant and on occasion convert to cereal production when sugar prices fall too low. Hence, the expanse of sugar varies somewhat from season to season. In a good year such as 1970, planters devoted 53,291 hectares to the growing of cane to feed the three modern mills, or centrals, that service the region.[17]

The enormous debris from the 1991 explosion of Mount Pinatubo (1,610 meters) has altered somewhat the physical shape of the Pampanga region, but the effects have mainly been felt in the lowland rice-growing areas. Some sugar farmers have even reported better yields as a result of the fallout of pyroclastic materials.

Pampanga has long benefited commercially from its proximity to Manila. Early on planters and middlemen shipped their product in light sailing vessels called *cascos* down the shallow streams entering Manila Bay. In the late nineteenth century the main trunk of the railroad that runs north from the capital reached Pampanga. Subsequently, feeder lines branched out to meet the industry's needs, and since then the raw sugar has gone mainly by rail, either to the port, from where it is shipped overseas, or to refineries that supply the insular market.

The sugar region encompasses eighteen towns of Pampanga, four of Tarlac, and one of Bataan, where cane has been grown on a significant scale. Provinces in the Philippines break down into town-sized municipalities subdivided into smaller communities known until recent times as barrios (currently *barangays*). In central Luzon, as elsewhere, each town has its commercial, social, and administrative core, usually called the *poblacion*, where stand the Catholic church, the municipal hall, the more substantial residences of the rich, a covered or open air market, and bigger shops, arranged around or near a central green plaza.

Change, however, is coming rapidly to the Pampanga region. The traditional homes of the wealthy with their wood and stone construction and sliding capiz-shell windows have given way to modern houses of cement and stucco with glass jalousies. The growing trend in the area is toward residential subdivisions separated from the commercial districts. The three biggest communities—provincial capitals San Fernando and Tarlac, as well as Angeles, now an incorporated city—have a somewhat different layout with their chief activities spread along main streets, and they have lost the old-fashioned hispanic character of the smaller towns with their plaza complexes. The former U.S. installation of Clark Air Force Base contributed to the distinctive character of Angeles.

In the barrios, usually comprising from one hundred to three hundred families, reside most of the workers in the area, including the tenants who actually grow the cane. They live chiefly in airy nipa palm and bamboo

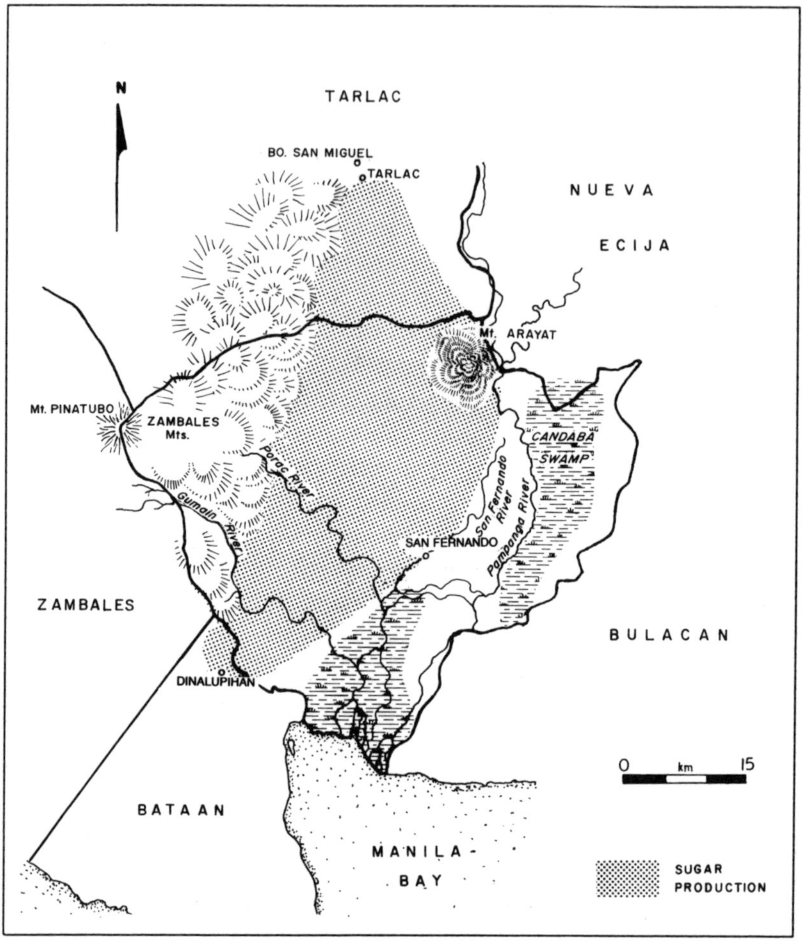

Map 2. Pampanga, Major Physical Features

houses and obtain their everyday necessities at small stores called *sari-saris*. Better-off farmers might have electricity, and a new feature of the countryside is the more permanent cinderblock house with metal sheet roof purchased with "Saudi money" earned abroad by the adventurous Capampangan. Within the past two or three decades barrios have become much more crowded, for Pampanga has the second highest density among all the provinces in a populous country. The 1980 census revealed that for the first time urban residents in Pampanga outnumber rural ones.

All the towns have in common a central place where barrio folk visit to transact business, to socialize, and to find entertainment. Communities in Pampanga are accessible by a strong network of local, provincial, and

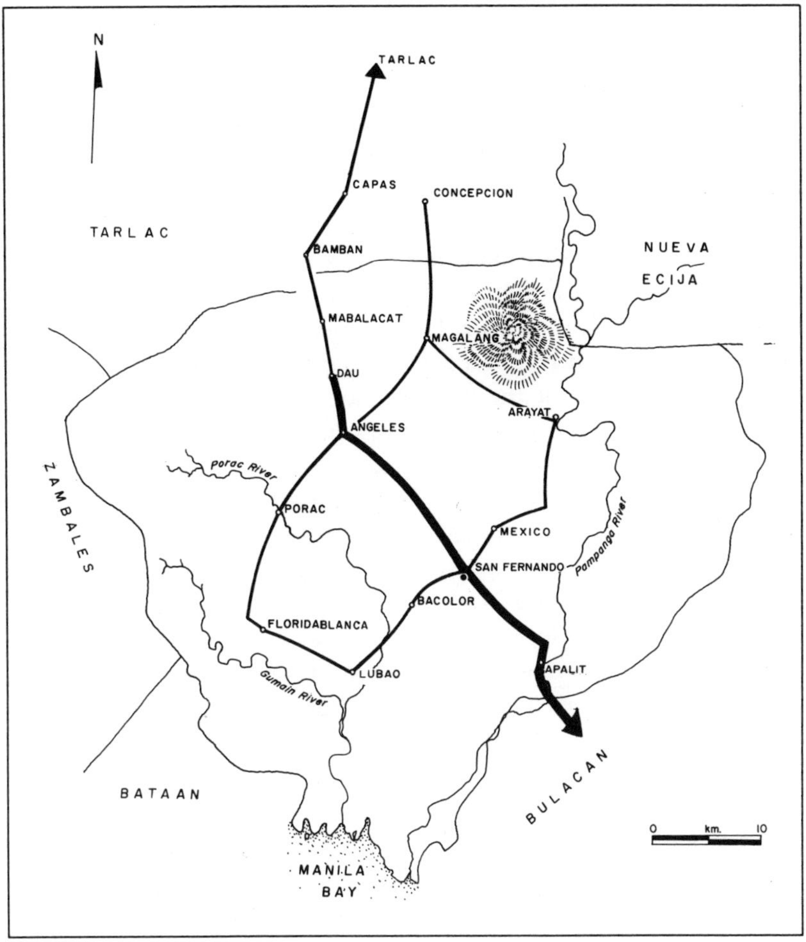

Map 3. Pampanga, Main Roads

national roads over which stream jeeps, buses, tricycles, and horse-drawn *calesas* that make travel easy and fairly inexpensive. The many roads and short distances between settlements have facilitated strong social interaction among the local denizens. The predominant language here is Capampangan, one of several important regional dialects in the country; however, one also hears the national language, Pilipino (Tagalog), spoken, especially in town centers. In Tarlac, Capampangan is interspersed with the Ilocano spoken by descendants of settlers from the northern Ilocos area who joined migrants from Pampanga on this nineteenth-century frontier.

The northbound expressway out of Manila passes by San Fernando and Angeles, bisecting the heart of sugar country; near Barrio Dau the highway becomes a typical provincial road as it proceeds toward more rural Tarlac. Arteries off this central highway offer entree to old towns with many fine examples of colonial architecture, as well as to barrios large and small (see map 3). In such communities people tend to be outgoing and curious toward strangers. Two things are likely to strike the contemporary observer: the myriad children one sees everywhere and the variety of economic activity. The province possesses not only a dense population, but a young one as well. The imperative of maintaining an economy for the many seems clear, and to meet that need enterprising Capampangan have sought numerous solutions in the face of a currently depressed sugar industry. Interspersed among the still extensive sugar fields are paddies, now double cropped and planted with strains of the "miracle rice." Padi dries everywhere, on cement roads, in house yards, and on basketball courts, and seed beds turn deep green with new seedlings. Piggeries appear frequently on roadsides, as do retail and repair shops and fruit and fresh coconut (*buko*) stands. Perhaps sugar will revive one day; in the meantime, the rice, pigs, housing subdivisions, and stores suggest that the Capampangan avidly seek to diversify their agricultural economy.

On Negros Island a forest-covered central mountain spine dominated by the dormant volcano Mount Canlaon (2,465 meters) separates the western from the eastern coasts (see map 4). Numerous rivers flow down the sides of this chain of peaks, carving deep cuts and providing irrigation and alluvium to the crop lands below. Gradually rising plains surround this cordillera from the northeast to the southwest, and where the slope is not too steep farmers plant their cane. The flatest sections of the coastal littoral drain too poorly for sugar, and there farmers grow rice or other crops; but not far inland, from Kabankalan to San Carlos, stands an almost continuous band of fields that identifies Negros as the premier sugar region.

Almost all the sugar lands lie within twenty-two municipalities of Negros Occidental[18] and the portion of Vallehermoso, Negros Oriental, that belongs to the San Carlos mill district. In 1970 Negrense hacenderos devoted 190,592 hectares to sugar cane—more than three times as much as did the Capampangan—which they shipped by truck or narrow-gauge railway to the region's thirteen centrals. Western Negros lacks good harbors, and before World War II exporters shipped mainly from Iloilo across the Guimaras Strait on neighboring Panay; however, raw sugar now reaches its overseas destinations via lighters that transport it from the long pier at Pulupandan or from the wharves along the shallow coastline near several centrals to oceangoing vessels off shore.

Bacolod serves not only as the capital of Negros Occidental, but also as its hub of commerce, entertainment, and transportation. While five other municipalities—Silay, Cadiz, Bago, San Carlos, and La Carlota—boast the status of incorporated cities, only Bacolod truly seems like an urban center. A sprawling market area with a variety of shops and restaurants abuts the large central plaza with its big church and other religious buildings. The city contains colleges, one of the most impressive provincial capitols in the archipelago, and the local offices of the major planter organizations; furthermore, its hotels, movie houses, and other amenities attract visitors from all over the region. From one of its several terminals commence all journeys through sugarlandia (see map 5).

Travel through Negros proves more difficult than through Pampanga because of the greater distances between communities, the poorer road system, and the less frequent, more expensive public transportation. A two-lane highway parallels the shore slightly inland all the way around the island, and through sugar country is mostly macadamized. Off that trunk, feeder roads and paths, frequently gravel and dirt, head inland. Since their main traffic is cane trucks, they become rutted, and access to and from most haciendas is best accomplished by private vehicle.

A highway running northeast from Binalbagan makes it possible to drive through the middle of sugar country. Part hard surface, part gravel, the highway passes through fields of tall cane that block the view on both sides. In the midst of this overwhelming expanse rest the quiet, spare towns of Isabela and La Castellana, for most of those who own land in the vicinity either reside on their haciendas or elsewhere. Not far beyond La Castellana the hills start to rise, and the road crosses the central chain near Mount Canlaon and connects with the main highway along the east coast just above Vallehermoso. From there it is only a short distance to the busy mill town and port of San Carlos.

Along this portion of the coast live speakers of Cebuano, revealing their origin on the neighboring island of Cebu. Only as one proceeds toward the great northern shelflands does the language gradually shift back to the Ilongo of the western Visayas, the dominant tongue in Negros sugarlandia. The northern cap contains large fertile tracts with the highest cane yields in the whole region. This section from San Carlos to Victorias, with its mixture of languages, its rich soils, its timber stands and newer towns, reflects its frontier status as recently as seventy years ago. The cathedral at Silay and the quiet Spanish plaza of Talisay with its stately homes and church offer a contrast to the structures in later-settled northern Negros. The closed sugar mill on the outskirts of Talisay not far from Bacolod serves as a reminder that the sugar industry currently faces a serious economic crisis.

While Negros Occidental has traditionally broken down into the same municipalities and barrios as Pampanga, sugar workers (*duma'an*) in the former area do not usually live in barrio communities but on haciendas in

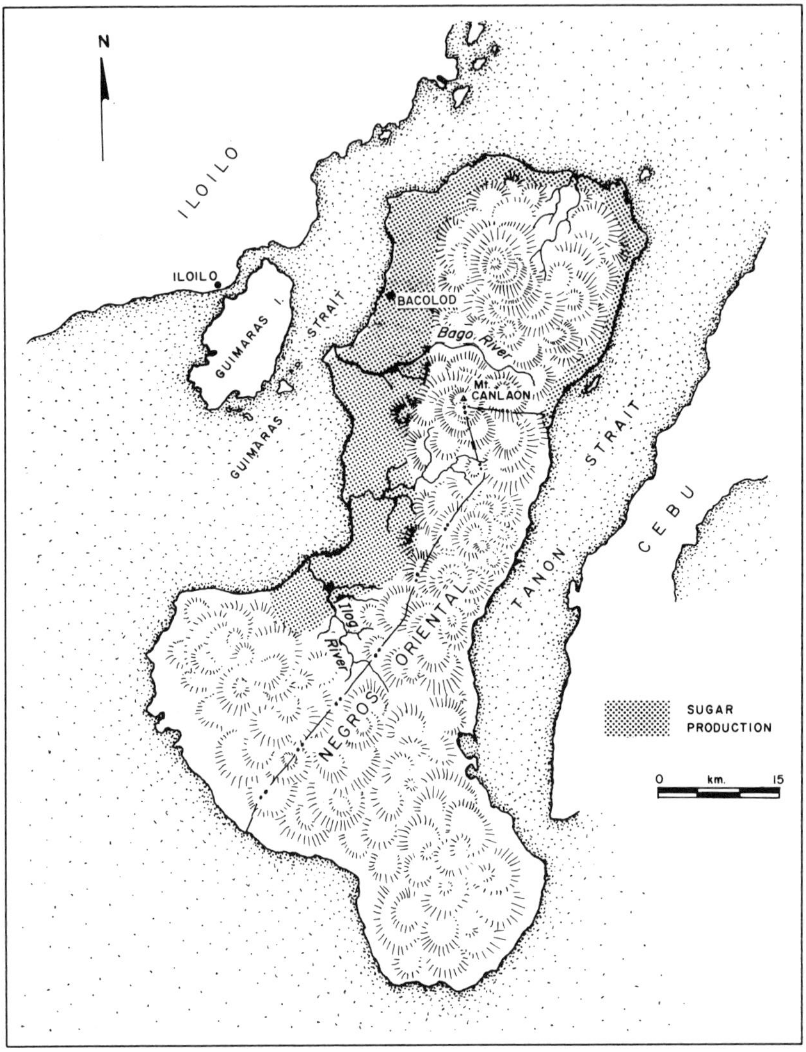

Map 4. Negros Occidental, Major Physical Features

the immediate vicinity of their employment. Such plantations vary in size from as small as five hectares to as large as many hundreds, and their borders do not necessarily coincide with any political boundaries.

Ruttan described the hacienda, a typical one, on which she undertook research in 1978, in the following manner:

> From the town plaza of Murcia, a sand and gravel road passes through several haciendas and leads after three kilometers to

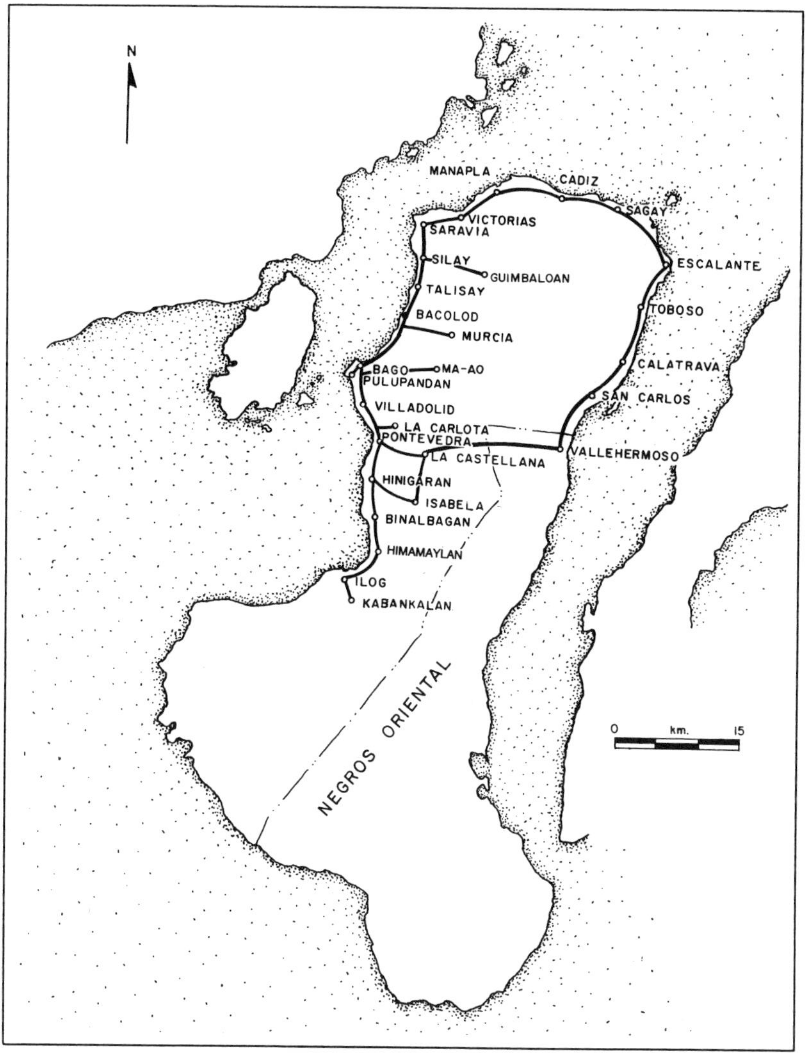

Map 5. Negros Occidental, Main Roads

Hacienda Milagros. A large acacia tree marks the place where the road splits in two, continuing to the left through other haciendas and entering Hacienda Milagros to the right. There is no gate or fence, but the boundaries of the property are known to all who live on its grounds. Two concrete buildings are situated close to the entrance. One is the warehouse (*bodega*) where the tractor and cane trucks are parked, the implements and sacks of fertilizer are stored, and where the small office is

> housed. It is the central place of the hacienda: here each morning the laborers assemble for the assignment of daily work, and here the weekly payment of wages takes place. The other building is the *sacada* house . . . , the living quarters of the migrant laborers during milling season, and partly occupied by the security guard and his family. Behind these buildings some twenty-two bamboo and *nipa* houses line a narrow, winding path. There are the houses of workers and salaried employees—the overseer and timekeeper, foremen and drivers. Across the fields on the northern side of the hacienda is a second group of ten houses built along a river, while a third cluster of six houses lies further downstream. Eight more houses lie scattered in the hacienda. Vegetables and fruit trees are grown in the small, well-kept yards. The house lots border on the sugarcane fields, and when the cane stands tall it hides the houses from view.[19]

Sugar laborers rarely leave the haciendas, for their workdays are long, and they can buy most necessities in shops on the premises. Their isolation, their strong dependence on their jobs, and their constant supervision by management personnel have made the duma'an shy—more so than the sugar tenants or *casamac* of Pampanga. Only recently have conditions in Negros become so harsh that on a number of estates some duma'an have resorted to protest and to union organizing. Nevertheless, the strongest opposition to landlord control remains among those who have joined the New People's Army (NPA) on the fringes of sugarlandia or among the political demonstrators in the streets of Bacolod.[20]

Hacenderos, at the same time, seem more outgoing and gregarious, usually eager to defend the vaunted Negrense way of life, by which they mean the planter style of doing things. Planting consists of borrowing from the bank enough money to have others place a crop in the ground in hopes of gaining great profits. If the balance sheets look good, spend those profits lavishly; if they look bad, borrow more and replant. These hacenderos perceive themselves as gamblers, forever ready to raise cane if credit is available; however, they do not appear as willing as the Capampangan to gamble on alternate investments to sugar. Despite a recent tightening of bank funds in the face of poor overseas market prospects, despite a deterioration in the quality of the soil, and despite the mounting threat of the NPA, the majority of Negrenses remain committed, more so than the Capampangan, to the monoculture that has sustained them, identified them, and shaped their way of life since the nineteenth century.

No matter how else the hacenderos from Negros and Pampanga differ, they respond alike to the physical elements that have long determined their agricultural calendar. Pampanga and western Negros have similar growing seasons susceptive to an annual weather cycle prevailing throughout tropical Asia. Usually the southwest monsoon begins to blow in May and brings an increased amount of moisture, frequently in the form of torrential rains, to fields left dry by the prevailing northeasterlies. The rains abate in November, and farmers commence the harvest of cane planted the preceding year.[21]

From the dissipation of the southwest monsoon until mid-May, gangs of workers take to the fields where they laboriously cut, trim, and load the cane onto assorted vehicles—carts, trucks or tram cars, depending on the location of the hacienda and on the milling district—for transfer to centrals. The cane reaches the central according to an intricate schedule designed to avoid backlogs that would allow the sucrose-laden stems to deteriorate. What complicates this process is that the Philippine sugar industry is structured differently from that in other countries, for the central operators do not, for the most part, own or manage the majority of farm property in their districts. Rather, these lands belong to numerous private planters who contract with the mills to process their cane for a share of the finished raw sugar. Thus, each central must arrange its grinding to accommodate the harvesting timetables of its numerous clientele.

Meanwhile, the emptied fields must be replowed, harrowed, fertilized, and planted once more with foot-long cuttings from the tops of the cane. In some select fields the stubble is cultivated, and another crop grows from the stools, a process known as ratooning. Later on, the young cane crop requires weeding and cultivating to assure good growth, and farmhands pass along the rows several times with plows and hoes accomplishing those chores. With the overlap of planting and harvesting that necessitates a large manual labor force, even women and children find employment in the fields. Planters also normally hire temporary workers from neighboring regions to cut and load cane.

During six or seven months each year, life in sugarlandia revolves around the frenzy of making raw sugar, but in May the pace slackens. As the southwest monsoon reasserts its domination, field work comes to a close, most mills shut down, and migrant laborers return home. All that remains of activity are the repairs around the haciendas. While the next crop matures, even the business of marketing sugar lags.

For those who still plant and mill cane the seasonal rhythms are old ones.

TWO

Foundations, 1565–1835

A riddle in the village goes like this: The head is downwards while the tail is upwards. The answer is sugar cane.

Historical Data Papers, Barrio San Pedro, San Simon, Pampanga (1953)

Although the sugar industry achieved a foothold in the Philippines between 1565 and 1835, it had little impact on native society and commerce. Sugar became a part of Filipino diet and a minor component of local and overseas trade; however, Spanish disinterest in cash crop farming and modest world demand hindered growth. Despite slow development, at the end of this era the industry was preparing for more rapid expansion. Knowledge of basic techniques of sugar production improved, new plantation areas began to open, and export houses appeared in Manila. By the early nineteenth century, Philippine sugarmen were poised to take advantage of improved international market conditions occasioned by the onset of the Industrial Revolution and revised colonial economic policies.

From Sugar Cane to Sugar

Prehistoric immigrants to the archipelago brought with them techniques for growing cane, but only in colonial times did sugar production and commercial uses for sugar develop under foreign tutelage. *Saccharum officinarum*, true sugar cane, has many relatives of the botanical family of tall, internoded grasses called *graminaceae*—cogon, talahib, and tigbao, for example—that grow wild all over Southeast Asia and the Pacific islands. It appears that at some indistinguishable time in the past sugar cane was domesticated somewhere in Southeast Asia and taken by Austronesian-speaking migrants to the southern Philippine Islands. From there its cultivation and use gradually extended northward.[1] Precolonial inhabitants of the islands chewed it as a treat or as a means of assuaging hunger. Mothers employed it as a pacifier for babies, and children ate it mixed with rice. When the fourteenth-century traveler Wang Ta-yuan visited the archipelago, he observed that natives in different places had acquired the skill of turning cane juice into wine. Perhaps this was the same process, described by Jesuit missionary Francisco Alzina in the seventeenth-century Visayas, of fermenting in Chinese jars cane juice mixed with a special tree bark to make an alcoholic beverage called *intus*. This traditional method of fermentation was preserved into the twentieth century by aboriginal Bacobos of Mindanao, who used a wooden press to express juice. Such a press, or one like it, may have originated in prehispanic times, but natives in the islands also extracted juice from some varieties of cane simply by beating two stalks together.[2]

What the early *indios* (native inhabitants) did not do was make sugar. When Magellan arrived in 1521, natives in the Mindanao area offered cane to his crew as a refreshment, while Spanish explorers of the Cagayan Valley in northern Luzon received similar gifts in 1591. But not sugar. Sugar was among the items of resupply requested from Mexico by members of the first permanent expedition to the archipelago in 1565. From 1571, when Manila became the established place of Spanish settlement, until the first decades of the next century, Chinese traders regularly imported sugar to the colony. The idea of manufacturing sugar and its byproducts came to the Philippines along the route of colonial conquest: across the Atlantic, via the Azores and Canaries; to the Caribbean; on to Mexico and South America; and finally, across the Pacific.[3]

Little information exists on how sugar technology initially entered the Philippines. Presumably Spaniards, who had a great taste for the sweetener, encouraged its domestic manufacture to save the considerable import cost from China. Methods of expressing juice from cane between two horizontal wooden rollers, boiling it down in earthen vessels, and crystallizing it were widely known in China and around the Mediterranean Sea, so that either Chinese or Spaniards, or possibly both, could have brought these techniques to the Philippines. Spanish friars played a considerable role in setting up sugar plantations in the first decades of the seventeenth century, and gradually, sugar making spread throughout the archipelago, first to Luzon and then to the Visayas. Local sugar slowly replaced the Chinese imported product, and as the Philippines became self-sufficient, the price dropped appreciably during the seventeenth century.[4] A kind of brown sugar, called *panocha*, crystallized in coconut shells with the aid of lime water, is still made today in the countryside and may date back to these early times. With increasingly widespread knowledge of how to derive sugar came a corresponding rise in its consumption by the indigenous population, especially the ruling class. Even before midcentury one Spaniard, Juan Diez de la Calle, noted that sugar abounded in the islands and served as evidence of native wealth; meanwhile, Moro (Muslim Filipino) sultans served cakes and preserves sweetened with cane syrup as a treat to special guests. Natives learned also to concoct a kind of sugar brandy, probably *basi*, and by the early eighteenth century, so widespread had its use become that the Spanish government felt obliged to forbid production of this beverage.[5]

While making ordinary sugar for home use spread generally throughout the archipelago from the mid-seventeenth century on, fabrication of more highly refined grades was restricted to the religious estates near Manila and to Pampanga Province. By 1708, estates like San Pedro Tunason and Makati produced pilon sugar, that is, sugar crystallized in clay molds, freer of the molasses found in more common grades of the *muscovado* type. Augustinians in Pasay and Jesuits in Nasugbu were making higher grade sugar by at least the 1740s, and the latter maintained warehouses on their property so that they could hold their product back until prices reached a high in Manila.[6] Processing of commercial grades of sugar may have gone back to the late seventeenth century in Pampanga, although specific references to that industry do not appear before the eighteenth. There native farmers grew cane and may even have undertaken the first stage of producing sugar, but Chinese merchants dominated the marketing end of the business, and in 1729 a Spanish governor of the province complained that the Chinese bought all the produce of the area so that they could resell it in Manila.[7]

Once sugar reached the capital city, no matter from where, the Chinese monopolized its processing and sale. They turned sugar into candy and syrup for drinks (e.g., *azúcar rosado*, a beverage made with caramelized sugar and citrus juice) and packaged it for the slowly growing export trade in native products. A census of Manila Chinese establishments in 1745 noted that the sugar dealers' guild consisted of sixty stores, and the sweetmakers' guild contained twelve.[8] At its inception, then, the commercial end of the Philippine sugar business came under the control of foreign hands with native participation only at the level of primary production.

The Philippine sugar industry has always depended on external market conditions for its progress and profit, and during the first two centuries of colonial domination Spaniards focused their attention on the renowned trans-Pacific galleons, ignoring the development of indigenously based economic endeavors. The galleon trade, sanctioned as a compromise between mercantile interests in Spain and the Philippines, turned Manila into an entrepôt, a place to exchange highly valued Chinese textiles and wares for Mexican silver, with profits in the archipelago going chiefly to the resident foreign community of Spaniards and Chinese. The Spanish crown remained amenable to maintaining the Philippines as a religious responsibility supported by its more profitable colonies in Latin America. Native produce had little role in this officially sanctioned commerce, although some sugar made its way onto junks returning to China.[9]

But Philippine international commerce did not consist only of what the Spanish government officially allowed; a substantial amount of semilegal and illegal trade also occurred, and Philippine goods found a minor outlet through these clandestine channels. Distance from the mother country made official supervision weak, and colonial servants learned ways to profit from overlooking the strict rules of colonial commerce. By the mid-seventeenth century, European vessels, including Dutch and British, visited Manila, and the British East India Company (BEIC) sent its first ship, *Seahorse*, in 1644, inaugurating trade on a more or less regular basis beginning in the 1670s. *Seahorse*, on its return to India, carried samples of Philippine sugar, and small quantities of it went into cargos of later BEIC voyages. By the 1750s, Nicholas Norton Nicols, a naturalized Spanish subject living in Manila, pointed out that substantial quantities of Philippine sugar reached both the Coromandel and Malabar coasts of India, Bengal, Persia, and China.[10] The early pilon sugar industry in the archipelago met those needs.

Still, the sugar industry could not grow beyond certain limits because Mexican silver, the currency of Asian trade, remained the chief object for ships coming to Manila. As late as 1789, export of Philippine sugar did not exceed 30,000 piculs, or 1,898 metric tons, per year, and even in 1819 birds' nests still outranked sugar in value as an export item.[11] Not until the Spaniards altered their economic policy and international demand for sugar picked up could sugar production really expand. These changes began to take place only toward the end of the eighteenth century. By midcentury falling demand for oriental textiles in Mexico and Spain started the Manila galleon traffic on its long decline toward cessation in 1815, a victim of its own anachronistic nature and the Latin American wars of independence.

To compensate for this decline and to put the Philippines at last on an economically independent basis, the government initiated several reforms following the British occupation of Manila (1762–64). Under a series of progressive governors, Spain sought to break the galleon near monopoly of Philippine international commerce, to encourage the growing of local agricultural produce for export, and to keep profits from this new trade in government coffers. In 1785 Governor José Basco y Vargas created la Real Compañía de Filipinas, designed to link private and government capital to foster a trade within the empire that trespassed even on the hitherto sacrosanct trans-Pacific route. But this endeavor ultimately failed because of a lack of interest and sound management. For example, while foreign merchants were exporting 14,892 tons of sugar between 1786 and 1802, the company shipped only 509 tons. Basco also established in 1781 la Sociedad Economica de Amigos del País de Manila to foster a new interest in, and publications about, agricultural crops, but again, lack of sustained concern defeated this project. One of the few tangible results of the society's efforts toward promoting sugar was an 1878 manual by Francisco Gutiérrez Creps on the art of growing and producing the sweetener.[12]

The increased international demand for sugar that followed upon the Industrial Revolution stimulated the rise in production. As a result of a petition of la Real Compañía de Filipinas, ships of foreign registry began legally to trade in Asian goods at Manila in 1790, thus inaugurating a process of fully opening the port to international commerce by 1834, when the company's charter ended. Initially, the chief beneficiaries of this new policy, as far as the sugar trade was concerned, were Americans who sought new sources of sugar and molasses for their tables and rum distilleries because the British West Indian market had been closed to them following their war of independence. By the mid-1790s, ships from the Atlantic ports, particularly Salem, Massachusetts, frequented Manila; and throughout much of this decade a resident American merchant, John Stuart Ker, acted as broker for U.S. vessels, procuring the cargos of sugar they carried home. As a result of greater sugar consumption among their workers, the English, too, increased their trade and established their first commercial house in Manila in 1809. By the 1820s, England had seven firms at the port, and America one; meanwhile, Americans began consular service in 1817, and the British followed in 1844. These two nations became the chief trading partners of the Philippines and remained so throughout the rest of the nineteenth century.

While figures on sugar export for the first quarter of the nineteenth century remain fragmentary, it appears that sometime in the second half of the 1820s sugar began a climb in output that continued more or less unabated until the end of the nineteenth century (see table 1). The official opening of Manila to world commerce in 1834 did not stimulate this rise; rather, the conclusion of the Napoleonic wars and the subsequent freeing up of shipping, as well as a growing demand for sugar in the United States and England, seem to have been the main causes. In 1836 sugar surpassed rice, abaca, and indigo as chief Philippine export and became one of the mainstays of the economy, a condition that has persisted until recent times.[13]

Table 1. Philippine Sugar Exports through 1835

Year	*Export (metric tons)*
Before 1780	less than 1,898 in any year
1789	ca. 2,846
1796	ca. 4,744
1786–1802	avg. 1,058
1813	949
1818	911
1828	7,276
1829	7,592
1831	13,432
1835	11,777

Sources: Manuel Buzeta, O.S.A., and Felipe Bravo, O.S.A., *Diccionario geográfico, estadístico, histórico de las Islas Filipinas*, 2 vols. (Madrid: José de la Peña, 1851), 1:222; Manuel Azcarraga y Palermo, *La libertad de comercio en las Islas Filipinas* (Madrid: José Noguera, 1871), p. 135; Tomás de Comyn, *Estado de las Islas Filipinas en 1810: brevemente descrito* (Madrid: Imp. de Repullés, 1820), p. 10; María Lourdes Díaz-Trechuelo Spinola, *La Real Compañía de Filipinas* (Sevilla: Escuela de Estudios Hispano-Americanos de Sevilla, 1965), p. 269; [Henry Piddington], *Remarks on the Philippine Islands and Their Capital, Manila, 1819 to 1822: By an Englishman* (Calcutta: Baptist Mission Press, 1828), p. 76; Yslas Filipinas, *Estado que manifestan la importación y exportación de esta ciudad en todo el presente año . . .* (Manila: n.p., 1818), p. 4; Angel Martinez Cuesta, O.A.R., *History of Negros*, trans. Alfonso Felix, Jr. (Manila: Historical Conservation Society, 1980), p. 365; Ramon Gonzáles Fernández and Federico Moreno y Jeréz, *Manual del viajero en Filipinas* (Manila: Est. tip. de Santo Tomás, 1875), p. 185.

Up to 1836, even as foreign trade developed, the manner of making and delivering export-quality sugar changed little from what it had been in the preceding century. Innovation came from China around 1800 with the introduction of stone vertical rollers in place of wooden ones and iron cauldrons (*cauas*) in place of earthenware ones; otherwise, the sugar business remained as American supercargo Nathaniel Bowditch described it in 1796 when he purchased a cargo of sugar in Manila for his ship *Astrea.*[14]

In most Philippine provinces output was small. The sugar was of poor texture and was mainly for local use; nevertheless, a few areas, particularly the Luzon provinces of Pampanga, Bulacan, Pangasinan, and Tondo, earned a good reputation for their product. The former was the most highly regarded for the quality and quantity of its pilon sugar, made from a high yield, deep red local cane. The success of these regions came in large measure as a result of their proximity to Manila, the center for sugar refining and the only sizable market for consumption of high-grade sugar.

In these provinces, cane, squeezed between stone rollers turned by *carabao* (water buffalo), released a juice that, when boiled sufficiently in a series of cauldrons, turned into a thick syrup that was poured into conical clay pilones. There, with the aid of stirring and some lime water, the mixture crystallized into a hard substance, a brownish yellow blend of molasses and sugar. Between November and June, traveling agents of refiners purchased pilones, each weighing about 63.5 kilos, from farmer producers and transported them in cascos down the main rivers and streams of Luzon, into Manila Bay, and on to the port area. At small refineries, called *farderias*, usually operated by Chinese but occasionally by a Spaniard, claying took place. Pilones were broken and sugar separated, the best grade being repacked in new molds. The sugar was then tamped, covered with a thin layer of special clay, and treated with water. As fluid seeped downward, the molasses dripped from a hole in the bottom of the mold into a container below, leaving a purer product, slightly gray on top with a yellow layer underneath. Once the sugar achieved its best color, the pilon was broken and the finest grades separated and dried in the sun; later the finished product was poured into sacks which, when filled, weighed one picul of 63.25 kilos, standard measure of the sugar trade. Merchant refiners stored these bags in warehouses (*camarines*) where they awaited sale to foreigners, usually from European and American houses supplying ocean-going vessels. Darker grades could either be reboiled, reclayed, or sold at home, since inhabitants of the Philippines made ample use of various kinds of sugar in their diet.

Another kind of Philippine muscovado, called "mat" sugar, achieved only minor importance in external trade before the 1840s, but found some outlet, mainly to China, Singapore, and Macao. Produced all over the archipelago, but especially in the Visayas, it sold for two-thirds or less the price of pilon sugar, because it was more heavily laden with molasses. In processing mat sugar, cane was passed between wooden rollers and boiled in cauas. Once lime was added to the thickened syrup, final crystallization took place on wooden tables. After drying, the sugar, dark brown in color and resembling a doughy substance, was placed in *bayones* (buri palm leaf bags of exceptional water resistance) weighing from eighteen to thirty-two kilos each, which were transported to Manila for repackaging and reshipment. Later on, an improved mat sugar garnered a much larger market share as worldwide sugar refining patterns changed, but in the 1830s pilon sugar dominated the trade; moreover, the government took special effort

Table 2. Sample Sugar Prices for First and Second Grade Export Sugar from Manila, 1796–1836 (pesos per picul)

	Price	
Year	*First Grade*	*Second Grade*
1796	7.00	4.50
1817	6.00	5.00
1818	9.00	6.50
1820	8.00	—
1830	7.50	6.00
1834	4.75	4.50
1836	5.25	—

Sources: Thomas R. McHale and Mary C. McHale, eds., *Early American-Philippine Trade: The Journal of Nathaniel Bowditch in Manila, 1796*, Monograph Series, no. 2 (New Haven: Yale University Southeast Asia Studies, 1962), pp. 29–47; Andrew Stuart to Secretary of State James Monroe, May 30, 1817, U.S. Consular Reports, Manila, U.S. National Archives; [Henry Piddington], *Remarks on the Philippine Islands and Their Capital, Manila, 1819 to 1822: By an Englishman* (Calcutta: Baptist Mission Press, 1828), p. 76; Andrew Stuart to Secretary of State John Q. Adams, April 20, 1820, U.S. Consular Reports, Manila, U.S. National Archives; Ramon González Fernández and Federico Moreno y Jeréz, *Manual del viajero en Filipinas* (Manila: Est. tip. de Santo Tomás, 1875), p. 238; *Centenary of Wise and Company in the Philippines, 1826–1926* (n.p.: n.p., n.d.), p. 101.

to preserve the quality of the product. In 1818, an ordinance passed in Pampanga prohibited adulteration of pilon sugar with darker grades.[15]

Because of market conditions, Philippine export sugar fell in price between 1796 and 1836, as indicated by figures in table 2. Some rise seems to have occurred about the end of the Napoleonic wars, before peacetime shipping fully returned, but, after that, prices did not revert to earlier levels because of changed circumstances in the sugar industry.

Pampanga

One of the first places the Philippine sugar industry took hold was Pampanga. Leaders of Pampangan society early on agreed to participate in the colonial order and duly benefited from that collaboration. The prehispanic social system was restructured and the population mobilized in the service of the native elite and the Spanish establishment. The contractual labor arrangement that resulted proved adaptable to the needs of the sugar industry as it began to exert an impact on the province.

Archaeological evidence indicates the existence of long prehispanic settlement in Pampanga, and when the Spaniards reached Pampanga, they

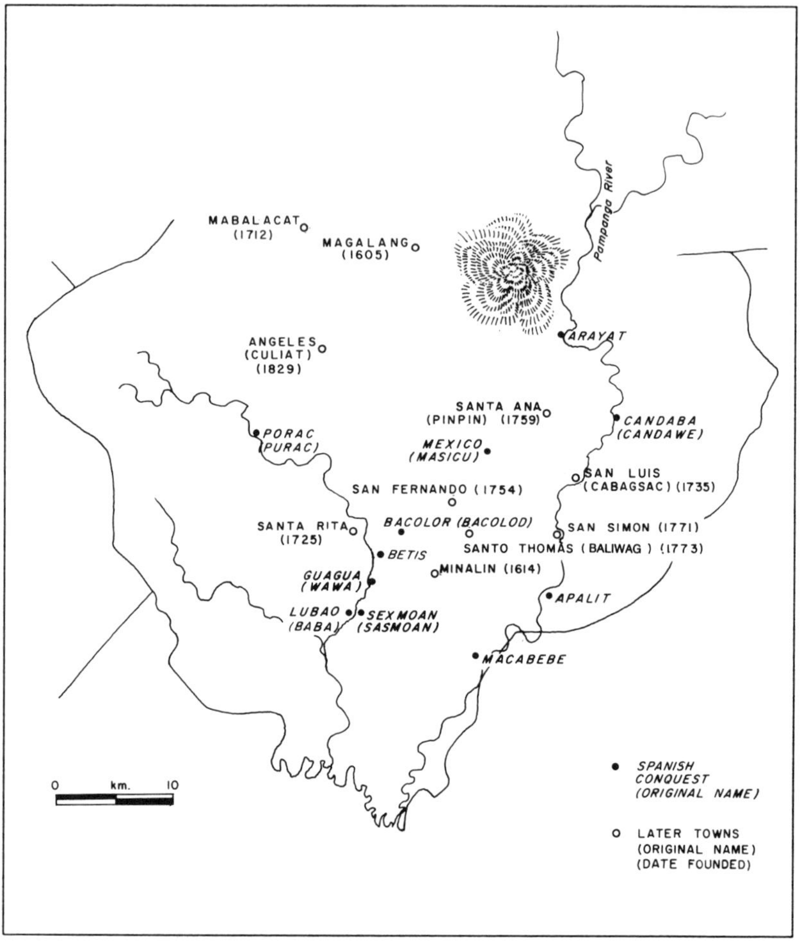

Map 6. Settlement in Early Pampanga

found at least eleven communities along the banks of the Pampanga River system (map 6). The name of the area, indeed, derived from the Capampangan word *pangpang* meaning "riverbank," and people of the region largely earned their livelihood from that body of water. The river nourished their crops, especially their rice; provided them with fish; and offered them access to interior jungles as well as to Manila Bay and beyond. In the course of their habitation of some of the best grain-producing land in the Philippines, Capampangan developed advanced agricultural techniques, knowledge in the working of brass, and navigational skills that took them to trading emporia of the Malay archipelago. Their use of imported ceramic wares indicated fairly constant commercial intercourse with merchants originating from the ports of southern China. In addition, Pampanga maintained contact with other parts of the islands through exchange of its excess rice for cotton needed in weaving local cloth. By the late sixteenth century, the delta had become sufficiently populous that Capampangan had moved up feeder streams to Masicu (later called Mexico) and Porac, thus extending their sway onto more elevated, drier portions of the great plain.[16]

Europeans encountered this aggressive and skilled people who dominated a fertile edge of the great forest covering the Central Luzon Plain and began reshaping their social structure and refocusing their economic activities. In 1574 Pampangan warriors were enlisted to defend Manila against depredations of the Chinese pirate Limahong (Lin Feng), thus initiating a tradition of more than three hundred years of military service to the Spanish regime. Subsequently, Spaniards employed their most trusted mercenaries to suppress rebellious natives and riotous Chinese residents, to guard the citadel of Manila, and to make war against the Moros of Mindanao and Sulu. In addition, Pampangan regiments fought overseas, in the Moluccas and Marianas in the seventeenth century and in Vietnam in the nineteenth. Such service brought substantial rewards to their leaders in terms of officers' commissions, even the exalted rank of *maestre de campo*, and, for a rare few, assignment of an *encomienda*, a tax-collecting sinecure almost never granted to indios. The most renowned Pampangan soldier of the seventeenth century, Maestre de Campo Don Juan Macapagal, received such an encomienda of three hundred tributes in 1665.[17] Military use of Capampangan provided an early occasion for collaboration between the native elite and the colonial regime, and other opportunities followed.

The Spanish government initially divided wealthy, strategic Pampanga into encomiendas; however, the malfeasance and ineptitude of early Spanish encomenderos made the system unworkable, so the crown moved to institute civil government. Small private encomiendas, like the one to Macapagal, continued to be bestowed until the mid-eighteenth century, but only for recognition of extraordinary service or for maintenance of charitable causes. After the early years of conquest, governance and major tax gathering in the province became the duty of an *alcalde mayor* (governor), a Spanish appointee of the governor-general, who served in both an executive and a judicial capacity.

Within the province indigenous personnel assumed substantial administrative responsibility because few Spaniards served there. With the disappearance of most encomenderos in the seventeenth century, only an alcalde, parish priests of the Augustinian order, and a handful of soldiers constituted the Spanish government community—in effect the whole of European society—for a law, on the books from the sixteenth century to

1786, prohibited Spaniards from living outside Manila, unless in an official or religious capacity. Spaniards in Pampanga never numbered more than fifty before the second half of the nineteenth century, and control of municipal government passed largely into the hands of gobernadorcillos and cabezas. Under the colonial system, parish priests exercised civil as well as religious authority; nevertheless, priests had to serve in very extensive parishes spread out over many square kilometers containing settlements often difficult to reach. Moreover, between 1773 and 1854 Augustinians did not even hold the Pampangan parishes, because of a clerical dispute with the bishop in Manila. During this time native secular priests represented the clergy, and by 1848 the total number of Iberians in this province of some 140,000 people had sunk to nineteen.[18] A native leadership thus possessed ample opportunity to maintain jurisdiction over the population, collecting taxes, assigning corvee duties, administering justice, and, in general, serving as buffer between the ruling Spaniards and the bulk of the Capampangan.

Mutual self-interest fostered the close collaboration between native leaders and Spaniards during this long era. Spain needed the military and logistical support of the Capampangan, and the local elite took up colonial service in order to continue their prehispanic leadership. In the old Pampangan barangay, authority had resided with the datu, a person exhibiting military, judicial, and administrative ability. The datu presided over a community of lesser datus, freemen (*timaua*), and debt slaves in which agricultural land was communally owned and distributed on the basis of need. Members of the community owed labor obligations to the datu in exchange for his leadership, provided he could sustain his authority by virtue of his strength and ability; he could be replaced by another datu if he lost his power.[19]

Sudden intrusion by Spain altered the old basis of authority, and the more ambitious among the datus readily adapted to the new order. Under the colonial regime, loyalty to the government became the main criterion for tenure, and chiefs could perpetuate themselves and their heirs in office merely by delivering goods and services and by not giving offense. In exchange for meeting their quotas, for facilitating native conversion to Catholicism, and for promoting peace and order, Pampangan leaders earned colonial recognition: the inheritable title of *cabeza de barangay*, head of a group of tribute-paying families. The new position offered its holders numerous advantages, most crucial of which was assurance of continuity. In addition, the cabeza received for his efforts, along with a title, exemption from certain taxes, corvee obligations, and legal liabilities. As a result of administrative reorganization near the beginning of the seventeenth century, the new position of *gobernadorcillo* came into existence, the highest office a native Filipino could aspire to under Spanish colonialism. This official, selected from among and elected by cabezas of a given *pueblo* (municipality), was ultimately responsible for delivery of the town's tribute. Gobernadorcillos and cabezas in each town of Pampanga became the dominant class in native society, and they and their families became collectively known as the *principalia*. Principales were addressed as "Don" and "Doña." Although the principalia became a ubiquitous institution in the archipelago, those in Pampanga were especially noted for their reliability and devotion to Spain.[20]

During the seventeenth and eighteenth centuries, the principalia converted their political authority into social and economic dominance of Pampanga as well. They used their tax-gathering power and their control of the Spanish system of labor obligation, *repartimiento*, to reduce the population to share tenants working on lands controlled by the elite. A two-class society, made up of those in charge who monopolized positions and wealth and those who furnished labor for principalia and colonial needs, gradually replaced the more complicated prehispanic society with its various gradations of class, rank, and labor obligations. In each town of the province, a group of families, perhaps a dozen or so, achieved this higher status and perpetuated it with Spanish acquiescence. In exchange for a guaranteed source of goods and services, Spaniards allowed native leaders to control the means of supply, and the population as a whole remained relatively free from colonial interference.

In 1784, perhaps the most astute observer of the techniques by which the elite perpetuated their position, the great reformist governor-general José Basco y Vargas, toured the province and recorded his findings in a decree issued on March 3 at Arayat.[21] In it he noted that farmers could have their implements and draft animals seized as payment for civil debts and that they could be imprisoned for debt during planting, plowing, and harvesting time, even if such incarceration meant loss of their crop. He saw cabezas and former gobernadorcillos avoiding all work on their farms, making others do the labor for no wages, even though legally only those who possessed eight cabalitas (2.24 hectares) of land were exempted from manual work. Principales also rented out land, an illegal practice. Basco observed widespread use of the *samacan* contract as well. Under this arrangement, a landowner and a laborer (*casamac* or *aparcero*) agreed to farm land on shares, the owner lending seed, food, and money to carry the worker through the season, with repayment coming at harvest time. Basco understood that great abuses occurred under this system because owners charged high interest on loans, forcing their tenants into chronic debt. Moreover, they loaned tenants rice when the price was cheap and demanded repayment in cash when the rice was dear. By these various methods the elite kept the lower class as the permanent underpaid labor force of the province.

Basco also described the process by which principales acquired control of most land in the province, the *pacto de retrovendendo* (pacto de retro, or pacto, for short). Through this contract, land was sold for less than its true value, but with the proviso that the seller had the right to repurchase within a specified time limit, with the addition of an interest charge. In essence this arrangement amounted to a way of pawning land to raise cash; however, the system was subject to much abuse, including excessive interest charges. Moneylenders employed the pacto de retro as a means of taking land from poor farmers.

But the pacto de retro was only the latest method for obtaining farmland; other practices had been going on for two centuries. When Spaniards first arrived, they claimed all land in Pampanga for the crown, but because of early datu support, they received large tracts as a reward. The government ceased bestowing such favors after 1626, and all other territory in the province remained royal lands or communal lands to be held by natives in usufruct, rather than in fee simple.[22] In other words, farmers and householders could take up agricultural and residential plots that, theoretically, when vacated became available for reassignment. Such lands could not be bought, sold, or otherwise alienated without court permission. In practice, however, the Pampangan elite acquired real property, purchasing, selling, and renting it out on shares to casamac without ever obtaining a formal right to do so; and they also gained the legal skills to defend their claims in court. Furthermore, they added to their landholdings by picking up, again without official permission, household lots in payment for debts. The principalia thus institutionalized a system of private ownership of land, even though based on faulty legal titles, despite Spanish attempts to maintain a communal system of property control.[23]

Finally, Pampangan officials enriched themselves by abusing the repartimiento system. They inflated the Spanish labor requirements, exempted their friends and kin from service, and charged others, mainly poor farmers, fees to avoid such obligations, which interfered with the latter's own vital agricultural activities.

Basco, ever anxious to increase output of Philippine produce to cut the dependence on imported silver, decreed that the above inhibitions to good farm practice should cease. He was especially concerned about the abuses in Pampanga, for it remained the most productive agricultural region in the Philippines. Despite his decree, however, the practices continued unabated, for they had become part of the provincial way of life, and the Spanish government had neither the will nor the personnel to alter the situation. By this time, samacan had become the main labor system of the province as well as an enduring form of social organization. Basco failed to realize the paternalistic characteristics of the system: tenants looked to their landlords for various kinds of assistance, social and economic, as well as for protection from the abuses of colonial authority.

The elite of Pampanga derived originally from prehispanic datus, particularly those who most cooperated with the new regime. From the few extant lists of town officials, there appears a marked continuity in the families that composed the earliest principalia down to about the middle of the eighteenth century, when a new group began to infiltrate elite ranks. Mestizos descended from early Chinese migrants to the province began to assert themselves, first as an economic factor, then as a political and social force when they intermarried with the indio governing class.[24]

A Chinese community throve in Pampanga after 1603, when merchants fled there following a massacre of their compatriots in Manila. The refugees established themselves in Guagua, chief outlet for the province to Manila Bay, and entered into commerce in produce that flowed to the Spanish capital from central Luzon. Being mostly single males, the Chinese took native wives, and in time, a mestizo society developed, first in Guagua, then in its economic satellite and capital of the province, Bacolor. By the mid-eighteenth century, Chinese mestizos formed a distinct community in those two towns where they organized their own *gremio*, a separate legal category under Spanish law, with their own chosen leaders (*capitanes de mestizos Sanglayes*). In a setting remote from the sources of Chinese culture, mestizos began increasingly to assume the culture of their native mothers, while remaining, initially at least, in business rather than farming. First they acted as collecting agents for established merchants of Guagua, buying, for example, the sugar that ended up in the farderias of Manila. Eventually, mestizos took commercial leadership when Chinese were excluded by law from the province between 1766 and 1849. Mestizos moved more and more into agriculture, too, as they made loans to farmers directly and through the pacto de retro, finally ending up as landowners themselves. They entered the ranks of the elite, partially as a result of their acquiring land and partly through intermarriage with the traditional indio ruling class, and from the late eighteenth century on, the principalia of Pampanga became increasingly Chinese mestizo.

The early emergence of commercial agriculture and cottage industry in Pampanga facilitated this rise to power and position. In the period from the Spanish conquest to the 1830s, rice persisted as the chief export of the province, providing the population with their main source of wealth; however, other products—sugar in particular, but also añil, cotton, oil of ajonjolí, fish from the Candaba Swamp, woods, palms, fruits, and vegetables—offered additional income. Descriptions in 1819, 1833, and 1860 stress the variety of crops shipped from Pampanga, as well as the wide range of local manufacturing pursued there, much of it for the interprovincial market. Among other activities, Capampangan made pottery, including water and sugar jars; built boats and other items out of wood and rattan; wove and embroidered fabrics; operated distilleries and limekilns; and did primary processing of the province's agricultural produce. Throughout the first half of the nineteenth century Pampanga's considerable wealth derived from this broad range of industry, with sugar only gradually assuming a primary role.[25]

As noted earlier, Pampangan sugar probably began to enter the export trade in the seventeenth century and became an important part of that commerce by the mid-eighteenth. Before 1786 Pampanga was already the largest sugar-making area in the Philippines, averaging between 1,150 and 1,288 metric tons per year; by 1796, output had climbed to 2,045 tons. In the early nineteenth century, Pampanga and Pangasinan together produced more than 7,000 tons in one year, more than 2,000 of which entered the foreign market, and sometime around 1838, sugar surpassed rice as the province's major cash crop. Farmers grew cane and made muscovado in most of the river towns until the upper region opened up to settlement in the mid-nineteenth century, and the center of the industry slowly migrated north. As sugar farming expanded, mestizos benefited most, first as agents for Chinese merchants, then as separate middlemen buying on their own account, then as credit suppliers to those switching from rice to sugar agriculture, and finally, as owners of sugar lands and makers of sugar. While sugar production in Pampanga showed a pattern of gradual increase, the 1820s and 1830s appear to have been a time, too, of active road and bridge building in Pampanga, due in part to the initiative of mestizo sugar planters eager to improve their access to markets and to interior portions of the province where new plantations sprang up.[26]

Demographic shifts in Pampanga during those two decades reflected the northward advance of population and sugar cultivation. Mabalacat, Magalang, and Porac, still on the frontier edge of settlement, grew very rapidly, as did most other towns that devoted considerable land to cane. Candaba was known for its mixed economy of fish and vegetables that derived from its swampy lowlands and that found their way to Manila's burgeoning markets; however, the town's residents turned its western elevated, drier portions to sugar. The general provincial trend was movement of people and sugar farming away from the river.[27]

Angeles provides a dramatic example of change. The community started to develop in 1796, when Don Angel Pantaleon de Miranda directed his servants and tenants to begin clearing land for cultivation in that remote northern place. De Miranda, former gobernadorcillo of San Fernando and a soldier by trade, removed permanently to Barrio Culiat with his wife Doña Rosalia de Jesus in 1811 upon his retirement from the service. Once there, de Miranda and Doña Rosalia supervised the growth of the new settlement, establishing the first church and primary school; at his instigation, Culiat became the municipality of Angeles in 1829. In 1822 he built the first muscovado sugar mill in town, as well as the first alcohol distillery. De Miranda's heirs married local Chinese and Chinese mestizos, and the progeny of these unions became the principalia of the newly founded town, providing the leading officials and landowners in succeeding generations. Angeles remained the fastest-growing community in the province throughout the rest of the nineteenth century.[28]

Negros

While Pampanga experienced considerable change socially and economically in the years between the coming of Spain and the 1830s, Negros showed little growth. At the beginning it might have been different. Between 1565 and 1571, the lieutenants of Miguel Lopez de Legazpi moved about the Visayas in search of a permanent base within the archipelago, first trying Cebu, then Arevalo on the island of Panay. Had either sufficed, Negros, known initially as Buglas, would probably have been transformed into a major supplier of food and a thriving agricultural community. As it was, the lure of gold, access to China, and abundant available food in the surrounding area dictated the choice of Manila, thus determining Pampanga's transformation and Negros's continued somnolence. Lack of good anchorage contributed to the colonial government's paucity of interest in and late development of the latter area. Spanish officials largely ignored Negros from that time on, and its way of life stagnated until demand for sugar radically changed everything more than two and a half centuries later. Isolation marked the intervening years.

Spanish pilot Esteban Rodriguez circumnavigated the island in 1565 and provided the earliest firsthand information on life in western Negros. He confirmed a story circulating among Spaniards that many Negritos inhabited the island, but he learned they resided chiefly in the mountain interiors, while the coastal lowland belonged to people of Malay ethnic background who practiced the common Visayan custom of tattooing their bodies.[29] Negritos so fascinated early Spaniards that they called the island "Negros" after them, allowing the original name to lapse. The new name exudes a certain irony, for the nonaggressive Negritos, whose sole economic role lay in trading small amounts of jungle exotica for staples, kept largely to themselves and never constituted more than a minority of the island's population.

Initial Spanish visitors to Negros had to tramp inland some distance to find settlements of Visayans, even though they noticed people along the shore as they sailed by. They came upon only one exception: a single large community situated where the mouth of a river, possibly the Himamailan, opened out on the Guimaras Strait. The position of most settlement inland and the reaction of fear or hostility the Spaniards encountered from inhabitants indicated that the people of Negros had experienced frequent difficulties with outsiders, probably Moro slavers, who raided Visayan shores.

Denizens of western Negros already depended on agriculture in 1565, and Rodriguez came across rice fields, while in a native vessel he found rice, yams, and fish. At this early period communities clustered along banks of rivers emptying out on the western and most populated side of the island toward Panay, and soldier-writer Miguel de Loarca observed in 1582 that these places produced much rice, swine, and fowl. Farmers could well have employed wet rice techniques, for they had the right terrain, ample water and, probably, some knowledge of the methods of paddy farming.

But Negrenses probably practiced dry rice agriculture as well, especially the swidden type, in areas away from rivers and on less even ground. Francisco Alzina, the great Jesuit commentator on seventeenth-century Visayan life, though not specifically mentioning Negros, did point out that slash-and-burn agriculture predominated in his time. Evidence suggests that wandering people of ethnic Malay origin farmed dry rice in the southwestern highlands and in forested interiors behind the sedentary coastal and riparian communities. Here they raised crops on temporary fields and gathered forest produce which they traded in the lowlands for cloth and other necessities. Known by such names as Carolanos, Bukidnons, Monteses, Mangyans, Mondos, and Ambaks, the most mobile bands have survived in less accessible portions of Negros for centuries, continually defying those who would change their way of life.[30]

An apocryphal version of the founding of Hinigaran goes as follows:

> As far as could be determined, the earliest people in these localities were the semisavage Mondos and Ambaks. Traders in sailboats from Panay used to land at [Barrio] Talisay to replenish their food and water supply and brought back to their home island (Panay) stories of the potentialities of fishing and farming in the land they had visited. Slowly but steadily Ma-

> lay settlers from Panay came and drove the Mondos and Ambaks to the interior. The latter called the intruding settlers "taga Higad," vernacular for "by the side," meaning those who were beside the sea.[31]

Such a story portrays the nature of the original settlement of western Negros, for that side of the island showed cultural, economic, and linguistic affinity with Panay from at least the time of the first Spanish observations of the place. For socioeconomic interactions, western Negros has always looked to Panay, eastern Negros to Cebu, because the waters of the Visayas have served as a link between people, and the mountains have kept them apart.

The pattern of Spanish neglect emerged at the onset of colonial rule, and by the beginning of the seventeenth century, Negros's position within the Empire had solidified; it stayed almost static over the next two hundred fifty years. A *corregidor* (military-political commander) at Ilog, first appointed sometime between 1608 and 1618, represented colonial authority on the island; tax payments in kind continued going directly to Panay until 1734. In that year, Spain transformed all of Negros into a single administrative and revenue collection district with its capital, or *cabecera*, at Ilog.

Corregidores seem to have done little to promote better conditions; however, these officials had some excuse for their inactivity, because they faced, without much help from Manila, frequent devastation from Moros who ravaged coastal areas as late as the nineteenth century. Each corregidor after 1734 had a military officer to assist him with defense; still, protection remained inadequate on the west coast, for throughout most of the eighteenth century the government stationed hardly any troops on Negros. At least some corregidores faced the Moro threat by removing to Iloilo, leaving the general population to escape danger by either fleeing temporarily or moving permanently into the interior.[32] The government left Negrenses without any real means of improving their welfare and with imperfect guarantees for their personal safety.

What little support Spain provided came chiefly from the Church. At any given time, from their parishes in the coastal lowlands, a small group of priests, sometimes members of friar orders, at others Spanish or Filipino seculars, offered sacraments, served as missionaries to the wandering peoples, and supplied comfort after Moro raids. From the 1770s until almost the mid-nineteenth century, native priests held responsibility for five very large parishes, including many *visitas*, that stretched from Cauayan as far north as Silay.

The vast expanse of these parishes meant, necessarily, that pastoral care was attenuated, and one Spanish commentator, Robustiano Echaúz, reported as late as the 1850s the persistence and prevalence, even in the lowlands, of many old Visayan superstitions and religious practices. Religious care on Negros, although more consistent and substantial than government services, proved deficient because of inadequate commitment on the part of the Church. The attitude of both Church and government in western Negros through the 1840s is reflected in that up until then not a single stone church or permanent public building existed in the region, so that Spanish Catholicism and royal authority were represented only by structures of the most perishable materials.[33]

Agricultural conditions on Negros scarcely showed any real change before the 1840s either. A government report of 1739 revealed that the island still met its tax obligations largely with the same produce as that shipped in the sixteenth and seventeenth centuries: rice; cabo negro, a palm fiber woven into ship's cable; and a variety of forest products. When the Frenchman Jean Mallat wrote about Negros in the early 1840s, he indicated that only a small crop of cacao and some coffee and tobacco were being planted in elevated areas behind the lowlands. On the plains, farmers still harvested mainly rice and some tobacco, cabo negro, and abaca, paying their government tribute in kind in these commodities. In some years harvests were so poor that alcaldes had to plead for understanding in the delayed collection of tribute, as happened during a long spell of bad times from 1832 to 1835. The only commercial activity on Negros involved some cottage industry weaving of such native fabrics as *lompotes* and *sinamay*, commissioned by great mestizo cloth merchants from Molo and Jaro, on Panay.[34]

Life in western Negros remained brutish and insecure up through the 1830s. Pillaging by Muslim marauders, hostilities with the mountain folk, and government neglect made habitation in the area dangerous for the indigenous population and lacking in amenities for foreign colonials. The first Moro raid reported in colonial times came in 1599, although they had probably occurred before the Spaniards arrived as well. Periodically thereafter Moros plundered the coastal settlements in search of goods and slaves, usually destroying what they could not carry away. Attacks appear to have happened most frequently in the second half of the eighteenth century, declining in the nineteenth. As late as 1829, however, Moros captured a hundred or so natives from Bacolod, Talisay, and Silay as slaves. They took Spaniards, too. In 1771 the governor of Negros was held captive, and sometime in the 1840s Don Agustin Montilla, Spanish founder of the settlement at Pulupandan, had to be ransomed from the Muslim south.[35]

A wall of distrust and dislike also separated Christians from pagans on Negros, making forays into the interior hazardous. Those who lived beyond the pale of colonial control and the sway of the Catholic Church included nomadic Negritos; other aboriginal groups; former lowlanders called *remontados* who preferred the isolation of the jungle to the colonial order; and a miscellany of wanderers, bandits, and escaped criminals known collectively as *cimarrones*. Often Spanish attempts to bring these people "under the bell," that is, within the orbit of civil and religious authority, induced hostile reprisals and armed attacks upon the coastal settlements; and in the 1840s Mallat still advised against overland travel between west and east coasts because of possible hostilities along the way.[36]

The thumbnail sketches of all major communities in both Pampanga and Negros in the mid-1840s that Buzeta and Bravo supplied reveal the sharp contrast between the two regions. The former contained wealthy towns, most with substantial churches, schools, permanent *municipios* (town halls), and private homes of stone and wood. A network of all-season roads connected these communities, bringing them into regular contact with one another and, via the port of Guagua and the postal road, with Manila; thus, Capampangan, at least those in the central poblaciones, received capital news, market prices, and mail weekly. In contrast, western Negros resembled much more a frontier area than a long settled place. The seven widely scattered main towns boasted few solid buildings, religious, governmental, or residential; and land transportation consisted of narrow, rough paths crossing rivers often unfordable during the rainy season. Access to the outside world, difficult and infrequent, depended on coasting vessels from Cebu and Iloilo; thus such important items as mail and commercial news were available only infrequently. The low depth of rivers and streams closed off interior communities to all save shallow-draft boats.

In the 1830s, Pampanga already possessed an entrenched native elite, infused with economically aggressive Chinese mestizos who controlled the land, monopolized town political offices, and dominated the local professions of soldier, priest, and lawyer, as well as the lower echelons of the colonial bureaucracy. They had already accumulated knowledge of cane agriculture and the art of sugar manufacture and were, indeed, prepared to take advantage of the expansion of commercial farming when it reached their region. The Negros leadership was not, either by virtue of their agricultural ability or by their absorption of entrepreneurial techniques. Two comments speak to the socioeconomic status and economic preparedness of the pre-1850 Negrense principalia:

> All the political power and wealth of the island belonged to one or two caciques in each town who possessed a smaller or larger number of carabao, some gold beads hanging around their necks, a few cavanes of rice, scarcely enough necessities

> to maintain their families, and houses enclosed with thin walls of bamboo.[37]
>
> In his memoirs, Nicolas Belleza, an old resident of Bacolod, originally from Molo, Iloilo, presents a very interesting list of gobernadorcillos from the capital of Negros, when that capital was still situated at Himamailan. The list begins in 1770. . . .
> Now then, very few of those distinguished family names from that remote time still exist within prominent social and economic circles in the province: such names as De los Santos, De la Cruz, Maguilan, Vivencio, Palandangan, Espino, Gabaton, Andicoy, Guiouin, Varientos, Dopillo, Muncal, Salomon, Laurente, Guiquin. . . . On the other hand, starting in 1840, at the dawn of the sugar era, mixed with some of those old names on the list appear new ones, new immigrants, new gobernadorcillos . . . some of whom were still living a short time ago.[38]

In short, the old elite in Negros was scarcely better off than the poor farmers around them.

However, western Negros began in the 1830s, and especially the 1840s, to receive more attention from the government and to show signs of emerging from its lethargy. Perhaps the most important circumstance that made change possible was the diminution of the Moro threat. Their raid along the coast in 1829 that netted so many prisoners proved to be their last big success, and from that time on, governmental protection and local resistance reached the point that, while occasional attacks took place, they did not have such devastating consequences. Governors Luis Villasis (1833–40) and José Saenz y Vizmanos (1840–48) attempted to shore up coastal defenses, and in 1844, when Don Agustin Montilla petitioned for official recognition of his new agricultural settlement (*estancia*) at the visita at Pulupandan, town of Bago, he assured the government that he could adequately protect his laborers from the Moros who stopped at the nearby island of Inampulugan.[39]

Montilla appeared as the first of a wave of new settlers to western Negros, beginning around 1840. Why they chose this area remains unclear, but it may well have had something to do with the extremely low price of land, extolled by Vizmanos and other government officials. Montilla, a Philippine-born Spaniard married to a mestiza from Iloilo, Vicenta Yanzon Locsin, appears to have been something of an adventurer who resigned from a military career before choosing commercial farming. He left the relative comfort of Manila and Iloilo to become a planter on Negros, raising in those early years rice, coconuts, cotton, abaca, maize, and mongo beans. He succeeded very well, as the estancia at Pulupandan represented an extension of his original settlement along the Bago River and involved the effort of 118 laborers. In 1844 he sought the assignment of a *teniente de justicia* to look after the welfare of those workers; three years later the community had grown so much that Montilla requested permission to erect a chapel, because it was too far for the more than eight hundred villagers to go to Bago for church on Sundays.[40]

Whatever his original motivation, Montilla did not go to Negros to plant sugar. Although he owned extensive cultivations along the Bago River and an iron cane-grinding machine when the English entrepreneur Nicholas Loney visited his hacienda in 1860, he had showed no interest in that crop in 1844.[41] It would appear that he learned about sugar from the second significant migrant to Negros, the originator of commercial sugar production on the island, Yves Leopold Germain Gaston.

A twentieth-century source asserts that in 1836 Negros milled 280 tons of sugar, and by the mid-1830s ships at Manila accepted for export Visayan type muscovado wrapped in bayones; nevertheless, the commercial sugar industry on the island really began with the arrival of Gaston in 1844. A sugar expert by profession, he came from Mauritius in 1837 to make sugar for Domingo Roxas in Batangas. That project failed, and Gaston transferred seven years later to Negros to enter business for himself. His application for permanent residence on the island had the enthusiastic endorsement of Governor Vizmanos, a booster of Negros agriculture. At Buen Retiro, his estate in Silay, Gaston constructed the first sugar mill (*trapiche*), built an *horno económico* (a more efficient furnace for boiling the syrup), and planted the first large crop of cane. By 1848 his influence had spread, and Negros production reached 3,000 piculs, around 190 tons, manufactured by four planters: 1,000 piculs by Montilla at Bago, 400 by a certain "Tia Sipa" in Minuluan, 900 by Gaston, and 700 by Eusebio Ruiz de Luzuriaga in Bacolod. The latter was one of a group of Spanish political refugees moving into Negros in the 1840s and 1850s to pursue agriculture, business, and the professions just as the tide in favor of commercial sugar was coming in. Spaniards from the Iberian Peninsula along with Philippine-born Spaniards and Spanish mestizos were to form a significant component of the emerging Negrense elite.[42]

The changing situation in western Negros is reflected in the rise in population from some 18,000 in 1818 to about 35,000 in 1845. The annual growth rate was substantial for the whole area—2.5 percent—but was most spectacular in that part north of the oldest settled area around Ilog.[43] Indeed, that the demographic center of gravity was gradually shifting is indicated by the movement of the capital of the province northward. In

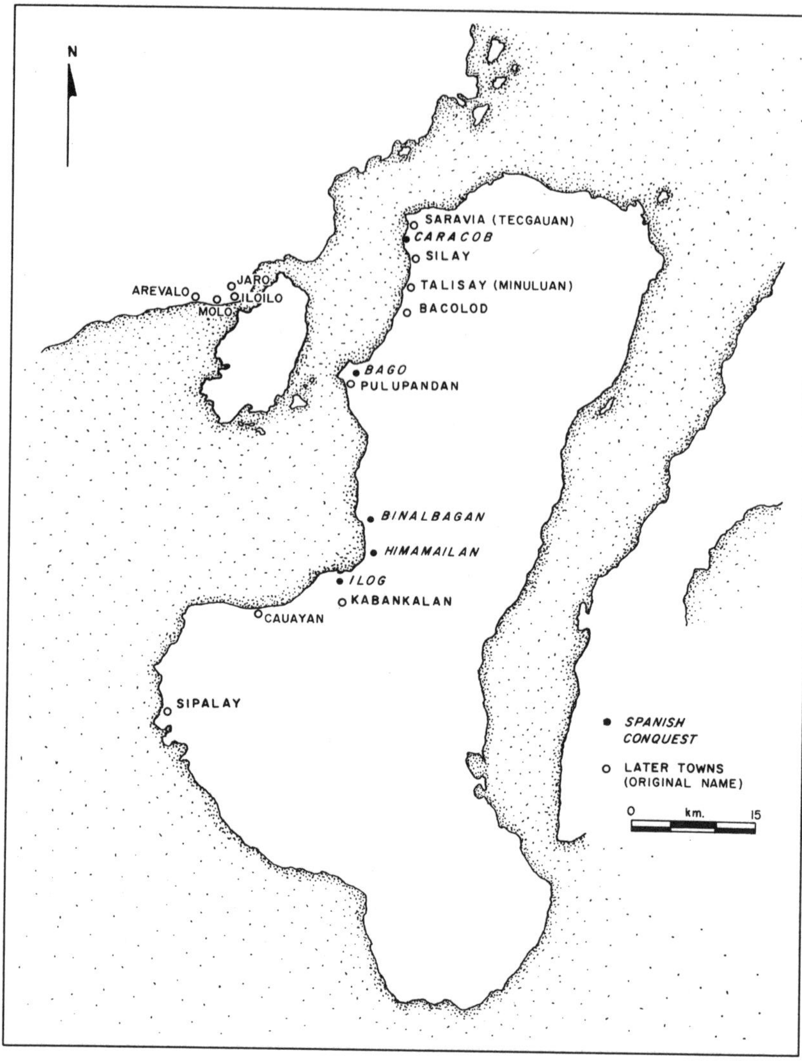

Map 7. Settlement in Early Western Negros

1790 it migrated from Ilog, where it had been since earliest colonial times, to Himamailan; then in 1849 it moved again to its present location at Bacolod (map 7). Population in the region not only increased rapidly, but people settled more permanently along the coast and moved toward new agricultural land where they grew more nonrice crops—all reflections of better security and an improved economy.

Immigration of agriculturalists and burgeoning population did not serve as the only evidence of economic development in western Negros; in 1834 mail service on a fortnightly basis commenced, connecting Himamailan with Manila via eastern Negros, Cebu, Leyte, and Samar.[44] And in 1849 the Recollect Order of friars acquired pastoral supervision of Negros, assuring more extensive religious assistance for the province and indicating that western Negros had reached the point that it merited more attention from the Church establishment.

Sugar and Early Philippine Society

In historical perspective, this first 270 years represents the extended infancy of the sugar industry in the Philippines, a time when sugar making reached and scattered throughout the islands, when local use of sugar became widespread, and when the first steps toward establishment of an overseas trade were taken. Despite the slow beginnings, one can see emerging, even at this early period, aspects that characterized the industry in its later, more advanced stages of development: heavy foreign participation, a compartmentalization of economic activity, and use of a plantation system. While this first stage proved a formative one for the industry, the industry itself exerted little influence at this time on the social and economic life of the archipelago.

That it stands as a foreign innovation is perhaps the most noteworthy fact about the origin of the sugar industry. Spaniards initially imported sugar to satisfy their own tastes and were later instrumental, along with Chinese entrepreneurs, in introducing manufacturing techniques throughout the archipelago, thus creating a widespread taste for brown sugar. Moreover, to the end of the Spanish regime the division of labor persisted between native Filipinos who grew cane and did the primary, crude boiling, and Chinese merchants, European or American agents, and Iberian managers of the great friar estates who did the processing, warehousing, and retailing of the higher grades for internal and external markets. Only from the mid-eighteenth century on did Chinese mestizos insert themselves into this hierarchy as provincial middlemen, acquiring in such places as Pampanga quantities of sugar for the big Manila Chinese dealers.

During the first 150 years of Spanish rule this division of labor meant little, for commerce in sugar amounted to only a small portion of the colonial economy. However, the distinction became more significant and began to shape the growth and structure of the industry as it waxed in the eighteenth century in response to early export demand. Gradually, regional concentration became more pronounced, as the areas near Manila started to specialize in the manufacture of pilon sugar, and native farmers there became linked to international commerce through a network of foreign and colonial entrepreneurs. For the locals, however, the only avenue of growth was through expanding their cane lands, and by the early nineteenth century, the first real plantations in the archipelago began to appear, first in central Luzon and later in Negros and other islands of the central Philippines. At the outset the pioneering projects of de Miranda in Pampanga and, later, of Montilla in Negros did not function as classic monocrop plantations, for although they produced for the market, they initially operated more as subsistence communities with a mixed-crop economy.

The labor pool and class stratification to launch sugar plantings also existed, especially in Pampanga where the samacan system already flourished. In western Negros itself a labor shortage prevailed; however, the nearby province of Iloilo possessed a large rural population upon which to draw for workers. Whether the original laborers came to Negros as tenants or as paid help is not clear, but the presence of so many European planters at the outset meant a much greater distinction between labor and management than in Pampanga where planters and tenants shared the same heritage.

The great inhibition to the expansion of commercial agriculture in the Philippines during this first stage was the lack of markets, partly caused by Spanish colonial policy but mainly a result of limited international demand. In fairness to Spain, if officials did little to stimulate trade, they did less to retard it. Content to make their money initially from the galleons and then through the salaries and peculation of colonial administration, the Iberians left commerce to foreigners. Americans and Englishmen, the chief buyers of Philippine sugar, increased their purchases only gradually, not fast enough to encourage investors to rush to sugar farming. Other crops and other activities—the fabrication of native cloths, for example—absorbed the attention of those seeking good business returns. Cheap land and labor in the archipelago made sugar cultivation a relatively easy field to enter; without the markets, however, there remained little incentive to do so.

As a result of this slow rate of growth, the commercial sugar industry had little impact on the two areas that would later become the archipelago's prime cane-producing regions. By the 1830s Pampanga had a flourishing, mixed economy based on a variety of jungle and agricultural products derived from its wet southern lowlands and the forested northern uplands. Its wealth was reflected in its prosperous towns, cottage industry, and extensive transportation system. The social order, a bifurcated structure held together by a close tenant-landlord relationship and headed by a native elite, had evolved over the preceding centuries of regular interaction with the regime. This infrastructure was ready for transfer to unsettled regions as soon as the demand for sugar arose. Negros, in contrast, having weathered the storms of Moro raids, governmental neglect, and separation from the main currents of economic life, barely survived into the 1830s. Further economic growth would depend on the infusion of new, outside talent and leadership, but only when enhanced trade conditions made such growth profitable. Subsequent change in both areas awaited new economic circumstances.

THREE

Frontiers, 1836–1920

The air was heavy with the never-to-be-forgotten fragrance of sugar cooking from the vats of the *hacienda* mills.
John White, *Bullets and Bolos* (1928)

The years from 1836 to 1920 constitute a distinct era in the history of the Philippine sugar industry, one characterized by enormous expansion in export and cultivation. During this period sugar society became firmly linked to the world market economy and responsive to its fluctuations. As never before, sugar developed into a separate, wealthy sector of the native economy, unique in the high degree of foreign participation. Sugar regions served as very models of a cash-crop society in the Philippines, and their leaders became among the most influential persons in the colonial order of the Spanish and American regimes. Sugar growers led the way to a transformation of the Philippine countryside as they converted deep jungle into extensive sugar haciendas, and major portions of western Negros and northern Pampanga felt this impact. Yet while the physical alterations looked the same in both regions, their socioeconomic structures developed along dissimilar lines, reflecting their unlike manners of settlement and their diverse backgrounds. Pampanga and western Negros grew up very differently.

Expansion of the Sugar Trade

The rise of the sugar industry in the Philippines during this crucial eighty-four-year period is inextricably entwined with foreign markets and foreigners. The world economy supplied an ever-increasing demand for sugar, and outsiders played a vital part in supplying the industry with credit and technology. As in the earlier era, native Filipinos made their greatest contribution to the sugar business in the cultivation sector, although in Negros they became responsible for the processing as well. Until near the end of the period Capampangan continued to depend on foreigners for the last step of their manufacturing, and the division of

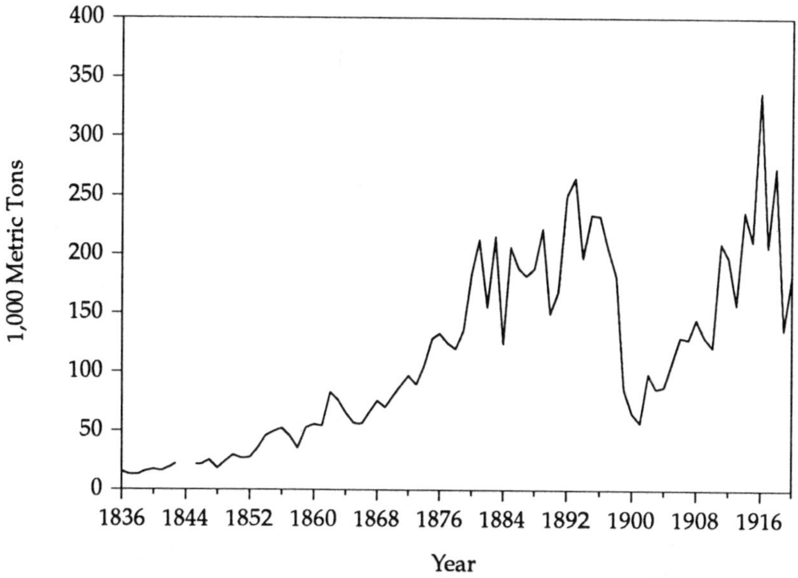

Figure 1. Philippine Sugar Exports, 1836–1920. Sources: Ramon González Fernández and Federico Moreno y Jeréz, *Manual del viajero en Filipinas* (Manila: Est. tip. de Santo Tomás, 1875), p. 185; M. J. Lannoy, *Iles Philippines* (Brussels: Delevingne et Callewaert, 1849), endchart, no. 5; Robert MacMicking, *Recollections of Manilla and the Philippines: During 1848, 1849, and 1850* (London: Richard Bentley, 1851), pp. 270–72; Angel Martinez Cuesta, O.A.R., *History of Negros*, trans. Alfonso Felix, Jr. (Manila: Historical Conservation Society, 1980), p. 365; Cárlos Recur, *Filipinas: Estudios Administrativos y Commerciales* (Madrid: Imp. de Ramon Moreno y Ricardo Rojas, 1879), p. 95; Russell, Sturgis and Company, "Principal Articles of Export in 1854 and 1855," *Market Reports*, January 7, 1856 (Baker Library, Harvard University); Alexander R. Webb, "The Sugar Industry in the Philippines," *U.S. Consular Reports* 31 (1889): 371; Edward W. Harden, *Report on the Financial and Industrial Conditions of the Philippine Islands* (Washington, D.C.: Government Printing Office, 1898), p. 20; *Sugar News* 7 (1926): 186, 698; Philippine Islands, Bureau of Customs, *Annual Report of the Insular Collector of Customs to the Honorable Secretary of Finance for the Fiscal Year Ended December 31, 1922* (Manila: Bureau of Printing, 1923), p. 69. The raw data for this chart can be found in appendix A.

labor throughout the industry between those who did the overseas marketing and those who produced sugar persisted during this time of expanding frontiers.

Figure 1 portrays annual sugar exports from the Philippines during the era and illustrates the extent of transformation of the industry. Between 1836 and 1916 exports rose some 2,135 percent, from 15,097 metric tons in the former year to 337,490 in the latter. By 1836 sugar had achieved first place on the list of exports; it continued to vie with abaca for that position throughout the rest of the nineteenth century (see table 3).

Foremost as an impetus to this dramatic transformation was an enormous heightening in demand for sugar that started even before the mid-nineteenth century, especially among industrial nations. Sugar consumption in Great Britain rose from an annual average of 16.4 pounds per capita in the years 1840 to 1844 to 90.8 in the five years from 1910 to 1914; meanwhile, the annual rise per capita in the United States went from 14.1 pounds in 1835 to 86 in 1920.[1] Only during periods of major war did the rate dip in either country. Furthermore, all the while per capita consumption was increasing, population, too, was multiplying, in the United States from 17 million in 1840 to 125 million in 1920 and in Great Britain from 19 million in 1841 to 42 million in 1921. Hence, although the Philippines remained only one of many suppliers, exploding world demand almost guaranteed the islands a bigger export market each year.

The destination of Philippine sugar exports varied considerably over the period, reflecting changing realities in world market conditions. Data in appendix B convey some sense of the shifting terminals. The United States purchased on the most consistent basis, but Great Britain bought more in the nineteenth century. Even so, these numbers may be slightly misleading, for some sugar originally consigned to Great Britain ended up in American East Coast refineries.[2] Australia, which served as a significant outlet at the advent of the era, faded after the 1870s as it began to acquire more sugar from other sources and to develop its own cane industry. In the 1880s and continuing through the rest of the period, China and, to a lesser extent, Japan became big buyers, taking up the slack as European purchases waned. Spain remained only a limited customer for its most far-flung colony, buying relatively small amounts of the very best grades of sugar available. More aggressive buying practices by British and American merchants in the Philippines partially account for this Spanish weakness, but Spain had other suppliers closer to home, in the Caribbean and in Europe. California, which early promised to be a large market, eventually came to depend on Hawaii's rising export as its chief source.

The complexity of shifting world markets created a need for good, current commercial intelligence, and British and American trading firms, including such giants as Ker and Company; Smith, Bell and Company; Warner, Barnes and Company; Russell, Sturgis and Company; and Peele, Hubbell and Company possessed the expertise, contacts, finances, and facilities to make the sugar trade a success. Throughout the nineteenth century these and other foreign houses controlled the export trade, al-

Table 3. Comparative Percentages of Chief Philippine Exports, 1846–1920

Year	Sugar	Abaca	Tobacco	Coffee	Coconuts and Coconut Products	Total of Export Trade (%)	Value of Exports (pesos/ $Mex)
1846	34	13	19	3	0	69	2,972,967
1847	37	13	18	3	0	72	3,126,141
1854	33	24	17	2	0	77	5,279,923
1855	27	44	14	2	0	86	5,937,150
1856	39	30	16	2	0	86	9,133,317
1857	36	23	21	2	0	82	11,895,821
1858	23	25	17	3	0	68	9,394,475
1859	39	22	21	3	0	84	9,082,868
1860	41	22	12	2	0	77	9,509,481
1861	37	20	14	5	0	77	8,065,530
1862	37	23	16	3	0	79	9,100,797
1863	31	21	27	3	0	83	10,056,818
1864	31	25	18	5	0	79	10,657,026
1865	29	25	17	4	0	75	10,466,309
1866	26	30	20	4	0	80	11,091,262
1867	28	34	21	5	0	88	11,003,402
1870	31	33	23	3	0	90	15,198,263
1873	58	22	10	5	0	95	23,522,529
1874	35	28	20	6	0	89	17,302,977
1875	49	21	18	6	0	94	18,920,475
1876	50	28	8	8	0	93	14,837,796
1877	54	22	8	9	0	92	16,347,450
1878	47	25	12	5	0	88	17,417,617
1879	41	21	7	6	0	75	18,775,727
1880	49	23	11	8	0	91	23,450,285
1881	50	37	3	4	0	94	24,579,007
1882	43	34	13	6	0	95	20,673,334
1883	46	29	11	5	0	91	26,380,727
1884	30	32	8	6	0	77	22,672,833
1885	42	27	11	4	0	84	24,553,685
1886	35	22	10	5	0	72	25,721,032
1887	32	42	8	8	0	90	25,257,139
1888	32	42	13	8	0	95	26,293,271
1889	35	41	9	7	0	92	34,926,969
1890	34	35	11	7	0	87	26,213,554
1891	27	50	10	5	0	92	26,905,102
1892	41	36	13	2	4	96	27,976,569
1893	47	35	11	0	2	95	36,187,966

Continued on next page

Table 3 (*continued*)

Year	*Sugar*	*Abaca*	*Tobacco*	*Coffee*	*Coconuts and Coconut Products*	*Total of Export Trade (%)*	*Value of Exports (pesos/ $Mex)*
1894	33	44	10	1	7	95	33,149,984
1895	32	35	12	0	2	81	36,655,727
1899	23	54	13	0	5	95	29,693,164
1900	10	58	10	0	14	92	45,980,746
1901	10	65	11	0	7	93	49,006,706
1902	12	67	7	0	9	95	57,343,808
1903	10	68	6	0	12	96	64,793,492
1904	11	72	7	0	7	97	58,299,000
1905	15	65	7	0	10	97	66,101,100
1906	14	60	9	0	13	96	65,285,784
1907	13	60	8	0	14	95	66,195,734
1908	18	51	9	0	20	98	65,202,144
1909	16	48	10	0	22	96	69,848,674
1910	18	41	11	0	26	96	81,256,926
1911	25	32	9	0	29	95	89,674,254
1912	18	40	10	0	26	94	109,846,600
1913	15	44	10	0	22	91	95,545,912
1914	23	39	9	0	21	92	97,379,268
1915	21	40	7	0	26	94	107,626,008
1916	27	38	8	0	16	89	139,874,365
1917	13	49	7	0	21	90	191,208,613
1918	12	43	10	0	27	92	270,388,964
1919	13	24	14	0	37	88	226,235,652
1920	33	24	13	0	17	87	302,247,711

Sources: Benito Legarda, Jr., "Foreign Trade, Economic Change and Entrepreneurship in the Nineteenth-Century Philippines" (Ph.D. diss., Harvard University, 1955), pp. 196–97, 222; Philippine Islands, Bureau of Customs, *Annual Report of the Collector of Insular Customs, 1922* (Manila: Bureau of Printing, 1922), pp. 49, 66–69, 73; U.S. Bureau of the Census, *Census of the Philippine Islands: Taken under the Direction of the Philippine Commission in the Year 1903* (Washington, D.C.: Government Printing Office, 1905), 4:54, 56.

though the Spaniards tried through tariff legislation to end that stranglehold in the 1880s and 1890s. Spain's efforts came too late, however, and the only change in leadership in the trade arose from the vastly increased role of Philippine Chinese exporters during the last decade of the nineteenth century. British, American, and Chinese firms maintained their dominance of that trade into the twentieth century as well.[3]

Constantly expanding world consumption explains the overall rise in sugar exports, but more specific events and factors account for short-term fluctuations. In the 1840s the decline of West Indian production resulting from the prohibition of slavery stimulated British demand for Philippine sugar. Sharp rises in the 1850s and the early 1860s followed upon temporary curtailment of alternate sources and greater military need associated first with the Crimean War and then with the American Civil War. Limitations of American cane production, especially in Louisiana, in the period following the Civil War favored increased use of Philippine sugar by American East Coast refiners.[4]

This upward course persisted until the mid-1880s when the expansion of the beet sugar industry, initially in Europe and later in the United States, offered new competition for cane. Germany, Russia, Austria-Hungary, and France put down extensive plantings of beets between 1850 and 1900, as did such American states as California, Michigan, and Ohio. To stimulate these fledgling industries, countries on the Continent legislated bounty systems rewarding local production of export sugar so that from the 1880s to the time of the Brussels Convention of 1903, they flooded the English and American markets with cheap, high-grade sugar. The McKinley Tariff Bill, passed in Washington in 1890, included a two cents per pound rebate on home-grown U.S. sugar, and although Congress repealed this bounty three years later, the Dingley Tariff of 1897 raised duties on imported sugar at a time when world prices remained low.[5]

In the 1840s world sugar prices dropped because of diminished processing costs; however, in the succeeding decades growing demand held the rate more or less steady. In the 1880s, however, prices fell by almost half; except for a brief surge in 1889, they remained depressed until the boom years of World War I. The bounty system represented one early factor accounting for low rates, but at the heart of the matter lay oversupply: too much cane and beet sugar combined. Manila prices did not fluctuate so drastically (see table 4), but the amount of sugar exported leveled off as the English trade permanently declined from its 1881 high. Only the increasingly active role of Chinese traders and the China and Japan markets for muscovado maintained Philippine exports at their previous levels (in 1893 they actually reached their nineteenth-century peak). But the Asian trade, especially that of China, demanded mostly the lower grades of muscovado at cheaper prices and did not compensate entirely for the lost Western markets in the better grades.[6]

The Philippine Revolution caused a further diminution of sugar exports, as disruptions at the port of Manila and combat in central Luzon curtailed deliveries from that northern island. Port facilities in Manila closed on and off in 1898 and 1899 while contending armies jockeyed for control of the city, and the archipelago's only refinery at Malabon shut down because of

Table 4. Prices of Muscovado Sugar at Manila, 1836–1920 (pesos per picul)

Year	*Price*	*Year*	*Price*
1836	5.250	1885	3.000–4.250
1837	5.250–5.375	1886	3.000–4.125
1840	5.000	1887	2.875–4.250
1841	4.000–5.000	1888	3.500–4.125
1844	4.125	1889	3.625–5.250
1846	4.125–4.250	1890	3.250–4.000
1847	3.750–4.250	1891	3.375–4.000
1848	3.438–4.125	1892	3.500–4.250
1849	3.375–4.875	1893	4.000–4.875
1850	4.375	1894	3.000–4.625
1851	3.750–5.750	1895	3.000–4.000
1852	3.250–5.500	1896	3.250–4.375
1853	3.250–5.250	1897	3.500–4.250
1854	3.000–5.250	1898	4.250–4.875
1855	3.000–5.000	1899[a]	4.500–5.315
1856	4.000–6.438	1900[a]	4.625–5.750
1857	7.750–14.000	1901[a]	4.500–5.750
1858	4.750–7.000	1902[a]	3.700–5.625
1861	4.625–5.000	1903[a]	4.000–5.625
1868	4.000–4.875	1904[a]	4.125–5.873
1869	5.000–6.000	1905	3.875–7.250
1870	3.875–5.250	1906[a]	3.750–4.375
1871	4.750–5.750	1907[a]	3.813–4.513
1872	4.750–5.375	1908	4.350–4.550
1873	4.500–5.563	1909[a]	4.450–6.500
1874	4.000–5.125	1910	6.320
1875	3.500–4.625	1911	6.320
1876	3.125–5.250	1912	6.320
1877	4.375–6.750	1913	5.060
1878	4.375–5.625	1914	4.750–6.250
1879	4.375–6.250	1915	5.410
1880	4.250–5.625	1916	5.650
1881	4.375–4.875	1917	4.750–6.250
1882	4.500–5.500	1918	4.500–5.750
1883	4.500–5.000	1919	11.380
1884	3.250–4.500	1920	23.660

Sources: Ramon González Fernández and Federico Moreno y Jeréz, *Manual del viajero en Filipinas* (Manila: Est. tip. de Santo Tomás, 1875), p. 238; *Centenary of Wise and Company in the Philippines 1826–1926* (n.p.: n.p., n.d.), p. 101; Rafael Díaz Arenas, *Memoria sobre el comercio y navegacion de las Islas Filipinas* (Cádiz: Imp. de D. Domingo Féros, 1838), p. 50; Jean Mallat de Bassilan, *Les Philippines: Histoire, géographie, moeurs, agriculture, industrie et commerce des colonies espagnoles dans l'Océanie*, 2 vols. (Paris: Arthus Bertrand, 1846), 2:348–49; Ramon González Fernández and Federico Moreno y Jeréz, *Anuario filipino para 1877* (Manila: Est. tip. de Plana, 1877), p. 79; *Singapore Free Press*, September 12, 1844; Current Prices, Manila (various files), Baker Library, Harvard University; Harden, p. 20; Willett and Gray, *Weekly Statistical Sugar Trade Journal* (1898–1920), *passim*; Philippine Islands, Dept. of Agriculture and Natural Resources, *Philippine Agricultural Review* 14(1921):132; Russell and Co., Price Sheet, Quezon Papers, National Library of the Philippines, Manila.

Note: Figures to 1898 are given in pesos and reales of eight (P0.125); after that, in pesos and centavos. The price range is supplied, where available; otherwise the average price is given.

[a]Figures available for the port of Iloilo only.

the disruptions and because this concern lost its chief customer for refined sugar, Spain. In the south, hostilities proved far less costly, especially in Negros, although the agricultural experiment station at La Carlota was burned. Shipments through Iloilo and Cebu dropped only modestly throughout the period of struggle against Spain. By and large, sugar farmers and merchants continued their straitened business as best they could.[7]

Declining exports in the early years of the American occupation had several causes including a disastrous outbreak of the cattle disease rinderpest that killed some 80 percent of the carabao, the main beasts of burden of the sugar industry. The disease had apparently arrived from French Indo-China in the 1880s but reached a high intensity for the first time only in 1897. Nearly one-third of the carabao in Pampanga and one-quarter of those in Tarlac died in 1902. An outbreak of human cholera in 1902 plus severe droughts and locust infestations added also to the miseries facing the population and the industry.[8]

Disease and war did not represent the only sources of hardship in that harsh time between 1899 and 1909, for the shortage of good outlets remained as well. The archipelago's production had to compete with that of Java for the China market, and Japan began to obtain more sugar from its new colony, Formosa, acquired as a spoil of the Sino-Japanese War. Except for a brief period during World War I, the English market never returned. The Dingley Tariff inhibited U.S. sales in spite of the fact that the Philippines received a 25 percent reduction in duty after 1903. Lessening of the Cuban duty by 20 percent coupled with the cheaper cost of transportation from Cuba plus free entry of Hawaiian and Puerto Rican sugar kept the Philippines at a competitive disadvantage on the American market.[9] Even as low world prices persisted, Philippine export stayed below half of what it had been ten years before.

Weak markets prevented recovery, especially in central Luzon; moreover, several old sources of credit to the industry had dried up by this time. The two American firms that had supplied so much cash and machinery in former years had gone bankrupt, Russell, Sturgis in 1876 and Peele, Hubbell in 1887, while a large British lender, Smith, Bell, faced deep financial trouble because of its inability to sell its overstock of sugar in New York. It took Smith, Bell from 1905 to 1909 to remove itself from debt and to begin rebuilding its cash reserves. Absence of credit led farmers to advocate the creation of the Agricultural Bank, launched in 1908; however, this institution made few loans to farmers, because they generally lacked the good, clear land titles acceptable as collateral. Furthermore, Pampangan farmers complained that too many government loans at the time went to

Negros. In 1916 the bank was absorbed by the far more successful Philippine National Bank (PNB).[10]

Philippine sugar producers began to focus on the need to garner tariff concessions on the American market, and here the government proved more helpful. Such efforts took time to succeed, however, for American beet and other offshore cane producers lobbied the U.S. Congress to limit preferences for Philippine sugar. It required the influence of William H. Taft, the first head of the Philippine Commission and later president of the United States, plus the efforts of other lobbyists for the Philippines to gain those import privileges. Under the Payne-Aldrich Bill of 1909, the Philippines received a 300,000-ton duty-free share of the U.S. sugar market, and in 1913 under the Underwood-Simmons Bill, even that weight limitation was dropped. Despite these concessions, however, the Philippines still competed with such heavy suppliers as Cuba, Puerto Rico, and Hawaii, and in most years of the 1910s it had to sell substantial portions of its product on the less lucrative Asian market.[11]

The underlying problem for Philippine export was the quality gap: processors turned out the same low-grade sugar they had for the past eighty years, but on a world market that now demanded a higher degree of purity. In 1813 an Englishman, Charles Howard, invented the steam-heated vacuum pan that, under reduced pressure, boiled sugar syrup more efficiently and quickly at a lower temperature. Invention of the centrifugal separator, a steam-driven cylinder that removed molasses from crystal sugar cleanly and rapidly, followed in the 1840s. By the late nineteenth century Java, Hawaii, and Cuba were already using these innovations; however, the cost of erecting a modern steam-run central ran very high, reaching the hundreds of thousands of dollars.[12]

The Philippines remained the last major world producer of cane sugar without centrals. The less expensive machinery introduced into the Philippines in the nineteenth century to replace the crude equipment of earlier times included steam-driven metal grinders; hornos economicos that, instead of wood, burned ground cane refuse (*bagasse*) as fuel; and batteries of open kettles (see figure 2). The first two used in tandem produced more efficient extraction rates of juice from cane; the latter improved the polarization of mat sugar. By the latter part of the century, Negros turned out a good sugar with an 85° average polarization (degree of sucrose content) that compared favorably with the finished pilon sugar of Pampanga; neither kind, however, matched the 96° of centrifugal sugar. For the introduction of even this cheaper equipment, credit belongs mainly to foreign risk takers: Nicholas Loney and Yves Germain Gaston on Negros

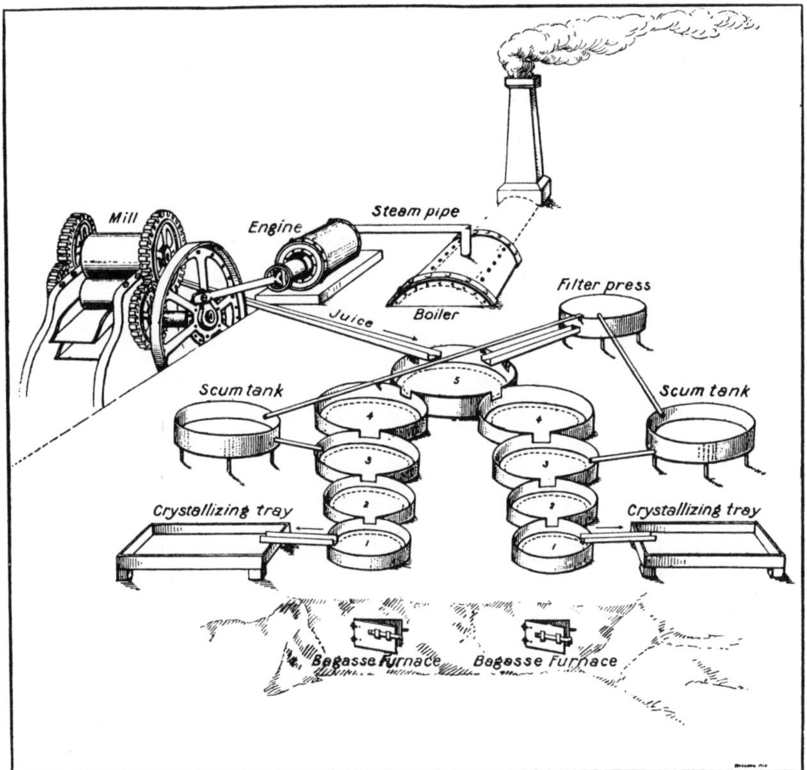

Figure 2. Advanced Muscovado Mill System. G. E. Nesom and Herbert Walker, *Handbook on the Sugar Industry of the Philippine Islands* (Manila: Bureau of Printing, 1912), pt. 2, p. 100.

Island and Paul de la Gironiere, Adolphe Delaunay, and M. M. Vidie on Luzon. The big trading houses supplied the machinery and financed its purchase when native planters followed the lead of those innovators. No one, however, attempted the erection of a complete central. The refinery at Malabon that functioned from 1887 until the outbreak of the Revolution had an array of modern equipment; even so, this plant's operation was limited in size by the circumscribed market for fully refined sugar.[13]

For the most part, Philippine growers did not even care to invest in better farming techniques to improve their profits, and the Philippines possessed the lowest yield per hectare of all the major sugar-producing regions of the world. A 1920 report indicated that Hawaii and Java had 6.66 times the per hectare yield of the Philippines; for Cuba and Puerto Rico it was 2.6 times, for Queensland, Australia, almost 3 times, and for Jamaica 2. Even beet-producing areas of Europe and America had higher productivity. Not until well into the twentieth century did planters begin regularly to fertilize their fields, rotate and irrigate their crops, and select the best cane for planting.[14]

In the mid-nineteenth century Philippine muscovado drew praise for its quality, but by the late 1870s criticism started to appear, and the new realities of the international sugar trade began to hurt the Philippines by the mid-1880s. Because of ad valorem duties on high polarization sugar brought into America and England (until 1874), it remained economical for these two countries to import 85° muscovado. But with the rising availability of high-quality beet sugar, first from the Continent and then from domestic growers, both countries began to insist on 96° centrifugal. As the century ended, muscovado was losing the competition for valuable European and North American markets.[15] The next decade proved an unmitigated disaster for Philippine sugar. Table 3 reveals that, even as overall Philippine trade continued to grow despite war and natural calamity, sugar's share of that trade declined from a high of 47 percent in 1893 to just 10 percent in 1903 and only 16 percent as late as 1909.

The major casualty of the sugar depression of the early twentieth century was the pilon industry of central Luzon and Pampanga's in particular. Before 1850, pilon sugar that was reclayed in Manila represented the top of the export trade and found its way readily to Western markets; however, an improved Visayan mat earned a significant share of those markets over the second half of the century. Pampangan farmers damaged themselves as well by lacing their sugar with molasses, a practice that drew criticism in the 1870s. Instead of improving their polarization, then, they became more dependent on the Manila fardarias to raise the quality of their product. By the 1890s annual exports from Manila, chiefly superior pilon, to North America and England began to drop drastically, while Iloilo shipments of Visayan mat to those destinations continued to rise. The Revolution savaged the industry in central Luzon; it never recovered. Sugar exports from Manila dropped from 127,000 tons during the 1887–88 milling season to nothing in 1909.[16]

In the next ten years Pampanga began to move away from pilon when some planters switched to making mat sugar by hiring sugar *maestrillos* expert in the Visayan boiling technique. In a more desperate move, other farmers after 1914 commenced sending their cane to the newly erected central at Canlubang, Laguna, despite the serious loss of sucrose content caused by the delay between harvesting and grinding.

Pilon no longer sold well, and only the best mat could compete for markets with the poorest grades of centrifugal. During World War I, the Continental beet sugar industry was incapacitated, and cane producers everywhere profited from the shortage as world prices touched extraordinary heights. In the Philippines, Asian and Western buyers vied with one another for Philippine sugar to such an extent that, for the first and only time, the United States bought small quantities of Philippine refined. Even so, muscovado sold for from five to more than ten pesos lower than did centrifugal; moreover, not every Western refinery could handle muscovado-quality sugar any longer.[17]

Despite the imperatives, potential investors in Philippine centrals faced formidable obstacles. First of all, there existed a problem of cane supply. To remain profitable, large, modern mills required that ample stocks of sugar cane be delivered throughout the milling season, and most centrals in other countries possessed guaranteed stocks through ironclad lease arrangements or through ownership of the surrounding fields. In the Philippines, however, acquisition of large tracts of public land was illegal, and there were insufficient private estates for purchase or lease.

Second, the matter of cost loomed large. Participants in the Philippine sugar industry generally lacked the resources and incentives to purchase expensive factories. The Spanish colonial government, more inclined to worry about paying its burgeoning bureaucracy, took little interest in aiding industrial development. Long-term depreciation of its silver-based currency over the last quarter of the nineteenth century as well as a large outflow of its precious metal reserves left the Philippines with a cash shortage.[18] Equipment that cost hundreds of thousands of dollars before the onset of World War I cost millions once it began. Local lending institutions at the time could not supply such amounts, and private families feared making big investments on their own, knowing little of the financing and construction of such enterprises. Lack of expertise constituted part of a bigger problem: confidence—or lack thereof—in the future of sugar. A decade of weak prices and fierce world competition made all but the most intrepid investors chary of perilous commitments. Again, it took foreigners to lead the way to change.

As to the first matter, the guaranteed sources of cane, several solutions emerged. The initial one involved a stratagem to avoid provisions of the Public Land Act of 1902 that prohibited the granting of public lands greater than 16 hectares to individuals and 1,024 hectares to corporations. This law, partially passed at the behest of American beet sugar interests, effectively prevented development of centrals along traditional lines by denying the centralists ownership of sufficient cane fields. But a careful reading of the law governing the disposal of the friar estates, newly acquired from the Catholic Church, allowed corporations to bypass the law on public domain and to buy extensive tracts of the land formerly owned by the religious orders. With the aid of Philippine Commissioner Dean Worcester, an American syndicate representing mainly Horace Havemayer of the American Sugar Refining Company purchased some 18,000 hectares of unused friar land in San Jose, Mindoro, in 1909, and subsequently erected a central there. The project ultimately failed because of the malaria that plagued the area, the peaty soil, and the unavailability of an adequate work force; nevertheless, a precedent had been set, and a central capable of milling some 1,500 tons of cane daily had been built in the islands.[19]

Before the Philippine legislature closed the loophole in the Public Land Law in 1914, California interests under the leadership of Alfred Ehrman and the Pacific Commercial Company acquired 8,000 hectares of the Calamba and Biñan estates in Laguna and used this property as the basis for erecting a large central at Canlubang. The enterprise flourished so well that in 1919 its owners put up another central in Del Carmen, a barrio of Floridablanca, Pampanga. Only at San Jose and Canlubang, however, did the owners acquire extensive plantations, and other investors in centrals had to look elsewhere for solutions to their cane problem.

The real answer to access to cane came with the establishment of the highly successful San Carlos Milling Company in 1912 and is indicated in the opening statement of the company's prospectus:

> Briefly stated, this Company has secured from the principal planters of North San Carlos District, Island of Negros, Philippine Islands, contracts to grind all of the sugar cane grown by them for the term of thirty years, and in return for this the Company is to receive forty per cent of the sugar manufactured.[20]

The long-term milling contract became the model arrangement used by other centrals erected in the Philippines and gave the archipelago a unique identity among the world's sugar-growing regions. San Carlos's success encouraged uncommitted planters to sign up with newly rising mills, and many farmers settled for less advantageous contracts containing a fifty-fifty split, especially during the boom years of World War I, when soaring prices promised great returns to those in the market.[21]

The difficulty of financing centrals was solved in several ways. The first involved large infusions of foreign capital, mainly American, as some of the biggest mainland U.S. and Hawaiian sugar concerns sought opportunities in the islands. At Canlubang, California interests came to the fore, and with Pasumil, the Spreckels West Coast refining interests joined Ehrman in supplying capital. Hawaiian money constructed the centrals at San Carlos and Silay, Negros Occidental (1920). Various firms representing long-time Spanish residents of the islands also became involved in central building: the Elizalde-Ynchausti interests financed a major factory at La Carlota that commenced milling in 1920, and Tabacalera, a Spanish company built out of the remnants of the government's old nineteenth-century tobacco monopoly, funded a large central at Bais, Negros Oriental, in 1919. Two other groups of Spanish investors put up small centrals at Ilog and Kabankalan in 1916 and 1917 respectively.[22]

Because of the shortage of domestic capital and available credit sources, native Filipino investors faced a more difficult challenge entering the central construction field. The Roxas family and Esteban de la Rama managed to erect small centrals on their own property at Calatagan, Batangas (1914), and at Talisay (1912) and Bago (1913) respectively, and Lizarraga Hermanos put up another little mill at Kabankalan (1914). Only Miguel J. Ossorio, however, could organize the private support to construct two big centrals, at Manapla (1917) and Victorias (1921). It took government intervention to assure that Philippine interests could afford to build centrals. The PNB, founded in 1916, loaned substantial amounts of cash for the erection of six large Filipino-owned mills: at Isabela (1919), Ma-ao (1920), Bacolod (1920), Talisay (1920), and Binalbagan (1921), all in Negros Occidental, and at San Fernando, Pampanga (1921). In the case of the five on Negros, these projects originated with prominent families, including the Yulos, Lizareses, and Montillas, who applied to the PNB for funds that included most of the capitalization.[23]

Reluctance to invest ceased during the second decade of the century, not just because of desperation over dwindling markets for muscovado, but because the American tariff situation promised better market opportunities than had existed for some time. In addition, the opening of the Panama Canal in 1914 reduced transportation time and costs to the East Coast refineries where Philippine sugar sold best. Indeed, inauguration of the Panama Canal meant much more to Philippine economic development than had the opening of the Suez Canal in 1869. The government, by founding the PNB and expanding railroad facilities, demonstrated its willingness to assist the industry, while prices during the war added to the sense of optimism and to improvement of the investment climate.

Out of the private sector and government service came technicians experienced in the financing and engineering aspects of central construction and operation. Almost all of the early specialists were Americans who advised investors on how to obtain and finance central machinery. A major journal, *Sugar News*, designed to promote the industry and to disseminate technical information, began publication in 1919. As a result of the availability of so much specialized information, investing in centrals became less of a mystery. By the end of the decade the first group of Filipino technicians trained in the intricacies of producing better sugar entered the industry. The era of the centrals might have started a little earlier except that the war created a shortage of shipping and machinery, so that rapid construction had to await the armistice. Not until 1921 did the export of centrifugal surpass that of muscovado.[24]

Negros Occidental: The Formation of Plantation Society

The peopling and exploitation of the western Negros wilderness between 1836 and 1920 shared much in common with the global frontier phenomenon taking place at this time. The expansion of agriculture onto hitherto underutilized territory of the Americas, Eurasia, Africa, and Oceania happened in response to social, economic, and political pressures, as well as to an imperative to feed the machines of the Industrial Revolution. The cycle of initial pioneering, succeeded by intense cash-crop agriculture, the encumbering of land, the harnessing of labor, and the gradual imposition of a full range of civilization's amenities and restraints, was repeated on Negros as on other frontiers. As elsewhere, forest lands were reduced and the local aboriginal population displaced as a rising entrepreneurial elite rapidly accumulated wealth. This era was indeed the heyday of unfettered capitalism.[25]

Figures in table 5 depict in gross terms the transformation of western Negros. Between 1845 and 1918 annual sugar production increased enormously, while population rose more than 1,021 percent, an annual rate of 3.35 percent. The extension of agricultural lands resulted from the creation of hundreds of new plantations out of areas heretofore primary and secondary jungle. Amidst these haciendas, permanent towns rose, built upon earlier settlements or upon missions recently established by Recollect priests.

In the mid-nineteenth century, new migrants to Negros included farmers who established homesteads, mainly subsistence, in coastal and interior Negros alongside the already settled Negrense smallholders. Here they grew chiefly rice, corn, or cash crops such as tobacco and abaca. The reasons for this early migration remain obscure, but they must have involved some degree of desperation, since much of this immigration did not have official sanction; moreover, local histories contain lore that some of these settlers came to avoid the law, the military draft, or various tax and labor obligations imposed by the government. Also, most arrived from overcrowded and depressed areas such as Bohol, Cebu, Antique, and the textile towns of Iloilo, suggesting that many of them sought simply to improve their material conditions, as homesteaders have done on other frontiers. Whatever the reasons, these early settlers had little effect upon the great changes

Table 5. Demographic and Commercial Change in Western Negros, 1845–1918

	Ca. 1845	*Ca. 1886*	*Ca. 1903*	*Ca. 1918*
Towns	8	23	34	24
Population[a]	35,007	154,408	303,660	392,292
Sugar production (piculs)	3,000	575,000	1,383,786	2,258,023
Animal-driven sugar mills (de sangre)	4	250–300	195	4
Hydraulic mills	0	60	45	29
Steam mills	0	200	291	396
Centrals	0	0	0	8

Sources: *Guía de forasteros en las Islas Filipinas, para el año 1847* (Manila: Colegio de Santo Tomás, 1847), pp. 338–39; *Memoria*, 1888, Negros, sec. 2, Philippine National Archives, Manila; Miguel Pérez el al., "Cronica semihistoria de Filipinas y en especial de las Islas Visayas desde 1877 a 1887" (Ms., Newberry Library, Chicago), p. 1; U.S. Bureau of Insular Affairs, *A Pronouncing Gazetteer and Geographical Dictionary of the Philippine Islands* (Washington, D.C.: Government Printing Office, 1902), p. 44; U.S. Bureau of the Census, *Census of the Philippine Islands: Taken under the Direction of the Philippine Commission in the Year 1903* (Washington, D.C.: Government Printing Office, 1905), 1:234; 4:328, 528, 530; Philippine Islands, Census Office, *Census of the Philippine Islands: Taken under the Direction of the Philippine Legislature in the Year 1918* (Manila: Bureau of Printing, 1920), 2:106–7;4: pt. 1, p. 570; *Handbook of the Philippine Sugar Industry*, 2d ed. (Manila: Sugar News Press), Table 1; Philippine Islands, Bureau of Commerce and Industry, *Statistical Bulletin No. 3 of the Philippine Islands, 1920* (Manila: Bureau of Printing, 1921), p. 43.

[a]The population increased at an annual average of 3.7 percent from 1845 to 1886, 4.06 percent from 1886 to 1903, and 1.72 percent from 1903 to 1918.

that occurred later. Many were subsequently absorbed into the hacienda labor force after having lost their land to the new breed of planters who took over the island.[26]

As noted previously, the original haciendas on Negros appeared in the 1840s and 1850s with the advent of such settlers as Agustin Montilla, Yves Germain Gaston, and Eusebio de Luzuriaga and his fellow refugees. Despite these early pioneering efforts and improving market conditions, Negros did not begin to attract large numbers of new hacenderos until the late 1850s. At least three factors seem to have featured in the delay. First, the threat of Moro coastal raiders lingered on and was not finally eliminated until the time of Governor Emilio Saravia (1855–57) who defeated them in the waters off Silay in 1857. Shortly after this engagement, the government stationed two steam gunboats to patrol the Guimaras Strait, discouraging further pirate depredations.

Second, Negros possessed a reputation as lacking the social and physical amenities of communities on the neighboring islands. The advent of the Augustinian Recollect friars to exercise religious control of the province served to alleviate somewhat this concern. Recollects assumed jurisdiction of Negros Island in 1848 and began establishing missions, then parishes, as well as taking up parishes vacated by the old native secular priests. Coincidental with the arrival of the Recollects was the governorship of Manuel Valdivieso Morquecho (1849–55) who, like his predecessor Vizmanos, sought to encourage economic development of the island. From his headquarters at the newly created capital of Bacolod, Morquecho began formally delineating a number of new town centers along the west coast and barrios that later became municipalities along the north coast.[27]

Third, there existed no pressing need earlier to consider Negros as a field for investment. By the 1850s, however, British cottons began to penetrate the Philippine market, cutting into the sales of indigenous textiles, a business controlled until then by Chinese mestizos from Panay. In addition, an influx of entrepreneurial Chinese into the Visayan region drove many of these mestizo merchants out of what remained of the native cloth industry and prevented them from finding niches in other branches of the wholesale and retail trades. Many held out until their market began to dry up rapidly between 1865 and 1873 in the face of renewed competition from imported cloth following the American Civil War. These conditions sent the mestizos in search of new arenas of economic activity, and, aware of a growing market for Philippine sugar abroad, they increasingly looked across the Guimaras Strait to Negros as an investment alternative. At a slightly later period Cebuanos from Cebu and Bohol began to turn to the eastern and northern coasts of Negros as regions to expand their sugar plantations.[28]

Other factors, too, began to exert a magnetic pull on potential investors. The immediate lift of the Crimean War, with its boosting of world prices, induced them seriously to consider risking the establishment of new plantations in the western Negros hinterland. To facilitate this movement came British Vice-Consul Nicholas Loney, who reached Iloilo in 1856. Loney, recognizing sugar's potential as an export industry, acted as a stimulus in several ways. On the positive side, he arranged for the flow of new British milling equipment, the provision of low-interest credit to pay for it, the construction of better port facilities, and the first foreign international shipments out of Iloilo, to Australia in 1859. On the negative side, by importing British cloth, he helped drive mestizos out of the textile business.

Loney established his own export-import company in 1860 and with his brother Robert acquired a hacienda on Negros a year later. In his early dealings, Loney took cash loans from the prominent American firm of Russell, Sturgis and Company, which put up its own branch at Iloilo in 1863. Subsequently, the other American merchant house in the Philippines, Peele, Hubbell and Company, and such British firms as Smith, Bell and Company and Warner, Barnes and Company entered the sugar business, encouraging the growth of the industry on Negros. Together these houses dominated foreign export of sugar from Iloilo and became the chief suppliers of imported goods and machinery, as well as a source of credit to Negros planters. Iloilo opened to international commerce in 1855, making it possible for exporters to bypass Manila as a transshipment point and thus to reduce shipping costs. By the mid-1860s Iloilo became the chief port for Negros mat, a position it held throughout the remainder of the period.[29]

The efforts of the first Recollect friars and Governor Morquecho, the opening of the Port of Iloilo, the activities of Loney and the other foreign investment houses, and, above all, constantly expanding world demand for cane sugar made the period from 1850 to 1886 the time of greatest intrusion upon the Negros frontier. Planters and small farmers sliced into the wilderness creating farming communities, and priests turned missions and parishes into new town centers. The chronology of town erections reveals the course of sugar estate expansion in western Negros (see table 6). Sugarlandia's major boundaries took shape during these prosperous market years of the nineteenth century.

The sugar frontier originated along the western seacoast, moved south from Bago as far as Ilog, and north from Silay, following along the coast to Cadiz. Growth also occurred along the eastern shore, out from Escalante toward Arguelles (Sagay) and Calatrava. San Carlos finally succumbed to sugar after the turn of the century. Settlement of the interior, up the rivers from the western coastal towns, took place slowly over the course of the entire period, and as late as 1920 virgin land still existed.[30]

Sugar flourished on Negros because of a new generation of entrepreneurs who created large plantations, employing imported and local labor to do initial clearing and then to work the estates for them. The entrepreneurs fell into two categories: actual settlers and speculators who bought or acquired estates by other means, fair and foul, combining, then developing, properties already cleared. Few of the old Negrense elite seem to have become successful hacenderos.

With his story of the Valderramas, Negros historian Modesto Sa-onoy provides a good example of a typical pioneer planter family. Catalino and Fortunato Valderrama, sons of a Chinese immigrant convert and his Ilongo wife, left their home in Molo on Panay at a youthful age, when the cloth business that had sustained their parents no longer produced profits. In the 1890s Catalino oversaw the clearing of some 300 hectares of frontier in Cadiz then opening up to settlement. During the following decade his younger brother established Hacienda Nazareth on 400 hectares in newly

Table 6. Municipal Establishment by Period and Region

Region	*To 1850*	*1850–86*	*1886–98*	*1898–1903*
West coast	Ilog Kabankalan Himamailan Hinigaran Bago Bacolod Talisay Silay	Binalbagan Pontevedra San Enrique Sumag Valladolid		Pulupandan
Interior west coast		Granada Isabela La Carlota Murcia	Guimbalaon	Eustacio Lopez La Castellana Ma-ao Soledad
North coast		Cadiz Saravia	Manapla	Victorias
East coast		Escalante Calatrava Arguelles		San Carlos

Sources: *Guía de forasteros in las Islas Filipinas, para el año 1850* (Manila: Los Amigos del Pais, 1850), p. 283; Felipe Redondo y Sendino, *Breve reseña de lo que fue y de lo que es la diócesis de Cebu en las Islas Filipinas* (Manila: Colegio de Sto. Tomás, 1886), pp. 284–91; *Guía oficial de Filipinas. 1886* (Manila: Ramirez y Giraudier, 1885), pp. 661–62; *Guía oficial de las Islas Filipinas para 1898* (Manila: Chofré, 1898); U.S. Bureau of the Census, *Census of the Philippine Islands: Taken under the Direction of the Philippine Commission in the Year 1903* (Washington, D.C.: Government Printing Office, 1905), 2:234.

founded Manapla. While pioneering was a game chiefly for the young, some older settlers also participated. Revolutionary leader Juan Araneta, who lost his lands in Bago during Spanish times, at thirty-nine and with his second wife penetrated the interior to start plantations in Ma-ao.[31]

Many of the arriving planter migrants utilized prior bonds to ease their entry into the Negros wilderness. Domingo Cuenca, a Spaniard, commenced farming in Minuluan (Talisay) when his brother Fernando, a Recollect, became parish priest in that town. Similarly, the presence of mestizo secular priests Eusebio and Ramon Locsin in Silay and Bacolod facilitated the movement of their Molo friends and relatives to these parishes. On a broader scale, groups tended to migrate to areas where they had preexisting contacts. Peninsular-born Spaniards, for instance, clustered in the municipalities of La Carlota, Kabankalan, Manapla, San Carlos, and Bacolod, while Boholanos and Cebuanos did the same along the north and east coast. Mestizos from Jaro and Molo fed the west coast settlements of Talisay and Silay, but migrants from the second-ranked Ilongo textile area of Guimbal-Miagao concentrated at Hinigaran and Isabela. Often, too, when planters imported labor, they recruited from their home town, so that small rural communities on Negros sometimes consisted of barrio mates from Panay or Cebu. As time went on, intermarriage and movement about Negros tended to break down this pattern, but some of the early associations between towns and groups still linger. The east coast towns, for example, remain Cebuano speaking until the present day, and the majority of Spaniards lived in the same five towns until at least the outbreak of World War II.[32]

Spaniards had to settle for a share of the plantations, but not a dominant one, and in no place, save in La Carlota and Kabankalan, did they become a major economic force. Indeed, like their predecessors Agustin Montilla and Eusebio de Luzuriaga, they tended to intermarry with the mestizo population, and their descendants were absorbed into the group broadly defined as the Negrense planter elite. Not all Spaniards made it to the top of the social hierarchy, for they held no privileged economic position in sugarlandia simply because of their nationality. Some became owners of small estates, while others served as hacienda managers or foremen.

Westerners from other countries as well as a few Chinese also entered the plantation frontier. Included among this group were Hugo Koch, a Prussian; the Swiss Frederick Luchinger, Charles and Samuel Bischoff, Paul Wuthrich, and the Jeanjaquet brothers; the English Loneys, Thomas Evans, and Frederick Ashton; Chinese such as Domingo Lazarte Yu-Bangco, Yap Waco, Lucio Echauz Tan-Suia, and Yee On; and, after the turn of the century, Americans J. Clayton Nichols, David Mulliken, and John Merrick. Eventually such foreigners either sold out, became absorbed into the local population, or like Luchinger and Loney concentrated on the exporting end of the sugar business.[33]

McCoy, in identifying the origin of the Negros planter elite, points to the continuity of names between the leading merchant families of Iloilo and the largest landowners subsequently on Negros, and certainly that correlation exists. At the same time it should be noted that settlers from other areas and groups sojourned to and succeeded on Negros and that the hacendero group became more than a mere extension of Iloilo society. The Ilongos Teodoro Benedicto, Isidro de la Rama, Teodoro Yulo, and Eugenio Lopez held thousands of hectares of land, but many of the other 485 hacenderos listed in the 1896 enumeration came from a non-Ilongo background. Moreover, intermarriage among the often large families of the era tended to blur some of the distinctions of origin. For example, descendants of the great Iloilo merchant Basilio Lopez (ca. 1810–ca. 1875), many of whom became Negrense planters, within two generations had intermarried into numerous other Ilongo families, but also with Cebuanos, Spaniards, Spanish mestizos, and Americans. Among the original settlers the Spaniard Agustin Montilla married an Ilonga, while the mother of Yves Gaston's children immigrated with him from the Tagalog-speaking province of Batangas. Montilla's daughter married Hugo Koch. The same 1896 census lists 151 Spanish men and 24 women, but also 332 Spanish mestizos.[34]

The image of the pioneer planter with spouse carving a hacienda out of the wilderness is slightly misleading. To be sure such individuals existed; however, planters coming in the 1850s and 1860s acquired land, usually along rivers and streams, mainly by buying the rice fields and unused property of local residents, often sitting or former officials. Heirs of these first arrivals would often clear and farm lands adjacent to the original settlements rather than move to the more dangerous interiors. In this way Negros grew out from the edges of prior settlement rather than from widely scattered nuclei in the middle of the jungle. Like many other pioneers, Juan Araneta did not live on his clearings, choosing rather to stay in his comfortable home in Bago. For a long time new haciendas and towns remained devoid of those amenities found in older settlements readily in contact by boat with the outside world. Furthermore, a high risk to health, especially from malaria, persisted for those dwelling in or on the edge of the jungle. Nicholas Loney probably died of that malady, contracted during a climb of Mount Canlaon in 1869. In 1902, Governor Locsin noted that malaria affected as much as 12 percent of the population and was particularly prevalent among workers dwelling in the interior portions of the province. With the threat of Moro raiders eliminated, the coastal town centers proved the more attractive places to live.[35]

The matter of titling lands remained informal, given the absence of government surveys, good records, and land offices, as well as the apparent availability of unlimited land. Early purchase agreements might include a hand-drawn map roughly outlining the property (see figure 3) or a statement approximating the location of the land. Descriptions of property did not specify exact dimensions; rather, lot sizes were described in terms of the number of *gantas* or *cavans* of rice or corn seedlings or *lacsas* of sugar cane cuttings necessary to plant the land. Larger properties were simply referred to as haciendas. Over time the acts of buying and selling of property provided one form of recognition of land ownership and offered a basis for formalizing titles when the government introduced programs of land registration.[36]

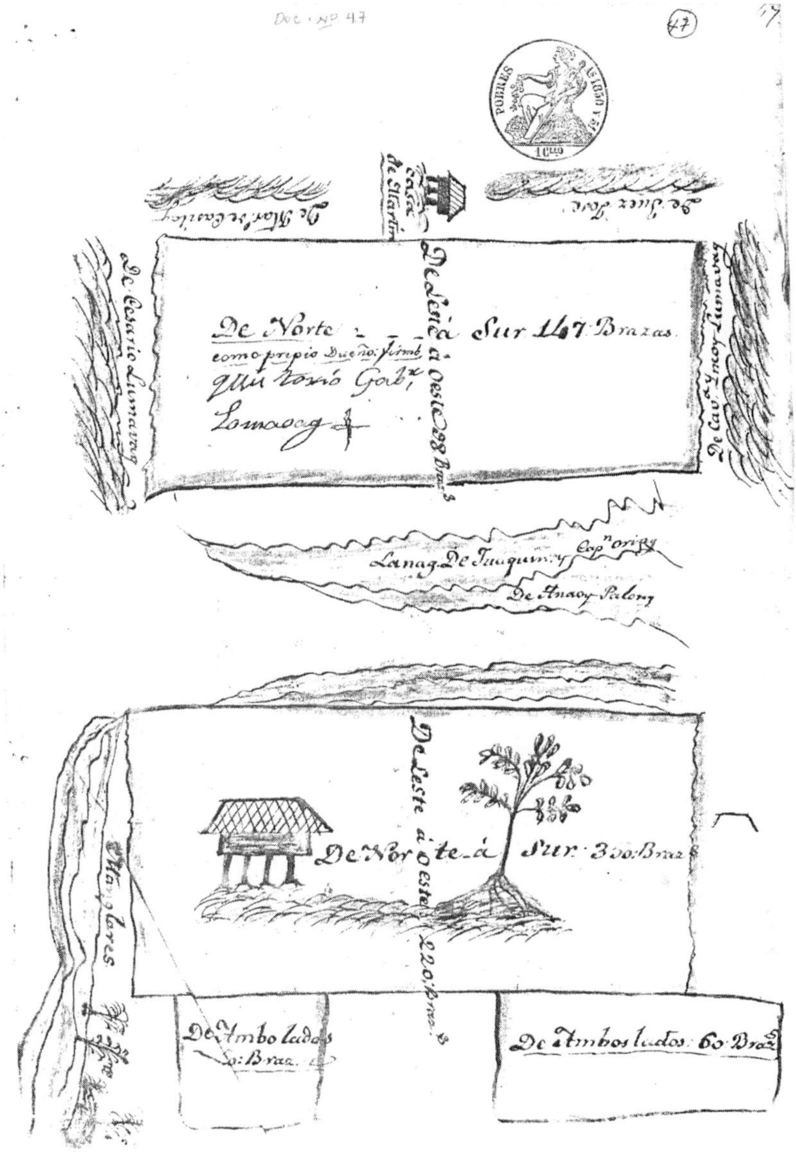

Figure 3. Map Accompanying Deed of Land Sale, Hinigaran, Negros Occidental, 1850. *Protocolos*, 1975, Negros Occidental, Philippine National Archives, Manila.

Legitimation for the acquisition of large blocks of agricultural land on Negros began in the mid-1870s when the Spanish government devised a program for distributing public lands (*realengas*), territory considered unoccupied at the time and, hence, belonging to the crown. Petitioners could purchase such lands at giveaway prices or with proof of prior cultivation (*denuncia*) could claim them gratis. Prices for realengas rose gradually over the two decades from one to two pesos per hectare to six to ten. The biggest purchasers on the list were Alejandro Montelibano and Teodoro Benedicto, each of whom obtained more than 1,200 hectares in this fashion. The majority of petitions involved properties of more than 100 hectares of frontier land. Martinez Cuesta's list of those granted free title based on prior occupancy includes many heirs of the first pioneers claiming lands settled by their parents in older, established areas. Lands offered by the government at such low prices accrued considerably in value and created great fortunes for the recipients. A 1918 estimate placed the worth of land in Negros at P100 per hectare for unimproved plots and as high as P500 for the choicest fields.

The U.S. colonial regime did not prove so generous in making large grants of the public domain, seeking rather to follow America's own ideal of turning the frontier into the realm of the yeoman farmer. The Homestead Act of 1902 granted a maximum of 16 hectares of public land per individual. Sixteen hectares still represented a substantial piece of land, and on the edges of the sugar frontier, in San Carlos for instance, numerous claimants came forth in the first two decades of the new century. The attempt, however, to preserve sugarlandia for small farmers failed.[37]

Actual registering of land presented something of a problem in Negros, for there was no functioning land office until about 1890, and the process of surveying property and legally establishing clear title proved cumbersome. Few owners, save those given public lands, had clear titles before the twentieth century. In 1902 the Americans instituted the Torrens system, which provided government-guaranteed titles, but the complicated nature of registration and the reluctance of planters to let a tax-hungry government know the size of their holdings reduced the number of early applications. By 1910 some owners in Negros, as elsewhere in the Philippines, were beginning to apply, but not in sufficient numbers to satisfy the government. In 1913, therefore, it inaugurated a cadastral survey of the whole Philippines, which included pro forma lawsuits intended to force all landowners to obtain Torrens titles, a monumental project that dragged on throughout the rest of the pre–World War II period. Negros Occidental was one of the first areas surveyed, and judges acted efficiently in settling the litigation, so that by 1922 legal titles for much of the best farming land in the province were available.[38]

During the process of claiming, amassing, and titling estates, planters sometimes displaced small farmers of the original Negrense population and those poor migrants who came to take up subsistence plots. The actual extent of this eviction and land grabbing (*usurpación*) must always remain a mystery, for they were carried out in various ways by hacenderos and their minions who made and kept the records. Sometimes removal occurred legally when planters with proper claims removed squatters who had simply occupied their land. At other times eviction took place with the aid of falsified documents obtained through collusion between corrupt officials and hacenderos. The planter group and their friends, relatives, and employees held almost all municipal and provincial offices as well as all judicial positions, and they had little difficulty turning such a monopoly to their own use. Finally, in unnumbered cases beyond the sight of witnesses, employees of the hacenderos forced peasants from their land. From the occasional evidence that does appear, a sense emerges that the taming of the Negros frontier was fraught with unrecorded violence. McCoy cites a complaint of Spanish farmers from La Carlota against the great landowner Teodoro Benedicto for his strong-armed removal of a group of Antique migrants who had worked the same land for years before Benedicto claimed it.

Such usurpacion still occurred at the end of the period, as evidenced by the case of some La Carlota homesteaders that came to the attention of Senate President Manuel Luis Quezon. Small farmers found themselves threatened by three of the most influential hacenderos in that district (see appendix C). In another case going on at the same time, Governor Matias Hilado of Negros Occidental faced a charge of land grabbing brought by another government official. Confronted with such pressure throughout the era, peasant farmers could only retreat further into the wilderness or stay and work for hacendero claimants to their lands.[39]

The plight of the aboriginal inhabitants of the island is more difficult to document but appears even more tragic, similar to the situation found on other contemporary frontiers around the world. As original owners of the interior they either farmed the land as swiddens or used the jungle for hunting and gathering. Since they possessed no formal titles, their land became officially crown property and could thus be granted to others. To resist the government directly or even indirectly meant to risk extermination. Governor Saravia supplied a frightening example of what could happen to an uncooperative population when in 1856 he caused the mass murder of non-Christians in Barrio Carolan, Kabankalan, while trying to bring them under colonial control. Hill people learned early in this era that retreat represented the better part of valor. The interior mountains and foothills became final havens for all the displaced, where they could practice their ways and avoid becoming part of a work force for the sugar economy and servile members of the colonial pyramid. Land grabbing burdens the modern history of Negros, and even today tension mars the relationship between uplanders and sugar people.[40]

A comparison of names of sugarland holders in 1896 with those who had made purchases at mid-nineteenth century reveals a considerable turnover of property ownership in the early years, demonstrating the high risk of venturing into sugar farming. Alongside early pioneers in the 1860s appeared speculators like Ricardo Mascuñana and Marcos Villaluz, who purchased agricultural land cheaply and sold it at a higher price to newcomers. In the 1870s wealthy merchants commenced putting together big estates for themselves and their relatives. In that decade alone Teodoro Benedicto purchased 5,590 hectares for P32,477, or about P5.813 per hectare. From this time on, some consolidation of ownership occurred, and by 1896 twelve families controlled almost one-third of the 53,211 hectares of sugarland in twenty of the twenty-six sugar-producing towns on Negros. About four hundred other planters having smaller haciendas possessed the remainder, so that the size of holding averaged about 109 hectares per owner. Investing in working plantations became a common way of entering the sugar business, and by 1887 the Iloilo newspaper *El Eco de Panay* carried advertisements for Negros haciendas complete with machinery, work animals, and crops in the field.[41]

Constant traffic in land serves as a reminder that transforming the Negros frontier was first and foremost a capitalistic enterprise, that haciendas represented investments first and homesteads second. Other forms of associated business activity included supplying agricultural credit, transporting sugar to market, and sugar brokerage. Foreign and native entrepreneurs, if they had cash, turned to these other activities, which offered greater and more reliable opportunities for profit. Owning several haciendas and leaving their day-to-day management to employees or relatives allowed bigger operators to concentrate on other economic pursuits. Teodoro Yulo over the course of his lifetime acquired seventy-five haciendas, some from his debtors, and ran his diverse financial kingdom, which included banking, from his home in Iloilo. The ultimate success story was Isidro de la Rama, a petty Ilongo cloth dealer who migrated to work a plantation in Minuluan. After seven years of farming, de la Rama switched to buying sugar and loaning money to fellow planters. Eventually, he moved into the shipping (interisland and international) and warehousing of sugar, and by the time his son Esteban took over his enterprises in the 1890s, the de la Rama fortune was one of the largest in the Philippines.[42]

Supplying credit offered the best entree into sugar-related business activities, for a shortage of working capital always plagued farmers on Negros. At the outset, the island boasted cheap, readily available land, but little else, and it took infusions of foreign funds to nurture the budding industry. Such foreign firms as Loney and Company; Russell, Sturgis and Company; Smith, Bell and Company; and Lim Ponzo and Company loaned money to planters chiefly to acquire rights to their sugar, usually at slightly below market prices. To obtain guaranteed deliveries, brokers sent agents throughout the province who would offer loans on favorable terms, sometimes as low as 8 percent and well below rates for other mortgages, which could top 30 percent. Such anticipatory crop loans worked effectively because they reduced some of the heavy competition among brokers for the sugar of the hundreds of planters spread all over Negros. Brokerage firms operated most actively in years of good market conditions when sugar was both expensive and scarce.

Foreign houses served as links in a chain of credit institutions with the large English banking concerns like Baring Brothers and Hongkong Bank at the top and planters at the bottom. Import-export firms borrowed from banks as well as from such private investors as the friar orders and Manila Spaniards. With this capital and their own earnings, the firms invested in crop brokerage, importation of Western goods, and local banking, providing a large share of the money for new plantations on Negros and elsewhere. A series of untoward circumstances led to the demise of Loney and Company in 1875, Russell, Sturgis in 1876, and Peele, Hubbell in 1887, putting a dent in the credit market just at a time when world sugar prices turned downward. In 1887 a group of Negrense farmers lamented the lack of cheap credit and petitioned the government to come to their rescue, and as late as 1918 farmers in northern Negros complained about usurious interest rates. Newer companies like Warner, Barnes and Company and the Chinese firms took up some of the slack, but they did not entirely replace the early pioneer lenders; nor did the alternate sources of credit provide capital at the same favorable rates. One of the most active brokers was Lim Ponzo, who lived in Iloilo but operated at least one store in Victorias and a warehouse in Silay. He loaned money to hacenderos in Silay, Saravia, Victorias, and Murcia in order to acquire their sugar for as much as 12 to 40 centavos below the prevailing market price—a considerable saving to himself. He charged interest for mortgages at rates from .2 percent all the way to 15 percent, still low by prevailing standards. However, farmers really in debt to him were required to buy hacienda supplies and rice for their workers at his Victorias store; also, they might have to pay an additional 12 percent interest on their loans, offer land as security, and pledge to deliver a given number of piculs of sugar to his bodega in Silay.

Aside from anticipatory crop loans offered by sugar brokers, hacenderos obtained mortgages and, to a lesser extent, pacto de retro contracts from private individuals and, infrequently, from sugar firms. Wealthy Ilongos like Teodoro Yulo, Isidro de la Rama, and Teodoro Benedicto made considerable money in mortgages, as did the occasional foreigner. When Yves Germain Gaston, founder and great pioneer of Negros sugar farming, died in 1863, the bulk of his P53,000 estate consisted of P40,000 worth of agricultural loans and a P9,000 investment in the Scottish firm of Ker and Company, the original Iloilo employer of Nicholas Loney. Rates for mortgage money commonly ran higher than for anticipatory crop loans and varied considerably in length, from as short as three months to more than a decade—as a rule, the longer the mortgage, the less favorable the terms. Lenders preferred land as collateral, but they occasionally took other forms of agricultural property; moreover, mortgages usually went on rather extensive properties valued in thousands of pesos. In 1915 the Spanish firm Ynchausti and Company picked up a hacienda as payment of an especially large debt of P112,500. That entries in the notarial records indicate few foreclosures in Negros reflects a high level of reliability on the part of the mortgagees; even so, lenders usually gave little money for agricultural land in terms of its true value.

Until creation of the Agricultural Bank of the Philippine Islands in 1908, and more especially its successor, the PNB, in 1916, even planters with good collateral did not have access to credit on really favorable terms. Government-sponsored lending institutions gave relatively larger loans on property, at 8 percent and 10 percent; even so, they only partially alleviated the credit problem, for they did not possess sufficient funds to meet the total need, and they demanded Torrens titles as security. Supplying agricultural credit persisted throughout the era as a lucrative business activity.[43]

Differences in the size of holdings created a two-tiered structure of wealth in Negros with the most influential families having the most capital, frequently living in and conducting their business from Iloilo. Out on plantations and in the towns of Negros dwelt working hacenderos who lacked the economic cushion to carry them easily through hazardous times without borrowing. The wealthy group not only knew more security, they had money to lend and could profit from hard times and, in promising times, invest in progressive changes. When sugar tramways, centrals, and shipping lines were to be built, they had the financial resources to profit and to increase their already extensive fortunes. Within the planter class of Negros considerable differentiations of wealth existed, and the gap grew wider as the era of the centrals approached.[44]

At the heart of economic and social life on frontier Negros lay the hacienda, locality for the majority of the province's inhabitants. In the 1903 census, organizers took the barrio as the smallest unit of enumeration in all provinces save Negros Occidental, where they used haciendas as well as barrios; furthermore, in the big Negrense sugar towns, haciendas represented a very large proportion of reporting units. In the earlier 1896 enumeration of the province, haciendas were the main unit. Haciendas varied in size, from a few hectares to several hundred; the 489 listed in 1896 averaged 74 hectares, and most included a mill—steam, water, or animal driven.

Lack of easy transportation on Negros caused most haciendas to remain isolated, self-contained communities. In Spanish times the only reliable road ran between Silay and Bacolod. Elsewhere, a trail roughly paralleled the island's western shore; however, along most stretches it was only a crude path and even in the better places was rutted during the rainy season and dusty during the dry. Furthermore, because so few bridges existed, the many creeks and rivers emptying out into the surrounding seas needed fording, and travel off main roads moved along narrow tracks or up shallow waterways. Americans took a more aggressive approach to road and bridge building; nevertheless, as late as 1916 only 142 kilometers of first-class highway covered the province. The best highways provided access to town centers and allowed for some automobile traffic, but large numbers of haciendas were then, as they are today, difficult to reach. Planters often had large families and on more remote haciendas created their own community. An officer of the Spanish Guardia Civil seeking to establish a post in an outlying community found the center of a particular hacienda as busy and with as many buildings as a proper town plaza.[45]

However, table 7 indicates that those wealthy enough to own a substantial home (*una casa de materiale fuerte*) chose most frequently to reside in town rather than in a barrio or on a hacienda. Towns, especially Bacolod, Silay, and San Carlos, possessed active social whirls, zarzuelas and other entertainments, large churches with regular religious services, business opportunities, and transportation facilities to other islands, as well as such twentieth-century niceties as electricity, ice houses, telegraph offices, and frequent mail service. In general, the focus of a family's business interests strongly influenced its residence pattern and social orientation.[46]

While absentee ownership became a common feature on Negros, each hacienda had a planter in charge, either the owner of a small estate, a

Table 7. Location of Substantial Houses by Municipality

	On Haciendas	*In Barrios*	*In Poblaciones*	*Total*
Bacolod	—	13	72	85
Binalbagan	8	2	7	17
Granada	3	—	3	6
Himamaylan	5	1	12	18
Hinigaran	1	1	5	7
Ilog	5	—	—	5
Isabela	5	12	9	26
Kabankalan	11	3	11	25
La Carlota	22	—	5	27
Manapla	14	6	11	31
Minuluan	20	1	43	64
Murcia	—	—	6	6
Pontevedra	3	2	7	12
San Enrique	3	—	—	3
Saravia	—	14	35	49
Silay	9	1	101	111
Suay	5	—	3	8
Sumag	—	—	6	6
Valladolid	—	7	13	20
Total	114	63	349	526

Source: *Estadisticas,* Negros Occidental, 1896, Philippine National Archives, Manila.

leaseholder (*arrendatario, acsa,* or *agsador*), or the owner's surrogate, an *administrador* or an *encargado* (overseer). No figures exist on how many owners actually operated their farms, but the sparse evidence suggests that the number diminished over the period. Hard times such as the decades of the 1880s and 1900s seem to have reduced the number of small planters, the kind most likely to run their own estates. A turn-of-the-century roster for the town of Eustaquio Lopez lists only four owner managers, all relatively small, out of forty planters. Owners of modest estates lived in houses little better than those of some of the paid supervisory personnel on larger haciendas.[47]

Leaseholding arrangements came with a complex set of options on Negros and altered according to prevailing economic circumstances and the changing lifestyle of landowners. Straight cash rentals seem to have been the least favored choice, for they provided tenants with the least protection against fluctuating sugar prices; moreover, owners did not prefer this option, because the lessees possessed little incentive to do long-term maintenance on hacienda machinery and land.

The acsa or agsador system of share rentals proved somewhat more popular, for it offered many protections not available under the cash tenant system. Acsas as mere share tenants farming their own plots date back to the beginning of plantations on Negros when owners personally managed their haciendas; however, as absentee ownership became more common, the acsa system changed character and became one of lease management, used by both native and European entrepreneurs. By the late nineteenth century ambitious young Spaniards eager to enter the sugar business came out from the metropolitan country to work as acsas on haciendas of Spanish and native owners.

On some estates, larger ones especially, an acsa leased a particular portion, supervising laborers and delivering cane to the mill. On other, smaller properties he managed the whole hacienda and paid the owner a percentage of the total sugar produced. Size of shares varied considerably, from 10 percent to 75 percent for the lessee, depending on the owner's and acsa's contributions of working capital, farm implements, and animals and according to prevailing economic conditions. With muscovado sugar, for instance, the division could normally range from one-third to two-thirds; however, if a central processed the sugar, the mill's share reached 40–50 percent and the tenant's dropped to 8–10. Of course, in the latter instance, he did not have to do his own milling, and the sugar sold for a better price. Acsas rented haciendas as small as ten hectares and as large as several hundred. Landowners of one hacienda might sometimes lease others. In all cases, the acsa acted as planter, taking complete responsibility for the successful performance of the estate. A rare firsthand description by an acsa of his farming activities appeared in the *Philippines Free Press* in 1912.

> I am working on the hacienda of my uncle where I cultivate my own sugar field. If the present price of sugar holds, I will make this year some P900 to P1,000 which is not a bad start.
>
> I also have pigs and farm birds, and I am cultivating, besides, a little patch of Indian corn that within three months will give me sufficient maize for the feeding of my hens and hogs. With that I hope to obtain enough to cover the costs of the cultivating of my cane.
>
> I go to the fields very early to begin the farmwork. As it is now cool, I can plow the ground by myself, at which activity I am engaged until nine in the morning. In the afternoon, when the sun no longer shines so intensely, I resume my work. And to these simple country folk it is amusing to observe, to pause before me and to express their astonishment, at seeing me work; it's not part of their comprehension that "amo [master] Ramon" holds a plow, being a student from Manila and a "gentleman."
>
> I have also two carabao and I care for them with great solicitude. The idea that they can die frightens me, because if that

> should come to pass, all my spirits, my hopes and my dreams will be buried with them. Lord, preserve them![48]

By far the most common system of sugar farming in Negros was owner or employee management of a hacienda of salaried workers. In 1911 *Renacimiento Filipino* published an article describing operations on a 2,700-hectare estate (one-third devoted to sugar) owned by the de la Rama interests in Bago. Under overall supervision of an administrator, the hacienda was broken up into eight units, each under the control of an encargado and each with its own complement of fields, mill, and workers. The administrator kept the books, oversaw the machine shop, supervised distribution of tools, and allocated use of the hacienda's three tractors. Encargados oversaw foremen, or *cabos*, responsible for the daily work activities of the hacienda's seven hundred permanent employees (duma'an, *jornaleros*) who tilled fields, ran tram cars (*bagones* or *bagonitas*), and operated mills. With variations in scale, machinery, and top administration, this plantation represents the typical sugar farm structure of Negros from the mid-nineteenth century to the advent of central milling.[49]

A chasm divided the Negrense hacendero families socially and economically from their workers. Some physical distinctions may have surfaced to separate the planter class from its more "indio-looking" help, but such differentiation was more likely a matter of social perception than of empirical reality. No clear racial division such as that between the Caribbean white planter and the black field hand or the migrant Hawaiian kanaka and the Australian planter existed. The gulf in Negros remained social, economic, and, increasingly, cultural. True, some bonds of paternalism formed on Negros haciendas, yet such ties usually remained at their core pragmatic and contractual rather than socially intimate—discipline could not have been maintained otherwise. The distinction between those who did manual labor and those who did not was the cutting edge of a differentiation in wealth, education, mobility, and wider economic opportunity.[50]

The permanent work force of the hacienda included persons with a variety of skills, responsibilities, and remuneration. The encargado, usually a relative or trusted employee of the owner, acted as hacendero in his absence and on bigger estates enjoyed a salary that allowed him and his family to live in a home of permanent materials. The following wry description, taken from Echaúz, illuminates the role of the estate supervisor (encargado or cabo-cabo):

> Heart and soul of the little hacienda where he ordains and arranges is the factotum, he who must know everything, he who overlooks nothing. . . .

> At dawn and dusk, he rings the bell, calls the roll with a thundering voice, distributes the work of the hacienda, and puts checks where he should not. . . .
>
> Riding a nag of little worth, he uses a European saddle, he accompanies his bosses to town or to nearby haciendas, and looks after the fighting cocks bound for fiestas of greater importance.
>
> During the cockfight he does not lose sight of the cocks held by the most trusted workers. . . . He collects the money if the cock wins and pays if things go badly.
>
> Knowledgeable about the lands of the hacienda, he consults his boss in passing (as a courtesy) about the work of the following day; after a brief conversation, he handles all civil matters—and some more not civil—reads letters, writes, adjusts accounts, and officiates, once in a while, as a Cupid without bow and arrow.
>
> Responsible for his actions, sometimes he is the intermediary between the worker who asks something for his sick mother, dead father or uncle, and the owner who pays. . . .
>
> He distributes rice among the workers, which always results in a reduced quantity, something similar to the miracle of the Loaves and Fishes.
>
> His handling of that cereal makes him friends and gives him influence, and when the owner complains about how quickly it is consumed, he always attributes the shrinkage to robbery, mice, or some other simple and innocent cause.[51]

Cabos carried out encargado's orders, providing formal and informal leadership and liaison between hacienda management and the labor force. If the encargado might sometimes have been a European, the cabo was always a native Visayan. According to Echaúz, the cabo lived closer to hacienda worker families, in a nipa house only somewhat better than their own. Often literate, he held supervisory responsibility for day-to-day agricultural activities but did not do manual labor; he received two or three times more pay than the most senior duma'an. Other personnel on the plantation included the maestrillos who supervised the crystallization of muscovado sugar, the machinists, and clerks, all of whom received pay according to their skills. A tax survey of 1894 indicated that Chinese immigrants may have constituted a significant portion of the work force at sugar mills.[52]

The bulk of the permanent labor force (duma'an) consisted of semiskilled workers, from as young as six to an advanced age, who prepared and maintained fields and looked after carabao and other stock. Duma'an cut cane points from sugar stalks, weeded around young ratoons (plant stools), and saw to the repair of buildings and carts. The number of workers depended on the size of the plantation, from as few as two or three up to hundreds of individuals; however, work varied little on all the estates. Living on or near the hacienda in nipa houses, duma'an were employed year-round, but they received little pay. Wages on sugar estates remain one of the more confusing and mysterious matters, because they varied so much. Foreman lists the duma'an salary at P4 per month in 1890; Landor places it at 25 cents per week, plus board, in 1902; and the *Manila Times* set it at P.50 a day in 1919. None of these figures took into account use of land upon which a worker might build his house or the availability of rice and cash loans, which also figured in the salary equation. Often, the hacienda ran a store at which duma'an, isolated from the towns, could purchase necessities on credit; interest charges often produced debts that lasted for years. Salary thus became meaningless, for duma'an essentially ended up as subsistence workers on estates. So tied did workers become to individual haciendas that some sales of estates included all buildings, machinery, field crops, and the help.[53]

November to April was the peak labor season: workers had to cut cane, make sugar, and put down a new crop simultaneously. Permanent workers could not handle all these burdens, and planters had to employ temporary help. To Panay, Cebu, Bohol, and other, smaller, offshore islands, hacenderos sent their agents with advance wages (*antesipo* or *anticipo*) to enlist migrant labor (*sacadas*) to come to Negros for from three to six months to cut and carry cane to the mills in exchange for a salary slightly higher than that of duma'an. Planters returned to the same poor Visayan communities annually to hire sacadas, or they engaged contractors (*contratistas, capataz*) to make those arrangements. Contractors often recruited workers from their own home town, loaned them money, paid their salaries and their transportation to and from Negros, and supplied their food and necessities on the haciendas. Opportunities for contratistas to exploit sacadas abounded; however, economic necessity drew many migrant workers back to Negros regularly, as long as they could handle the field work.

Plantation work was (and still is) repetitious, dangerous, and physically rigorous, and only a closely supervised, industrious labor force could produce sugar profitably. Obtaining such a work force persisted as the ongoing challenge for planters throughout the period. Complicating the problem was their need to obtain such labor cheaply. For Negros sugar to contend successfully on the world market required that production costs be kept to a minimum, especially after the onset in the 1880s of the challenge from European beet sugar. Since Philippine yields per hectare remained the lowest among the world's sugar-producing areas, maintaining a permanent poorly paid labor force on the haciendas and seasonally bringing in low-cost, migrant labor appeared to hacenderos the most reasonable solution to their dilemma.[54]

Negros did not originally possess an available pool of hacienda labor, since the peasant population planted rice in the south and swiddens in the interior. Hence, workers had to be imported to begin sugar planting. To expand the agricultural frontier required that more labor come in, that the Negrense peasants move to the haciendas, and/or that the aboriginal population join the plantation work force. Labor migrated from other islands, and some independent farmers were absorbed into the hacienda system as their lands were usurped. Peasant farmers had a choice either of moving to new homesteads, working on plantations, or joining one of the bands of outlaws and cattle rustlers that preyed upon haciendas and towns. Recollect friars attempted for both religious and economic reasons to persuade the aboriginal population to become part of lowland society and the sugar work force, an effort at which the priests had little success. Curiously, Philippine Constabulary officers in the American period sought the same goal, in part as a matter of public order, in part to "civilize the natives." The constabulary, too, failed in this endeavor; thus, migrants and locally absorbed peasants fed the island's plantation labor force.[55]

Once on plantations, workers usually found themselves bound there for life. Local judicial and executive authority, justices of the peace, and town officials were selected by and usually from among hacenderos and those who worked for them in the communities and on estates, so that legal controls supported the domination of the sugar elite. Runaway workers could be jailed for debt and returned to their amo, and laws still on the books in the American years supported these actions. The pattern of chronic indebtedness and lack of an alternative means of livelihood were the chief forces holding duma'an on plantations; however, in a frontier setting, with their farms remote from legal supervision and restraint, planters sometimes employed force as well. White noted that two legal codes existed on Negros: one for planters and one for the poor. Hacenderos possessed firearms and used them, along with other forms of physical abuse, to keep workers docile and acclimated to the discipline of hacienda work. Laborers might occasionally flee to a neighboring work place, but they seldom escaped from the system.[56]

If planters easily controlled the permanent work force on their haciendas, they had less success coping with the sacadas who came annually to work the cane harvests. When the first migrant workers traveled to Negros remains uncertain; however, they probably did not arrive before production made very rapid advances in the 1870s. Loney does not mention them in his extensive account of Negros in 1861, and one of the first references to their periodic journeys to the island appears in del Pan's description published in 1878. Ideally migrant laborers offered hacenderos a high degree of economic flexibility, for they worked only in response to seasonal demand. In practice, however, sacadas proved less malleable than duma'an, demanding more money for their part-time labors and working only when they chose to. Planters and their spokesmen often complained of the scarcity of labor, meaning that sacadas came in insufficient numbers to meet planter desires. Hacenderos became desperate enough to give advances to migrants and contratistas, although sometimes sacadas simply took the money and did not show up or left the fields early. Planters frequently spoke of a need for vagrancy laws as a way of coping with this flight, for, they presumed, culprits took the money and spent it on various vices in the towns.

Some disreputable workers and contractors may, indeed, have set out to defraud hacenderos, but others may simply have fled certain haciendas because conditions of employment and living became intolerable. A government report of 1911 stated (without intended irony):

> In Occidental Negros local conditions seem to be the chief causes of the crimes against chastity, which are designated as being the most frequent in said province, in the same categorical line as crimes against property and person.
>
> They are mostly committed at the time of the cutting of the sugarcane, and particularly, at the rice harvest time—from November to April—owing to the fact that during the sugar-grinding season a great number of laborers are gathered on the estates with their families, who live in crowded and narrow dwellings [*quartels*]. . . .
>
> In the said dwellings, which would hardly hold 3 or 4 persons, 3 or 4 families live and sleep closely and promiscuously, there being no separation of men from women, of the married from the unmarried, of old men from young men. As a result of the immorality growing out of this mode of living, the crimes of adultery, abduction, rape, and seduction are committed.[57]

Hacenderos never completely solved the dilemma of controlling migrant labor, and another often-heard planter plea in the twentieth century was for importation of Chinese and Japanese workers, who had a reputation of industriousness and docility. Americans, ever fearful of an inundation of "Asiatics," always dismissed such demands.[58]

Despite incidental difficulties with labor supply, the Negros plantation system functioned well, to the advantage of hacenderos. Planters ruled absolutely, managing estate finances, fixing the schedule of agricultural activities, making technical choices, and setting work requisites. Few restrictions, save those of the marketplace, interfered with their control over property and workers. Colonial governments for the most part chose to support agricultural expansion by, among other things, not meddling with management of haciendas; meanwhile, the Church sided with hacenderos in almost all matters, for parish priests depended mainly on their largesse for survival. Negros plantations came to resemble, in many respects, those of the American antebellum South and the late eighteenth- and early nineteenth-century West Indies: worlds unto themselves, with the hacendero the unchallenged master. Flexibility built into the labor system allowed larger hacenderos to expand or contract their plantings according to market demand. Furthermore, in periods of economic downturn enterprising planters profited by absorbing the lands of the failing ones.[59]

Wealth generated by sugar farming served as a springboard into other activities as well. The Valderramas, for example, went into lumber, for although large stands of Negros timber were cleared to make way for plantations, the northern region from Cadiz to Escalante became in the second decade of the twentieth century one of the first important Philippine lumber-producing areas. Lesser endeavors included one organized in 1919 by a group of Negrense planters to build a hotel near the health spa at Mambucal Springs in Murcia. Bigger entrepreneurs extended their empires beyond Negros, to Iloilo, Manila, the Visayan region, and the international arena. Children of the planter aristocracy not choosing to enter farming often used public and private primary and secondary schools in the province as a springboard to more advanced study in Panay, Manila, Spain, and the United States. A corps of Negrense professionals—doctors, lawyers, engineers, and technicians—serviced the island's communities and entered the ranks of government employees. Privileged families exploited sugar farming to create new economic activities and to reduce their dependency on agriculture as their sole source of livelihood. Their wealth presented them with the opportunity to participate in the social and political life of the archipelago, increasingly focused on the capital city of Manila; and Negrenses like Jose Luzuriaga, Rafael Alunan, and Esperidion Guanco became leading politicians during the early American period.[60]

Conversion of the Negros frontier into a plantation society represented a complicated process involving both foreigners and native Filipinos from all sectors of society: pioneer farmers, boatmen, rural workers, entrepreneurs, agricultural specialists, representatives of organized religion, and government officials. From all these elements Negros society developed, similar in many ways to the rest of Filipino lowland society, yet different in others because of the nature of the frontier experience with its opportunities for the accumulation of enormous wealth. Despite rough surroundings, poor roads, and an atmosphere of violence, visitors wrote glowingly of the opulent planter lifestyle. A Negros planter might walk around his hacienda all day with a pistol on his hip, but at night he would shed it and dress in elegant clothes to dance with his family at a lively ball, one of the province's favorite entertainments.

Absence of societal and governmental restraints in a climate of unfettered capitalism permitted the lavish expenditure of resources, land grabbing, and exploitation and abuse of labor to go unquestioned. Surviving and thriving on the frontier entailed great risks, and many entrepreneurs did not succeed. Those who did felt that the risks taken justified their monopolization of wealth. Further, absenteeism and use of migrant labor on Negros reduced the sense of paternalism that marked other agricultural regions. Workers on Negros probably felt less sense of security than those in other, more settled agricultural regions. One son of Negros in this period simply and eloquently expressed their plight: "To the laboring class or the peasants belonged the miseries of life."[61]

Pampanga: The Formation of a Tenant Society

In 1863, after a disastrous flood along the Paruao River, residents of Magalang, Pampanga, rebuilt their town center several kilometers to the south, away from that tributary of the Rio Chico, on its present location close to the foot of Mount Arayat. This transfer situated their settlement in the midst of an expanding region of sugar farming that included Mabalacat, Porac, Mexico, Arayat, and Angeles, as well as northern parts of San Fernando and Bacolor. In general, sugar cultivation moved onto higher, drier ground, forested and remote from the original riverine core area where rice farming still predominated. Wherever growing sugar proved feasible, Capampangan of the mid-nineteenth century took up that endeavor. The new Magalang, its poblacion laid out in a symmetrical grid pattern of streets with a central plaza, became a prosperous sugar community boasting a stone church and substantial government buildings.[62]

Pampanga exhibited a far less dramatic response to the upturn in sugar business than did western Negros. A comparison of figures in table 8 with those in table 5 reveals that, whereas population in Negros rose more than ten times between 1845 and 1918, the population in Pampanga did not even double between 1852 and 1918. Furthermore, Negros had three times as many municipalities in the latter year as it did at mid-century, while the

Table 8. Demographic and Commercial Change in Pampanga, 1852–1918

	Ca. 1852	*Ca. 1890*	*Ca. 1903*	*Ca. 1918*
Towns	21	23	23	21
Population[a]	131,798	223,187	222,656	256,058
Sugar production (piculs)	174,531	1,000,000	226,368	1,199,815
Animal-driven sugar mills (*de sangre*)	919	1,125	48	73
Hydraulic mills	0	32	15	14
Steam mills	0	158	131	350
Centrals	0	0	0	1

Sources: *Memorias*, 1853, 1890, Pampanga, Philippine National Archives, Manila; U.S. Bureau of the Census, *Census of the Philippine Islands: Taken under the Direction of the Philippine Commission in the Year 1903* (Washington, D.C.: Government Printing Office, 1905), 2:236; 4:328, 528, 530; Philippine Islands, Census Office, *Census of the Philippine Islands: Taken under the Direction of the Philippine Legislature in the Year 1918* (Manila: Bureau of Printing, 1920), 2:107; 4: pt. 1, p. 570; Hugo H. Miller, *Economic Conditions in the Philippines* (Boston: Ginn, 1920), p. 144; Philippine Islands, Bureau of Commerce and Industry, *Statistical Bulletin No. 3 of the Philippine Islands, 1920* (Manila: Bureau of Printing, 1921), p. 44

[a]The population increased 1.4 percent from 1852 to 1890, decreased .05 percent from 1890 to 1903, then again increased .95 from 1903 to 1918 (these are annual averages).

number of Pampanga's towns did not change. Considering that the latter province began the era as a much more settled region, already well populated with many long-established villages, it could not sustain the same spectacular rate of growth as did Negros. Pampanga also encompassed a smaller area than did Negros and could not expand to the same degree. In areas of Pampanga where sugar came to play an important role, however, population shifts over the period were impressive (table 9). For the Capampangan of the time, parts of northern and western Pampanga and southern Tarlac represented a real frontier. Because of Pampanga's long commercial associations with Manila, other economic factors besides a concentration on sugar figured in the growth pattern of its towns. The Capampangan produced a variety of foodstuffs—fish, vegetables, and nipa wine and vinegar—as well as craft items—baskets, pottery, and ironware—for the archipelago's markets, and communities that specialized in such products continued to maintain a strong local economy throughout the period. Despite this economic diversity, however, towns with the most lands suitable for large-scale sugar cultivation tended to swell more rapidly than did older rice municipalities.[63]

A major change occurred with the 1892 opening of the Pampanga portion of the Manila-Dagupan railroad. This line ran through the middle

Table 9. Changes in Population in Pampanga's Towns with Relation to Crop Specialization

	Main Farm Crop	*Population 1839*	*Population 1918*	*Absolute Growth*	*% Growth*	*Annual Growth Rate (%)*
Angeles	Sugar	3,640	17,948	14,308	393	2.02
Floridablanca[a]	Sugar/rice	3,110	8,477	5,367	173	2.39
Santa Rita	Rice/sugar	3,325	8,989	5,664	170	1.26
Porac	Sugar	3,660	9,810	6,150	168	1.25
Mabalacat	Sugar	3,718	9,258	5,540	149	1.15
Lubao	Sugar/rice	9,220	21,614	12,394	134	1.08
Magalang	Sugar	4,680	9,780	5,100	109	.93
Sexmoan	Fish	3,510	7,224	3,714	106	.91
Bacolor	Sugar	8,548	15,302	6,754	79	.74
Candaba	Rice/ vegetables/ sugar	8,155	14,434	6,279	77	.72
Mexico	Sugar	9,345	16,151	6,806	73	.69
Arayat	Sugar	8,055	12,302	4,247	53	.54
Apalit	Rice/sugar	7,910	11,880	3,970	50	.51
Minalin	Rice	4,965	7,219	2,254	45	.47
San Fernando[b]	Sugar/rice	14,250	20,622	6,372	45	.47
Guagua[c]	Rice/sugar	11,127	15,962	4,835	43	.45
Santa Ana	Rice	4,880	6,528	1,448	34	.37
San Simon	Rice	5,560	6,992	1,432	26	.29
San Luis	Rice/sugar	8,115	9,830	1,715	21	.24
Southern Tarlac						
Capas	Sugar	870	7,633	6,763	777	2.75
Tarlac	Sugar/rice	4,345	23,888	19,543	450	2.16
Bamban[d]	Sugar	842	4,539	3,697	439	2.55
Concepcion[e]	Sugar	10,898	17,487	6,589	60	1.12

Sources: Philippine Islands, Census Office, *Census of the Philippine Islands: Taken under the Direction of the Philippine Legislature in the Year 1918* (Manila: Bureau of Printing, 1920), 2:107–8; Jean Mallat de Bassilan, *Les Philippines: Histoire, géographie, moeurs, agriculture, industrie et commerce des colonies espagnoles dans l'Océanie*, 2 vols. (Paris: Arthus Bertrand, 1846), 1:197; Marshall S. McLennan, *The Central Luzon Plain: Land and Society on the Inland Frontier* (Quezon City: Alemar-Phoenix, 1980), p. 355; *Memoria*, 1853, Pampanga, Philippine National Archives, Manila. Crop emphases based on figures from the 1918 census.

[a]First population figure is for 1876, because this town was established only in 1865.

[b]First figure includes Santo Tomas, which was absorbed into San Fernando in 1906.

[c]First figure includes Betis, which was absorbed into Guagua in 1904.

[d]First population figure is for 1852, because Bamban earlier was part of Capas.

[e]Concepcion came into existence when it split from Magalang in 1863, and the first population figure is for 1876.

of the province, passing between Apalit, San Fernando, Angeles, Mabalacat, and on through Tarlac, so that the latter four towns gained direct access to the port city for their sugar. Additional spurs to Magalang (1906), Arayat (1914), and Floridablanca (1918), plus completion of many kilometers of all-weather roads, largely eliminated dependence on water transport for sugar. These additions opened up new portions of interior Pampanga to sugar production while diminishing the prominence of Guagua as a sugar terminal. Angeles and San Fernando emerged as the two most thriving commercial centers of the province, and the latter replaced Bacolor as provincial capital in 1904. Expansion reached into neighboring Tarlac Province and probably slowed population growth in Pampanga, for numerous Capampangan migrated to towns in Tarlac, especially Capas, Bamban, Concepcion, and Tarlac, from the mid-1800s on. By 1918 these four towns had become adjuncts to sugar-growing northwestern Pampanga.[64]

Settlement of Pampanga's sugar region resembled the pattern found in Negros in several ways. Large tracts of forested land gave way to extensive sugar plantations as entrepreneurs directed groups of workers to clear jungle and plant cane. Small towns and mission settlements became large, flourishing communities, and a feeling of wilderness disappeared as aboriginal Negritos retreated to neighboring mountainous regions. Yldefonso de Aragon found in 1818 the northern part of the province sparsely populated, heavily forested, and teeming with game. By 1880 Frenchman Alfred Marche visited a transformed northern Pampanga and southern Tarlac of sugar plantations interspersed with occasional cattle ranches. Because of rinderpest, the ranchers, mainly Spaniards in Porac, Floridablanca, and Lubao, gave up stock raising in the 1890s and switched to sugar.[65] Sufficient public land for additional plantations continued to be available in Pampanga into the new century, although depression and war slowed growth from the mid-1890s to 1909; it picked up again only about 1915.

Perhaps the most notable difference between the frontier experiences of Pampanga and Negros was that in Pampanga expansion occurred mainly under the aegis of an indigenous elite rather than under that of outsiders. Capampangan planters had grown cane and produced sugar for a century on lands contiguous to the new territory; moreover, they controlled a local labor force and possessed the legal expertise to acquire unclaimed real estate. In the 1830s the landowning group consisted of a traditional indigenous elite increasingly infiltrated by Chinese mestizos, but ninety years later it was overwhelmingly Chinese mestizo with a sprinkling of Spanish mestizos, Spaniards, and Tagalogs. Despite this change, however, landlords still remained closely linked to one another through ties of intermarriage, a commonly shared Pampangan identity, and decades of economic interaction and interdependence, for newcomers augmented the old elite rather than superseding it. After 1849 mestizos largely abandoned the commercial sector and limited their pursuits mainly to farming and to supplying credit for agriculture. Through the course of these transformations they assumed the culture of a hispanized upper class. A classic example of this metamorphosis was Ceferino Joven, related by marriage to the prominent de Leon, Liongson, and Ventura families and a planter, owner of a pilon factory, and patron of local theater, who began his career in the retail trade in Binondo, the Chinese district of Manila.[66]

Pampanga had far fewer Spaniards among its landowners than did Negros, for reasons not entirely clear. Perhaps general unavailability of large tracts, save in the western section, and a tight hold on property by indigenous landowners discouraged European investment in Pampanga; or maybe difficulty in obtaining labor prevented foreign entree to sugar farming. Names of just a few Spanish families—Gil, Toledo, Puig, Valdes, Arrastia, and Herreros among the most prominent—appear on turn-of-the-century lists of those holding sugar properties, and those who remained after the advent of American rule seem to have rather quietly integrated into the local population or taken up residence elsewhere in the Philippines. Among those of Spanish descent owning land in the province (in Floridablanca and Magalang) who chose to reside in the capital was Trinidad H. Pardo de Tavera, an original member of the U.S. Philippine Commission. Aside from the Spaniards, few outsiders joined the provincial upper class. In the nineteenth century a small number of Tagalogs, including Don Pio Nepomuceno in Angeles and the prominent politician Felipe Buencamino in Apalit, married daughters of wealthy sugar farmers, but they remained the exceptions. Even fewer Americans became planters, and one discerns little of the cosmopolitan mixture that characterized Negrense hacenderos.[67]

The Chinese who returned after midcentury did not join or interact socially and politically with the landholding elite, even though these new arrivals did come to perform an important economic function. They grew in number from 153 in 1848 to 1,100 by 1893, and they clustered in the three towns of Guagua, San Fernando, and Angeles, where they remained registered on their own gremios and chose their own gobernadorcillos. Though by law they could not farm, they did participate in the sugar industry in several ways. Some bought sugar in the province and transported it to their contacts at refineries in Manila; others operated distilleries that converted molasses into rum; and many of the poorer Chinese laborers ran the steam machinery on sugar farms. Finally, as the Chinese reclaimed their role as itinerant peddlers, they drove their mestizo competitors into agriculture.

Sugar expansion, then, was undertaken mainly by the same group of planters and their descendants who farmed sugar and rice in southern portions of Pampanga. This phenomenon had several important consequences. First, the Pampangan elite, bound early by common ethnic ties and through intermarriage, utilized different sources of credit to facilitate their agricultural expansion. They depended much more on the pacto de retro for capital than they did on such outside credit sources as the foreign export companies that supplied loans to Negrenses. As noted earlier, the pacto de retro could be used under certain circumstances, particularly between rich and poor, as a means to acquire land, and historians have tended to regard it as an especially pernicious instrument. As a contract between approximate equals, friends, or relatives, however, it could serve to raise cash for additional agricultural and commercial endeavors. Such contracts proved a pervasive form of credit because with them both buyer and seller obtained many options. They could lease the land, work it, rent it to others, or use such contracts as a first step toward a final sale. Notarial registers for Pampanga contain many more entries for pacto de retro sales than do the ones for Negros. Up to 1920, even as other credit instruments became available, some Pampangan farmers still continued to employ this older form.[68]

Retro sales involved parcels of land as large as several hundred hectares and as small as two or three. One contract in the records ran for thirty-eight years, but the usual arrangement lasted between two and ten. Wills of some wealthy Capampangan show that substantial portions of their estate consisted of land held with right of repurchase, land they nevertheless bequeathed to their heirs. Many farmers worked their own fields under pacto de retro for long periods; however, it would appear that few gave them up as a result of foreclosure.

Another example of the Capampangan ability to find more local sources for investment is their use of the rural credit associations, created by the insular government in 1914. These institutions were underfinanced and required iron-clad titles before granting loans; however, they were fairly widespread and effective among the Capampangan with their closer sense of community. In 1920 Pampanga possessed sixteen branches of these credit associations, compared to only two in western Negros; a decade later the ratio had grown to twenty to four.[69]

A second consequence of the way frontier Pampanga became settled was that farmers tended to have scattered holdings rather than big haciendas. Large tracts of public land in western Lubao on the border of Bataan

Province as well as in interior Porac seem to have been granted outright or sold to Spaniards by the colonial government during the first half of the nineteenth century. One such parcel, Hacienda Mamada de Pio, consisted of 190 quinoñes (532 hectares) belonging to Don Felino Gil, the first of several generations of his family to settle in the area. Most of the other Spanish grantees sold their lands to native farmers who broke them up into smaller lots. Still, Porac, western Lubao, and, later, Floridablanca (created out of portions of those two towns) harbored the province's biggest estates, one or two as large as one thousand hectares, often referred to as "haciendas." To this region to take up farming in 1854 came Gil's nephew, Roberto Toledo, from Valencia, Spain. By the end of the century his son, also named Roberto, had enhanced the family's holdings to more than three thousand hectares, some in very large pieces. The younger Toledo stayed on as one of the most progressive sugar planters in the province.

Apart from the Toledos and a few others, the overwhelming majority of landowners, even if they possessed extensive lands, cultivated smaller plots, often in more than one town. The biggest fields, which might run to 100 or 200 hectares, usually existed in later settled frontier areas of the province, in Mabalacat, Angeles, Magalang, and the towns of southern Tarlac, for example. A sample of data from wills and other documents for the years 1889 to 1896 reveals holdings ranging from 13 to 1,033 hectares, but such estates included mixed rice and sugar lands, lands held in fee simple and through pacto retro contracts, and land in and out of production. A 1910 survey showed 419 sugar planters farming 14,903 hectares, an average of 35.6 hectares per farmer, but this year represented only the first in an upturn following an extended period of depression, and probably more and larger plantations became reactivated subsequently. The tendency among landowners to sire large families and the prevalent system of equal inheritance among children tended to reduce the size of even the larger pieces.[70]

Capampangan raised sugar through one other arrangement—leaseholding—under which a lessee (*inquilino*, or *mamuisan* in Capampangan) rented land for a fixed price in cash or in pilones of sugar. Properties rented sometimes included machinery and warehouses, and in most cases the lessee acted as a landlord and engaged aparceros to farm smaller portions of his leasehold. Notarial registers contain entries for some rentals as small as several hectares and for others as great as several hundred, with the majority for parcels larger than twenty. Rent periods ran from four years to indefinite time spans. Straight leases appear to have involved two types of lessors: those either by age or infirmity no longer able to farm themselves or wealthy entrepreneurs interested in pursuing other economic endeavors. Lessees included some of the more energetic farmers, those seeking to expand their planting beyond their own holdings. While the number of farm rentals remained small compared to that for absolute sales, it should be remembered that numerous farmers also leased land, in this case their own, through clauses of the pacto de retro contracts so frequently employed in the province.

A third consequence was that owners commonly possessed both rice and sugar lands and sometimes kept one foot in the north and one in the south. Although the northwest, being higher and drier, concentrated on sugar, and the delta on rice, all towns save two or three devoted at least some lands to both crops. Further, in times of poor sugar markets, owners and their tenants with experience in rice cultivation preserved a degree of flexibility in crop choice that could alleviate their distress.

A fourth consequence of the settlement pattern was that Capampangan transferred their traditional labor system to newly tamed lands. The samacan contract had originally evolved in the delta's rice-growing agriculture, and the elite subsequently adapted this arrangement to sugar production. Whereas with rice, landowners and casamac squared accounts in kind, with sugar they did so in coin. One of the earliest available descriptions of customary sugar contracts appears in Buzeta and Bravo's work of 1850, and turn-of-the-century portrayals by Sawyer and Forman reveal little change in their stipulations during the succeeding half century.

Under the terms of the contract, the landlord normally furnished cash loans, land, cane cuttings, processing equipment, and mill workers; the aparcero contributed his own tools, labor, and draft animals. Tenants planted, harvested, and transported the cane to the mill, where they assisted with the sugar processing. Sometimes, too, they had to supply half the cane cuttings. They paid and fed any additional hands required, but most often casamac relied on the *sugu* system of mutual help, thus reducing their expenses to the feeding of sugu during harvest time. After the completion of the sugar making the landowner sold the pilones to the Chinese merchant or his representative and then settled in cash with the aparcero. Proceeds were divided fifty-fifty, unless the landlord provided the carabao, in which case the tenant received only 25 percent.

Further variations within the contract depended on the quality of land and the degree of access to transportation networks. In practice, tenant farmers rarely profited from sugar farming, and almost all counted on credit from owners to survive through the agricultural season. Whatever the specifics of the contractual relationship, landowners monopolized profits because they owned the milling equipment, did the accounting, sold the sugar, added the molasses to their own share, set prices paid to tenants, and supplied agricultural loans. A detailed survey conducted in Pampanga around 1915 confirms that few tenants gained the opportunity to better their socioeconomic position, and it proved easier for a landlord to become a casamac than for the reverse. Occasionally aparceros emerged as small proprietors, but troubles for sugar from the 1890s on, especially the onset of rinderpest, seriously reduced tenants' expectations in the twentieth century.[71] Scarcity drove the price of animals out of the reach of many aparceros, and their income from sugar farming suffered accordingly.

At several points the 1915 report implies that sugar tenants fared better than rice tenants, but it is difficult to confirm this speculation because many casamac grew both crops either on alternate plots or at alternate times. Tenants often borrowed both cash and rice and repaid them both, although landlords usually charged more interest on rice. Since sugar tenants dealt more in a cash market, however, they seem to have held a slighly better chance to improve themselves than did the rice farmers, who lived more purely in a world of subsistence farming. In times of prosperity farming sugar offered more abundant opportunities for profit, while during depressions landlords provided some economic safety, and sugar tenants sometimes temporarily switched to rice.

Sugar planters in Pampanga made little use of migrant workers, at least before passage of the Payne-Aldrich Act. References to wage labor on sugar lands do not date back to the nineteenth century, and early twentieth-century observations stress the prevalence of tenantry in cane production. With the upturn in the American market and the move away from pilon sugar, the bigger hacenderos began to import seasonal workers from northern Luzon and a few from the Visayas. The advent of centrals further raised the need for such help, which numbered in the tens of thousands by the time the new era commenced; nevertheless, in 1920 tenant farmers and their families still served as the major source of planting and harvesting labor.[72]

A final implication of Pampanga's settlement pattern was that planters carried to new lands their old forms of sugar production, methods difficult to change because of extant socioeconomic relations. During the frontier era sugar output in Negros grew by 751 times, compared to only 5.8 times in Pampanga. The latter area already turned out substantial quantities of sugar at the outset and could not accelerate as rapidly as the former, which started almost from scratch; still, Negros consistently proved more responsive to new market demands. Greater influence from outsiders on its economic life meant it more quickly turned to new machinery and made more rapid adjustments in processing techniques than did Pampanga. The more independent Negrense planter continued freer to innovate than the Pampangan landowner bound by a complex web of commercial and labor relations. The aparceria system possessed social as well as economic dimensions, and landholders could not easily retrain their semi-independent peasant labor force or hire an alternate source of workers.

Between 1836 and 1920, sugar seemed to transform Negros more than it did Pampanga, but appearances aside, Pampangan society altered significantly. The landowning class became more oriented toward the business dimensions of farm management, prospered despite the depression at the turn of the century, and widened the social and economic gap between themselves and their poor tenants. The upper class earned a reputation for their extravagant lifestyle, hospitality, and cultural achievements, and the province itself became recognized as one of the most progressive and wealthiest in the islands. Despite similarities in social structure and geographic extension, the up-to-date province of 1920 hardly resembled the sleepy agricultural region of nine decades earlier.

To prosper within the cash-crop environment of the nineteenth century, Capampangan required economic acumen and managerial skills largely unknown to the eighteenth-century cacique described by Basco. In this new climate foreclosures and farm failures occurred, and on occasion former landowners ended up as tenant farmers. The pacto de retro presented dangers as well as opportunities for enterprising planters, and all agriculturalists had to sell their sugar on a competitive market. Purchase and maintenance of new processing equipment, employment of mill workers (often Chinese), keeping of tenants' accounts, and, perhaps, leasing land all demanded a new level of ability from planters and made them as much managers as agronomists. A talent for business, knowledge of market conditions, and comprehension of technical changes not only separated the nineteenth-century hacenderos from their predecessors, but also determined the degree of success planters had in the shifting economic conditions of the era.

Landed families in Pampanga did not comprise a single, homogeneous economic group; rather, they fit along a continuum that ranged from extremely rich hacenderos down to inquilinos not much better off than their share tenants. At the beginning of the era, much more uniformity characterized the principalia, but the growth of a cash-crop economy occasioned more differentiation as those with entrepreneurial skill, ambition, and good fortune progressed in a climate favorable to native capitalism. By the end of the period, one could usefully separate the elite into three rough groups: extremely wealthy entrepreneurs, average landholders, and urban professionals.

Almost all the very rich created their fortunes by supplying credit mainly through the pacto de retro: loaning money with land as collateral in good times and bad offered the surest way to profit. In the mid-nineteenth century, Jose Mariano Panlilio of Mexico, Pampanga, and Don Vicente Lim-ongco of Guagua both aggregated extensive holdings through pacto contracts, and by the 1890s a Spaniard named Jose Puig, after a decade of buying land with pacto de retro, established a thriving business that included sugar mills and other farming equipment. During the first years of the twentieth century, Mariano Pamintuan of Angeles converted his retro buying into an estate of some 3,227 hectares and emerged as one of the richest men in the province. Others who achieved great wealth dealing in land and credit included Jose L. de Leon and Roman Valdes of Bacolor, Manuel Escaler of Apalit, and Isidoro Santos of San Fernando. The truly wealthy knew as well how to benefit from harsh economic times: entrepreneurs like Pamintuan, de Leon, Santos, Manuel Urquico, Valdes, and Escaler purchased large parcels of land cheaply through absolute and pacto de retro sales just after the Philippine Revolution. Besides providing credit local magnates invested in other commercial ventures; de Leon, for example, joined such big planters as Honorio Ventura of Bacolor and Miguel Heras of Floridablanca as well as prominent businessman E. J. Valdes of Tarlac in founding the Pampanga Electric Light and Power Company in 1919.[73]

Pamintuan, de Leon, Toledo, and Augusto Gonzalez probably did not amass fortunes as grand as those of Esteban de la Rama, Eugenio Lopez, or Teodoro Yulo; however, aside from such Negrense moguls, wealthy Capampangan compared favorably with other great southern planters. Those Capampangan, along with a handful of others, ranked among the wealthiest in the islands and could truly be called sugar barons. By the end of the nineteenth century, Capampangan had earned a reputation throughout the Philippines for wealth and ostentation. When novelist–national hero Jose Rizal wanted to indicate in his classic *Noli me Tangere* the immense fortune of his character Capitan Tiago, he identified this Chinese mestizo as one of the big landowners of Pampanga.

Comparisons of Pampangan landholders with those in other provinces is difficult, given the paucity of similar information for provinces throughout the archipelago; however, as an example, Soledad Borromeo-Buehler notes that during the Philippine Revolution the very rich in land-poor Cavite Province, just south of Manila, owned estates of P50,000. At about this time, the will of Don Florentino Dayrit of Angeles, married to Doña Antonia Pamintuan, revealed assets of more than P176,000. Dayrit was rich by local standards but certainly not the wealthiest in his town. From another comparative vantage, a worker in a sugar mill earned 50 centavos a day.[74]

No measure precisely defines boundaries for membership in the landholding class of Pampanga, especially at the lower end of the scale. Sugar planters generally did not do manual farm labor, but even those peasant proprietors owning perhaps one to ten hectares might choose to contract laborers or rent their fields rather than work them personally. Productivity of land varied so greatly because of fertility and other physical factors that amount of hectarage owned did not always differentiate landholder from peasant proprietor either. Net income figures rarely surface in the data from the era; therefore, one gains only an impressionistic view of what constituted in provincial terms a landlord.

The following estimates of farm income of three Pampanga planters, each of whom owned a small sugar mill, appeared in testimony before the U.S. Congress in 1905:

	*Land Planted (balitas/has)**	*Sugar Produced (piculs/tons)*	*Price Sold (pesos per picul)*	*Net Profit (pesos)*
Juan Nepomuceno	220/61.5	2,560/40.5	6.00	3,000
Joaquin Linginao	120/33.5	1,200/19	5.00	1,200
Antonio Consunji	60/16.8	900/14.2	5.50	1,500

*one balita equals .2795 hectares

As part of the same testimony, a hacendero from Floridablanca estimated that 95 percent of Pampangan planters produced between 20 and 200 tons of sugar annually. By way of income comparison, in the same period Pampanga's governor received annually P3,200; the provincial fiscal (attorney) made P2,700; the provincial treasurer, an American, collected P4,800, and a justice of the Supreme Court of the Philippines earned P20,000.[75]

No data exist for this time on the amount taken in by a peasant proprietor; however, in 1913, when economic conditions had improved considerably within the province, a report indicated a range of incomes for such families of 100–300 pesos from agriculture. If they received less than a hundred pesos they had to supplement the amount with income from off-farm work.[76]

Given the absence of savings institutions in the archipelago, the elite of the province invested their earnings in farmland, urban real estate, farm equipment, warehouses, jewelry, and other negotiable items. Agricultural property in particular provided the most security and served as an important element in conferring social status, and ownership remained concentrated in the approximately 10 percent of the population that comprised Pampanga's landed elite.

Besides holding all economic power, members of Pampanga's landholding families dominated those political and bureaucratic offices available to indigenes under the colonial regimes. Few of the ultrarich took time to participate personally in local politics either under the Spanish or the American regime, concentrating, instead, on managing their vast fortunes. They left local political offices to their less well-heeled townmates (*kabalen*), especially those who formed the landholding class of the province. For example, Ceferino Joven, gobernadorcillo of the old capital town of Bacolor, became the first American-appointed, then elected, governor of Pampanga. He was succeeded by Macario Arnedo (1904–12), of Apalit's most influential planter family that included prominent Tagalog politician Felipe Buencamino. Honorio Ventura, governor from 1914 to 1921, subsequently became secretary of the interior in Manila and, briefly, acting governor-general, as well as an opponent of Manuel Quezon in archipelagowide political circles. Members of less wealthy and less notable families filled other offices, becoming municipal mayors and councilmen and barrio lieutenants. Strategic jobs like justice of the peace, notary, and head of the telegraph office—all positions that conferred local control and provided access to information—remained the monopoly of the planter class or those in their service.[77]

Access to educational facilities in the province and beyond buttressed elite dominance of local political and economic power, for the poor seldom had the chance to attend school beyond the first two mandatory primary grades. Americans placed great stress on public schooling, but the major beneficiaries of their efforts were the sons and daughters of the rich. Many landholders furthered their education at colleges and universities in Manila and Spain and, later on, in the United States. This educational advantage allowed the wealthy to turn the legal system to their benefit, to function in a complicated market environment, and to undertake such complex activities as registering property according to the stipulations of new land laws. The cadastral survey of sugar lands in Pampanga was largely completed by 1935, and the program worked almost exclusively to the benefit of the landholding elite.[78]

Because of Pampanga's smaller size and better roads, Capampangan landowners focused more of their social life on town centers than did the planters of Negros. Churches, schools, markets, and stores clustered near the poblacion, and sometimes residence there kept them closer to their scattered holdings. Wealthier landowners often maintained a residence in town and a country place near their farms, traveling between the two as their social schedules and business demands dictated.

The largest town homes usually contained a *sala* grand enough to host balls, the favorite provincial form of upper-class entertainment, often sponsored by such social clubs as the Circuito Recreativo Pampangueño of San Fernando. The social occasions provided more than mere amusement, for they also created an environment to encourage the marriages among the elite that held their property within a tight circle of families, despite the practice of equal inheritance among all the children. The endless round of dances and parties that introduced travelers and outsiders to the elite of the province ironically served the function of perpetuating Pampanga's landholding class as a closed society.[79]

In the second half of the nineteenth century towns already boasted regular mail service and telegraphic communication with Manila, and by 1900 Bacolor, Guagua, and Angeles claimed theaters for the performance of plays, especially *zarzuelas*, musicals written either in Spanish or in the local dialect. Temporary platforms set up in plazas allowed traveling drama companies to perform in other municipalities throughout the province. By 1913 automobiles traveled the local streets and all-weather roads, and before 1920 the larger towns featured boxing matches, jazz concerts, vaudeville shows, and silent movies. About this time electric lights started to appear in homes in central San Fernando, Guagua, and Angeles. The pull of urban life drew the provincial elite first to core areas of the province's most progressive towns and then, a select few, into the Manila orbit.

Urban activity and the educational system helped create an adjunct to the provincial upper class, a group of town-dwelling professionals and government functionaries who served the demands of the agricultural community. Lawyers, pharmacists, engineers, office workers, teachers, and minor officials found employment in the poblaciones, especially in Guagua, Bacolor, San Fernando, Angeles, and Tarlac, where commerce and legal business concentrated. A prominent example of this new category among the elite was the Abad Santos family. Vicente Abad Santos, the son of a merchant, received legal training and in the late nineteenth century practiced law in his native San Fernando. He was chosen to the position of *juez de ganados* (superintendent of livestock) and did well enough to acquire several residential lots and educate most of his children before he died in 1894. His eldest, Pedro, began his legal education at the prestigious Letran College in Manila.

To achieve full elite standing within the province and to hold higher political office persons in this professional group had to own agricultural land. For example, Honorio Ventura, ancestor of a later governor with the same name, was admitted to the bar in 1851 and practiced in Pampanga. He and his children improved the family's social status by transferring to sugar planting, which conferred the greatest prestige within the province. Similarly, among the children of Abad Santos, some became hacenderos, while three, Quirino, Jose, and the aforementioned Pedro, took up legal careers.[80]

During the nineteenth century the standing of these urban professionals appeared modest, but in the twentieth it rose appreciably in the face of mounting commercial and political activity. In 1916 Attorney Pedro Abad Santos, though still not a landholder, was elected to the Philippine Assembly from Pampanga, and other of his contemporaries served as municipal mayors and in high provincial office. This group also supplied many prominent members of the provincial literati: poets, playwrights, essayists, and journalists who wrote in the dialect and in Spanish and made the province at the turn of the century and afterwards one of the most important cultural centers outside Manila. As the twentieth century progressed, Pampanga's elite began to shift their social and cultural orientation toward Manila and the United States, but up to 1920 the province still served as the focal point of their interest. Professionals and Chinese merchants made life in the urban centers of Pampanga comfortable, active, and profitable even as extraprovincial diversions appeared on the horizon.

The bustle of Pampanga's towns substantiates the prosperity sugar brought; nevertheless, as in Negros that wealth remained maldistributed, for while the landholding mestizo families grew rich, their indio tenants continued at the subsistence level. Hard data on the condition of Pampanga's peasantry in the nineteenth century is difficult to find, and those for the early twentieth prove spotty at best. Old peasants did not recall any improvement in their livelihood in the early twentieth century, and records do not reveal any success stories of peasants rising to landholding status. The samacan system, with its seasonal loans of cash and staples and the inheritability of family debt, kept tenants perennially at the bottom of the socioeconomic ladder. Regardless of the paternalism inherent in the tenant-landlord relationship, catastrophes left the poor vulnerable. After battles of the Philippine-American War destroyed crops in Pampanga in 1900, starvation beset barrios of the province during the subsequent season.

Two notable changes took place in Pampanga between 1900 and 1910 under the impact of disastrous occurrences. First, as already mentioned, rich proprietors with cash to lend took advantage of the dearth of credit to increase their holdings. Their gains came at the expense of small proprietors and planters without sufficient resources to weather the continuous years of hardship. Unfortunately, no data exist on the number of landholders forced out of business at this time, and strong family support probably reduced the losses; furthermore, the government offered tax relief to stave off foreclosures. Nevertheless, enough landholders failed to allow Jose L. de Leon and others to profit from the downturn in the economy. Second, Pampangan farmers wherever possible shifted from sugar to rice cultivation. This temporary solution permitted them to improve their subsistence and to enter the rice market once again. By the end of the decade and for the first time in years, Pampanga produced a surplus of rice. So long as sugar prices stayed depressed, planters stuck to rice, for despite its limited profitability, it allowed them to retain their relationships with their casamac.

The situation for muscovado remained so poor that, despite the passage of the Payne-Aldrich and Underwood bills, Capampangan devoted more attention to rice than to sugar production during the second decade of the twentieth century. A steady demand for the grain in the archipelago and a severe rice crisis in 1919 discouraged planters from returning to cane. An estimate made about 1890 placed hectarage in Pampanga devoted to rice at 51,732, to sugar at 36,252; in 1921 the figures were 72,099 to rice and 36,500 to sugar. The province's sugar planting had not grown in three decades—but change was imminent.[81]

Access to American markets and the extraordinary wartime prices for sugar encouraged Capampangan to consider moving to better milling. Pasumil (Pampanga Sugar Mills, Inc.) was a central built with American money, the same interests that had constructed the factory at Canlubang, Laguna. Undoubtedly the fact that Pampangan planters had previously been shipping enough cane to extract 4,000 tons of sugar at this latter facility encouraged its owners to build a second plant in the north. Pasumil received strong encouragement from big planters Roberto Toledo III of Floridablanca and Martin Gonzales of Lubao and constructed the central near their haciendas; nevertheless, the company drew cane from all over Pampanga and as far away as Tarlac. Pasumil signed contracts with planters that split the output fifty-fifty and, to encourage farmers to begin milling with them, offered mortgages on their crops at 8 percent. The central experienced few difficulties obtaining contracts and was an immediate success, shipping about 19,400 tons to American West Coast refineries by 1921. Its clientele subsequently included big Spanish and native planters as well as a few Americans, Warner, Barnes and Company, and the Catholic archbishop of Manila.[82]

The other factory, Pasudeco, stood as a monument to native entrepreneurship and provincial solidarity. In response to a need for increased modern milling capacity, the leading planters and businessmen in the province met in 1918 and organized a stockholding corporation that borrowed money from the PNB and erected a central at San Fernando. Unlike comparable enterprises in Negros, Pasudeco was funded not by a single powerful native family or by foreign capital, but by a group of individual and family interests in a kind of cooperative effort that reflected the homogeneity, trust, and myriad interrelationships that existed among the

Pampangan elite. Under the leadership of founding members Jose L. de Leon, Augusto Gonzalez, sugar broker Manuel Urquico, Governor Honorio Ventura, former governor Francisco Liongson, Assistant Secretary of Justice Jose Escaler, and prominent planters Jose P. Henson and Tomas Lazatin, the agricultural interests raised sufficient internal capital for a down payment on a P5,000,000 central. Even more unprecedented in terms of provincial cooperation was that individuals like magnates Emiliano J. Valdes and Mariano Pamintuan and great planter families such as the Davids, Hizons, Lucianos, Felicianos, and Jovens gave Jose L. de Leon power of attorney over all their properties to secure the loan from the PNB. Through their financing program the Pampangan group lowered the amount they needed to borrow from the bank and became the first native corporation to redeem their mortgage. The rapid success of the central also came about as a result of the planters' great willingness to switch to centrals from rice farming and from muscovado production.[83]

Because of increased demand for sugar and the subsequent rise in milling capacity, new sources of credit became available that eventually led to a reduction in use of the pacto de retro. Loans at 8 and 10 percent from the Agricultural Bank and its more active successor, the PNB, provided big planters with cheap money, and Calamba and Pasumil began to offer mortgages to encourage planters to mill with them. Pampangan Chinese sugar brokers and local native houses like Valdes and Urquico vied with one another to provide credit in loans and in anticipatory crop sales to guarantee their supplies of sugar. Planters found it relatively easy in this period to obtain mortgages on their crops, processing machinery, houses, and draft animals if they would sell their produce to a particular broker. After years of economic drought, 1915 to 1920 turned into the best years in the whole frontier era.[84]

The advent of centrals portended significant change for the social and economic structure of the province's sugar society. For planters with sufficient wealth to invest in the new centrals the future promised big rewards, for such investments allowed them to profit from both the farming and milling sides of operations. Hacenderos who had previously done their own milling now had to split the output fifty-fifty with the central. The higher prices obtained for the centrifugal sugar and the better markets available helped offset the reduced share, but planters still had to split their portion with their tenants, further reducing profits. In general, those with ties to the processing side of the sugar industry fared better than those who only planted.

As more and more planters switched to the centrals and as the price of sugar rose, the use of the aparceria system came into question among hacenderos and sugar specialists. It is almost axiomatic in the Philippine sugar industry that when the price for finished sugar goes up hacenderos prefer to pay fixed wages, but when prices descend they like tenants to share the depression with them. In Pampanga the shift away from share tenancy remained mostly talk before 1920, but the future did not bode well for the aparceros.[85]

Sugar and Philippine Society, 1836–1920

From its modest origins in the nineteenth century the sugar industry emerged as one of the archipelago's economic giants. In 1920 it represented almost one-third of all Philippine foreign trade; moreover, the industry boasted the islands' most advanced manufacturing technology. For all its economic strength, however, the sugar business was vulnerable, because its prosperity depended largely on world demand and access to the duty-free U.S. market. While improved milling facilities represented a degree of industrial modernity to the Philippines, they did not stimulate growth of other kinds of processing, save distilling.

Yet the very status achieved by the sugar industry worked to the detriment of other Philippine enterprises. Sugar soaked up much of the private and governmental credit available to local commerce. Further, because of peak harvest labor demands and low field productivity, hacenderos discouraged cultivation of other crops, including important foods, with the result that their activities contributed to the Philippines' becoming a net rice importer from the end of the nineteenth century onward.[86] Absorption of peasant farms and open lands in northern and western Negros and upper Pampanga did more than add to planter holdings: it destroyed an alternate way of life for sugar workers and tenants.

During Spanish times collaboration between sugar planters and colonial officials served to sanction the political and economic hierarchies of Philippine society. Moreover, patterns of agricultural management on sugar farms as well as the economic gulf between rich and poor profoundly shaped the exercise of political power within society and precluded any real possibility of instituting participatory democracy, despite American efforts to install such a system. Political domination by the elite in Negros and Pampanga was complete; although sugarlandia's politicians had to share power with representatives from other regions, the sugar barons, by virtue of their economic power and size, had their way in important matters of finance at the insular level as well. The stronger the voice sugar interests gained in Manila and Washington, the more dependent they became on colonial support and protection.

Ironically, the very influence planters held with colonial governments sometimes hindered development of their own industry. In the matter of taxation Spaniards never instituted an exaction on agricultural property, and Americans imposed only a very modest one; instead, both administrations drew their major revenues from monopolies, head taxes, tariffs, and excises that shifted the burden onto others often less able to pay. Even with its modest levy on land, the American regime, rather than foreclose on their properties, allowed tax relief to planters during the early years of crisis. No other group received gentler treatment at colonial hands than did the landholders of sugar country. Accordingly, colonials never raised sufficient revenues to construct good infrastructure that would have aided agriculture and related activities in the two sugar areas and elsewhere in the archipelago.[87]

The period from 1836 to 1920 encompassed the establishment in the Philippines of a great network of family-owned sugar plantations. At the same time in Java, Hawaii, and Cuba, businessmen formed estates based on large, efficient central mills. In those places agro-industrial corporations directly controlled most of their cane supply, either through ownership or rental of fields. Filipino planters continued far longer as the primary producers of both cane and sugar, preserving for themselves a substantial share of industry-generated returns. When centrals finally arrived in the islands, hacenderos already occupied a protected niche within the industry, and through their milling contracts they persisted as active participants, sharing returns that elsewhere frequently reverted to foreign concerns.

Survival of family-owned and -managed landholdings prolonged traditional socioeconomic patterns in sugarlandia, often to the detriment of its inhabitants. In Pampanga a tenant system scarcely found in commercial crop zones lingered on as a vestige of a peasant economy, as farmers maintained the tenant-landlord pattern of their riverine heartland. Despite the impact of so modernizing a force as the sugar industry, the Capampangan, unable easily to change their methods of production, lost access to more desirable markets until late in the era.

Negrense society reflected its plantation structure. For all the wealth generated there, highways on Negros remained inadequate, central markets barely suitable, and public schools only average. The want of amenities serves as further evidence of the weaker sense of community that characterized frontier Negros. Planters might come together for entertainment and to assist one another in times of crisis, but society as a whole consisted of a series of segmented, producing units. Town centers played a less important role in social life than in Pampanga, and hacienda workers lived a more isolated existence than did casamac in the north.[88]

In both Negros and Pampanga the chief beneficiaries of the frontier era were the entrepreneurs of sugarlandia who gained wealth, prestige, and influence from their exploitation of rich new lands. Class differentiation between planters and workers became more pronounced as time passed, and the duma'an of Negros and the casamac of Pampanga found themselves increasingly trapped through debt and low returns in a permanent subsistence condition. As it did elsewhere, the sugar industry enchained Philippine field hands, casamac and duma'an, and left them little recourse against further exploitation.

FOUR

The Mind of Sugarlandia

A letter came saying that the Women's Association of Silay was composed mostly of rich families, and that, although they belonged to the elite and that they studied in big schools in Iloilo and Manila, nevertheless, in their meetings and sessions, they used their own dialect instead of English and Spanish. This was worthy of praise. Hence, I have no doubt that this association composed of twenty girls who belonged to the rich families, will without doubt prosper.

Makinaugalingon (Feb. 8, 1916)

Though it has waned, changed, been buried
Santa Iglesia is first among religions
In time to come it will again arise
Reappear, coming to us.

Santa Iglesia Brotherhood,
"Song of the Flag"
(trans. Linda Ty-Casper)

The preceding chapter dealt with the establishment of sugar society in Negros and Pampanga during the formative years from 1836 to 1920; the present one seeks to explore some ideas, perceptions, and attitudes of participants in that society as it solidified. What events shaped the thinking of sugar people, and how did they react to the changes wrought by the coming of large-scale production? One can more readily discern the social and economic structure that sprang up in sugar country during the frontier era than penetrate the outlook of sugarmen, their *mentalité,* in the argot of intellectual historians. The relationship between farming practice and world outlook is a subject only recently considered by historians, and success in such studies depends on having ample statements by the participants themselves. But expressions of discontent and satisfaction, of aspirations and disappointments by the sugar people of the Philippines are not so plentiful as are data on landholding, wealth, agricultural practices, and the other circumstances of livelihood. It is, therefore, difficult to differentiate the opinions of wealthy and modest planters and of rich and poor casamac and sugar workers, if indeed there are differences. To gain even a general notion of the outlook of sugarmen, one must comb their scarce statements and those by others who wrote about them, as well as consider their group behavior. Such an endeavor risks distortion and can lead to overly broad conclusions; however, an initial foray is worth undertaking, for during the decades of the founding of the modern sugar industry, attitudes and predilections developed that carried over into subsequent times and affected the way the industry evolved.

Hacenderos

Several important phenomena shaped the thinking and behavior of sugar planters and landowners: conquest of the frontier; acquiescence, even encouragement, on the part of the colonial government in this endeavor; strong participation of foreigners in that undertaking; and dependence on international market conditions.

Perhaps the most significant result of the transformation of the frontier into thriving sugar plantations was the considerable wealth generated, despite years of economic depression that sometimes afflicted the industry. During this era no other enterprise yielded more profit than did sugar, and the title of hacendero became synonymous with material riches. Contrary to the romanticism about heroic conquest of the wilderness that suffuses the work of writers like Robustiano Echaúz and Mariano Henson, both planters themselves, the fact persists that at its heart the taming of the frontier remained for the hacendero an economic activity, the conversion of the soil and other natural resources into investors' profits.[1]

With rare exception so-called pioneers of the industry—ex-servicemen like de Miranda and Montilla; former tradesmen and artisans like the mestizos of Iloilo and central Luzon; and erstwhile colonial civil servants, Spanish and American—moved into agriculture from other pursuits and did not actually do farmwork themselves. Advertisements of complete estates for sale on Negros appeared in nineteenth- and twentieth-century Visayan newspapers, and rentals continued to offer a door to planter status. Among later generations, a similar situation prevailed. Consider, for example, Justo Arrastia, member of a prominent Pampangan Spanish mestizo family. He finished engineering studies at the University of the Philippines, undertook graduate studies at Cornell, worked for the Bureau of Public Works, and taught at his alma mater, all before turning to farming.[2] The following note from an Iloilo newspaper conveys an impression of the way many planters approached their occupation: "A tea party will be held in 'Union Juvenal' tomorrow afternoon in honor of Mr. C. R. Fuentes and his family. They are leaving Iloilo to farm in Murcia, N.O."[3] As easily as investors moved into sugar, they just as quickly departed. At the turn of the century, Pampanga's farmers left their land fallow or turned to rice in the face of failing sugar markets; meanwhile, under similar harsh conditions, many Negros planters simply abandoned their haciendas.[4]

One gleans a sense of how hacenderos viewed their enterprises from some observations by Francisco Liongson. A physician educated in Europe, he subsequently served as governor of Pampanga and senator from the Third District; as well, he owned extensive sugar lands. In 1911, the *Philippines Free Press* interviewed him on matters pertaining to sugar farming, and his remarks sparked a debate on a number of issues related to tariffs and agricultural labor. On the state of sugar farming in his province, he commented:

> The sugar industry in Pampanga occupies the first place, for it is the only product exported abroad and so is the article which brings in big returns or revenues to the province. It is true, other products of Pampanga, such as rice, are also important, but this cereal does not go abroad but only to neighboring provinces. Pampanga produces about 700,000 piculs of sugar and when the price for a picul does not go higher than P5, the hacendero pays only his expenses, interest of 8 per cent on the capital employed, and as administrator receives for his own services only P50 a month. As a result, with sugar at P5 a picul, there is no clear profit to pay him for his trouble. And this on the supposition that everything goes well, and there are no locusts, or fires among the sugar cane, or baguios [typhoons]; and over and above all this, that none of his carabao die. But when some of these calamities come, with sugar at P5 a picul, he is headed directly for bankruptcy.[5]

Investors certainly had to learn the economics of planting and processing if they hoped to flourish, but maximization of profits remained their chief concern. Overseers and tenants took care of the everyday business of making the soil yield its fruit. Low productivity directly resulted from failure by Filipino hacenderos to pay close attention to farming methods and from their tendency to entrust supervision of their properties to employees or tenants. Some planters actively involved themselves in cane production, but many more either lacked the experience and knowledge of how to farm efficiently or showed no interest in that aspect of the business. To raise productivity required infusions of technological expertise, personal attention, and capital resources—three commodities they often sparingly offered.

Because of low labor costs and an abundance of land, however, planters earned high returns from sugar farming during the best decades of the frontier era. One of the more astute American residents in Negros, John

White, a Philippine Constabulary officer assigned there during the early American years, commented:

> But beyond other Philippine pueblos that I have known Isabela possessed a distinctive flavor; whether it was the carelessness engendered by the proximity of constant danger or because of the large number of *mestizos* and Europeans on near-by *haciendas* I cannot say, but Isabela was always gay. The *babaylanes* [local insurgents] might be raiding the *haciendas* by day; but there would be a *baile* [ball] at night. Despite many years of insurrection and outlawry there was plenty of money in circulation. Let the price of sugar rise ever so little and the *haciendas* fairly ground out wealth from the black volcanic soil. Did the *babaylanes* burn the buildings? There was abundant bamboo in the foot-hills to be rafted down the river, and a *camarin* (storehouse) could be erected in a day or two.[6]

Rather than using their gains to raise agricultural productivity, hacenderos spent money elsewhere. The most entrepreneurial found ancillary activities in which to invest, or they turned to other financial outlets: shares of commercial banks and trading houses, money lending, trade, urban real estate, and utilities. Nevertheless, colonial policy severely limited opportunities in the broad area of manufacturing, and savings institutions did not exist before the twentieth century. Other planters utilized their profits to purchase jewelry for security against hard times or to educate their children as a way of diversifying their economic expectations. Many simply indulged in conspicuous consumption in the form of large houses, imported merchandise, gambling, religious processions, automobiles, and an extravagant lifestyle.

Sugar hacenderos became known for their liberal spending, as this quote from the *Philippines Free Press* suggests:

> With sugar at eight pesos a picul it looks as if the halcyon days of yore were on the wing for the planters of Negros and Panay. . . .
>
> Now it looks as if even P8.00 might not constitute the limit and that the register recording saccharine prices might not stop until it strikes an even P10. All of which means mortgages wiped off and plantations free and unencumbered and a healthy balance in the bank and large purchases and a revival of the ancient splendor and glory and royal magnificence and lavish entertainment for which Negros was formerly famed.[7]

Capampangan, too, earned a similar reputation for wealth, as evidenced by descriptions from numerous foreign travelers to the province. For instance, José María Mourin, a Spanish visitor particularly observant of matters material, recorded at Christmas time 1876:

> For our next activity we headed to San Fernando and went up to the house of the former Capitan [gobernadorcillo] named Paras, who lived with his family, among whom the one who stood out, a pleasant mestiza named Juanita.
>
> Not only did the good construction of this house surprise me, but also even the reliefs on the doors were well done, and the spaciousness of it, besides the profusion of furnishings that adorned it, and the good taste and beauty of many things, among others that caught my attention, a mirror in the Venetian style with a frame also of mirror, magnificent busts worth at least five hundred pesos each, and a superb sideboard for silver plate in the dining room (which is a room separate from the interior gallery), that went for no less than one hundred pesos; and all that hardly benefits this rich family, since it has few needs, and only on great occasions do they light the lamps and show off the furnishings.

On a later visit to the Paras house, Mourin added:

> While the others were eating . . . I could not help but focus on the contrast between the luxury, the splendor of this house, the exquisite platters, the delicious wines and all the refinements of modern civilization, with the calico shirt of Paras, his bare feet shod with light slippers, spending on this meal solely in order to entertain his guests, without having a fondness for those eating and drinking; and it's probable that a little ball of rice and viands, with their dried fish, solely constitutes the repast of Paras and his family. Undoubtedly it is worthwhile studying the indio with his mixture of plainness and ostentation, of vanity and indifference and the other multitude of contrasts that would be extensive to enumerate.[8]

Mourin's observations coincide sometimes even in small detail with those of such other tourists as Ferdinand Alençon, a French nobleman who visited Pampanga around 1850, and Edith Moses, an American who visited half a century later. Compare Mourin's remarks, too, with those of English businessman John Foreman about a hacienda in northern Negros in the early 1880s:

> From Victoria[s] to Cadiz Nuevo, the route is still worse, and one has to ford several streams and a number of insecure bridges to reach the town. Instead of going directly to Cadiz Nuevo, I turned off to a place called Bayabas—to the property

> of a half-cast Chinese planter, whose acquaintance I had made in Yloilo. His estate-house is the neatest and prettiest I have ever seen in any Philippine plantation. The spacious airy apartments are well furnished and decorated, whilst the exterior calls to mind a country gentleman's residence in fair Andalusia. Moreover, the furniture of the house was chosen with rare taste, whilst the vestibule and lobbies are void of that miscellaneous lumber generally found in Philippine farmery.
>
> The owner, Don Leandro, and his *Señora* shewed me every attention. Ponies were at my disposal for riding round his splendid property—a basket chaise was always ready if I wished to go into town. I could bathe in the house, or I could swim in the river, the *Italon diutai*—with its shaded banks, two minutes walk from the house.[9]

Whether in the poblaciones of Pampanga or in the more rural settings of northern and interior Negros, foreigners encountered a form of hospitality purely indigenous in provenance. As early as 1521, a datu treated Ferdinand Magellan and his officers to a grand feast served on imported porcelain platters.[10] By the nineteenth century the ritual had changed little; only its main diplomatic purpose of putting strangers at ease had given way to a more informal function of providing visitors with respite from the journey and with evidence of a family's local standing. Furnishings and settings were more likely to be Western, reflecting intervening centuries of colonial influence.

Besides elegant meals, sugarlandia's hosts frequently treated their guests to an evening of dancing such as the ones attended by John White at the turn of the century.

> The people of Negros delighted in dancing. Rarely a week passed in any pueblo but that a baptism or a birthday offered excuse to get together a few guitars or a more pretentious orchestra, clear the polished hardwood *sala* (hall) of some house, and tread a maze of waltzes, polkas, and *rigadons* (square dances) from 9 P.M. to daybreak.[11]

The first ball that White attended in Bacolod honored the visiting governor-general. Mourin was also invited to such affairs during his stay in Pampanga.

Other travelers to nineteenth-century Negros and Pampanga shared Mourin's view of the newly rich quality of the planter life there, of the elegant possessions out of sync with the hacenderos' own more plain, rustic lifestyle. Recent penetration by Chinese mestizos and others into the planter group at a time when the taming of the frontier created new fortunes likely accounted for their need and ability to acquire status symbols, the fancy goods so proudly exhibited. As the period closed, however, later, better-educated generations behaved in a more sophisticated manner and became more comfortable with their use of such possessions. Edith Moses, a visitor in Apalit's most distinguished home, confirms this transition in the following comment:

> The dinner was good, but dining or rather the feeding of one's guests is a serious affair in the Philippines. . . . After dinner we had music and dancing, and were delighted with the young uncle of the girls. He is a charming young man educated in Europe, yet not spoiled by his sojourn there. He was gay, unaffected, and simple in his manners. He is clever, too, and manages the large estate owned by an elder sister, who, it appeared, is a woman of character and position in Pampanga. She did not appear at the dinner and we did not see her until just as we were leaving, when a tall dark "Indian woman" appeared, who was dressed in a straight narrow skirt and a cotton jacket. She extended a hand in greeting, and our young host presented her with all due deference and courtesy as a lady who had never learned Spanish. No one seemed disturbed by her sudden appearance and there was no attempt to keep her in the background, but this dispenser of diamonds and dinners, for she owned the house and all it contained, preferred to superintend the kitchen maids and be presented to her guests later.[12]

At least one version of the contemporary social ideal of the planter class appeared in "A Remarkable Filipino Family." Written by Negrense planter/journalist Ramon Navas, the article, which was published in the *Philippine Free Press*, dealt mainly with the four daughters of a planter from Cadiz. Of them, he wrote:

> But it is not so much that they play the piano and the violin so well, and that they shine in both Negros and Iloilo society, that the Lopez girls elicit admiration. Personally, I admire them most when they are at home.
>
> Last week I had an opportunity of visiting their home in Faraon. While traveling for the FREE PRESS I saw many Filipino homes, but I have never been in one where so much of that right and sane Americanism, mingled with all that is best in our own native manners and customs, is to be found. As one enters the house one sees on the left a stand of books, on

> the table on the other side, books again, and copies of the *Ladies Home Journal, The Delineator, Woman's Home Companion, Collier's, Everybody's Smart Set, Popular Mechanics,* and half a dozen other magazines, besides Manila and Iloilo and local newspapers.[13]

By the second decade of the twentieth century, this ideal of blending American culture with native refinement had spread widely among the Filipino upper class, in part because of the broad access to education provided by the colonial regime and because of closer economic ties encouraged by the Payne-Aldrich Act. In sugarlandia, moreover, familiarity with Occidental ideas and tastes became even more pronounced because of interaction with Spaniards and Americans through the industry and through intermarriage, especially with the former group.

Cultural refinement, a good education, and a reputation for lavish hospitality stood as important achievements to members of planter society, and they spent liberally to attain those goals. The image of the freewheeling, free-spending planter came to symbolize both independence of spirit and action to the hacendero class and to other Filipinos as well. Francisco Varona, a Visayan author of the 1920s and 1930s, wrote a book that revealed his admiration for the great entrepreneurs whom he described in almost heroic terms. For example, he portrayed one of them as follows:

> They still recall the pomp and opulence of D. Jose Domingo Frias, the magnate who competed from La Carlota with Capitan Orong Benedicto, Sambi Hernaez and Isidro de la Rama in financial matters. Of Frias they said that, through his capitalization of haciendas and hacenderos, he could have built a larger fortune, had he been a man of greater ambition. He could have owned a number of haciendas that today would represent one of the grandest fortunes in the Philippines. But Don Jose Domingo Frias contented himself with having what, at the time, was considered the maximum in riches, with his million in properties, lorchas and cash, the product of his loans; he bridled his ambition, satisfying himself with pursuing his business at a moderate pace while he rewarded himself by living a splendid life of a nabob generously shared with his family and all his friends. He created and maintained at his own expense, and for the personal delight of his palatial household, the best and largest orchestra, the orchestra Kandaguit, and in his immense dining room he maintained a perpetual banquet for guests who came regardless of the day of the week.

> It is said that, once, when D. Jose Domingo Frias was playing cards, people approached him with a proposition for sale at a seductive price of a beautiful hacienda with mature cane. The potentate Don Jose Domingo did not want to listen to the proposition so as not to bother the friends who were playing with him. Well, this hacienda, having been purchased by someone else, was paid for from money produced by the sale of sugar milled from the harvested cane.[14]

In Pampanga, independence was also highly esteemed, but the more cautious Capampangan frequently tied prestige to public service and the professions as well. Being a sugar planter meant having social standing in Pampanga, and great entrepreneurs like Roberto Toledo, Jose L. de Leon, and Augusto Gonzalez were all highly admired; nevertheless, most smaller landholders needed further attainments to rise to the social pinnacle. Jose Ventura, son of a planter and nephew of Governor Honorio Ventura, acquired an advanced education in England and Spain and achieved prominence as an attorney and financier; furthermore, he married Carmen Pardo de Tavera, daughter of a member of the Philippine Commission.[15]

The ideal of the independent and achievement-oriented planter clashed with the reality of the prevalence of debt in sugarlandia, since hacenderos frequently found themselves dependent on loans. For every Jose Domingo Frias willing to supply credit, there existed numerous farmers borrowing from him or from others. Credit and debt is a phenomenon woven into the fabric of Philippine society and is prehispanic in origin. It stands at the heart of patron-client bonds such as the tenant-landlord relationship that tied Pampangan society together and was used in various ways in other businesses in the islands. Social and political relations have long operated on a ubiquitous system of favor and obligation. In the sugar industry, however, the system of loans grew out of proportion to the availability of credit and took on more of the character of a strict business obligation.

Negrense farmers freely admitted their personal dependence on credit and its role in sustaining the sugar industry on their island. Confronted with a market crisis in 1886, a group from La Carlota and Pontevedra sent the government a petition of relief that included the following remarks:

> From 1860 to 1877 was the time of the development of agriculture in the Archipelago, thanks exclusively to the special help of the foreign commercial houses that unlocked financial credits for both machinery and clarifying equipment to establish haciendas, especially for cane sugar. [The credit], if not all that was necessary, [was] at least enough to produce [sugar] under conditions of [hacenderos] being able to redeem annu-

ally, if not all their debts, at least two thirds or three quarters of them with some exception. [It was] all that some hacenderos could accomplish under the most favorable circumstances and with their best efforts.

In this whole period, due to the fertility of the soil and to the newly opened lands, even with little intelligence on the part of the majority of the farmers, the fields produced sugar in abundance so that from year to year came such enthusiasm for agriculture that peninsular and locally born Spaniards and natives who figured at least that even though they dedicated insufficient [funds] to create haciendas, by relying always from the start on the credit that they would get from the above mentioned houses, and, with the good conditions of the years cited up to 1877 and beyond, there was such abundance of production that in those years there was a feeling of well-being because the rewards more than compensated for all the anxieties of the work. The savings sugar afforded them they gradually returned to the farm as improvements that haciendas needed for completion, and in this manner at the end of each harvest and sale of sugar it always roughly came out that if they did not break even with their creditors, having very little debt they could later resort to a loan for the succeeding harvests.[16]

With the frequent downturn in market conditions from the late nineteenth century onward, the plea for low-interest credit grew into a steady refrain in sugarlandia, somewhat more strongly heard in Negros than in Pampanga. Through newspapers and reports of the provincial governors, the call for loans and mortgages came from planters and their spokesmen. Timoteo Unson, a newspaper writer and planter farming in Negros, spoke most eloquently on behalf of distressed planters in a 1913 article in the *Philippines Free Press.* After detailing the preceding years of disaster and pointing out that most planters did not have resources for luxurious living, he concluded:

There you have the true causes of the present crisis and it is not attributable to improvidence or mismanagement on the part of the farmers, since it has been shown how if the farmers of Negros know how to spend 100 or 200 thousand pesos on silks and jewels to please their wives and daughters, they also know how to spend eight million on work animals; if they know how to spend 100 thousand pesos on automobiles, they also know how to spend 6 million on agricultural machinery and cultivation equipment, and for such people who know how

> to allocate their expenses, it is an injustice to say that they spend money on luxuries and feasts.[17]

The Iloilo newspaper *Makinaugalingon* (Native ways) sometimes served as the conscience of southern farmers, and, apropos agricultural loans, its editor wrote:

> Many of the farmers from Negros have no clear account books. Hence, many of them were victims of a loan shark—especially if the loan money was not spent properly, but was, instead, used on things unrelated to farming, for example, gambling, diamonds, politics, automobiles, and other luxurious things. If so, the hacendero will certainly fall into the pit of bankruptcy, and, hence, his hacienda will be taken by the loan sharks. Thanks to a law introduced by Commissioner Jaime de Veyra, all luxury goods must be paid for by the owner. Perhaps this kind of law will curtail the unnecessary expenditures of some hacenderos.[18]

In reality, hacenderos and landholders employed credit in a variety of ways: to farm, to invest in newer equipment, and to retire prior debts, as well as to grant loans to their tenants and duma'an. Planters also borrowed to buy luxury goods and to invest in nonfarming enterprises. Critics and defenders of the planter way of life could find many examples of the misuse of and the need for credit, and the numerous references to this subject suggest that it remained a pressing topic in sugarlandia, particularly in the last few decades of the frontier era.

Especially in times of distress, partisans of the hacenderos spoke often and loudly of the need for survival loans; however, during good years only occasionally did anyone from the inside point to risks inherent in extravagant expenditures. In 1920, the following rather isolated news item appeared: "Representative Lope Severino of Silay recently announced that he is not happy with the luxury of the hacenderos. They should think of the future because the price of sugar might go down and the little saving they have might just disappear like a dream."[19] Here surfaces a rare testimony on a harsh reality of planter life: that big rewards from sugar farming came only intermittently. Credit remained the vehicle by which hacenderos transported themselves from one crisis to the next.

Planters in Negros and Pampanga perceived no difficulty in turning to the government for aid with their financial problems because in the past the regimes had provided them economic relief. The planter class stood as a powerful political and economic prop for the colonial administrations, and the latter sought to assure landholders' support by following policies that would not alienate them.

To obtain such support from the government, hacenderos had learned to make use of petitions, a custom that dated back at least to 1886, when Negrenses sent Manila a nine-point proposal. By the twentieth century ad hoc agricultural associations in Pampanga and Negros, with prominent spokesmen like Liongson, Jose Escaler, José de Leon, Rafael Alunan, Matias Hilado, and Tito Silverio, regularly petitioned Manila on various financial matters related to their benefit. Additionally, under the United States, planters enjoyed increased say over government financial policies when sugarmen were elected first to the Philippine Assembly established in 1907 and then to the Senate after 1916.[20] The following item from the *Free Press* reveals how planters interacted with the government on their own behalf:

> News of the possible postponement of legislative action on the project for a national bank so alarmed the farmers of Occidental Negros that a meeting of them was held in Silay last Sunday for the purpose of devising some means to avert the impending calamity. It was decided to send former assemblyman Esperidion Guanco, who was president of the first agricultural congress, and Carlos Locsin to Manila to urge upon the legislature the necessity of immediate action on the bill. According to Mr. Guanco, unless the legislature approves the national bank bill, the withdrawal of two million pesos of government money from the planters during the next harvest crop, and the shutting down of credit by the British houses on account of the war, will mean the grave of Negros agriculture.[21]

Within two years Guanco was elected to the Senate, where he ended up on the banking committee overseeing policies of the newly created PNB and supervising the activities of rural credit associations. By 1920 the leaders of the sugar industry were already influencing government policy in the Philippines; more and more sugarmen were moving to Manila to enjoy the benefits of urban life—and also to lobby for favorable legislation for their industry.[22]

As a group, hacenderos adopted a conservative stance toward the use of government in support of the common weal; rather, they supposed its purpose was to aid planters so that they could afford to help others. As noted in the last chapter, owners paid little in the way of land taxes, and the government accordingly functioned on sparse income. In 1920 the provincial government of Negros Occidental sought permission from the governor-general to solicit private contributions for the construction of roads and bridges.[23] Many public expenditures in Negros and Pampanga depended on private donations, a sort of noblesse oblige, and local newspapers abounded with stories of elite generosity, among them the following:

> Agustin Ramos of Himamaylan, Negros, donated to the municipality a concrete school house which cost him P15,000. People rejoiced at this exemplary act.[24]

> The high esteem for public instruction in this province exists, perhaps because said branch has the necessary support for its promotion and development. One may say, if no school buildings are being raised, that they begin to raise them and that they will probably raise them. Bacolor rates among others with its School of Arts and Trades; Arayat with its intermediate school; San Fernando with its high school. The erection of these buildings is through voluntary contributions of the citizens and through donations by the municipal, provincial and insular governments.
>
> Angeles and San Luis have already collected enough money, in spite of the hard times, to build in their respective jurisdictions spacious intermediate schools. It mounts into the thousands of pesos the money gathered by voluntary contribution. Not much time will pass, if the eagerness for instruction continues as it has up to today, before all the towns in this beautiful region may count upon their own school houses.[25]

Numerous items from the local news make it clear that provincial schools, public as well as private, relied on the generosity of the wealthy, and this situation caused a writer for *La Igualdad* to wonder if democracy could flourish under a system where public education depended so heavily on private largesse.[26] But Negrense planters felt that they made education effective. In 1901, when the Philippine Commission met with local officials to discuss formation of a civil government, the following observation appeared:

> Referring to the subject of education, [a representative from Bacolod] did not think the present system in Negros left anything to be desired. He referred to the town of Bago, where there are over four hundred children attending school. The president of that town had paid money out of his own pocket for clothing, so that the children might appear decently attired; and all this upon the initiative of the present government of Negros.[27]

Like so many conservatives, hacenderos feared that too much government would cost them money better used elsewhere. In deliberations over creation of provincial administration for both Pampanga and Negros, questions of officials' salaries arose and were strongly debated. On the matter of taxation, the following comment appeared in the minutes:

> Senor Ramon Orozco [of Bacolod], who offered to speak in English if desired, showed credentials making him the floor representative of five towns of Western Negros. . . . His towns, he said, were also pleased with the proposals as to the land tax and distributing more equitably the burdens of supporting the government. . . .
>
> Orozco, however, went on to say that the "proletariat" class, not owning land, would pay nothing under this system, while their wages are now about eight dollars a month and on these they live very comfortably. The onus of taxation would fall on the rich, who would gradually lose their land.
>
> Another speaker interrupted to recommend a direct tax of two dollars gold per year on the proletariat class. At present they have to pay $1.50 gold for cedulas.[28]

This last remark reveals a strong planter belief that the functions of government did not include rectifying the income imbalance between rich and poor. Furthermore, it shows the distinct limitations on the sense of paternalism felt by the elite of Negros.

By virtue of their wealth, political position, education, and cultural orientation, the elite attained a familiarity with foreigners that made it easier for them to exert influence upon the colonial regime. Western merchants, government officials, and travelers regularly sojourned at Pampanga and Negros, where they interacted with hacenderos officially and unofficially. On Negros there existed a situation virtually unknown elsewhere in Southeast Asia, where citizens of the metropolitan country actually worked as inquilinos for native landholders. In no other area outside Manila did such an easy relationship between Europeans and the native elite spring up as in the sugar provinces. With Americans it took longer for such an interaction to develop, in part because of racial prejudices and stereotyping the new rulers brought with them and also because of the language barrier; nevertheless, when the first military officers and civilian administrators arrived in Pampanga and western Negros, they were quickly introduced to children of the elite already able to speak English, often learned in Hong Kong.[29] Official contacts between representatives of the two peoples were followed by formal social engagements that eventually led to more personal relations. To be sure, outright social equality did not exist, and Americans usually proved more standoffish than did their predecessors; nevertheless, greater dependence on native participation by the new administration eventually eased the formality of the relationship. In no other colony in Southeast Asia did a group of natives immediately play such an influential role as did that in the Philippines. Consider that, of the original three Filipino appointees to the Philippine Commission, two—Pardo de Tavera and Luzuriaga—held sugar lands and a third—Benito Legarda—while not having sugar properties, owned other agricultural lands and a nipa palm wine distillery in Guagua, Pampanga. The general attitude of sugarlandia's elite toward foreigners appears most clearly in its response to the Philippine Revolution, against both Spain and the United States.

The Revolution, Asia's first major nationalistic movement against a Western power, stands as the most complex series of events in the archipelago's history, and the body of literature on this subject is enormous. Historiographic disagreements about the meaning and extent of revolutionary activity abound, and it would require at least a monograph to elucidate these debates; nevertheless, recent work on the Revolution in Pampanga and Negros has provided some insight into sugar elite behavior during those trying times.[30]

Between 1872 and 1896, members of the Filipino intelligentsia led by Jose Rizal and Marcelo del Pilar launched the nonviolent Propaganda Movement among students and intellectuals of the Christian lowlands to encourage political, economic, and religious reform of the Spanish regime. While the movement's main actions occurred abroad and in the areas in and around Manila, the turmoil reached into Pampanga when a small number of landholders such as Ceferino Joven and Mariano Alejandrino joined "subversive" Masonic lodges in San Fernando and Bacolor. A crackdown on Freemasonry in 1892 resulted in punishment of both men, the harsher sentence falling on Alejandrino, who was exiled to northern Luzon. Capampangan also shared in the student ferment in Spain, where Jose Alejandrino (son of Mariano) and Francisco Liongson joined Rizal in discussions of the colony's future under colonialism. Although large numbers of Capampangan did not participate openly in the various organizations, many undoubtedly quietly shared the sentiments in favor of reform. The province was so close to the center of agitation that the political currents of the times could scarcely have gone unnoticed or unfelt there. In Negros, however, there appears to have been little enthusiasm for the Propaganda Movement from elite residing either in the archipelago or in Europe. Negrenses studied at those same educational centers where the burning issues were discussed, but only a few converted to the cause, including Juan Araneta, a student contemporary of Rizal and Jose Alejandrino at the Ateneo de Manila and in Europe.

Open revolt against Spain broke out in the Tagalog provinces in August 1896 and culminated in victory when revolutionary troops gained control over almost all of Luzon during June 1898. The First Philippine Republic, based on the Malolos (Bulacan) Constitution, was inaugurated under the leadership of President Emilio Aguinaldo on January 23, 1899. As the fortunes of Spain declined, Capampangan and Negrense allegiance to the mother country faded as well.

Despite attempts by the Republican forces to involve Pampanga in their struggle, the province remained uncommitted during the first year. On October 15, 1897, the last Spanish governor of Pampanga, José Cánovas, wrote to his superiors:

> [Since the outbreak of fighting] there was not a single moment of indecision: from the first moment until today, all the towns declared allegiance to Spain, have stayed and will stay at her side, accepting the same fate as the Spanish flag, rejoicing with the triumphs of our arms and suffering for the cause of Spain's persecution, blockade and plunder by the rebels who, on different occasions, have shown to the Pampangos who have fallen into their hands indignities for [the rebels'] having encountered in this province one of the most formidable obstacles to their intent, because Pampango loyalty has been a model of continuity for the soldiers of five provinces. . . .
>
> A call was sounded to gather resources for Pampangos who died or were wounded in the lines of [our] army, and the province with great generosity offered her help; ask for donations for the [Spanish] patriots and at once the province will heed the call without pressure of any kind.[31]

For all its contributions, Cánovas hoped that the government would award Pampanga a permanent title such as "Muy Heroica y Siempre Fiel," or "Muy Noble y Muy Leal," or even "Muy Española."

Pampangan loyalty began to wither in late 1897 when guerrilla units of the Republican cause began to filter into the province, providing evidence that Spain could no longer control the military situation. A Capampangan from Tarlac, General Francisco Makabulos, commenced organizing clandestine revolutionary cells in every town; and the Spanish population, facing increased hostility, started one by one to evacuate the province. By the time of Dewey's victory over the Spanish fleet at the Battle of Manila Bay in May 1898, Pampanga had committed itself to the Republic, raising local troops to expel remaining Spanish forces.

The Negrenses, too, initially declared their allegiance to Spain and, more tangibly, committed men and money to the Loyal Volunteers, a locally raised force of Spaniards and natives who joined the fighting against Aguinaldo's army from November 1896 to April 1898. The Negrenses did not support in any significant way the Republican cause, although several planters including Juan Araneta were arrested and held on suspicion.

As long as Spain appeared able to hold the upper hand in the conflict, most Negrenses stayed loyal to the mother country; however, with Spain's defeat at Manila Bay and its subsequent losses to the armies of Aguinaldo and the United States, the hacenderos began to distance themselves from their old ally. By August 1898 several towns in Negros Occidental had formed central and local revolutionary committees, and Generals Aniceto Lacson and Juan Araneta acted as regional commanders of the northern and southern sections respectively. Planters created local military units and drafted their sometimes reluctant workers to fill the ranks. Lacson even resorted to hiring Macabebe mercenaries from Pampanga to provide himself with reliable soldiers. In a move coordinated with revolutionary groups on Iloilo, Negrenses used their superior numbers to defeat small pockets of Spanish troops in Bacolod and Himamaylan between November 5 and 8, thereby ending more than three centuries of Spanish occupation.

Negrense leaders then took a unique step: instead of affiliating with the Malolos Republic, they immediately formed their own provisional government with Lacson as president and Araneta as war delegate. During the next month they created the Cantonal Government with local branches in every town of the island and opted for autonomous status vis-à-vis Malolos. This course of action did not sit well with leaders on neighboring Panay, for leaders there had hoped to include Negros in a new federal government of the Visayas they were then creating. The decision taken at Bacolod and endorsed by most planters can perhaps be seen as further evidence of a growing social and sentimental separation of Negros from its parent settlement across the Guimaras Strait.

The third and final phase of the Revolution commenced in February 1899 when the Philippine Army battled the forces of the United States, which now claimed the archipelago by virtue of the Treaty of Paris signed the preceding December. The First Filipino Republic ended in April 1901 upon the capture of Aguinaldo and his taking the oath of allegiance to the United States; nevertheless, sporadic guerrilla operations persisted in widely scattered areas including Pampanga and interior Negros for months, even years in the case of the latter. Despite continuing incidents of violence, the inauguration of civil government on July 4, 1901, signified to the elite of sugarlandia the finale of the Revolution.

Within a week of obtaining the Spanish surrender and before the signing of the Treaty of Paris, the government of Negros forwarded to the Americans a petition seeking alliance, signed by Lacson, Araneta, Melecio Severino, and other high-ranking officials. After Iloilo fell to American forces in February 1899, representatives from Negros accelerated that search. Members of both the Malolos and U.S. governments acknowledged that this defection of Negros seriously damaged the morale and prestige of the budding national government. Thereafter, in several stages, the island moved toward provincial status under the new regime, a status confirmed on May 1, 1901. These actions earned the enmity of the Aguinaldo government, and the Negrenses subsequently had to ask for help from the Americans in dealing with Republican dissidents who had secretly entered their province and harassed planters declaring their allegiance to the United States.

Leaders on Negros justified their actions in this way:

> Holding the current responsibility that we have contracted before the civilized world [and] . . . considering that, having assured the internal order of this territory, we have also the duty to take precautions against the attacks of Spain or of any other foreign power, that if this event should occur, it would be the beginning of the destruction of all that exists on this fertile, rich and coveted soil, because we are prepared to repel with all our force all unjustified aggression; having deliberated with wisdom about this most essential point that demands immediate solution and making use of the authority we are demonstrating:
>
> The provisional revolutionary government of this independent territory has agreed to take refuge as a protectorate of the Grand Republic of the United States of North America.[32]

At the turn of the century Philippine nationalism scarcely reached rural areas, and the sugar elite of Negros placed local concerns above those of a newly formed, shaky government dominated by a small group of leaders from central Luzon. From their own vantage, Negrenses could hardly have acted otherwise.

The south also faced another worry, where to sell its sugar. Exports from Iloilo had begun dropping off, and the demise of Spanish authority made existing international market arrangements unpredictable. That the possibility of renewing access to the U.S. market and of penetrating the Dingley Tariff wall occurred to leaders on Negros is obvious from the following hint contained in a letter, dated May 27, 1899, from President Aniceto Lacson to President McKinley:

> The Island of Negros, inhabited by sons of toil engaged almost exclusively in agriculture, produces more than half of the total amount of sugar exported from the Philippines, and for this reason its inhabitants are in the majority peacable, and have gladly accepted American authority, because it is the incarnation of work and material progress, and is the generator of moral progress also.[33]

Economic interest coupled with political realism informed basic decisions made by the Negrense leadership during the Revolution.

The third phase of the Revolution proved far more devastating and divisive for the Capampangan, since a large share of the fighting happened on their turf, leaving their land ravished and many of the poor famished. No neat political swings occurred, and questions of loyalty became confused because of shifting military control, physical and psychological coercion, and the raging guerrilla warfare that engulfed the province. Broadly speaking, Capampangan began this phase overwhelmingly in support of the Republic, but by the time the period ended, with the creation of Pampanga Province under the American civil government in February 1901, a majority of the elite backed the new colonial regime. Many local civilian leaders participated in the Malolos government, and Maximino Hizon and Jose Alejandrino as well as Servillano Aquino and Francisco Makabulos from Tarlac served loyally in the top ranks of the army. Residents in the province provided soldiers, logistics, and moral support to the cause, even as U.S. forces began to invade its borders.

For roughly the next two years, the provincial elite found themselves trapped between two contending parties, each demanding their allegiance. Guerrilla intimidation of planters to hold their loyalty was matched by U.S. coercive pressures to end their support for the Republic. Murders, kidnappings, burnings, and robberies marred tranquility until the Americans finally mastered sufficient control of the countryside. As peace returned, more and more hacenderos—including such former loyalists as Liongson, Joven, and Enrique Macapinlac—committed themselves to the new order. Others, such as Hizon, Alejandrino, and Pedro Abad Santos, even after their capture remained true to the cause.

The majority of the elite in Pampanga seemed to swim with the tide of whichever side controlled the province, but such an observation obscures a more complex reality. The elite espoused a conservative ideology that called for order and the sanctity of private property, and they gave their allegiance to the government—Spanish, Philippine Republican, or American—that appeared to provide them the best guarantee of stability. At times when it was not clear which faction would win, many Capampangan paid a heavy price for making a choice, suffering death, injury, and/or loss of property. When the Americans emerged at last as the victors and supported the traditional order, the elite backed them, even at considerable risk to themselves. While their revolutionary experience differed, the sugarmen of Negros and Pampanga shared, finally, a common desire for tranquility, peaceful commerce, and the preservation of their own estates, aspirations the Americans promised to respect. To those ends, national independence took a back seat.

Planters of sugarlandia subsequently subordinated their desire for political freedom to their need for markets. No more striking evidence of this attitude can be found than in debates over passage of the Payne-Aldrich Act in 1909. This tariff bill offered duty-free access to the U.S. market for large quantities of Philippine agricultural commodities, including sugar, in exchange for free entry to the archipelago of American manufactures. Filipino nationalists opposed this bill, correctly anticipating that it would create an economic reliance on the United States that would delay political independence.[34]

Sugarmen did not begin their quest for American tariff preferences with the idea of compromising Philippine independence, and not all hacenderos favored the 1909 arrangement; however, in the end, the majority of them chose economic advantage over other considerations. In September 1901, scarcely had civil government come to the provinces when planters in Negros and Panay petitioned Governor-general Taft for reduction of duties under the Dingley Tariff, and this plea continued for the next eight years with planters from the south even taking their case directly to the halls of the U.S. Congress.[35] Spokesmen for the Negrense planters did not view tariff relief as a brake to the drive toward liberation but rather as part of a package of relief for their depressed industry. In his report for 1906, for example, Governor Melecio Severino, after outlining the economic hardships confronting Negros, wrote the following:

> Such being the calamities afflicting agriculture, with which the planters must necessarily and desperately contend, it cannot be hoped to bring about an improvement of agricultural conditions by their unaided efforts or without the decided protection of the Government.
>
> It therefore becomes necessary for the Insular Government to exert itself on behalf of the Islands for the enactment of legislation which shall free from customs duties agricultural

> machinery and implements; which shall encourage the establishment of agricultural and mortgage banks, and which shall reduce or abolish the Dingley tariff on sugar. It would also be advisable for the Philippine Commission to appropriate Insular money for the extermination of locusts and grasshoppers and to enact a law regulating plantation labor.[36]

Capampangan, in contrast, because of their proximity to the capital and its politics and because of their closer ties to the old revolutionary cause, showed greater understanding of the dangers inherent in tariff concessions. In 1905, a group called "Comite de Intereses Filipinos," made up of more than a hundred of the province's most influential agriculturalists and professionals, sent a long petition to Secretary of War Taft, listing thirty desired changes. Unlike the usual solicitation from Negros, the document encompassed all the points of the current nationalist agenda, including demands for a specific date for independence, formation of a legislative assembly, trial by jury, revision of the sedition and libel laws, reform of the constabulary, change in the composition of the Philippine Commission, reduction in the alcohol and land taxes, and equal pay for Filipino and American officials. All these changes and others preceded pleas for tariff consideration for local commodities. Indeed, the petition raised so many politically sensitive issues that the senior inspector of constabulary for Pampanga secretly investigated the origins of the document and reported on its organizers to his superiors.[37]

Because of differing political traditions and perhaps because Pampanga possessed a more mixed economy than did Negros, Capampangan remained more divided on Payne-Aldrich than did Negrenses. At the time of the passage of the bill, debate in Pampanga, pro and con, raged "red-hot," in the language of the *Philippines Free Press*.[38] Nevertheless, confronted with the reality of their dire economic conditions, hacenderos supported the compromise. As Governor Arnedo, himself a sugarman, wrote in his annual report:

> As to the general opinion regarding the results expected from the Payne Bill after enactment thereof by the Congress of the United States, so far as the agriculture of the province is concerned, this bill was in general well received by the majority of the inhabitants of the province, and although a small minority appeared to sustain the contrary opinion, in the sense that the effects of this bill, instead of being beneficial, will be detrimental to the interests of the country in general and the province

> in particular, it may be affirmed that this was but a play of party politics.[39]

In Negros the reception of "Bill Payne" was even more enthusiastic, although even in the south some reservations about its political implications surfaced. Governor Severino wrote in 1909:

> By the foregoing brief statements of the prices that prevailed in the Iloilo market, it will be seen that sugar quoted highest when favorable news of the bill was received.
>
> The rise in prices naturally caused the planters of Occidental Negros to form a favorable opinion of the Payne bill, although this opinion was divided with respect to the considerations relative to its transcendental influence on the political future of the Islands.
>
> The majority of the planters, realizing the palpable results which will accrue to agriculture in the future from the enactment of the Payne bill, as it will create a market for Philippine sugar, paid no attention to the efforts made to make a failure of every public meeting held in its favor, and in important assemblies convoked by the municipal presidents of different places, not only said that they favored the bill and asked for prompt enactment, but also would accept free trade, provided that Philippine sugar was admitted duty free into the United States.[40]

After enactment of Payne-Aldrich, sugar farmers of both provinces, although they gave occasional lip service to the idea of independence, cast aside any reservations once favorable market conditions appeared and came to rely almost entirely on sales to the United States. In 1915 the Agricultural Association of Pampanga, representing the most influential of the province's agriculturalists, wrote to Resident Commissioner Manuel L. Quezon in Washington, asking his help to continue the existing tariff preferences, for without them the Philippines could not compete with Hawaii, Puerto Rico, and U.S. domestic producers for a piece of the American sugar market.[41]

The following year the U.S. Senate added to the pending Jones Bill the Clarke Amendment that promised independence for the Philippines within two to four years. While this amendment ultimately met defeat, it evoked the following response from Jose Ledesma Jalandoni, a Negrense planter whose opinion represented that of a strong segment of sugarlandia:

> I am not opposed to independence, but I believe that ample time for preparation should be allowed us so that we can devote all our efforts and energies to the development of the vast

> agricultural resources of our country. Let us urge the establishment of agricultural banks, sugar centrals, railroads and all that is necessary to develop our national resources, for, with the individuals prosperous as they should be, the government which derives from them shall be able to establish coast fortifications, a respectable navy, a well organized army and acquire sufficient war implements and ammunitions to enable it to meet other nations shoulder to shoulder, or breast to breast. . . .
>
> The great majority of our professional and ignorant politicians are actually insisting upon independence under whatever form without calmly considering the responsibilities that it brings with it. They have flattered and seduced the people into this belief, call us "traitors" without stopping to ascertain that the interests of our country are dearer to our hearts than to theirs. Let us not be deluded by the emotion of beholding our dear flag unfurled on the shaky mast which may break never to rise again.[42]

Demand for a stable market, like the need for a steady source of credit, imposed sharp limits upon the economic and political choices of these otherwise powerful and independent-acting planters.

Casamac and Duma'an

Before World War II, the Filipino poor left little printed testimony concerning their reactions to events that changed their lives. Moreover, many of those in the past who claimed to speak for tenant farmers and laborers exhibited little understanding of or empathy with them. Often these putative spokesmen represented the interests of the upper class rather than those of their adopted charges. Historians recently have pointed out that, in several instances at least, the rural farmer's world view differed widely from that of the landholder, that the two outlooks were positioned at a greater distance from one another than is normally implied in the great tradition–little tradition dichotomy. Patron-client paternalism did not necessarily produce the kind of symbiosis that allowed planters to fathom the thinking of those who labored in their fields; rather, opportunism, a patronizing attitude, and even adversariness characterized that relationship. Evidence suggests that workers in sugarlandia shared this same fate of being little or badly understood by litterateurs.[43]

In 1964, as part of my research on local history, I conducted an anonymous informational survey among older men in Pampanga concerning their memory of their lives before 1920. Among the respondents, 149 former sugar tenants and thirty landowners provided data about their residence, education, and employment in the sugar industry during this century's first two decades. Aside from brief, biographical answers, many of these interviewees, who ranged in age from 69 to 104 years, volunteered more extensive comments about their work experience. Their insights, given to the local teachers and college students who acted as surveyors, offer some unusually frank comments on tenant-landlord relations. The forty-four intervening years, eventful and tumultuous as they were, did not erase for some of these old men vivid memories of their days laboring in the sugar industry.[44]

Perhaps the clearest notion that emerged from these interviews was the contrast in perceptions between landlords and casamac about their relationship: landholders considered that their tenants felt a deep sense of gratitude toward them for the treatment they received, while tenants often expressed resentment and fear. The following statements demonstrate this contrast, the first from a landholder in Angeles:

> My brother and I tilled the soil—our own land—and had helpers, wards of my father. We treated them like members of our own family. They lived with us. We supplied their necessities and we did not maltreat them. I remember they loved us very much. My father saved one of them from the Guardia Civil during Spanish times. My father held the position of cabeza.[45]

A retired school teacher and hacendero from Guagua described the samacan system in these terms:

> We were like one big family. They treated us like their parents and we treated them like children. When the planting began and they came to the house for the cuttings, they brought along firewood of their own volition, and I was thankful for their gesture of kindness.[46]

Another planter, from San Fernando, added:

> My father was a farmer with around a three-hundred-hectare hacienda. . . . The sharing of crops was fifty-fifty and the expenses were also on a fifty-fifty basis. The tenants loved my father. They would come and help us during fiestas, bringing us gifts of fruits, chickens, and sweets.[47]

While some tenants considered their landlords paternalistic, the majority were more resentful. An 84-year-old tenant from Porac gave the most positive comment about the relationship:

> The tenant and the landowner share fifty-fifty. . . . The landowner calls for the tenant when the Chinese buyer comes—

> everything is done in their presence and with their consent. No interest on money and rice. The landowner (Hipolito Coronel) was very humane. He treats his tenants as member of the family. The tenants are served their meals at the family table.[48]

On the other side, a casamac from Guagua stated:

> The tenants would serve the landlord by cutting wood for fuel for him, cleaning his yard and his house, and giving him gifts of chickens, firewood, and carabao milk whenever he had a fiesta. No request of the landlord was ever turned down. Of course, the landlord had a way of discriminating among his tenants. It must be kept in mind that the landowner has foremost in his mind the increase of his production. Nevertheless, there were times when a landlord would remove his tenant from his farm for failing to please him. There were even cases when the landlord cut out the ration of the tenant altogether.
>
> A common practice of the landlords at that time . . . was that every weekend when the tenant's wife went to see the landlord for the next week's ration, she was made to clean the yard, the house, or made to cook the landlord's meal before she was given the ration, which time was usually shortly before noon or even later.[49]

Another, from Angeles, said:

> My landlord would ask me to do odd jobs for him without pay, even to the extent of cutting wood, which was about three carloads, and delivering it to his house. My wife used to clean clothes and clean the house of my landlord. She, too, received no compensation for it. At the end of the milling season our debts were cleared. Of course we were the poor, then oppressed by the rich. I did not complain. We were not allowed to, and nobody dared to.[50]

Fear of landlords appeared in numerous comments, including one by a tenant, 73, from San Fernando:

> I started selling firewood at the age of about ten or eleven years old. We were very poor. My father was a tenant farmer. He had no carabao. . . . At that time we were much afraid of our landlord. My father could not answer back for fear of be-

> ing removed from his work. My father's landlord cheated my father.[51]

One from Mexico testified:

> My landowner was the kindest among the Panlilios. I was formerly a tenant of Don Vicente Panlilio, but something happened. I asked him once if he thinks that the price he gave to my crop was too low. But it happened that he was out of mood at the time I asked him. I have always considered myself one of the most faithful tenants, but that time he got angry with me and he started shouting at me. Plenty of co-tenants heard me because we were in the fields at the time. They were angry at me because I didn't assert my right. They said I was a weakling. All of them were mad at Don Vicente. Then it happened that Don Bengang Panlilio, his cousin, needed one more tenant, and I asked Don Vicente if I could transfer to his cousin's hacienda. He was no longer angry at that time and he refused to let me go. My landlord was just temperamental. I understood his moods because I knew he has some Spanish blood.
>
> Later on Don Bengang asked Don Vicente if he could spare one, and that was when I transferred to Don Bengang's hacienda. He was a very kind old man—very fatherly; although he also had some bad moods, he was very kind compared to Don Vicente. There were even some brothers of Don Vicente who whipped their tenants.[52]

That whippings occurred on occasion was confirmed by another Mexico tenant, age 78, who revealed:

> During those times even grown men got beaten when the landlord, Pablo Panlilio, did not like what he did. We said a tenant was given "two cavans" if he gets whipped fifty times, because one cavan was equal to twenty-five gantas. . . . And the whip he used was not just an ordinary kind, it was especially made for the purpose of whipping tenants. It had a leather case, the handle was made of a metal and gold plated, and the stem was of thick rounded leather. When the landlord asked his servant to bring out the whip, everyone in the barrio trembled in fear. Even how much one hated the tenant being beaten, one felt pity when the whip was taken out. Everyone gathered to see, and the family most of the time cried for mercy. The landlord rarely used the whip, however. He used it only in extreme cases, but I did see him use it once when I

> was a small boy, and the memory stayed long in my mind. The tenant was not like a human being when he was being beaten. During the first few whippings he shouted in pain, but after that he did not cry anymore, because he became numb.[53]

If Pampangan tenants expressed a sense of helplessness in the face of planter power and authority, they also conveyed a sense of hopelessness as well. A 76-year-old tenant from San Fernando offered a common sentiment of the era:

> Although the sharing of crops was on a fifty-fifty basis, the tenant shouldered his expenses on the farm. Whatever he got from his landlord in cash or kind (cigarettes, rice, sugar) he paid back. He worked for his landlord like a slave. . . . What was not quite nice was that most landlords cheated their tenants. . . .
>
> The tenant does not get his share of the harvest because he has no place to store it and he does not have connections with big buyers like the Chinese, et cetera.[54]

The endlessness of unrewarding work appeared further in a statement from a 100-year-old tenant from Angeles:

> I was supposed to receive one fourth of the sugar production which we placed in pilones. No sugar and no money was given to me in return, for my share was kept in my landlord's storehouse. He sold my share as he pleased without my knowing the selling price. I was just informed of the cost of my ration every time I came to get it. At the end of the next harvest, I was informed of the balance of debts. I got so fed up with such treatment that I gave up the work. My son who was then quite big worked in my stead.[55]

Landholders at their most paternalistic expressed their reluctance to loan money, for it encouraged long-term indebtedness, and three of them commented:

> I used to limit the loans of my tenants, because I wanted them to make a little sacrifice for their future. I did not collect interest on money I loaned them. I even gave them lessons on how to produce more, once in a while.[56]

> When I lent my tenants any amount of money, I charged twenty percent interest to prevent them from borrowing often and spending the money for gambling. When my father died, I canceled all debts of my tenants.[57]

> My father . . . always gave his tenants money as often as they came to borrow, so that when I took over, I found many of the tenants with debts as big as five hundred pesos, six hundred pesos, and a thousand pesos. There seemed to be no way by which they could pay their debts, so I forgave them their debts and told them to start anew. I often gave them lectures on thrift. There were two bad traits I observed common to most tenants—indolence and extravagance.[58]

Despite these charitable sentiments most tenants borrowed to survive, and most landholders loaned them the cash, the majority of the latter charging some interest rate between 5 percent and 20 percent for cash. And this system resulted in a recurring round of indebtedness that left tenants without hope of breaking free. A 95-year-old tenant from San Fernando revealed his thoughts in this manner:

> The landlord at that time would give you any number of pilones of sugar as he pleased. We could not complain for fear of being removed from our work. We were much cheated and we poor people were treated as servants. We worked as tenants to pay for the debts incurred by our parents, and our children would in turn work as tenants to pay for our debts to our landlords. We worked day and night. The landlord's word was law.[59]

Perennial debt and inability to alter their situation informed the thinking of casamac in Pampanga; however, these attitudes did not necessarily determine their reaction to a specific hacendero. Rather, along with adequate subsistence tenants expected, even insisted upon, fairness from landlords. Casamac opinion about their relations with others as well depended on this need for fairness, and wrong was measured by just how inequitably someone treated them. The following narrative concerning the arrival in 1916 of the cadastral survey in Magalang reveals a long-remembered slight harbored by a 74-year-old tenant of that town:

> I remember clearly—the police came and gathered us. They told us to go to the *tribunal* [municipal building]. But we were afraid of the police then, and we never wanted to go near the tribunal for we associated it with being imprisoned. They told us to register our land, but we didn't want to have anything to do with the police. We didn't go to the municipal building, and they came and asked us why. We told them we were very busy working in our fields. They then told us that a man would register our land for us. We were ignorant at the time

> and we were happy that this man would register for us. We found out later he registered it in his name.[60]

Most tenants in this era possessed no legal claim to land, only traditional rights through the samacan, and the registering of titles did not directly affect them; however, the perception of inequity on the part of those associated with the survey made many tenants view the cadastral program negatively.

Casamac operated on a basic sense of justice in dealing with landholders; and above all the implied paternalism, they needed to be satisfied that they received enough and that their contracts operated fairly. A tenant from San Fernando expressed this sentiment succinctly:

> During that time the landlord bore all the expenses on the farm, and all the production went to the storehouse of the landlord. He gave us our necessities—food, clothes, shoes, and other things—and we did not know our share. We just lived buried in debt to our landlord. We were like members of his family. He disciplined us and we were afraid of him. We were not given enough subsistence and we left him.[61]

The samacan functioned in such a way that tenants seldom improved their economic condition, largely because opportunities to profit all remained in the hands of hacenderos. The latter kept the books, warehoused and sold the finished product, set interest rates, and often loaned stores, equipment, and draft animals. Choosing where to profit at the expense of tenants remained a matter of individual landlord style, and the manner selected often determined casamac reaction. Charging moderate interest on loans did not appear to cause undo reaction, providing other parts of the contract proved acceptable; charging no interest compensated for other exactions by the hacendero. A satisfied tenant from Guagua described his relationship this way:

> My share of the sugar was paid in cash to me by my landlord, usually a peso less than the current selling price. The molasses went to my landlord. Any amount of money I borrowed from my landlord did not bear any interest. The relationship between us was paternal.[62]

By far the biggest perceived inequity on the part of tenants dealt with the matter of selling finished sugar to brokers. Planters often did not seem to realize the distrust they created with these financial dealings; rather, they believed that they did the casamac a favor (or fooled tenants into thinking so) in handling the complex negotiations. Three landlords gave different justifications for dealing alone with the Chinese brokers:

> During those times tenants were treated very well by us. We did not ask any interest. . . . They were free to ask for help anytime they needed it. Only we were the ones who purchased the whole crop, including theirs, because they might be cheated by Chinese merchants.[63]

> When we sell the sugar I got the average price of sugar and I multiplied it by the number of piculs. That was how I gave an accounting to the tenants. Sometimes I sell several piculs at a certain price and the week after I sell several other piculs at a higher price. I get the average of all these prices and that was the price I based the accounting on.[64]

> If I sold a pilon of sugar at twenty-five pesos, I charged it to [the tenant] at twenty-four pesos. My gain was one peso, which was in the form of a gift to me for selling my tenant's share.[65]

No matter how hacenderos justified their negotiations, tenants found them the greatest source of injustice in the samacan contract. Two representative tenant comments reveal the hostility and misperception that underlay the Pampangan labor arrangement:

> In sugar production we farmers were cheated most of the time. If a pilon of sugar cost twenty-five pesos in the market, the landowner will first tell the poor farmer any amount he wishes to tell him. Any complaint by the farmer in this accounting will mean his firing from his job.[66]

> The landlord treated us kindly in words. I know very well that they were cheating me, especially in sharing the crop, which is supposed to be on a fifty-fifty basis. . . . And when it comes to sharing harvested sugar, the crop was first put in the bodega of the landlords. Then they did everything they can to cheat us. However, they lend us money without interest, provided it will be paid back in not longer than one year.[67]

Tenants who sold their own share usually defended their samacan relationship as fair, but such individuals remained a small minority. Perceived inequities as early as the first two decades of the twentieth century threatened the social order that had developed over the preceding years.

In 1970 a similar survey collected responses from duma'an and other sugar people from Negros concerning their life in the two decades before

World War II.[68] Among the interviewees were eighty-two duma'an from 70 to over 100 years of age who supplied observations concerning their early days working on haciendas. Because of the time lapse between the two surveys and the different period emphasis of the later one, the data collected are not quite comparable; nevertheless, these older Negrenses did offer recollections of the late frontier period. And their comments on their working life contrasted in some ways with those of Pampangan casamac.

Duma'an evinced somewhat more satisfaction with their conditions than did their northern counterparts, perhaps reflecting the better market conditions that prevailed in Negros in the the early twentieth century. While no hacienda laborer admitted to improving his circumstances, they generally felt their subsistence needs were met. An 80-year-old retiree from Murcia supplied this response:

> My life as a hired worker of the hacienda was much better during that normal time, even though wages were so small as compared to wages now. At the rate of fifty centavos a day I could still support my family, since prices of foods were very much lower as compared to prices now. I can also let my children go to school, but, due to their [negative attitude], they didn't even reach the intermediate grade.[69]

Several of the comments, however, contain a certain ambivalence: their wages had to suffice, because no alternative sources of livelihood existed. Three examples from octogenarians in Hinigaran, Isabela, and Himamaylan exemplify this sentiment:

> We received no *consumo* [rations]. . . . Life was hard but I couldn't complain about my financial problems for fear of losing my job. I had to work in the field every day, even when I wasn't feeling well, since my earnings were paid on a daily basis.[70]

> We were given consumo and the amount was deducted from our salary. I was contented with my earnings. It was a hand-to-mouth way of life. I supported my family with my meager income. Everything was cheap during that time, so no worry at all, although this income was not enough to meet daily needs.[71]

> There were no major troubles, although the landowner didn't give any privileges to his laborers. They couldn't get any cash

> loans from him, nor get any help in bad times. Laborers would just have to bear the kind of management they have.[72]

The remarks of the minority who proclaimed dissatisfaction with their hacienda wages contained overtones of a fear and helplessness that bonded them to their poor situations. Three retired duma'an, two from Pulupandan and one from Binalbagan, made representative comments in this vein:

> There were no labor troubles. If you do good in your work you won't have any trouble at all. They were treated well by the owner, if they only follow what the owner would like them to do.[73]

> Laborers couldn't complain—otherwise they'd be ousted. They just waited for instructions and payday. They never complained because they reasoned that the landlord wouldn't help them anyway.[74]

> I just obeyed orders. At times I complained to the cabo because of too much work, but the cabo didn't listen to my complaints. I just worked and obeyed orders.[75]

Not so surprisingly, the only statements that revealed open resentment came from or referred to sacadas. As noted earlier, the one group over which hacenderos complained they exerted little control and which caused them the most trouble were these seasonal workers from neighboring islands. Many sacadas later settled on Negros haciendas and became duma'an, but so long as they remained transients, they maintained an independence unavailable to permanent staff. A 70-year-old duma'an from La Carlota commented:

> Trouble arises only if the amount paid to the laborers in the *pakyaw* [piece work rate] was very low. Laborers would stop working if the landowner would not raise the salary.[76]

Another duma'an from La Carlota remembered the time around 1920 when he came from Antique Province, Panay, to cut cane on Negros. He observed:

> Labor troubles arose only during payday when the laborers couldn't receive their salary, especially those under the pakyaw system, and recruited by the contratista. There were sometimes contratistas who didn't give the salary to the laborers but, instead, used the money for themselves.

> During those times laborers were treated like animals. There were foods served for the laborers, but foods which weren't prepared well—like rice which was not cleaned well.
>
> There was also a laborer on one of the haciendas in Bago, owned by a Spanish mestizo. He tied the laborer to a tree and let the ants bite him, because of the cane that the laborer wasn't able to cut because he didn't feel well.[77]

A comparison of the collective responses of Pampanga casamac and Negros duma'an points to a similar harsh perception of conditions on the sugarlands of northern Pampanga and the Negros plantations. The casamac, however, appeared to see more unfairness in their relations with landholders than did the duma'an, or at least they expressed their sense of the injustice more often. But such a comparison might be misleading. The surveys involved the memories of old men, some of whom volunteered fuller answers than others. Further, the years between 1920 and the 1960s and 1970s witnessed vastly different political experiences within the two areas, and the replies of the casamac may have been colored by the politically charged atmosphere of 1964 Pampanga. Negros Occidental in 1970 harbored a far more repressive and orderly climate. It is possible, of course, that different cultural backgrounds, living arrangements, and conditions of employment in the two regions accounted for the dissimilarities in declarations of injustice. Perhaps the Capampangan expressed themselves more openly because they possessed collective ways to reveal their resentment. Does other evidence buttress or discredit these disparities in actions and expression?

While direct corroborating testimony does not exist, reactions among rural farmers to two turn-of-the-century messianic movements, one in Pampanga, the other in Negros, tend to confirm the differences in attitude and outlook expressed by the elderly casamac and duma'an. Folk leaders Felipe Salvador—Apong (Saint) Ipe to his followers in Luzon—and Dionisio Sigobela, the Negrenses' Papa (Pope) Isio or Dionisio Papa, seemed to have parallel careers in their respective regions; however, the nature of the support they received reflected regional cultural and historical differences that gave each movement a distinctive flavor, despite a common impact on both of the Philippine Revolution and an expanding sugar industry.

Salvador distinctly belongs to an old Philippine tradition of chiliastic leaders who draw upon folk Catholic themes and practices to express peasant world views. Movements in a similar vein to his own sprang up in central Luzon from Laguna to Pangasinan from at least the mid-nineteenth century onward. In 1894 he formed his own group, Santa Iglesia

(Holy Church), among followers of a sect founded in the late 1880s by Gabino Cortes of Apalit, Pampanga. Salvador himself grew up in the nearby Tagalog town of Baliwag, Bulacan, and spoke that language as his native tongue; nevertheless, he had strong influence within the Capampangan-speaking community. He eventually held sway in the rural barrios of Bulacan, Nueva Ecija, Pangasinan, and Tarlac as well as Pampanga, communities that he visited first from his base in Barrio Camias, San Miguel, Bulacan, then from hidden centers on Mount Arayat and in the Candaba Swamp.

At the onset of the Philippine Revolution in 1896, he shifted away from his initial, strictly religious focus and created a militant arm to fight for independence, his troops first confronting Spanish forces in San Luis in 1896. After a retreat to Biak-na-Bato (near Camias) to join Aguinaldo, Salvador's army of church members fought again in February 1898 at Apalit and Macabebe, in both cases suffering considerable losses. With the arrival of the Americans, the soldiers of Santa Iglesia took to the field again and achieved success in capturing a hundred rifles from the Spanish garrison at Dagupan, Pangasinan. This feat and others earned Apong Ipe the rank of colonel in the revolutionary army, and in July 1898 he paraded with five hundred of his followers triumphantly through the streets of Candaba.

Despite these contributions to the cause, local elite officers from Pampanga refused to treat Salvador as an equal, abused soldiers of Santa Iglesia and their families, and accused Apong Ipe himself of desertion in the line of duty. In a reasoned defense to Aguinaldo, the religious leader made it clear that Pampangan principales objected to his troops' loyalty to him and their combining military with religious activities. The elite felt they deserved to command the poor of the province and resented this threat to their authority. Because of his appeal and his loyalty, Salvador earned a favorable ruling from his commander in chief on the charge of desertion and retired to the Candaba Swamp area in time to organize a guerrilla campaign against the American army. Captured in 1902, he escaped—to the wonder of his followers—and subsequently conducted religious services and directed a guerrilla war for independence, long after other Pampangan officers had sworn allegiance to the new regime.

For eight years Salvador and his apostles wandered the rural barrios of central Luzon preaching devotion and brotherhood. The military wing under the command of Manuel Garcia, known as Capitan Tui, made lightening strikes against unsuspecting constabulary outposts in such places as San Jose, Nueva Ecija (1903), Mabalacat (1903), and Malolos, Bulacan (1906). The constabulary killed Garcia in mid-1906, and military raids diminished thereafter; however, as late as 1910, in the fateful year of the appearance of Halley's comet, peasants and former soldiers from south of Manila to Lingayen Gulf still looked to Apong Ipe to revive the Revolution and expel the Americans. The colonials and cooperating native elite still considered Felipe Salvador a danger to public order. His capture came about at his home in Barrio San Isidro, San Luis, in the midst of the Candaba Swamp on July 24, 1910, the result of a joint effort between secret agents from Governor Arnedo's office, municipal policemen, and constabulary troopers. The government charged him with sedition and on April 15, 1912, at Manila's Bilibid Prison, executed him by hanging.[78]

Santa Iglesia did not vanish with the disappearance of its leader. In 1913 Governor Liongson reported confidentially to the executive secretary in Manila that the Salvadoristas still congregated peacefully and regularly. Evicted from a barrio of Angeles, 150 of the faithful removed to the slopes of Mount Arayat, the old haunt of their slain Apong Ipe. The governor ordered their leader, a man named Cortez, to appear before him, and this spiritual guide dutifully did so, accompanied by Angeles vice-mayor Ireneo Abad Santos, a planter and younger brother of Pedro. Cortez seemed to agree to disbanding the group, and Liongson considered the matter closed, attributing the whole incident offhandedly to opponents of independence. However, in 1970 I visited the Santa Iglesia headquarters, still in Barrio San Isidro, San Luis, and found that elderly adherents maintained two churches in that community. One of the original apostles of Apong Ipe, Victor Larin, who was 101 years old, presided over one of the structures and asserted that the Santa Iglesia never died, although at that time its membership consisted only of very old parishioners living in the surrounding barrios.[79]

While Salvador centered his movement in the wetter, rice-growing portions of Luzon, his sway reached into sugar-growing Pampanga. From his vantage on Mount Arayat he possessed easy access to the rest of the great plain that stretched out from its foot. After their attack on Mabalacat in August 1903, his raiders fled north to safety in Tarlac, where Salvador had a considerable following. Driven from Arayat town center in 1910, he found sanctuary for a time in the sugar community of Floridablanca. Finally, as Salvador notes in his abbreviated spiritual autobiography dictated on the eve of his execution, he received hospitality from two *tatcheros* (those who boil sugar), indicating a kind and enthusiastic reception from those in sugar country.[80]

Papa Isio derived from another Philippine folk tradition, the *babaylan* or native priest, a holdover from prehispanic society. The religion flourished in rural, especially mountainous, areas of the western Visayas, where babaylanes performed a variety of functions including conducting services on important occasions that propitiated natural spirits and supplying *anting-anting,* charms that warded off evil and harm in many forms. Babaylanism as an institution survived in part because of the shortage of Catholic priests to minister intensely to Visayans, including those who lived on or transferred to Negros. Along the central cordillera and in the southern foothills where dwelt upland farmers, victims of usurpacion, and lowland refugees from hacienda exploitation, animist priests ministered to those outside the plantation system.

From as early as the seventeenth century, some babaylanes had taken on the added role of leading peasant revolts and customarily supplied anting-anting that protected their adherents from bullets. Hence, when Isio became a babaylan in Negros, his combining of military and religious leadership fit longstanding local traditions. Authorities believed that he fled to this world after wounding or killing a Spanish hacendero. Information about his life—even about his given name—is conflicting, but the story of this murder at least indicates Isio's longstanding hatred of foreigners. In 1896 at age 50 he joined the revolution against Spain and confronted the Guardia Civil in hard-fought battles in central Negros.[81]

Isio's actions reveal that he despised colonials because they sanctioned, indeed instigated, the sugar industry with all its attendant inequities and injustices. That sugar stood as the root problem to him and his followers is evidenced in an 1899 report by General James Smith:

> The Babaylanes came down to the outlying haciendas, and by specious representations that the lands would be repartitioned among the people, that machinery would no longer be permitted in the island, and that nothing but palay [rice] would henceforth be planted, succeeded in persuading the ignorant laborers of about fifty haciendas to join them and to destroy by fire the places which had given them employment.[82]

Initially his men, known collectively (and incorrectly) as babaylanes, attacked just Spanish plantations, in the belief that only native Visayans had rights to the land of Negros.

When the just-formed Negros government sought American protection in early 1899, a disillusioned Dionisio Papa directed his attacks against native planters who collaborated with the new colonial power. Isio made his targets explicit in a letter written to his next-in-command, Rufo Oyos, on May 19, 1900:

> It is advisable to punish by decapitation all those who go with the Americans; but it is necessary first to ascertain the existence of the crime, and it should appear that they are real spies

> of the enemy, they must be beheaded immediately without any pretext whatsoever against it [being accepted].
>
> You, Captain Antonio and Judge Cornelio must perfectly understand what this order says; when the wealthy are Americanistas, you must seize all their money, clothing and other property belonging to them, immediately making an inventory of the property seized.[83]

From March to July 1899 Papa Isio's troops pillaged Spanish and native Negrense plantations, mainly in the sugar district from La Carlota south to Isabela, an area skirting the central mountain spine that provided raiders sanctuary from pursuing American soldiers. These attacks reduced the island's sugar output, and the U.S. Army eventually committed three battalions to the task of quelling them. Marauders under the command of Rufo Oyos also operated effectively in towns in southern Negros.

After midyear the army provided better security for planters around La Carlota, and the babaylanes moved west to Ma-ao, where they made several forays against the property of, among others, Juan Araneta. Further raids brought them to Himamaylan and Pontevedra, but as they approached the coast the insurgents enjoyed little sanctuary. Additionally, big hacenderos like Araneta, Aniceto Lacson, and Pedro Yulo employed private guards to protect their lands from destruction and their workers and themselves from capture. Finally, planters began to organize programs of registering duma'-an to ensure none supported the insurgents. Isio and his troops fought their last major battle of this campaign at Bacolod in late July and suffered a loss of 170 men. From this time on he adopted more sporadic hit-and-run tactics.

Despite defections from his ranks and pursuit by American forces, Isio and his remaining troops harassed plantations and towns in western Negros on and off for eight more years. Although loyal to the cause, he received only reluctant recognition from Aguinaldo, who preferred to deal with faithless hacenderos of his own class, like Araneta. Finally, the last Republican commander, Miguel Malvar, commissioned Isio a colonel in May 1902; at the time of his surrender the latter had served the Revolution more continuously than any other officer. The Philippine Constabulary replaced the American Army in the law-and-order campaign on Negros in 1902, and newly appointed Lt. John White attacked Isio's mountain bases shortly thereafter. Oyos capitulated in April 1903, and Isio carried on the struggle alone. After a final foray against Kabankalan in 1907, Isio, now an old man, surrendered; he died in Bilibid Prison around 1908.[84]

The careers of Apong Ipe and Dionisio Papa reveal many similarities due to the common impact on Pampanga and Negros of faltering economic conditions and revolution. Depressed markets, spreading epidemic diseases among people and farm livestock, political change, and military destruction damaged the lives of casamac and duma'an, and millenarianism offered them solace and a rallying point for organized protest. Removal of the Spanish clergy as a mechanism of social control and unwillingness on the part of Americans to enforce some of the more onerous restraints upon sugar workers allowed some opportunities to release pent up hostility to the system that subjugated them. That the two religious leaders emerged and flourished during the same time span proves no coincidence, and other regions just then experienced similar religious outbursts. Each movement, however, was shaped according to the local culture of its adherents.

Salvador moved through central Luzon in flowing robes, conducting prayer sessions and giving sermons that spoke of brotherhood and a future that included land redistribution. While Isio constructed a church at a mountain retreat where he maintained his own utopian community, his chief religious function was to issue anting-anting to his followers to ward off injury when they attacked government forces. His agents at the same time destroyed plantations and tried to induce workers to swell rebel ranks on the promise of a more equitable land settlement. Isio also demonstrated a better grasp of modern notions of secular leadership and closer touch with the larger political issues of the day. His captured letters, written in Spanish by a clerk, contained practical instructions on how to conduct a campaign of guerrilla warfare. A note of March 4, 1901, to Rufo Oyos, revealed that Isio knew that American politician William Jennings Bryan somehow featured in America's future plans in the Philippines:

> I have received from Luzon an order to proceed more rapidly with my operations this month, because Bryan ordered Emilio to keep the war going vigorously until April, and he also said that if independence was not given the Philippines by that time, he, Bryan, and his followers would rise in arms against the oppressors.[85]

Nothing in Apong Ipe's biography approached such a practical or secular tone.

Despite differences in style and mode of operation, Salvador and Isio endured the long, hard struggle for Philippine independence for the same reason. The two leaders finally achieved commissions as colonels, but both faced continuous hostility from such patriots as Maximino Hizon, Liongson, Lacson, and Araneta. This enmity existed because those in control of the Malolos government and its provincial branches quite accurately understood that, whereas they fought for political independence, Apong Ipe and Papa Isio struggled for social and economic changes repugnant to the elite.

In his annual report for 1902 Governor Locsin wrote the following:

> The society of Babaylanes (believers in superstitious and idolatrous things) is a mixture of confused socialistic principles, anarchistic instincts, and an aberration of religious and fanatic ideas. They are a crazy and criminal sect, and at the same time pray to God and preach the distribution of wealth, and looting and murder.[86]

Undoubtedly his awareness that Isio persuaded duma'an from plantations bordering the central mountains to desert their jobs to join his ranks and that the babaylanes promised to redistribute land and eliminate the sugar industry colored Locsin's judgement. That widespread fear of social revolution afflicted Negrense hacenderos emerges from the following item in a local newspaper:

> The presidente of Silay, Sr. Lucio Jaime, convoked on December 17th [1899] a junta of property owners and hacenderos of the pueblo, also with the assistance of [Negros Government] Secretary of the Interior Sr. Locsin and American Lieutenant Hanagan, and they resolved to adopt effective means, not only to repel the bandits who try to claim the shelter of a political idea which they do not comprehend or know, but also to prevent the workers on the haciendas from being infected with the virus of banditry. The junta is organizing a system of vigilance of such workers so that they have to be enrolled on each hacienda, so that by this means they can be better watched.[87]

During this period planters all along the west coast offered to support American forces in suppressing Papa Isio and his movement.

Government forces on Luzon expressed similar judgements about Apong Ipe. A constabulary report in 1906 explained his movement this way:

> The society purports to be a religious one, the members being given or sold crucifixes or rosaries by Salvador and using forms of worship similar to those of the Catholic Church. Salvador preaches socialistic doctrines to the believers, practices polygamy, and promises them that land and other desirable

> things will be distributed among his followers when he shall have overthrown the Government and taken possession of the country himself, that there will soon be a great flood or fire that will destroy all unbelievers, and that after this purging of the country there will be a rain of gold and jewels for the faithful.[88]

Like their counterparts on Negros, establishment Capampangan placed themselves at the disposal of the Americans in bringing about the downfall of this social revolutionary.

Comparison of the practices and aims of the two religious figures proves helpful in understanding their thinking and that of their adherents; as well, such comparisons provide insight into regional cultural diversity. But what does one learn of the attitude of sugar people toward these millenarian leaders and toward their own social and economic circumstances, so affected by the impact of war and a sugar economy? The support varied considerably and does provide evidence of differences in outlook between Capampangan and Negrenses.

In Pampanga and Negros Occidental the Philippine Revolution generated several splinter patriotic movements; moreover, simple banditry, a longstanding problem in both provinces, proliferated during these years of distress. Nevertheless, among all these antigovernment, antiestablishment activities, the organizations of Dionisio Papa and Apong Ipe attracted the most support from the indigenous population and the most attention from colonial authorities. Additionally, no other dissident movement survived nearly as long as Santa Iglesia and Isio's babaylanes.

Each leader, however, operated in a different manner and evaded arrest for separate reasons. For many years Apong Ipe moved freely about farming barrios in central Luzon, including the sugar areas of Pampanga and Tarlac, praying with his apostles and preaching love and brotherhood. What appears most remarkable about his experience is that, even in those harsh economic times, no one turned him in despite the P2,000 reward for his capture. A 1910 constabulary report observed:

> Felipe Salvador, the well-known bandit leader who deserted from the Filipino insurrectionary forces years ago, and who has been lurking since in the low and swampy regions of Nueva Ecija or neighboring provinces and around Mount Arayat, showed considerable activity last spring after having been long quiet. The people of whole barrios, minor officials and all, joined him, and a large gathering was formed on Mount Arayat, apparently with the intention of attacking some

> detachment of Constabulary. Strenuous efforts were put forth by many Constabulary detachments from the near-by province, but they were unable to locate or capture Salvador, who was aided practically by the whole population, though the activity of the detachments prevented his doing any harm and caused his band to dissolve and himself to again go into hiding.[89]

As he himself notes in his autobiography, so long as he stayed away from town plazas, the abode of officialdom and rich landholders, he did not face danger. Like Jesus at the Garden of Gethsemane, Salvador, to test his disciples' faith, led them to pray at the town plaza in Arayat. People of the poblacion proved fearful of approaching him, and soldiers eventually began firing at the religious group. However, among the barrio folk and the very rare hacenderos who remained sympathetic to the Revolution—loyalists like Anselmo Alejandrino (brother of Republican General Jose)—Apong Ipe received a hospitable reception to the end.[90]

Papa Isio, in contrast, depended for backing on mountain folk, people in the nonsugar foothills in the far south, and escapees from haciendas abutting the central cordillera. The greatest defections of duma'an to his ranks came between February and July 1899 when he ravaged inland sugar plantations in the La Carlota district. Defeats at Ma-ao and Bacolod essentially ended this support from sugar workers, and afterwards Isio remained at large chiefly by hiding in the inaccessible central mountains, shunning plantations and making occasional forays against towns chiefly in the south. Whereas Salvador worshipped among the lowland poor, Papa Isio avoided them.[91]

The diverse manner in which the two rebels operated accounts in part for this difference in receptivity. Apong Ipe circulated in a peaceful manner, not destroying farms where casamac earned their livelihoods. Santa Iglesia directed its raids mainly against military and police outposts, seeking weapons and other supplies. Isio, initially at least, ravaged the farms of both Spaniards and collaborating Negrenses, not necessarily discriminating between harsh and generous hacenderos. His activities thus displaced duma'an in a region where alternate forms of labor hardly existed; moreover, White indicates that the babaylanes sometimes kidnapped women from haciendas, an action certain to alienate the local population. If oppression existed on many haciendas, Dionisio Papa's methods did not necessarily provide the means of ending it.[92]

Salvador also traveled freely through sugar country because of the structure of rural communities in Pampanga. As municipalities took on a more urban face in response to a cash-crop economy, the social division between towns proper and barrios grew. The former became the space chiefly of planters, bureaucrats, merchants, craftsmen, and laborers, while the latter communities remained the realm of tenants and small proprietors where casamac lived freer of hacendero supervision. Certainly representatives of the establishment kept in touch with more remote hamlets, but oversight remained less effective than in Negros. In the latter region, duma'an resided on plantations under the close watch of encargados and hacenderos, and this structured environment offered little opportunity for sugar workers to support without detection Papa Isio's movement.

Finally, an important part of the explanation of Apong Ipe's warm reception had to do with the great appeal of his message to Capampangan casamac. The way communities developed in Pampanga affected social attitudes, and Salvador's message of sharing blended with those rural values. Tenants dwelt near their fields, and because of the scattered pattern of landholding, aparceros contracted by several different owners might reside in the same barrio. In contrast, all those farming for a single individual might inhabit one community, especially in recently settled territory where more extensive holdings still prevailed. In any case, Pampanga's tenants mixed more freely with one another than did duma'an of Negros. The need to deal with landlords, often weekly, and to go to central markets, as well as the shorter distances between communities and better roads, generated tenant socializing.

Because of the labor pattern of Pampanga's sugar industry, share farmers forged two sets of relationships: one vertical with landholders, the other horizontal with fellow tenants and barrio denizens. A common ethnic heritage, generations of intermarriage and family ties, and a shared barrio existence provided the bases for social security in harsh times and joint action in the face of disaster. Poor farmers might depend on the rich for certain forms of economic support, but barrio mates and relatives provided the final protection against threats from nature and other outside forces. Rice tenants reciprocated planting and harvesting labor more so than did sugar tenants, but harvesting and milling cane provided some occasions for mutual help. What information casamac gained about market conditions they frequently passed among themselves, and as landlords grew increasingly distant, horizontal ties had to provide compensatory bonds of support. Such a change did not happen quickly or dramatically, and one can still discern strong patron-client bonds operating well into the twentieth century. Nevertheless, crises like those at the turn of the century encouraged cooperation and mutual support among rural folk. Two old residents of the province spoke in interviews on this matter of provincial cooperation:

> The people then loved one another more than they do now. Your neighbors would rally to your side whenever you need their help.[93]

> Life is not so hard because everything is cheap and neighbors then are ready to help those who need help.[94]

Into this environment came Apong Ipe with his message of brotherhood and sharing. A recurrent theme in his autobiography is the partaking together and voluntary giving of food that becomes a metaphor for communalism, spiritual and social. In the biography Salvador also refers to several occasions when he and close friends formed a cooperative venture to cut and sell firewood to obtain their sustenance. At San Luis members of Santa Iglesia formed a successful cooperative market to which came rural folk to buy their food. Through such ventures Salvador demonstrated his theme that joint endeavor provided both physical and spiritual advantages. Concerning the appeal of this message to the farm folk of central Luzon, Ileto notes:

> We can also conclude from the narrative that people were attracted to Salvador, not merely because of his individual traits, but because through their association with him certain possibilities of existence were realized. In 1904 Salvador in passing referred to the Santa Iglesia as a katipunan. In the narrative, Salvador talks about what "katipunan," or brotherhood, is all about. The minute descriptions of the bringing of gifts and food, the cooking and sharing of meals, and the conversations; the sharing of work and earnings; the pervading atmosphere of damay [emotional sharing]—all these point to how the katipunan idea is being realized. In each of Salvador's encounters with people, "katipunan" is experienced.[95]

Sympathy for Apong Ipe and his message of both prayer and communality encouraged Capampangan to harbor this religious rebel in their midst for years, despite the antagonism of the landholding elite and the government. No similar situation existed in Negros, where duma'an proved unwilling and perhaps unable to hide the babaylanes from the purview of hacenderos. Dionisio Papa did have a priestly function and a social message: gain political independence and dismantle the sugar industry. However, if he possessed a vision of a better society he did not make it easily available, because he did not preach and pray among sugar hands. His only writings contained orders and threats, while his personally established home community lay hidden in inaccessible and mysterious mountain reaches. Dionisio Papa lacked the means to communicate with the great bulk of Negrense poor.

Even with a well-articulated social message, however, it seems unlikely that Papa Isio would have found a *simpatico* response on haciendas, for duma'an had not developed the sense of community that existed in Pampanga's tenant barrios. Whereas the latter region began with communities upon which the sugar industry was grafted, in Negros the social units were a creation of that industry. The duma'an inhabited isolated plantations where they were closely watched. They had limited occasions for concerted action and for socializing with workers on other haciendas. They might well have practiced the everyday forms of small resistance adopted by the poor all over Southeast Asia; the hacenderos did, after all, carry guns when they made their rounds of their estates.[96] Such acts of defiance, however, would have gone largely unnoticed by most, since they were carried out subtly and individually, for the duma'an would scarcely have acted overtly and risked the wrath of the plantation bosses. Even sacadas had more freedom to speak out in concert than did workers on haciendas. This inability to function collectively reduced the duma'ans' ability to confront inequity and to express dissatisfaction with it.

Of social life on plantations in general, Beckford has written:

> Within [the] plantation community, interpersonal relations reflect the authority structure of the plantation itself. In every aspect of life a strong authoritarian tradition can be observed. Any one with the slightest degree of power over others exercises this power in a characteristic[ally] exploitive authoritarian manner, and attitudes toward work clearly reflect the plantation influence. Overseer types never do manual work which is degrading to their social dignity and laborers consistently devise ways and means of getting pay without actually doing the work—it is simply a case of always trying to beat the system. On the whole the plantation has a demoralizing influence on the community. It destroys or discourages the institution of family and so undermines the entire social fabric. It engenders an ethos of dependence and patronage and so deprives people of dignity, security, and self-respect. And it impedes the material, social, and spiritual advance of the majority of people.[97]

While this description applies most aptly to Beckford's own Caribbean world, its claims about society appear to fit the situation in Negros as well.

Sugar workers recently drawn from several surrounding islands and diverse language groups and living in isolated, atomistic units scarcely constituted a population likely to share a common notion of the ideal community. Papa Isio's social vision probably had little chance of being well received or even comprehended by those to whom he most needed to appeal.

Thus, differences in expression of resentment and sentiments toward social protest in the statements of casamac and duma'an seem to find corroboration in the responses of each to local rebels. The two regions had grown along different lines, and not surprisingly, their work forces had developed disparate social attitudes that reacted to events in separate ways. In the broadest terms Pampanga's spirit of community and the Negrense notion of individuality emerge as the two major social legacies of the frontier era, ideals that would carry over into the years when centrals dominated the landscape.

Plate 1. Pedro Abad Santos. From Florence Horn, *Orphans of the Pacific: The Philippines* (New York: Reynal and Hitchcock, 1941), photo section.

Plate 2. Successful Negros Hacendero Yee On. From *Sugar News* 14 (1933): 92.

Plate 3. Cane Cutter. From *Sugar News* 1, no. 15 (1920): 55.

Plate 4. Loading Sugar on Lorchas in Negros. From G. E. Nesom and Herbert S. Walker, *Handbook on the Sugar Industry of the Philippine Islands* (Manila: Bureau of Printing, 1912), pt. 2, plate 9, fig. 2.

Plate 5. Pilon Sugar in Storage. From *Sugar News* 1, no. 9 (1920): 19.

Plate 6. Sugar Mill in Action. From Nesom and Walker, *Handbook*, pt. 2, plate 6, fig. 2.

Plate 7. Furrowing Out Rows and Planting Cane Points. From Nesom and Walker, *Handbook*, pt. 1, plate 11, fig. 1.

Plate 8. Loading Railroad Cars with Cane. From *Sugar News* 1, no. 14 (1920): 20.

Plate 9. Cascos of Sugar at the Manila Wharves. From Frederic H. Sawyer, *The Inhabitants of the Philippines* (London: Sampson Low, Marston, 1900), p. 161.

Plate 10. Aniceto Lacson House, Talisay, Negros Occidental. From the Museum of History and Iconography Archive, Ayala Museum, Makati, Metro Manila.

Plate 11. President and Mrs. Quezon at Their Pampanga Farm. From Manuel L. Quezon, *The Good Fight* (New York: Appleton-Century, 1946), p. 198.

Plate 12. Central Azucarera de La Carlota. From *Sugar News* 1, no. 10 (1920): frontispiece.

FIVE

Centrals, 1920–1934

"I want to go to Negros and learn how to plant sugar cane," Don Sixto Lopez, the once irreducible Batangas revolutionary leader one day told a Negros woman sugar planter.

"Do come," she said, "and we will not only teach you how to plant cane but also how to go into debt."

Philippines Free Press (April 7, 1928)

My being a Capampangan is a source of pride to me,
For it is the only treasure I shall bring to my grave.
I am a Capampangan in thought and aspiration,
Heart and soul, flesh, blood and bone.

Capampangan poet Juanito Goingco

The years from 1921 to 1934 brought unprecedented prosperity to the Philippine sugar industry. The U.S. tariff system provided the islands' crop privileged access to American markets and for several years protected the industry from the worsening effects of the Great Depression. Production accelerated at an extraordinary rate as processing facilities multiplied to accommodate overseas demand. The central, with its tall, distinctive, barnlike structure and protruding smokestacks, became the symbol of this new age.

More efficient milling, increased sugar hectarage, and guaranteed markets infused massive amounts of capital into the sugar industry and augmented the wealth, power, and prestige of its leaders. Added to the top of the structure was a layer of centralistas, those, including Americans, associated through investment, management, and/or technology with the manufacture of a competitive grade of export sugar. These millers converted their economic strength into political clout, which they brought to the halls of colonial government and to the U.S. Congress. To realize how powerful the industry became, one need only observe how the leadership manipulated the resources of the Philippine National Bank. As never before the sugar industry influenced life in the Philippines and affected the shape of the colony's future.

Economic change brought tensions to sugarlandia, between millers and planters and between sugar hands and those for whom they labored. Negros experienced social, political, and labor unrest, but the opposition to the changes taking place was unfocused and spread out among groups with divergent concerns. In Pampanga, economic deterioration affected the resilient and resourceful sugar casamac somewhat later, when quotas were about to become a reality and just when an intelligent, articulate spokesperson for their grievances was emerging on the scene. Despite all the changes during the period, cultural distinctions between the two regions that had formed in earlier times remained unaltered.

A New Era for Sugar

Unusual circumstances in the international sugar trade brightened the dawn of this new era for Philippine sugarmen. World War I temporarily destroyed the largest contributor to world sugar supplies, the Continental beet industry, and global output dropped from 18,008,380 tons in 1912 to 15,212,772 at war's end. Europe's recovery took until about 1927, and beets never again retrieved their relative share of prewar world production. Events particularly favored Cuba, which increased its yield from 1,593,867 to 3,967,094 tons over the same period. Wartime witnessed a steep rise in prices, but nothing compared to those in the two years following armistice. In early 1920 New York raw sugar touched a phenomenal high of 20.8 cents a pound, which translated in Manila to P54 per picul for centrifugal. Better markets might have prevailed longer, but Cuba had already so increased its output as to fill much of the gap created by European losses; hence, prices slipped rapidly to preboom levels and below by the end of the year and into 1921 (see figure 4). In 1923 a temporary production shortfall of more than a million tons lowered world supplies, so that Philippine centrifugal briefly reached P20.50 per picul; thereafter, price direction followed a generally downward slant as global output once more outgrew demand.[1]

Despite the short duration of the era of extravagant prices, euphoria reigned in Philippine sugar circles. Speculation in the Visayas for the 1920 crop became unusually vigorous as other optimistic indications appeared. The end of hostilities brought a sharp reduction in overseas freight rates, further improving the salability of the archipelago's agricultural produce. Additionally, under three separate tariff acts between 1916 and 1922 the U.S. Congress moved to raise duties on foreign sugar imports from 1.560 to 2.2060 cents per pound, and from 1.0048 to 1.7648 per pound on Cuban sugars, while continuing duty-free status for the Philippine product. Even

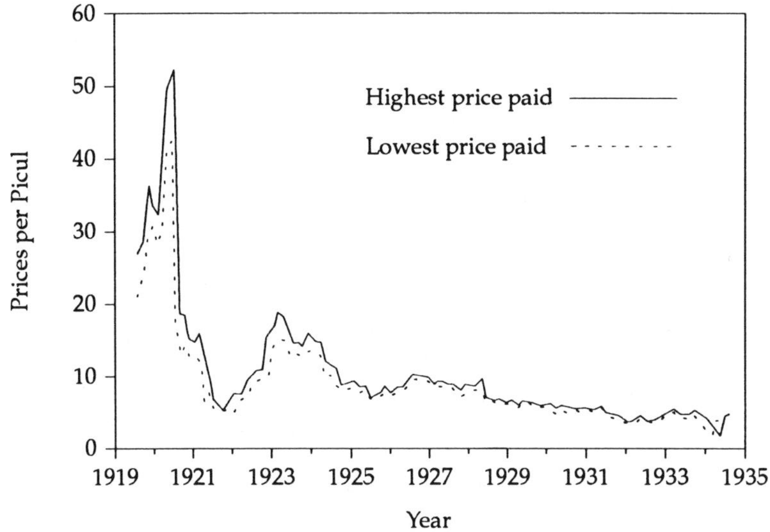

Figure 4. Sugar Prices on the Manila Market, 1919–34. Based on monthly quotations, but excluding slack period of July, August, September, and October. *Sugar News* 1–15 (1919–34).

though sugar prices never again approached their immediate postwar highs, America absorbed on favorable terms all the centrifugal the Philippines could produce, and this accessibility stimulated the growth of export throughout the period (see table 10). Despite particularly poor weather conditions in parts of sugarlandia in 1923 and 1926, sugar exports grew at an annual rate of 11.2 percent.[2]

The differential between the protected New York price for Philippine sugar and the London world price ranged from 30 to 150 percent, so that tariff preference led insular exporters to an almost complete reliance on the American market. Meanwhile, the decline of muscovado exports from 127,433 tons in 1921 to just 603 a decade later signified the demise of both the China and Japan markets, which previously absorbed all of the lower-grade product.[3] When the Depression deepened, sugar purchases by U.S. refiners came to represent 60 percent of the archipelago's export income, as opposed to 30 percent in the early 1920s.

To profit in the face of falling prices Philippine sugarmen raised their output of high-quality sugar by augmenting advanced milling capacity and by growing more cane. In 1922 twenty-six large and small centrals turned out 233,770 tons of centrifugal, whereas the 1933–34 yield was 998,123

Table 10. Philippine Sugar Exports, 1921–34

Year	Amount (metric tons)	Value (pesos)	Pesos per Ton	Value of All Exports (%)	To U.S. Amount (tons)	To U.S. % of All Sugar Export
1921	289,876	51,037,454	176.07	29	150,479	52
1922	362,072	51,165,110	141.31	27	244,852	68
1923	271,983	69,038,246	253.83	29	230,555	85
1924	357,830	83,736,173	234.01	31	300,865	84
1925	546,832	91,028,005	166.46	31	403,989	74
1926	411,232	64,459,268	156.75	24	341,306	83
1927	553,324	100,591,919	181.80	32	508,317	92
1928	569,938	95,085,879	166.84	31	534,229	94
1929	695,868	106,488,298	153.03	32	670,953	96
1930	743,980	104,480,451	140.43	39	737,195	99
1931	752,932	99,926,210	132.72	48	752,284	99
1932	1,016,568	119,603,769	117.65	63	1,016,266	99
1933	1,078,653	128,666,851	119.28	61	1,078,596	99
1934	1,152,841	130,909,161	113.55	59	1,152,679	99

Source: Philippines Commonwealth, Bureau of Customs, *The Port of Manila, Commonwealth of the Philippines, 1940: A Year Book Devoted to Foreign Commerce and Shipping of Manila and the Philippines* (Manila: Bureau of Commerce, 1940), pp. 64, 71.

tons manufactured at forty-five plants. Aside from one in Batangas and two in Tarlac, other centrals constructed in the 1920s on Luzon, Panay, Leyte, and Cebu tended to be smaller, testimony to the difficulties encountered in financing major projects. While export increased almost four times, cane plantings in the archipelago grew by some 27 percent, from 241,345 hectares in 1921 to 305,890 in 1934.[4]

Hacenderos in both western Negros and Pampanga ceased grinding in the old-fashioned muscovado factories, and the change in method netted from their cane about 20 percent more sugar of a uniformly higher grade, as well as quantities of alcohol obtained from new syrup distillation.[5] Greater output derived from expanded capacity at the existing centrals rather than from the addition of big new centrals. The former region had seventeen factories in 1922 and just eighteen a decade later; the latter region went from two to four factories (see map 8). The twelve largest centrals in the two provinces, however, increased their production significantly over this period (table 11).

Western Negros expanded its sugar hectarage by 44 percent, while Pampanga's grew only 14 percent; instead, Pasumil and Pasudeco added to

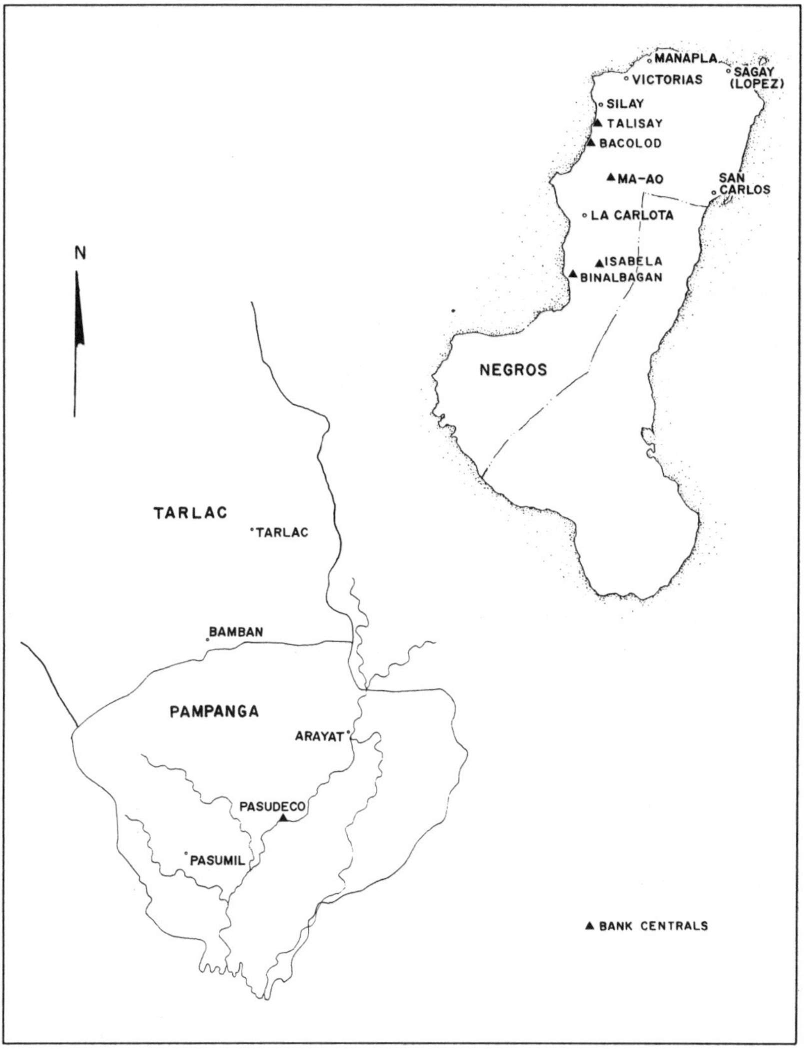

Map 8. Main Sugar Centrals in Pampanga and Western Negros, 1934

their stocks of cane by drawing from plantations in nearby Bataan and Tarlac. The two large centrals constructed in 1927 and 1929 in Tarlac reflected the lack of room for expansion in Pampanga and the need for the industry to move further north.

As table 12 indicates, the quantity of sugar per hectare also rose. Likewise, all centrals raised their productivity at this time; however, they did so at disparate rates and by stressing amelioration of different phases of their operations. Comparable data on sugar processing for each of the

Table 11. Growth in Major Centrals' Production, 1922–34 (metric tons)

	1922	*1933–34*
Negros Occidental		
Bacolod	9,912	63,152
Binalbagan	13,843	65,329
Silay-Hawaiian	14,844	66,168
Isabela	4,681	45,369
La Carlota	26,537	90,825
Ma-ao	13,712	59,077
Manapla	9,081	89,612
Talisay	10,027	57,792
San Carlos	16,638	48,422
Victorias	11,431	62,627
Total	130,706	648,373
Pampanga		
Pasudeco	15,571	90,508
Pasumil	26,022	84,118
Total	41,593	174,626

Source: *Sugar News* 3 (1922): 586; 16 (1935): 480.

central milling districts no longer exist, making broad comparisons of productivity impossible; however, annual reports of the Hawaiian-Philippine Company offer especially good information on how improvement came about in one case.[6]

Hawaiian-Philippine Company was founded in 1918 by corporate members of the Hawaiian Sugar Planters' Association in an effort to employ Philippine labor locally rather than across the Pacific in Hawaii. After failing to reach a satisfactory arrangement with planters in Pampanga, organizers decided to erect a central in Silay, drawing cane from the surrounding area and milling on the basis of a fifty-five–forty-five percent split of extracted sugar between hacenderos and central respectively. Planters who contracted with the new factory formed the Silay-Saravia Planters' Association in 1919, and grinding began January 15, 1921.

The central enjoyed rapid success and by October 1929 redeemed its initial capital indebtedness of P5,496,000 to its Hawaiian creditors. The company paid its first 6 percent dividend on 197,428 outstanding shares of stock in 1927, and thereafter shareholders' returns went up to 12 percent. In 1931, even as the Depression deepened in the United States, Hawaiian-

Table 12. Centrifugal Yield by Major Milling District, 1922–33

	1922–23 Season (piculs per ha.)	*1923–33 (piculs per ha.)*
Negros Occidental		
Bacolod[a]	58.38	74.68
Binalbagan[a]	54.51	74.95
Silay-Hawaiian	66.24	121.70
Isabela[a]	47.00	79.00
La Carlota	63.44	98.86
Ma-ao[a]	74.00	82.35
Manapla	—	112.71
Talisay[a]	65.00	108.21
San Carlos	66.09	142.98
Victorias	—	119.90
Pampanga		
Pasudeco[a]	—	59.92
Pasumil	42.41	88.97
Philippines	57.00	82.20

Source: *Sugar News* 6 (1925): 529; 14 (1933): 609–10.
[a]PNB-financed centrals.

Philippine Company gave shareholders a two-for-one stock split, at par value of P20, plus additional cash for a payout of P4,422,185. High dividends continued throughout these early years of world economic crisis.

Silay's productivity can be gauged from the following figures:

	1921–22	*1933–34*
Extraction	95.59	92.79
Hectares available to cane	10,777	11,353
Hectares harvested	4,525	9,484
Tons of cane per hectare	26.66	63.79
Tons of sugar per hectare	3.29	6.98

The central raised its milling capacity substantially, and its quality of production compared well with that of plants in other parts of the world, as evidenced by its extraction. "The efficiency of milling is generally expressed in terms of the percentage of total sucrose in the cane that is extracted in the juice (sucrose in juice per cent [of] sucrose in cane). This figure is known as the sucrose extraction or more briefly the extraction."[7] Concurrently, Australia matched Hawaii's extraction at 95.5, while Java managed 94, and Louisiana and Cuba were slightly lower at 93. Silay's varied from a high of 96.23 in 1923 to a low of 92.679 in 1931. The effects of weather on the quality of cane and the volume of cane milled influenced the extraction and may account for Silay's lower rate, but generally speaking the mill's performance met the world competition, despite some decline as the era closed.

In field productivity Silay milling district made large gains in cane per hectare. Aside from its contribution in greater milling efficiency, the central also provided planters with expanded field transportation, access to fertilizers, and interest-free fertilizer loans. Further, the central maintained experimental facilities to study cane varieties, supplied samples of high-yielding strains, and offered technical advice on field management.

Many hacenderos belonging to the Silay-Saravia Association responded positively. The district contained some of the most experienced farmers in Negros, and more farseeing ones understood the multiplier effect: that modern farming methods netted correspondingly much higher crop yields and, hence, better returns on investment and that good agricultural practice offered the best hedge against falling prices. Two of the district's leading sugarmen, hacendero Cesar Gamboa and technologist Carlos Locsin, stressed this point in articles for major sugar publications. In numerous ways planters contributed to higher productivity: they increased their use of fertilizer, dug drainage canals, employed irrigation pumps, set up cane seed beds, used better seed selection, and undertook deep plowing with tractors. These actions added sufficiently to yields to make Silay in 1933 the third most productive (after Bais, Negros Oriental, and San Carlos) Philippine sugar district. Gamboa's 1927 record of 129.04 piculs per hectare placed him among the most efficient farmers both in his district and in western Negros. In 1933 the top planters in North Negros Sugar Company (Manapla) included the Philippine Chinese Yee On with an extraordinary 179.82 piculs and Catalino Valderrama (of the famous lumber family) with 127.91 on his best fields.[8]

Centrals, by virtue of their size and wealth, could undertake activities on a larger scale to support planters. For instance, Pasumil purchased tractors and rented them to farmers so they could deep plow the dry, hard soils of northwestern Pampanga. Ma-ao acquired a limestone crushing plant to supply inexpensive fertilizer, and the very progressive Victorias Central conducted advanced research on various farm activities, including studies concerning the deterioration of burnt cane. Centrals normally became involved in provincewide campaigns to eliminate such plagues as rinderpest and locusts. The government helped in numerous ways, not the least of which was through studies on seed strains conducted at its major research facility, La Carlota Experiment Station. Its findings appeared in the quarterly *Philippine Agricultural Review*, published by the Department of Agriculture and Natural Resources.[9]

Not all milling districts reached the same level of productivity, and those in Pampanga did not succeed as well as ones on Negros. For instance, Pasumil district, which developed the highest yields on all of Luzon, in 1923 produced only 24.55 tons of cane per hectare and 2.67 tons of sugar per hectare, compared with Silay's 30.95 tons cane and 4.19 tons sugar. Experts proffered two explanations for the disparity: weather and outdated farming practices. Central Luzon experienced more pronounced wet and dry seasons than did Negros, and the long rainless spells affected cane growth in the north; hence, technologists recommended that Capampangan invest in major irrigation projects to assure adequate water supplies. Such waterworks, however, materialized only after World War II. In the matter of cane selection Capampangan had a more feasible opportunity to raise yields but did not take it. Despite all the research on new strains, as late as 1932 Luzon planters still sowed their fields with 57 percent old, low-yield, native varieties of cane, compared with just 28 percent in Negros. Finally, the more worn soils of Pampanga required heavier applications of fertilizer than did the fields of Negros, and many Pampangan farmers lacked financial resources to meet those demands.[10]

Even the highest Philippine yields did not compare with those in other major world cane areas: for example, in 1932–33, the number of tons of sugar per hectare in the thirty top Philippine milling districts—5.8—was second worst among Hawaii (17.3), Java (15.7), Puerto Rico (9.9), and Cuba (4.9). And whereas the most modern planters on Negros averaged between one hundred and two hundred piculs per hectare, centrals on Hawaii regularly produced more than two hundred, while some Javanese fields employing the latest, best strains of cane reached four hundred.[11] Although various factors—including a longer growing season, more centralized management, and more intense research in the other areas—accounted somewhat for these disparities, the poor performance of the PNB-financed centrals reduced significantly overall Philippine averages.

Bank centrals (as they were often called), though founded in an era of great optimism about sugar's future, could not have been launched at a worse time. Machinery prices had steadily risen throughout the war and the immediate postwar periods, fueled by a scarcity of parts and high wages; hence, investors had to borrow heavily to finance these projects. The new factories quickly evolved into investment and management nightmares because original cost estimates proved so low that initial loans did not cover all the construction. In several cases the new central operators

Table 13. Performance of PNB-Financed Centrals, 1918–35

Central	Building Period	Original Financing (pesos)	Debt (pesos)		Production (piculs)	
			1922	1935	1922–23	1933–34
Isabela	1918–19	1,700,000	3,725,738	1,189,000	94,387	717,289
Ma-ao	1919–20	6,350,000	10,822,633	1,881,000	265,127	934,008
Bacolod	1919–20	2,900,000	6,806,646	1,300,000	222,723	998,441
Talisay	1919–20	3,500,000	6,248,942	—[a]	230,757	913,703
Pasudeco	1919–21	4,500,000	4,758,102	—[b]	291,724	1,430,948
Binalbagan	1920–21	5,000,000	10,896,543	3,330,000	231,532	1,032,866

Source: Sugar central data supplied to Manuel Luis Quezon, Manila, July 30, 1935, "Outstanding Obligation of Bank Centrals as of June 30, 1935, Compared with December 31, 1922," letter from General Venancio Concepcion, President of PNB, to the Board of Directors of PNB, June 21, 1920, Quezon Papers, National Library of the Philippines, Manila.

[a]Debt paid May 1929.

[b]Debt paid September 1927.

did not have money to lay down sufficient railway track to reach contracting planters in their district. PNB extended further loans (see table 13) and mortgagees, mainly local planters, had to put up as further collateral most of their fields, often evaluated at inflated prices. Moreover, PNB estimated the payback time on the assumption that extraordinary wartime prices would prevail for several years longer. When sugar dropped precipitously in 1921, bank centrals could not meet even their interest payments. There followed a series of crises, and the government found it necessary to create the Philippine Sugar Centrals Agency, a special branch of the PNB just to supervise management of the six plants. Ownership of several of these ventures changed hands; and for his gross mismanagement of bank funds, especially with regard to loans to sugar interests, PNB president Venancio Concepcion eventually went to prison (see appendix D).[12]

By 1923 sugar experts correctly concluded that, given the inflated debt structure of bank centrals, all save Pasudeco lacked sufficient milling capacity to meet their minimum payments and that only by expanding extant facilities could they become viable enterprises. PNB, which had recently faced a situation in which its ratio of outstanding loans to deposits was woefully inadequate and in which 52 percent of those loans was already committed to bank centrals, moved conservatively to become involved in further expansion. Nevertheless, pressure from the presidents of Bacolod and Isabela centrals, Rafael Alunan and Emilio Montilla, and from knowledgeable American sugar technicians overrode the conservative advice of financial advisers, and PNB provided money, first to Talisay, later, in smaller amounts, to Isabela and Ma-ao, and finally, to Bacolod in 1924.[13]

But the bank's troubles did not end at this point, for both Talisay and Bacolod overdrew their extension loans, the latter by P2,102,970! Unsurprisingly, the annual report for 1925 noted that the bank centrals' total debt in outstanding loans and unpaid interest exceeded by almost two million pesos the obligations owed in 1922. When the 1925–26 planting season on Negros proved a disaster, PNB at last called a halt to serving as an open wallet to the centrals. Not until 1927 did they all begin to show positive results from their enlarged milling capacity and to pay down on their enormous debts. Pasudeco, the best-planned operation with the smallest outstanding obligation, paid off its mortgage that year, and Talisay followed in 1929. Extremely productive seasons in the early 1930s seriously reduced the debt of Bacolod, Isabela, and Ma-ao. By the mid-1930s, only Binalbagan remained a problem.[14]

Throughout much of its early history, a combination of corruption and maladministration associated with Binalbagan's financing and operations caused PNB, the government, and local planters serious difficulties. Originally founded by the Yulo family, Binalbagan changed hands in 1919 because its owners feared losing their lands while raising necessary capital to meet increased construction costs. An American named Philip Whitiker managed to acquire the major interest, almost solely with bank credit; moreover, he presented PNB president Venancio Concepcion with more than P600,000 worth of stock "for services rendered." Senator Esperidion Guanco acted as the company's vice-president at this time when the Binalbagan estate owed PNB P12,000,000. Eventually the credit pyramid crumbled, and the bank, under a new president, took over ownership of the plant.

More than a year of bad management ensued, and hacenderos complained of losses incurred during milling. In late 1923 a minority shareholder, Enrique Echaús, attempted to buy the factory. He failed, despite obtaining a PNB loan with his land serving as collateral, and the bank now had invested P14,000,000 in a factory valued by some outside experts in 1923 at P4,000,000. It seems that Echaús employed his loan to make high-interest crop loans to Binalbagan planters; moreover, he found himself locked in combat with the unpopular manager, an American named Locey. In early 1924, Echaús engaged 250 armed men, invaded the factory grounds, evicted Locey, and began to ship out sugar held in the central warehouse. Order subsequently returned, and lawyers for the bank and Echaús sorted out the tangled web of debts. PNB, still the owner, in 1927 turned operations over to John Dumas, a highly efficient manager who so boosted the central's production that it achieved its first million picul season in 1934. PNB general manager Rafael Corpus served as president of Binalbagan and succeeded in reducing its debt considerably; nevertheless, it remained the only plant under the bank's ownership until after World War II.[15]

Bank centrals did not have the same resources as privately funded centrals to raise productivity and profit margins. Investors owed PNB for construction costs, and since many of them were also planters, they had to pay off crop loans as well. The bank, already overcommitted to the centrals, proved miserly with funds for improvements and did not sponsor the kind of research that increased yields in the private milling districts. Talisay, for instance, appears to have operated far more effectively after it returned completely to private control in 1929.[16]

On three occasions between 1920 and 1926, the government and PNB entertained offers to sell their interest in the bank centrals to private American financiers—Philip Whitiker, Pacific Commercial Company (PCC), and Hayden, Stone and Company. Each time, however, Filipino leaders and American officials turned down the bids, either because the financing was inadequate or on the grounds that it was important to maintain a strong Filipino presence in milling.[17]

Native opposition to these various offers did not imply a hostility toward all American participation in the Philippine sugar industry. Indeed, in no other endeavor did Americans become more active or cooperate with native entrepreneurs more fully. Political leaders like Manuel Quezon and Rafael Alunan made it clear that U.S. capital remained crucial to the continued development of Philippine agriculture.[18] On many issues Filipinos and Americans shared a common interest and point of view, so that sugar represented the business area of most cosmopolitan interaction.

The launching of centrals brought to prominence a group of U.S. sugarmen, some with prior experience in the Philippines, some, including the Hawaiians at San Carlos and Silay, new to the islands. Laws inhibited foreign ownership of land, and Americans became most numerous at top levels of finance and management and in the construction and technical operations of centrals. The experiences of two early American businessmen offer good examples of the origins of U.S. participation in the Philippine sugar industry.

John Switzer's career coincided with the rise of PCC, which had its origins as California-based Castle Brothers, Wolf and Company, selling produce to the U.S. Army in the Philippines since 1899. Castle Brothers became involved in scandal involving commissary supplies but evaded prosecution, and the firm grew into the largest American export-import firm in the Philippines. Meanwhile, Switzer, a veteran of the Philippine-American War, achieved financial success on his own in Cebu, where he developed diverse commercial enterprises.

A major change occurred in late 1911 when Maurice Lowenstein, an employee of Castle Brothers, acquired the firm and reorganized it into PCC with better financing. Switzer merged his Cebu interests into the new corporation and became its general manager. Stockholders and members of the board of this new company included Galen Stone of Hayden, Stone and Company; Andrew Preston of United Fruit; and Francis Hart of Old Colony Trust Company of Boston. New York's prestigious Sullivan and Cromwell acted as the company's legal council. PCC had by this time branch offices in Cebu, Iloilo, San Francisco, New York, Kobe, and Sydney. Under Switzer's guidance PCC went into sugar milling. Along with Alfred Ehrman, Switzer in 1912 finessed the friar lands at Calamba, Laguna, and established Canlubang Sugar Central. Several years later Ehrman and PCC, backed by the resources of the powerful West Coast Spreckels sugar interests, constructed Pasumil, and PCC continued as agent for these two major centrals throughout much of the pre–World War II period.

The firm in 1917 became a branch of the umbrella conglomerate Pacific Development Corporation. Among the most important new investors and members of the board were William Endicott of Kidder, Peabody and Company and Herbert Fleishacker of the Anglo-London Paris National Bank of San Francisco, which had become chief fiscal agent for Calamba Sugar Estate as well as its largest shareholder. Anglo-London included among its stockholders Governor-general Francis Burton Harrison (1913–20). Besides their connections with Harrison, Lowenstein and Switzer maintained personal ties with Clarence Edwards and then Frank McIntyre, successive chiefs of the U.S. Bureau of Insular Affairs (BIA), the liaison office between the Philippines and the U.S. government. These ties proved very helpful, for both Harrison and the BIA provided useful assistance in the establishment of Pasumil.

Switzer departed the Philippines a wealthy man in 1919, having served PCC and Pacific Development well. He had brought into the firm very talented personnel like sugar agent Alfred D. Cooper (taken from San Carlos Milling), central managers John Dumas and R. Renton Hind, executive Horace Pond, and publicist Lorenzo Thibault, former editor of the *Manila Times*. A staunch Republican, Switzer firmly held the view that for economic reasons the United States should postpone as long as possible granting independence to the Philippines. As head of the New York office of PCC until the mid 1920s and as a member of the board of the Philippine-

American Chamber of Commerce he continued to use his influence in this cause. Even in retirement he unofficially advised his old friend, senate, then commonwealth, president Manuel Quezon on economic and political matters. Meanwhile, under General Manager Horace Pond PCC remained an active participant in the milling and export ends of the sugar business.[19]

As an individual George Fairchild probably had more sway over the industry than any other American. Arriving from Hawaii in 1912 with considerable experience in sugar manufacture, he became involved in one or more phases of the construction of at least five centrals. He also formed Welch, Fairchild and Company, a major sugar trading and management firm that had among its clients Silay-Hawaiian Central. Like Switzer, Fairchild remained a solid Republican wedded to retention for both political and personal economic reasons. In 1920 he purchased (curiously, with the help of Manuel Quezon) the *Manila Times*, and for six years used that paper as his forum against independence. He also helped found and actively participated in the American Chamber of Commerce to promote his cause. His greatest influence, however, came through his role as cofounder and longstanding secretary-treasurer of the Philippine Sugar Association (PSA).[20]

Established in 1922 as a technical forum for all participants in the industry, the PSA within a decade became an organization representing the collective voice of more than 80 percent of the central millers in the Philippines. From the dawn of the central era the Philippine sugar industry became a game of statistics in which chemists, engineers, and agronomists played an increasingly important role, and it remained for such privately employed individuals to isolate new strains of cane, to raise field productivity, and to ameliorate milling procedures. The PSA acted as the clearinghouse for their findings. Even at its outset, however, PSA maintained a legislative committee to keep track of insular and metropolitan government actions affecting Philippine sugar; and this subgroup, which included Fairchild and Felipe Buencamino, Jr., received regular intelligence from the BIA in Washington. As time passed and membership in PSA grew, the legislature committee greatly augmented its activities and achieved added importance within the organization. Initially about one-third of the centrals belonged to PSA, but that number grew in the late 1920s and early 1930s as schemes for the imposition of tariffs and/or import restrictions began to attract attention in Congress.

Through PSA Filipino, American, and Spanish millers united as a single force to compete with Cuban, Puerto Rican, Hawaiian, and U.S. beet interests for privileged access to the American market. Officers of PSA came from the upper ranks of mill owners and managers and constituted a cosmopolitan mix. In succession, American R. Renton Hind (Pasumil), Filipinos Rafael Alunan, Wenceslao Trinidad (Pasudeco), Cesar Ledesma (Talisay), and Alunan again became the organization's presidents, while Fairchild (Silay-Hawaiian) served as permanent secretary-treasurer. Vice-presidents, such as Spaniard J. M. Elizalde (La Carlota), and other members of the board of trustees represented all other participating centrals. Even PNB president Rafael Corpus in his capacity as president of Binalbagan joined the association's ruling council. The PSA therefore included practically all the most influential and wealthiest sugarmen and the most outstanding professional managers and technicians.[21]

Despite PSA efforts and claims to represent the entire sugar industry, it did not. As new centrals came on line in the late 1910s and early 1920s, planters in each milling district formed associations to protect their interests. They hired their own technicians to check the centrals' test results and to supervise the distribution of cane and sugar among member planters and between hacenderos and centrals. In 1924 four planter groups—those milling at Talisay, Bacolod, Ma-ao, and Isabela—founded the Confederation of Associations and Planters of Sugar Cane (La Confederacion de Asociaciones y Plantadores de Caña Dulce, Inc.). Working with a subsidy of two centavos for every picul of sugar milled, this umbrella organization gradually attracted to its ranks planter groups from all the other major milling districts on Negros and from Pasumil in Pampanga. The confederation, representing 52 percent of centrifugal output, did everything from securing better loan terms from PNB to lobbying through its president and chief spokesman Amando Avanceña in Manila and Washington. Planters at times adopted an adversary relation toward millers and tended to take their own stand on the twin issues of immediate independence and free trade.[22]

The struggles over Philippine independence and economic arrangements have captured considerable attention from scholars, and only the critical role of sugar in those deliberations needs emphasis here. On the American side, a major—perhaps the chief—impulse toward Philippine independence came from agribusiness: sugar and dairy people who wanted to exclude Philippine sweetener and coconut oil from the duty-free U.S. market. Politicians and lobbyists for the U.S. Beet Sugar Association, American Sugar Cane League, American Farm Bureau Federation, Hawaiian Sugar Planters' Association, Association of Sugar Producers of Porto Rico, as well as corporations heavily involved with Cuban centrals such as National City Bank, United Fruit, and Hershey's Chocolate, all joined the campaign. Although Philippine sugar never represented more than a fraction of the total production within America's tariff walls, its share of imports grew dramatically from 7.6 percent in 1921 to 24 percent twelve years later, alarming American competitors. As world supply became overabundant and prices skidded, they somewhat incorrectly viewed the Philippine product as a substantial threat to their profits and in some cases to their survival.

The Philippine movement for independence had its roots in the nineteenth century, and by the early twentieth century it involved partisans from every region of the archipelago. In Philippine politics, the Nationalista party with its platform calling for immediate, absolute independence captured the hearts and minds of most Filipinos in elections after 1907. The two main leaders of that party, Manuel Quezon of Tayabas Province and Sergio Osmeña of Cebu, rose to power on that platform and never wavered from that stand in their public utterances.

Several factors impeded the road to swift independence, however. In the United States many members of the Republican Party continued to share the view of Governor-general Leonard Wood (1921–26) that the Philippines was simply not ready for self-government. Also, those who profited, either as importers of American goods to or exporters of Philippine produce from the archipelago, those who had invested their lives and savings in the Philippine economy, as well as others with strategic concerns favored gradual devolution of power to native hands. Filipinos who feared the economic and global political dangers of independence expressed, albeit softly in the face of strong contrary opinion, a need to postpone total autonomy until some indefinite time in the future. Payne-Aldrich had accomplished what many nationalists feared it would; it had made the Philippine economy, especially the pivotal sugar industry, dependent on American preferences. Against this background, the drama of Philippine national and international politics unfolded.[23]

Between 1924 and 1933 American interests in and out of Congress attempted by various means to curb the access of Philippine sugar. In the Fairfield Bill (1924) they sought to do so by granting the Philippines early independence, but actions by John Switzer, members of PSA, and other Filipino politicians prevented their success. In 1928 Congressman Charles Timberlake of beet-growing Colorado introduced a resolution seeking to cap Philippine imports, but Switzer, the PSA, Governor-general Henry L. Stimson (1928–29) and former BIA chief Frank McIntyre, among others, managed to bury his proposal. Likewise, Cuban and American interests tried to cut imports of duty-free Philippine sugar in the Hawley-Smoot Tariff Act of 1930, but again Stimson, now Herbert Hoover's secretary of state, intervened, and free Philippine entry remained. While the Philippine sugar interests escaped American legislative efforts against their industry, they also refused to participate in the Chadbourne International Sugar Agreement of 1931, which planned to limit world production.[24]

As Philippine independence loomed, the thinking among Philippine political and economic leaders clarified as they contemplated the consequences of losing duty preferences. Some sought means to protect that access as the best way of preserving economic health, even as they worked toward the highly desired goal of self-rule. Others concluded that the quicker Filipinos obtained independence, the sooner they could begin taking charge of their economic destiny. This dichotomy of thought appeared in the remarks of leading sugarmen, some of whom became directly involved in independence negotiations. Urbano Zafra, an administrative secretary of the PSA and sometime Washington lobbyist, wrote the following in the procentral *Sugar News*:

> Taken as a whole, with all its imperfections, the tariff relationship between the United States and the Philippines, under which the trade and commerce between the two countries have been developed for the past 33 years, has resulted in mutual benefits to the Philippines and the United States. To the Philippines it has opened to the products of these Islands the great American market—a prize for which the nations all over the world are striving—and has been responsible for the attainment of our present economic progress. . . .
>
> Irrespective of what political relations may be established in the future between the United States and the Philippines, it is to the advantage of both Filipinos and Americans to continue, even in modified form, the present reciprocity in Philippine-American commerce.[25]

On the other side, leading planter spokesman Amando Avanceña declared:

> The sugar planters of Negros, however, are always disposed to forego at any time the advantages offered by the American market, provided the loss of such advantages will bring independence to the Philippines, not a nominal independence but one real and complete. We are therefore disposed, moreover, and so we ask, that America concede to the Philippines its independence without any period of transition, although this may mean that we have to abandon the planting of sugar cane and must produce other products; but such independence should be real, in other words, once she has granted independence to the Philippines, the United States should not have

> any military or other reservations within the territory of the Philippine Islands.[26]

Manuel Quezon, the consummate politician best able to clarify Philippine sentiment, bridged the dichotomy in the arguments when he offered these thoughts in a letter to John Switzer in 1931:

> I will not advise my people to oppose immediate and complete independence without free trade if it is the purpose of Congress to grant it. On the contrary, I would advise them to accept it. The present situation is getting to be intolerable and rather than continue it indefinitely, not knowing what is to come next, we had better face whatever consequences the loss of free trade might involve.
>
> . . . And if the only means to do away with [the present] government is through the loss of free trade with the United States, I am ready to lose it. For one, I am willing to compromise on the question of immediate independence and let it be postponed, if thereby I can prevent poverty to my people and make independence more secure when it comes. But under no circumstances am I willing to compromise on the question of self-government.[27]

The two independence bills, Hare-Hawes-Cutting (1933) and its near clone the Tydings-McDuffie Act (1934), contained provisions both beneficial and detrimental to Philippine sugar. The main provision of the bills, a ten-year commonwealth period, represented a triumph of American agricultural and Cuban sugar interests in Congress over the wishes of President Hoover and other Republican retentionists, who wanted a longer transition period. However, the final independence bill included a sizable quota of 850,000 long tons of sugar—800,000 centrifugal and 50,000 refined—allowed duty-free entry into the United States during the first five years. Then would follow a 5 percent duty increase in each of the next five years. All sugar over the limit and all imported after ten years would be subject to the full foreign tariff. The limitation represented a sum larger than American farmers had demanded.[28]

In all these deliberations Philippine sugarmen, especially centralistas, spent heavily to forward their interests. The PSA opened a New York office in 1929 and paid for it with an assessment on every picul produced by its member centrals. The funds also supported negotiators and lobbyists taking care of business in Washington. PSA did not rely just on Philippine officials and businessmen to advance its cause; it hired influential Americans as well. In 1933, following his retirement from the Senate, Harry Hawes of Missouri, one of the authors of the first independence bill, became PSA's leading lobbyist. He had served as chairman of the Senate Committee on Insular Affairs, and in 1930 traveled to the islands on a fact-finding mission. Hawes also came to know Quezon and other Philippine leaders and subsequently solicited their thinking on legislative matters in Washington. After retiring, he devoted much of his time to protecting Philippine quota rights. For several years Joseph Tumulty, formerly a personal adviser to President Woodrow Wilson, joined Hawes in those lobbying efforts.[29]

In the political struggles between Manuel Quezon and Sergio Osmeña, sugarmen generally supported the former and helped him become the first president of the Philippine Commonwealth. Quezon numbered among his most important allies both Rafael Alunan and Amando Avanceña. Almost all sugar legislators backed Quezon, including Senators Sotero Baluyut (Pampanga) and Gil Montilla (Negros Occidental) and Representatives Felipe Buencamino, Jose de Leon, Emilio Yulo, and Enrique Magalona. An important exception, however, was Benigno Aquino, Sr., of Tarlac, who kept faith with Osmeña. Even so, most of the big-money contributors like the Elizalde family and M. J. Ossorio helped Quezon.[30]

While consideration of the two independence bills proceeded apace in Washington and Manila, New Deal administrators sought to uncover means of alleviating America's farm crisis. Since Hawley-Smoot tariff legislation had not succeeded in raising prices sufficiently to aid the plight of sugar producers, the government turned to restrictions on production as a means of coping with the industry's dilemmas. Congress amended the Agricultural Adjustment Act (AAA) of 1933 to incorporate more reasonable production limits suggested by the administration. Approved on May 9, 1934, the Jones-Costigan Act provided quotas for all domestic, insular, and foreign suppliers to the U.S. market, the total amount adjusted to annual American consumption. It was hoped that a decline in output would stimulate a rise in American prices. To minimize the economic sting of limitations, producers would receive proceeds from a sugar-processing tax. Congress made provisions of the bill retroactive to January 1, 1934.

Throughout the negotiations Philippine sugar interests lobbied energetically for higher limits. Hawes, Alunan, Governor-general Frank Murphy (1934–35), and many others either testified before committees or corresponded with officials to prevent cutting the insular quota, despite efforts of fiercely competitive rivals to accomplish such reductions. What finally emerged in the Jones-Costigan Act was a 1934 export quota of

1,015,186 short tons (920,970 metric tons) of sugar, including 79,661 short tons (72,268 metric tons) of refined. Again Philippine advocates had prevented the worst from happening to their industry.[31]

Difficulties associated with the administration of Jones-Costigan initially created confusion in Philippine government circles and caused considerable anxiety among sugarmen. Several problems immediately surfaced, the most salient of which centered on matters of scheduling. Because the law applied retroactively to January 1 and the milling and crop seasons ran from November to May, what limits should, or could, be placed on the 1933–34 crop, the one just harvested and milled? Allotments to various centrals and planters could not be applied rationally, for by June of 1934 shippers had already sent to market quantities equivalent to the 1934 quota, and some large centrals had not yet completed their milling season. Should the government stop further shipments?

A second set of problems centered on equitable quotas. Given a maximum figure for export each year, what basis should determine each central's share of that amount? Two plans surfaced: one, favoring older, larger factories, called for averaging production for calendar years 1931, 1932, and 1933 at each plant, and then giving each one a proportional share tied to that number. A second option, favored by smaller centrals, including seven that had only recently started up, proposed taking each factory's single best year as the figure on which to divvy up the quota. The choice involved considerable differences in the size of allocation to each central and led to sharp cleavages among the membership of PSA. Felipe Buencamino and Esteban de la Rama among others favored the latter method, while spokesmen like L. Weinzheimer of Pasumil and Avanceña, on behalf of many planters, favored the former. The matter precipitated something of a credit crisis as well, for PNB became reluctant to offer crop loans until it had some idea of how many hectares each hacendero could plant.[32]

In June 1934, Governor-general Murphy set about laying down the rules and building the machinery by which the Philippine quota would be administered. He opted for the system of average central output as the basis of allocation, thus pleasing the larger centrals, and he decided that sugar should continue to go to the United States throughout 1934, the amount over the quota (some 400,000 tons) to be held in bonded customs warehouses for sale after January 1, 1935. He thus postponed the hardships of output reductions until the following year and allowed himself sufficient opportunity to emplace the insular quota system. During the remainder of the year local advisers and AAA officials from Washington helped him turn out the legislation and establish the bureaucracy to give each central and each planter an exact share of the dwindled pie.

By mid-December, all plants had their 1935 allocation, based on a total export of some 552,000 tons. At the same time the first 195 planters in Silay received their quotas, and others were on the way. Despite troubles in 1934 and the prospect of a bleak future, the Philippines exported its largest crop ever, a fitting conclusion to the prosperous central era.[33]

Sugar Society and Centrals

New mills brought change to sugar society. At the top of the revised socioeconomic pyramid stood the centralistas, Filipino, Spanish, and American owners and executives managing either corporate or family interests. Americans included Fairchild, Renton Hind, and Horace Pond, all pillars of the expatriate community. Miguel Ossorio, the Elizaldes, and officials of Ynchausti and Company and Tabacalera represented the Iberians, while Jose de Leon, Augusto Gonzalez, and the Montillas, Aranetas, and Lizareses were the leading Filipino capitalists. Lines of nationality tended to blur, however, for Ossorio became an American citizen and Angel Elizalde married Mary Huntington Spreckels, thus forging bonds between Spanish-owned La Carlota and the Pasumil-Calamba U.S. combine.

Intermarriage inextricably enmeshed native central families as well. For example, Eusebio Lopez, founder of Sagay Central, married the sister of Cesar Ledesma, vice-president of Talisay Central. One of the daughters of that union married Nicholas Lizares, president of Talisay; another wed lawyer, entrepreneur, and PSA executive Salvador Araneta. Meanwhile, Ledesma's son Ricardo married a daughter of Carmen Yulo, who possessed holdings in Binalbagan Central; thus ownership of three centrals was linked by kinship. Beyond Negros, too, the centralistas formed affinal ties. In November 1926, Fausto Gonzalez Sioco, brother of Pampangan magnate Augusto, married Amparo de la Rama, and wedding gifts included 350 shares of Central Talisay from her father, Esteban, and 100 shares of Pasudeco from his relatives.

The new class of central owner-operators did not spring sui generis from the establishment of the sugar factories but rather derived from some of the most entrepreneurial planter families of old. Lopez, the Elizaldes, de Leon, and Gonzalez all had substantial haciendas first. Ossorio represented fairly new money when he organized Victorias and Manapla, but the Lizareses and Aranetas planted well before they became mill proprietors. Their collective initiatives in modern processing made them even wealthier, the richest, most powerful people in their industry and society. In 1930 Carlos Locsin calculated that, depending on crop yields, profits from direct investments in centrals doubled or trebled those from investments in sugar lands.[34]

Equities of central corporations were traded regularly on the Manila exchange, and sometimes planters received shares in their centrals in lieu of cash payments. During the 1920s those grinding at PNB centrals agreed to buy shares worth 25 percent of their net profit as a condition of not selling the plants to foreign buyers. But by the late 1920s centrals yielded good returns and appeared to have a profitable future, so shares became scarce on the open market and remained closely held by the largest investors.[35]

Wealth bred further wealth, and several millionaire millers diversified with outside investments, some close to the sugar industry, some quite far afield. Ossorio purchased a seat on the New York Sugar and Coffee Exchange, de la Rama added new vessels to the family fleet, sugar merchant and investor Jose Ledesma bought PNB bonds, while Jose de Leon sat on its Board of Directors. Ynchausti and Company owned not only three centrals, plantations, and a distillery, but also paint, lumber, and shipping companies. The Elizaldes bought Ynchausti. Jose Gomez, general manager at Ma-ao, took an active interest in the construction of the very important shipping facility at Pulupandan; and Jose Escaler, who held a similar position at Pasudeco, acquired a major stake in the Philippine (copra) Oil Company. Pasudeco's Wenceslao Trinidad founded in 1931 the Luzon Investment Corporation and in 1933 the National Life Insurance Company. In the latter endeavor two of his coinvestors were Jose de Leon and Cesar Ledesma. Nicholas Lizares, Ledesma, and Salvador Araneta were among those who joined with the entrepreneurial Lopez family of Iloilo in forming the pioneering air passenger company in the Visayas. Sugar money penetrated almost every area of Philippine enterprise from agriculture and food processing to mining.[36]

Philippine politics, whether a person was running for office or supporting other candidates, demanded considerable cash and time; hence, only the wealthiest members of society—for example, the centralistas and biggest hacenderos—could afford the game at the provincial level and higher. In Negros two of Manuel Quezon's chief lieutenants, Gil Montilla, associated with Isabela Central, and Rafael Alunan, vied to control offices. Montilla became successively representative, governor, and senator during this time and acted as political *lider* (local boss), influencing the choice of local slates. Alunan, though for a while serving as a legislator, preferred cabinet positions and the role of eminence grise in provincial elections. Negros's top officeholders tended to come from centralista ranks or centralista-supported candidates, men such as Mariano Yulo, Emilio Montilla, and Hermenegildo Villanueva; otherwise they tended to be big planters like Jose Locsin, Isaac Lacson, Emilio Gaston, or Enrique Magalona (see appendix E).

In Pampanga the system worked somewhat differently, because Americans operated one of the two big centrals, and at the other, leading executives de Leon, Gonzalez, and Trinidad chose to concentrate on business. However, the latter three owned clout by virtue of their wealth and position, and Quezon solicited their support in his various local initiatives. Pampangan sugarmen had to share power with rice land proprietors; nevertheless, those connected—either through employment, shareholding, or family ties—with Pasudeco achieved success at the highest levels of insular government. Sotero Baluyut, from a relatively obscure local family, acquired an American education as an engineer and went on, following employment at the central, to become Pampanga's governor and senator.[37]

Central owners gained numerous advantages from holding so much political power, including their ability to affect the legislative outcome of key bills. For example, despite growing labor agitation for passage of an eight-hour-per-day labor law, PSA managed to delay such legislation—at least as it applied to sugar central workers—for more than a decade. PSA, with the aid of such high-priced legal talent as Jose Yulo and the American Clyde Dewitt, also prevented the imposition of added taxes on processed sugar.

Yulo represented a category of appointed politicians who looked after sugar from the executive branch. After representing Pasumil-Calamba in numerous matters and acting as PSA attorney, he became secretary of justice from 1934 to 1938. Salvador Laguda typified the active hacendero in politics. A former newspaperman, he served successively as assemblyman, vice-president of the first Agricultural Congress, vice-president of PNB, secretary of commerce and communications, and president of Lopez Central. Honorio Ventura of Pasudeco was chosen chief of the executive bureau from 1921 to 1925, then secretary of the interior between 1925 and 1933. From these vantages such administrators could influence government policy on crucial matters relating to sugar. In 1931, when strikes began to affect the sugar industry in the western Visayas, Ventura ordered the Philippine Constabulary to intervene if necessary to prevent violence and the disruption of central operations. Of all groups associated with the sugar industry, the centralistas clearly commanded the most influence in the halls of government.[38]

The division between planters and centralistas contained a nationality component, for up to 91 percent of hacenderos were Filipinos while perhaps

50 percent of central owners were not. Not only did Americans and Spaniards directly possess from one-third to one-half of mill production, but local central-owning families with long residence in the Philippines sometimes held foreign passports. Miguel Ossorio acquired American citizenship, and the Elizaldes remained Spanish subjects. Foreign planters, who constituted a distinct numerical minority, came mostly from Spain but included a few other Europeans and a handful of Americans like H. B. Ross and W. J. Fassoth in Pampanga and Richard Nolan in Negros. Such outsiders possessed little influence on industry policy, unless they were, like Nolan, married into an influential local family, in his case the Lizares-Alunans. On national issues, planters tended to adopt a more consistently proindependence point of view, whereas centralistas, reflecting their mixed loyalties, assumed more flexible positions.[39]

With the creation of a supraclass of millers, planters lost power and prestige as well as income, and the economic condition of many became more precarious as a result of the change. For the biggest landholders, centrals initiated more efficient operations on their estates and provided them with opportunities to improve crop productivity. The rich could also diversify their sources of income so that they did not have to depend exclusively on the whims of sugar's fortunes for their livelihood. President Corazon Aquino's father, Jose Cojuangco, in addition to cultivating some 15,000 hectares of Tarlac sugar plantings, also held considerable banking interests. Juan Nepomuceno, who became one of the biggest hacenderos with Pasudeco, also operated the electric companies of Angeles and Magalang. Planters such as Segundo Montilla, Roberto Toledo III, and Timoteo Unson, who had the highest production of roughly 15,000 to 50,000 piculs per harvest, earned an excellent livelihood from the industry. Others with careers outside the sugar industry dabbled in cane production as a sideline and as a way of gaining status. Manuel Quezon, for instance, possessed some 52 hectares of farm land in Lubao and 200 in Arayat.[40]

For those smaller planters who derived their main livelihood from their harvests, the central era brought some peril. Thomas McHale, a former sugar executive at Victorias Milling, summed up their new circumstance thus:

> The new central mills clearly represented a quantum jump in technical and economic efficiency. Drawing cane from many sources and with no direct vested interest in the specific problems or prosperity of individual cane planters, however, the mills tended to be highly impersonal in their dealings with planters. As a result, planters began to complain that the contracts were onerous in that they required them to plant cane

> irrespective of weather cycles, disease infestations, price movements or other problems and that the mills had the right to take over management of their land if they didn't comply with their contract regardless of the reason. . . . While planters were aware that from a practical point of view the mills had little control over the quality and quantity of cane they produced under their contract, they were also aware that if they wanted the cane made into sugar, they had no alternative to the one mill to which they were bound.
>
> As corporate organizations with professional engineering and management personnel, many of the new sugar mills tended to treat their contract planters with condescension or patronizing formality rather than as business partners and equals. Their attitude was partly due to differences in social and technical backgrounds on the personal level; it was also a result of the fact that the mills, with their wider access to credit, were usually in a strong bargaining position with invariably less well-financed planters.[41]

Large-scale renters, too, began to feel economic pressures. The leaseholder (arrendatario; inquilino in Pampanga) had long been a respected agriculturalist in Negros, though less frequently appearing in Pampanga. In the south, owner-planters sometimes added to their production by renting additional fields. According to his study of Negrense hacienda economics, Carlos Locsin estimated that 50 percent of farms in his two sample mill districts were leased. New grinding contracts, however, made the arrangement less desirable for renters. Centrals received normally 45 percent of milled sugar in Negros and 50 percent in Pampanga. Rents varied but usually ran about 10–12 percent, so that leaseholders obtained a 40–45 percent share, from which they had to deduct expenses. They frequently borrowed cash from centrals or other credit institutions, thus adding interest costs. As prices fell toward the end of the 1920s, renters saw their margins shrinking to the point of extinction. Lessors, especially those charging fixed cash rents, large owner-planters, and centrals all had hedges against deflated prices, but lessees (all but the biggest) and small planters lived ever closer to desperation fearing bankruptcy and/or loss of their lands.[42]

Mateo Guanzon, a small farmer from Kabankalan, lamented to *Makinaugalingon* in 1930 that, whereas hacenderos used to have tenants, the former were now the tenants of the centrals, that is, that the factories currently made milling, marketing, and credit decisions that planters used to handle themselves. This observation reflected the commentator's social anxiety rather than legal reality. The fear of becoming a tenant, an acsa (also agsador) paying shares to a landholder, pointed to a significant socioeconomic distinction within sugar society: possessing land not only provided security, it conferred status as well. Owners, large or small, sought, for both social and economic reasons, to keep their property, despite new pressures to lose it.

Before the central era the distinction between sugar acsas and arrendatarios had blurred, since both manufactured sugar at hacienda muscovado factories and paid their rent in cash or produce to the owner; however, the separation became pronounced again under the influence of the new milling system. Arrendatarios signed formal contracts with landholders and might possess property in their own right. They managed their leasehold alone, dealing personally with the central and receiving *quedens* (plant vouchers often used in lieu of cash) in their own name. Furthermore, they obtained direct loans from PNB and tended to rent larger estates from 10 to 200 or 300 hectares. In contrast, acsas frequently emerged from the ranks of duma'an and cultivated but 2 to 8 hectares that often contained both rice and sugar. Their annual share, established by verbal agreement, came from the hacendero who held the central milling contract and who provided cash advances and other necessities. Some acsas worked land themselves, but others only supervised paid hands. Acsas made a better living than duma'an and exercised some control over farm management, but they lacked the flexibility and status that belonged to arrendatarios. While reliable statistics do not exist, sugar acsas clearly cultivated only a small fraction of Negros sugar lands.[43]

Lessees and small planters frequently lacked the incentive, skills, or cash resources to make prescribed improvements in irrigation, seed selection, fertilization, and farm mechanization. Centrals such as Silay, Ma-ao, and San Carlos constructed shoreline loading docks, and Pasumil built new railroad tracks, all to reduce their transportation and handling expenses; however, cost-cutting innovations remained sporadic among their contracting hacenderos. The technology gap between planters and central operators pointed to an unequal socio-cultural, as well as economic, response to the introduction of modern processing.[44]

A revised system of credit distribution emphasized the changing hierarchy in the sugar industry as well. Centrals and PNB replaced export-import houses and wealthy private individuals as major sources of loans, although a few entrepreneurs still continued to supply money to smaller farmers. Exporters like PCC, Warner, Barnes and Company, and Ker and Company offered mortgages, sometimes tied to sales of fertilizer, to their customers; however, these transactions were confined to the Negros sugar area and remained infrequent compared to the business of the centrals.

Most Chinese lenders withdrew from the sugar industry with the decline of muscovado exports. Thereafter they concentrated on the distribution of imported goods, making infrequent crop loans and occasional purchases of sugar for resale to bigger exporters.

Credit remained the essential lubricant of the sugar industry during the central era, but a major difference persisted between conditions in Negros and Pampanga; planters in the former region still depended much more on government funding than did those in the latter. PNB's program of crop loans granted directly to Negrense farmers or indirectly to them through the five bank centrals year after year sustained their sugar plantations. In 1925, of a total of P6,003,260 in PNB crop loans, P5,545,060 (92 percent) went through the Bacolod and Iloilo branches. Najeeb Saleeby, representing the hemp industry, complained as early as 1922 about sugar's monopolization of bank loans, and four years later Juan Alegre, a senator from another district, commented that businessmen had no faith in PNB, describing it as "only a collection agency, its resources being buried in the Negros cane fields."[45]

About this time an official of PNB wrote to Quezon:

> The crop loan to Pampanga is less than P600,000 for the present 1925 crop—the biggest they ever had—and [as of] now 95% is already paid to the Bank although the milling season is not yet finished. *No planters of Pampanga Sugar Development Co. owe the Bank any amount, outside of crop loan and on the first milling season in 1920 the planters paid up not only their crop loan but their original debt to the Bank.*[46]

This comment indicated a major socio-cultural as well as economic disparity between residents of the two regions.

A 1927 *Free Press* article contrasting Capampangan and Negrenses contained the following insight:

> The difference between us, the planters of Negros, and those of Pampanga—told us by a very knowledgeable woman sugar planter of the south three years ago, with notable frankness—is that they do not know how to owe, while we start with little or no capital, charging everything against the productivity of our fields. . . .
>
> But now that the Pampanga Sugar Development, the only mill in Pampanga financed by the National Bank, has just redeemed itself totally, paying all of its debts to the Bank, the commentary that involuntarily comes to our lips is that the Pampangan planter, if he does not know how to owe, on the other hand knows how to get out of debt. . . .

> We use these terms only by way of comparison, and to mark better the dividing line between the one and the other, for we all know that the Negrense is intrepid, extravagant and optimistic; the Pampango is conservative, foresighted and prudent. All this, naturally, speaking in general terms.[47]

This perceived difference touches on only partially accurate cultural stereotypes. Indeed, hacenderos who invested in the cultivation of wilder portions of the two regions shared a common outlook, both "optimistic" and "foresighted"; even so, Negrenses, on the whole, earned more money than their northern counterparts and could afford the more "extravagant" lifestyle their reputation implied. But, more to the point, each region had a markedly different credit system.

Capampangan still arranged credit through local sources: mortgages with Pasumil, Pasudeco, and (after 1929) Tarlac Central, plus smaller mills at Mabalacat, Arayat, and Calumpit, Bulacan; through private mortgages on both land and crops; through the old pacto de retro; and, to a limited extent, through little local institutions like People's Bank and Trust. Although associated with Pasudeco, Emilio J. Valdes of Angeles and the de Leon-Joven family of Bacolor still provided agricultural credit. All these sources kept PNB business to a minimum.

Closer-knit ties among the Capampangan made possible the Arayat Cooperative Marketing Association, formed in 1934 in the face of a credit squeeze caused by the pending imposition of quotas. A joint stock company, the cooperative provided 12 percent mortgages, with milled sugar as the main security, to small farmers in eastern Pampanga from San Luis to Magalang. Collateral ranged from a high of 1,500 piculs to a low of 20, with the average around 250, and loans were for no more than P1 per picul. The subscribers and stockholders included members of the Alejandrino family of Arayat, all relatives of Revolutionary War hero General Jose Alejandrino. Officers of the cooperative included a local farmer and a director of the small Arayat Central, who followed the policy of making modest loans available to farmers to enable them to put down next season's crop. The modesty of the venture contrasted with the large, impersonal loan policy carried on by PNB in Negros.[48]

Relations between Negrenses and their chief creditor, PNB, proved unsatisfactory in that hacenderos became heavily reliant upon the bank. The policy of providing crop loans based on estimates of forthcoming harvests sometimes left planters overextended if the crop failed for some reason. Furthermore, PNB, perhaps responding too much to industry pressure, set loan amounts too high for planters to pay back comfortably. In 1922 PNB gave P3 per picul, and the sum rose to P4.90 by 1930. All the while sugar prices continued to drop from the P10 range down to around P6.50 in the early 1930s. Interest charges ran from 7 percent to 12 percent, depending on the degree of risk of the loan. Furthermore, as part of agreements made in the mid-1920s, contracting planters at bank centrals had an obligation to pay off a portion of the accrued debt of those plants. Hence, PNB became the prop not only of the five centrals, but also of the farmers who milled there. One estimate of 1927 noted that PNB money financed 30 percent of the crop at Isabela Central, 60 percent at Binalbagan, 70 percent at Ma-ao, 80 percent at Talisay, and practically all at Bacolod. Negrense sugarmen enlisted their planters' associations, politicians, central officials, and journalists in efforts to coerce bank officials and senior government administrators to keep funds flowing in an ever-faster stream.

Bankers became worried about these investment patterns in view of the failure of some planters to repay, for the health—and perhaps very survival—of PNB came to depend on the sugar industry. By 1926 the threat of numerous farm loan failures loomed, though PNB officials revealed a reluctance to foreclose. In a 1929 petition to lower interest rates and refinance loans, officials of the Bacolod-Murcia Planters' Association admitted that 20 to 25 percent of planters' debts consisted of accrued interest. PNB sought to reduce loans in 1930 but had only partial success. The bank branch at Bacolod slated for closure in 1932 remained open, though with a reduced staff, because of a persistently high volume of business there. A revised policy went into effect in 1933, with PNB offering smaller loans to Negrenses and seeking to make credit available on a modest scale in Pampanga.[49]

Sugar planting not only depended on a continuous supply of credit and good international markets, it proved incapable of generating additional off-farm industry. Instead, the sugar business produced a regular outflow of plantation-derived capital. The erection of centrals initially drew off cash, and profits from foreign plants regularly fled to Spain, Hawaii, and the United States. Gains from locally owned centrals also left in the form of expenses for fertilizers, mechanical farm and transportation equipment, and conspicuous consumption, another notable trait of the Negrense lifestyle. Outside the centrals, sugar created some additional service industry and little more. In 1939 the number of chauffeurs (2,361) for private auto owners surpassed that for all categories of nonsugar manufacturing save carpenters, embroiderers and dressmakers, and sawmill workers.

Negrense sugarmen spent prodigally in the 1920s, often acquiring big obligations along the way. American Baptist missionary W. B. Charles wrote the following from Bacolod in 1922:

> The hacienderos [*sic*] (in the main sugar planters here) plunged deeply on possible continuous high prices on sugar. Invest-

> ments in machinery needed and useless also ran high. Luxuries of all kinds were purchased on time payments. Borrowed money was lost at the gaming table. . . . The inevitable crisis left many woefully in debt.[50]

The very rich set the tone for this lifestyle with stunning examples of extravagance. The Elizaldes formed their own polo team and played in international competition. In 1925 the *Free Press* wrote the following concerning the five daughters of Gil Lopez:

> The parents of the girls believe in education by travel, so years ago they spent weeks and months traveling on the family's steam cutter, making trips over the Visayan islands. On the boat they had their musical instruments, such as the piano, violin and cello. They took their teachers with them during these trips.[51]

The same paper announced in 1928 that Miss Consuelo Lopez (not of the same family) would wear jewelry worth P250,000 during her crowning as carnival queen of Negros Occidental.

The smaller Negrense farmers could not match the lifestyle of the very rich; nevertheless, they too had diversions befitting the Negros image. Foreign travel; gambling; tea dances in town and, for students, in Manila; beauty contests; jewelry; and, above all, automobiles absorbed planter resources. Despite the fact Negros had relatively rough roads and poor bridges crossing its many rivers, in 1925 the province boasted ownership of 1,038 cars, highest for any area in the Philippines save Manila. Some planters began to take out mortgages on their crops and other property in order to purchase vehicles.[52]

Capampangan, too, spent on such luxuries, but, as befit their image, they did so generally on a smaller scale; hence, the problems of debt associated with Negros do not seem to have afflicted Pampanga, at least not on the same alarming scale. Some Capampangan lived in the grand manner: Florentino and Tomasa Pamintuan became residents of Washington while their children attended school there; the province claimed ownership in 1925 of 322 autos, fifth highest in the archipelago; and the beauty pageants at the provincial carnival attracted daughters of the leading planters. Nevertheless, social life among the hacendero class had a practicality about it that seemed lacking in Negros. The carnivals, for instance, though very elaborate and costly, were in actuality trade fairs designed to attract investment. Social clubs like Circulo Fernandino did conduct frequent dances, but other groups formed in the period—the Pampanga Cooperative League (1920) and the Pampango Youth League (1933), for example—had mainly professional and political purposes. Although usually more conservative than southern hacenderos, Pampanga's landlords gained sufficient freedom to participate in their province's active town social life and, for some, to take up residence in Manila.[53]

For several reasons comprehending changes in living conditions among sugar hands as a result of the inauguration of modern mills is difficult. Comparative material for previous and subsequent periods continues hard to accumulate; worker well-being remains, to some extent, as much a matter of perception as of physical reality; and several categories of workers existed, each with its own history. Nevertheless, certain observations about life in the central era emerge from available sources.

Modern developments brought new jobs to sugarlandia to replenish those lost when muscovado factories closed. Workers at centrals, trainmen on central railroads, sugar weighers (*manugpisar*), paymasters (*pagador*), bookkeepers (*tenedor de libro*), and warehousemen (*bodeguero*) replaced maestrillos and others who made sugar the old-fashioned way. In 1929 a plant the size of La Carlota employed 118 workers and 9 foremen. Carters (*pakyador*) and truckers found extra work moving some cane to mills, and there now existed additional demands for tractor drivers, herdsmen (*bakero*), timekeepers, watchmen (*ronda*), and other supervisory personnel to fill the jobs created by expanded production. Furthermore, the opening of piers along the Negros shore, while it diminished the number of dockworkers at Iloilo, provided a new source of employment to Negrenses as *cargadors*, loading sacks onto ships. Centrals thus created more jobs, both in the fields and out, than were lost. Whether this labor force enjoyed a better life, however, represents another question.

A 1970 information questionnaire about their livelihood in the 1920s and 1930s, administered to 255 Negrense duma'an and to rice and sugar agsadores from the ages of 56 to over 100, drew a wide range of responses, from how hard their life seemed to how much better it was before than in 1970. They continued to work long hours at strenuous, sometimes debilitating jobs simply to earn a livelihood. The *Sugar News* in 1929 offered the following description of wages and work in the Negros fields that, generally, coincides with data provided by the older hands themselves:

> Movement of hand labor is more important in Negros than in Luzon, because the system of tenants is less widely established. Permanent hand labor is derived from laborers living on the land with their families, having at their disposal a bit of land and sometimes possessing a team of carabao. They do the usual labor of cultivation according to their age and sex. The

men do the plowing and harrowing, establishing and maintaining the canals and ditches. Their usual wage is P2.50 per week plus seven kilos of rice which is given in daily rations.

The boys do the lighter work, such as weeding and hoeing and taking care of the animals. The average salary is P1.50 with seven kilos of rice per week.

The women and girls plant the cane generally by contract [pakyaw]. They are paid for each 10,000 [laksa]: P0.50 for stripping and P2.00 for planting and covering up, which bring the cost of planting a hectare up to P6.25 to P7.50, depending on whether 25,000 or 30,000 points are planted. . . .

Daily farm wages are as follows:

	Maximum	*Average*	*Minimum*
Men	P1.10	P0.78	P0.45
Women	P0.70	P0.51	P0.32
Children	P0.62	P0.41	P0.22[54]

The only discrepancy between this description and the questionnaire comments lay in the number of gantas given: of those who acknowledged receiving daily rice, few earned more than three to four gantas a week. No matter that planters garnered P40,000 a year for 120 hectares; they paid their hands about P100 for a season's work.

It may have happened that as the central era progressed more duma'an labored on the pakyaw system, that is, having their pay set according to the number of hectares plowed or fertilized, rows weeded, and tons of cane cut, loaded, or transported to the mill. Almost two out of three interviewees stated that they worked either totally or part-time on pakyaw. One planter, Ramon Ramos of Bacolod, noted that he moved to pakyaw from daily wages in the 1930s and that performance-driven work presented obvious advantages to planters confronting lowered prices. Nevertheless, more comparative evidence from years preceding the 1920s needs to become available before this trend can be confirmed.[55]

As yearly production expanded, the outlook for wages and employment continued bright for farmworkers throughout the 1920s. *Sugar News* and other publications complained about shortages in the fields and urged that officials curtail labor migration to Hawaii and Mindanao. Industry leaders like John Dumas and Rafael Alunan revived the notion of bringing in "Oriental" immigrants to work during milling season and then to retire docilely to government-provided homesteads. By 1930, however, when sugar prices had slipped to dangerous levels, *Sugar News* changed its tune, insisting that the labor force be reduced and carping on the high wages paid to Philippine sugar workers, compared to those in Java and elsewhere. In

1932 and 1933 large numbers of duma'an usually hired throughout the year found themselves unemployed when harvesting ended. Governor Isaac Lacson then initiated a program of ensuring that public works jobs went first to Negrenses needing work.[56]

Numerous duma'an noted that although wages stayed low, so did commodity prices. They expressed contentment often in terms of eating three meals a day, of times remaining peaceful and their place uncrowded. Some described their existence as hand-to-mouth, but more that it was comfortable. None commented that the coming of centrals either appreciably improved or worsened their lot. For many, satisfaction rested upon their ability to supplement low hacienda wages with some other source of income, because many hacenderos did not pay wages during the slack season from June to September, called *tiempo muerto* (dead time) or *tiempo tinggulotom* (starvation time). Some duma'an had permission to plant either rice or sweet potatoes (*camotes*) and vegetables on fallow fields, while others served as ronda or as part-time agsadores on hacienda rice lands. Duma'an also found a variety of off-hacienda work as fishermen, vendors, carpenters, house help, firewood and rattan collectors, *tuba* (palm wine) makers, and cargadors. A few returned to their original home provinces, where they farmed or stayed with relatives.

Comparisons with workers' salaries in other regions make little sense because of differences in living conditions, but as an indication of the sorry state of Visayan economic life elsewhere, sacadas from neighboring islands risked travel to Negros on crowded vessels to accept poor wages because they could earn more than by staying at home. Carlos Locsin estimated that Negros needed 15,000 sacadas to handle the 1927 crop; by 1931 that number had grown to 20,000.

Even when planters enhanced the anticipo to one-third of their seasonal wage, they had no assurance that the workers would materialize or stay. Hacendero Ramon Ramos noted an additional problem: that sacadas unprepared for the rigors of hacienda labor did not do good work. Locsin estimated that 25 percent of the work force could not perform their job adequately. Negrenses tried to solve the migrant labor problem by several means. A scheme to establish recruiting stations in Antique and Cebu failed for lack of cooperation, as did one to register and fingerprint all sacadas when they arrived to keep them from escaping from one hacienda to another. Planters sent encargados and cabos, even went themselves, to outlying islands to enlist help, but sacadas generally preferred to work for a contratista from their own community.

Sacadas I interviewed expressed mixed attitudes toward Negros. Some went annually because they needed money to support their families, others occasionally for the adventure. A few took their wives, some of whom also cut cane. Most disliked the place and felt homesick. They brought back from P20 to P70 for an entire season's work, depending on their strength, and all observed they could not earn as much at home. A considerable portion of the rest of their wages went to the contratista to pay for their food and any medical expenses they incurred. More experienced and daring hands might eventually go to Negros on their own, thereby avoiding having to share their money with the capataz. Usually hacenderos provided money for their passage to Negros, but sacadas paid their own return fare, and transportation costs ate into salary as well, equal to as much as ten days of work. Amador Española of Barrio San Francisco, Tibiao, Antique, recalled paying P0.40 for a bus from Ma-ao to Pulupandan, P1.50 for the boat across the Guimaras Strait to Iloilo, and P3 for the truck (bus) to his hometown, a barrio along the main road on the narrow coastal plain of eastern Panay. Several hours of walking from the bus stop awaited those living in Guba' and Bugtung Bato ("Destroyed" and "Lone Stone" in the local dialect), remote *sitios* (hamlets) of Bugasong, Antique, high on the slopes of the province's mountain spine. Despite all the difficulties facing sacadas, however, contratistas every year filled to overflowing the passenger boats plying the waters of Negros.

In a sense sacadas participated only peripherally in sugar society, despite their crucial economic role. They came for four to six months, remained largely to themselves, and returned to their own world. Many stayed in Negros, however, and became part of the permanent labor force, so that 40 percent of the workers surveyed had a birth place outside Negros. Sacadas thus transformed into duma'an, and occasionally a contratista became a cabo or encargado.[57]

Much better wages awaited those sacadas or duma'an fortunate, ambitious, and adept enough to become skilled and lower-management personnel. Cabos regularly made P30 to P40 a month, and encargado salaries ranged between P30 and P180, depending on the level of responsibility assumed. Truckers earned P30 to P40, while tractor drivers received from P1.25 a day to P50 a month. Even watchmen could garner a salary of P3.50, more than the regular wages of field hands.

At centrals the scale reached even higher, up to P220 for a locomotive mechanic and P160 for an electrician. Sugarmen relished pointing out to social critics and others that mill personnel enjoyed the highest standard of living and most perquisites of any laborers in the Philippines. Mills offered permanent housing, health benefits, and recreational facilities to their help, for management fully comprehended the value of maintaining a healthy labor force. Moreover, centrals needed the medical help because of the numerous industrial accidents experienced by those who regularly worked around the machinery and chemicals during the long, hard hours of milling season.[58]

While the south remained committed to a paid labor system with a plantation hierarchy, the Capampangan still opted for tenancy. On the typical Pampanga sugar farm, a landholder contracted with casamac, from one to a hundred or more, depending on the size of the holding. Larger plantations concentrated in the newer northern towns. Under the more or less loose supervision of an owner or his representative, called *palsunero* or *katiwala*, tenants grew both rice and sugar on plots of 2 to 7 hectares, sometimes alternating the crops in succeeding seasons. They and the landlords normally split harvests fifty-fifty; however, with loans of cash and, sometimes, draft animals, the sharing favored owners. The two parties divided most expenses equally, but landholders supplied cane points (*tabtab*) and casamac paid the people (*sakul*) who planted them. Tenants delivered cane to factories, and landlords kept the milling records and settled accounts seasonally.

Casamac bound to a particular landowner clustered in the same community, working on adjoining fields. They selected their own barrio lieutenants, although in a few places the palsunero held the title. Often related to one another, casamac frequently employed the sugu system of ganging together to accomplish chores. Occasionally on bigger estates, hired migrants from the Ilocos region to the north harvested cane, but more often casamac saved money by doing the work themselves.

The system generally provided tenants who planted sugar with a satisfactory livelihood, according to their own estimation. They earned sufficient income, often stated as around P150 to P200 a year, and some even made enough to provide schooling for their children. Managing their holdings, they possessed access to a variety of local resources so that when harvests came up short, they could supplement their income with fishing; trapping crabs, frogs, and locusts in paddies; raising animals for meat; collecting materials for craft work; gathering firewood; and growing produce in home gardens. All these items had value in local markets. Besides acting as vendors, women and children performed extra housework in wealthy homes, while men did carpentering and other forms of day labor. Casamac thus exercised more control over their economic lives and gained more independence than did the duma'an of Negros.

Tenancy in Pampanga baffled observers who could not understand its persistence, from either the point of view of the planter or the casamac. An editorial in *Sugar News* in 1924 contained the following appraisal:

> Under the existing system . . . namely, the tenant system, the high cost of cane, or the low return for cane, is passed on to

> the tenant. It is an idiosyncrasy of Filipino character that he will willingly work under the tenant system on his own time in the production of cane and be quite satisfied if, at the end of the year, he has averaged but thirty, forty or fifty centavos for each day of labor, his return being based on the price per tonne paid him by the hacendero or the Central. This same laborer would scoff at any offer under eighty centavos or one peso a day for a day's work of from ten to twelve hours.[59]

That casamac had long labored under this arrangement, preferred its managerial autonomy and economic latitude, and relished their barrio life, escaped the purview of outsiders. Plantation efficiency may have offered a better means of meeting production demands, but it scarcely satisfied the needs of the soul.

Specialists contrasted low productivity in Pampanga with higher Negrense yields and urged management reform; however, landholders, like their tenants, resisted change. The diversified two-crop farms of central Luzon provided a hedge against unfavorable market conditions, and tenants absorbed lower sugar prices with diminished shares. Owners profited from sugar, despite receiving on average a 5 percent lower share from centrals than did their counterparts in Negros. In addition, casamac took better care of land and tools than did hired workers, and the system in general reduced administrative costs while at the same time providing a stable, reliable labor force. Even when ownership changed hands, casamac tended to remain with the property.

Modern production delivered prosperity to sugarlandia but did not change the basic settlement and cultural patterns that had previously developed in the two areas. Negros still demonstrated something of its flamboyant character, while Pampanga continued to exhibit a more traditional lifestyle in its stable communities. Having room to expand and more commitment to sugar, the former area experienced far more rapid population increase than did the latter. The annual growth rate of 3.55 percent in Negros Occidental greatly exceeded the 2.12 percent for the archipelago as a whole, while Pampanga's 1.83 percent fell considerably below both. However, towns in southern Tarlac absorbed Capampangan seeking new sugar fields to plant.[60]

Perhaps the greatest alteration in the Negros landscape, besides the appearance of smoke-gushing centrals with their veins of narrow-gauge railroad tracks reaching onto vast expanses of cane, was the port at Pulupandan and the offshore loading facilities near the mill towns. These new docks and wharves not only denied business to Iloilo, leading to its demise as a major commercial center, they also kept more Negrenses at home to conduct affairs. Bacolod, the capital and fastest-growing city on Negros, stole much of the luster that had formerly accrued to the city across the Guimaras Strait.

Centered on its newly renovated plaza, Bacolod emerged as an attractive, bustling community with markets, department stores, and amusements. Carnivals with the accompanying round of balls annually drew the Visayan sugar community to the city. The Arco Theater went up in 1926, and planters who formerly journeyed to Iloilo to see films could now watch them on their own turf at one of the largest picture houses in the islands. They could attend meetings and conferences or just hobnob at the popular University Club; meanwhile, the Negros Golf and Country Club provided an opportunity for centralistas and hacenderos, Americans and Filipinos, to meet in a more social setting. The Bacolod Sporting Club offered bowling, and the Negros Jockey Club introduced regular horse racing to the province in 1934. Whatever sense of isolation had previously existed on Negros ended through the easy communication with Manila and the outside world that followed inauguration of daily mail in 1924, long distance telephone calling in 1927, and airplane travel via Iloilo in 1931. Much improved passenger boat service supplemented these other facilities and made it possible for tourists to visit such spots as the nearby Mambucal spa. Symbolic of its improved status, the city became the seat of a new Roman Catholic bishopric in 1933.[61]

Other communities, especially some of those with large centrals, harbored an active urban life as well. Silay, despite new docking facilities, continued as the grand old center with theaters, the province's most beautiful church, and after 1928, its second high school. Facing toward Cebu and with a large Cebuano-speaking population, San Carlos turned into the most active settlement along the eastern shore, boasting new sugar-loading facilities, three cinemas, a new church, and other amenities. Visitors also commented on the transformation in the center of La Carlota. Even smaller towns now obtained electric lights and telephone service, and Pulupandan offered a hotel to the travelers who appeared daily at its port. More than in prior times town plazas became places where the local elite congregated, held their club meetings, and enjoyed the attractions of the modern world.

May Coggins, a Baptist missionary who operated a girls' dormitory in Bacolod, wrote home in 1925 that people in Negros seemed to possess an anti-American attitude and clung to the old Spanish Catholic culture; however, despite her observation, lifestyles had certainly altered. During the 1920s—as novelist Nick Joaquin now laments—old Filipino-Spanish culture and values gave way to the manners and norms of the new conquerer, and the sugar industry undoubtedly provided means and motives for the change. While Spanish and Ilongo remained the languages of choice among many planters, American English increasingly served as the medium of business and government. U.S.-style public schools and American teachers played a very important role in this transformation. Furthermore, baseball, golf, beauty contests, vaudeville, jazz, movies, and radios all served as carriers of change, replacing the zarzuela and other traditional forms of native entertainment. In 1923 Negros even claimed a world boxing champion: flyweight Pancho Villa of Ilog, the son of a duma'an. Negrense youth responded easily to their times, and the dowagers of San Enrique sought to impose a P50 yearly tax on girls who bobbed their hair.[62]

Pampanga experienced similar changes, and San Fernando, home of the provincial hospital and public high school, led the way. The most rapid growth occurred in towns with centrals and large expanses of sugar. The province was linked to Manila by two bus companies, railroad service, and car travel. Tourism flourished after the government developed a spa and park at the base of Mount Arayat, as well as other attractions, and arriving visitors feasted on the vaunted native cuisine. Intertown travel also remained more frequent than in Negros.

Long-settled Pampanga clung more tightly to its well-developed native culture, despite the presence of electric service, long distance telephones, a dozen movie theaters, bowling halls, and other seductions of the Jazz Age. The province boasted seventeen brass bands, and President Diosdado Macapagal as a young man in the 1930s still toured with a company of players performing Capampangan zarzuelas, some of which were written by his father. Evangelina-Hilario Lacson describes the era this way:

> The Kapampangan literary world of the third and fourth decades of the twentieth century comprised many writers, all of whom were productive and delightfully festive. They made the period a bountiful one of writing, the writers as lively as birds in a wide-spreading molave tree—the magical tree lording it over the Athens of Pampanga, the town of Bacolor. In other Pampanga towns the same liveliness obtained—in Hilario's birth town of San Fernando; Yuzon's Guagua; Macapagal's Lubao; Punsalan's Magalang; Sanchez's Angeles, and in almost all the other towns of Pampanga.[63]

Besides its venerability, another reason for the survival of so much native culture was the large professional class in the towns. Capampangan prided themselves on their educational achievements, and local yearbooks

Table 14. Comparative Educational Statistics, 1932

	Negros Occidental	*Pampanga*
Number of schools (public)	208	165
Number of teachers	1,048	666
Total enrollment (primary, intermediate and secondary)	51,232	30,710
Number of secondary students	1,290	1,103

Source: Philippine Islands, Department of Agriculture and Commerce, *Statistical Handbook of the Philippine Islands, 1932* (Manila: Bureau of Printing, 1933), pp. 3, 11, 15.

always touted those with professional success more than those who had been successful exclusively as farmers. Capampangan placed greater importance on intertown communication and support of education than did their counterparts to the south (see table 14). Although the school-age population of Pampanga was 40 percent less than that of Negros Occidental, Pampanga had almost as many public high school students. Pampanga also boasted more private schools. Negrenses depended much more on the casual generosity of planters to maintain local public schools, in town and on haciendas, so when economic times turned bad, schools faced being closed for want of money.[64]

Despite the expansion of modern culture in western Negros, the province still exhibited characteristics of its frontier past, especially in its interior and on its northern fringes. Homesteading continued in the north, as did incidents of land grabbing, and the Philippine Constabulary chased and arrested cattle rustlers and robber bands. *Makinaugalingon* reported on persistent plantation violence, and even in the towns where new centrals sprang up, trouble occurred between managers and workers and between foreign and native laborers. Use of guns during arguments was ubiquitous in the province. Northern Pampanga and southern Tarlac exuded something of the same atmosphere, but not to the same degree. Overall, Pampanga gave the impression of being more stable and sedate than its southern counterpart. In both places, provincial character had been set by 1920, and nothing that happened during the central era or since has changed that essence.[65]

Tensions

Prosperity during the central era did not necessarily generate harmony within the sugar industry, and the maldistribution of profits created tensions. Planters observed stockholders at centrals, particularly private ones, receiving high dividends while they struggled under debt burdens, and they concluded that a bigger share of those rewards should go to them. Although locked mainly into thirty-year contracts, hacenderos sought to improve their situation in a shorter time.

The first signs of hacendero pressure surfaced sometime in mid-1929 as Negrense planters began approaching politicians about improving their share of milled sugar—called participation—from an average 55 percent to 60 percent. Within a year planters instigated their first legislative proposal to change the terms by statute, a bill the legislature narrowly defeated because Senate President Quezon opposed it on the constitutional grounds that it went against the laws of contract. Despite his legal objections, Quezon sympathized with the hacenderos and supported Amando Avanceña's proposal that the government have the bank centrals voluntarily offer higher participation. In early July, however, PNB declined to change the terms at its centrals. Centralistas proffered the sanctity of contracts argument and the somewhat specious contention that landowners, rather than planter-lessees, would benefit most from a change in terms. The second reason lacked validity in that only a fraction of planters rented lands; besides, in July 1930 landowners belonging to the Federation of Planters of Negros Occidental agreed to reduce rents by five percentage points in the event of altered participation.

Angered by their defeats, hacenderos adopted a more militant attitude. During August they threatened (1) to vote for the opposition Democrata party, (2) to halt purchases of fertilizer for the coming year, and thus (3) to reduce cane production. Suggested compromises that centrals, landowners, and planters share their fertilizer costs more equitably and that PNB lower its interest rates did not appear to soften planter ire. The protests failed, the centrals reported a bumper crop for 1930–31, and Negros remained a Nationalista stronghold.

By 1931 the situation began to improve slightly for planters. In January, Quezon, backed by a plea from Negros Occidental Governor Isaac Lacson, endorsed a plan to have Isabela Central raise hacendero participation by 5 percent and even advocated that another 5 percent go to mill hands. PNB responded by granting the planters a 5 percent bonus, thus keeping the prior contract intact. The central did not offer workers anything extra. The idea of providing bonuses instead of altering the contract caught on, and other centrals adopted it. Binalbagan gave 5 percent in the form of shares of stock, and Talisay and La Carlota returned the equivalent of 25 centavos per picul. In the event that sugar prices turned upward, centrals could then revert to the old standard. The confederation still pressed for a uniform 60 percent, but many centrals resisted, and only hacenderos at Ma-ao and some at San

Carlos received the higher rate. With the prospect of limitations came added planter clamor for sixty-forty; however, centralistas increasingly resisted the appeal, and the bitter dispute continued. Some Negrenses favored a planter strike in 1932, and by August 1933 some growers advocated, to no avail, abrogating all contracts and selling cane directly to centrals. As the era of quotas dawned, the issue remained unresolved.

Despite the fact that planters in Pampanga received a smaller participation than did those on Negros, hacendero protests in the former area did not arise until 1934 when quotas loomed. Perhaps, as *Sugar News* suggested, the minimal amount of leaseholding made a difference in the planters' attitude; then, too, Capampangan also owed fewer debts and paid less interest than did southerners. While both Negrenses and Capampangan derived much of their income from sugar, the latter also grew rice as a cash crop so had diversified sources of livelihood. The tenant system as well had the effect of cushioning Luzon planters against losses incurred by low prices. Possibly, too, planters simply enjoyed better relations with centrals than was the case in Negros.[66]

Without effective organizations and influential spokespersons, field hands in sugarlandia lacked the means to protect their interests or to voice their objections to changes occurring around them. For the most part the poor remained dependent on the casual, often insincere generosity of powerful and wealthy patrons for whatever benefits they derived from the newfound wealth. The evidence of prosperity and modernity in towns contrasted sharply with the poverty and unchanging life of barrios and haciendas. Poorer wages and working arrangements among plantation workers and diminishing shares for casamac led sugarlandia's labor force to begin pressuring planters, just as hacenderos leaned on the centrals. Old forms of folk protest reappeared alongside more up-to-date expressions of dissatisfaction.

Inadequate medical services meant that faith healers in Pampanga continued to attract a following among the rural poor, and certain of these practitioners enjoyed a wide reputation as possessors of strong curative powers. One healer, Mang Tanong, caused considerable alarm among authorities. This former carpenter appeared in 1931 in Arayat, the site of Felipe Salvador's earlier religious passion, and drew a large crowd of poor folk from the surrounding area. Reminiscent of Apong Ipe, Mang Tanong claimed that six years before he had lost his way on Mount Arayat and returned a changed man. Local officials observing his success ordered him to cease his activity, and the healer desisted. Clearly, however, the tradition of messianism persisted in Pampanga, and followers of Santa Iglesia still held services in the depths of the Candaba Swamp.[67]

Millenarianism made a rare appearance in the western Visayas in the mid-1920s and elicited only limited enthusiasm from duma'an throughout Negros. From a palatial home in Iloilo, Emperor Florencio Intrencherado preached the coming of a reign of justice throughout the Philippines, based on independence, reapportionment of national wealth, and removal of the Chinese. An attractive feature of his program for the poor was his plan to reduce the head tax from P2.20 to 20 centavos. His agents fanned out to surrounding towns, signing up members for his paramilitary organization and selling them pictures and medals.

Historian David Sturtevant has traced Intrencherado's life and career from his early years as a petty merchant along the Guimaras Strait to his incarceration and death in 1937 in a mental asylum. Here one need only mention a few points concerning the response of sugar workers in Negros. Intrencherado's flamboyant style and urban location brought him considerable notoriety, and the government, ever on the alert for signs of rural unrest, paid particular attention to this highly visible figure.

On May 13, 1927, in the face of Intrencherado's imminent departure for mental examinations, five protests occurred in Negros, the two most serious in Victorias and La Carlota. In the first town, two policemen were killed, tax and land records were destroyed, and Chinese stores were pillaged by an estimated three hundred supporters led by the Montarde brothers. In La Carlota a policeman died and another was wounded. In Bago and Silay local officials and the constabulary prevented any serious violence, and in La Castellana three Spanish hacenderos and a Swiss were flogged. All these events happened the same day, and no others followed. The constabulary arrested fifty-six of the putative three hundred rioters in Victorias but released most of them shortly thereafter. Some supporters in Victorias and Murcia were beaten and sent home by the constabulary, and fifty-nine adherents from La Castellana served six-month terms in jail; the ringleaders, however, all received long sentences.

Newsmen reported on Intrencherado during the asylum years, keeping his name before the reading public and making him the most noticed messianic figure in Philippine history, but it does not appear that he attracted much of a following among the poor of Negros. Lists taken by the constabulary from his house claimed that he had 14,275 followers in the towns of Negros Occidental; however, there exists no clear notion of just what constituted membership. Did that number represent all those who paid P2.50 to enroll in the organization, those suspected of joining, or those who simply purchased a picture or medal as a talisman? Among older sugar hands interviewed in 1970, only 75 out of 257 had any recollection of Intrencherado, and of those, 29 had heard his name but knew nothing else about him or his movement; furthermore, another 7 confused him with someone else. An additional 15 possessed only negative memories, dismissing Intrencherado as a madman, fanatic, or flimflammer. Altogether, only 8 admitted to paying dues to the organization, and of that number, just 3 could recall in some detail the medals, pamphlets, and uniforms they acquired, while 1 admitted to being a sergeant in the organization. The distinct impression emerges that few comprehended much about Intrencherado, sympathized with him, or had any faith in his movement.

The movement never achieved any provincewide cohesion, and in only five of the province's twenty-six towns did any incidents happen, and then on only one occasion. Furthermore, among the interviewees knowledge of the Victorias and La Carlota raids was confined to individuals living in or near those towns. Heuristic evidence suggests that in the three towns where any violence occurred, local tensions between duma'an and a landlord or landlords served at least as a partial cause. Perhaps the clearest evidence of the movement's weak reception rests in the experience of Policarpio Montarde, known locally as "Karpo," the chief agent of Intrencherado and leader of the attack on Victorias. Following the raid Karpo fled to other islands because he could find no sanctuary on Negros, and upon his return two years later to eastern Negros, he was quickly captured.

Negros's single flirtation with messianism seems to have affected little those oppressed who might otherwise have sympathized with such movements. Perhaps the cellular nature of the hacienda system made it difficult for Intrencherado or his followers to reach duma'an. He rarely, if ever, traveled to the province. Or possibly messianism—as opposed to shamanism—better suited peasant societies like Pampanga than the plantations of Negros. Perhaps the historical ties of Negros and the western Visayas to babaylanism simply precluded success for a millenarian movement.[68]

Attacks upon isolated Negrense haciendas persisted into the central era, and marauders still found sanctuary along the mountain core where traditional religious practices flourished within isolated, poverty-ridden settlements of aborigines, *kaingeros* (slash and burn farmers), and lowland escapees. In these backwoods communities, memories of Papa Isio still survived. In late June 1928 policemen in Barrio Camangcamang, Isabela, confronted a band of forty *pulahanes* (bandits) led by Lucio Brender, a former member of Papa Isio's movement. Brender, pardoned by Governor-general Wood in 1922, returned to his old haunts and formed a new group called Siete Sagrados (The Sacred Seven) to whom he explained the hidden messages of his former chief. The sect exhibited all the trappings of babaylanism: the anting-antings, secret signs and words, black robes and priestesses. Members took nicknames redolent with dissent and folk heroism, names like "Quintin Intrencherado" and "Bernardo del Carpio." The police managed to fend off the attack, killing or capturing several gang members, meanwhile having nine of their own seriously wounded. Brender fled, only to die in another engagement with the constabulary in rural Isabela. Those captured received prison terms, and the raids ceased. Babaylanism, however, continued to thrive in the province's interior wilds.[69]

Alongside traditional protest, more secular forms began to appear in sugarlandia, often led by aspiring politicians. As conditions worsened for workers and as the modern sugar industry encroached upon their lives, they turned to leaders and organizations that proffered help in dealing with governments and solidarity against the economic and political power of the big hacenderos and centralistas.

Perhaps the most blatant manipulation of hacienda and central workers for political ends involved two mutual-help societies, Kusug Sang Imol (The Strength of the Poor) and Mainawa-on (Merciful), that operated during the 1920s. The idea for such groups did not originate on Negros and may have come from Panay, where they had existed since at least 1919. The societies functioned primarily to offer members or their widows financial help in the event of personal catastrophe or death. This type of organization with its local chapters fit the autonomous nature of the plantation labor structure while presenting workers with some insurance in an insecure world. For an initiation fee of 1–5 pesos, plus 20–50 centavos a month in dues, one became a member, wore the triangle ring of Kusug Sang Imol (KSI) or the eagle ring of Mainawa-on, and enjoyed other benefits. Supporters regularly attended services for their deceased colleagues, conducted flag-raising ceremonies on special occasions, and in the case of KSI, received a twice-weekly newspaper. Membership of the two organizations included not only laborers, but also doctors and lawyers who provided services to members and Chinese merchants seeking to maintain good community relations and to guard against possible intimidation.

Despite its economic attraction to the poor, at its establishment in Bacolod in mid-1922, KSI had basically political aims. The founder, Felix Severino, a former newspaperman and nephew of revolutionary leader Melecio Severino, induced General Emilio Aguinaldo, Manuel Quezon, Manuel Roxas, Senator Esperidion Guanco, Governor Gil Montilla, and Assemblyman Vicente Jimenez Yanson to act as honorary patrons. Such important leaders agreed to affiliate with a group supposed to appeal to workers because, as McCoy notes, the real power behind its formation was Montilla himself, who used the organization to ensure his election as governor in 1922. Severino took advantage of these connections too: when

Emilio Aguinaldo visited Negros, members appeared on daises everywhere with the Revolutionary War hero. Also, after the court of first instance came down with a ruling unacceptable to the association, its leaders felt confident in writing Quezon to have the judge transferred.[70]

Jealous of Montilla's success and anxious to build a counterforce, opponents in late 1922 introduced Mainawa-on from Panay to Negros. The latter group included as its sponsors Iloilo politician Julio Hilado, planter Federico Lazarate, newspaperman Esteban Vasquez, and Cesar Barrios, president of Iloilo's main wharfage and shipping concern, Visayan Stevedore Transportation Company (Vistranco). Both associations quickly spread to all towns in Negros and lined up with locally powerful liders. For instance, Assemblyman Enrique Magalona and Jose Ledesma headed the Saravia chapter of Mainawa-on. To reach out into the countryside both groups began at this point to stress the mutual aid facet of their organizations.

Mutual-help societies proliferated in Negros during this period, usually possessing brief life spans, limited areas of operation, and small memberships, numbering in the hundreds; however, KSI at its height had an estimated twenty thousand adherents throughout the province. Its following included policemen, justices of the peace, contratistas, cabos and other supervisory personnel, and central employees as well as acsas and duma'an. So prominent had the organization become that local authors composed a zarzuela and a fox trot titled "Kusog Sang Imol." Mainawa-on, constructed along the same lines, enrolled a slightly smaller constituency, perhaps fifteen thousand, drawn from essentially the same clientele. The charge lodged by KSI that Mainawa-on more clearly represented the rich does not seem justified, either by contrasts in membership or by the nature of the leadership. The major differences seem to have been that KSI was larger and more powerful than Mainawa-on and that the former originated in Negros and later established chapters on Panay while the latter followed the reverse course.[71]

If any distinction existed, it lay within the membership of each group. Town proper residents involved themselves more in the societies' social activities, while rural workers participated mainly in their mutual-aid programs. This compartmentalization became most apparent when competition between the two societies escalated into violent conflict. From late in 1923 to mid-1925 Negros was transformed into a battleground as KSI and Mainawa-on vied for control of politics and other financial resources. Incidents varied from a scuffle between the heads of the two groups to the assassination of the justice of the peace in Escalante. Most towns witnessed Chicago-style gang warfare, coercion, and corruption as local policemen and toughs sided with the two organizations in the struggle. At this time Negros Occidental became notorious for violence. Meanwhile, rural workers went on paying their dues and assisting their friends in trouble.

Severino apparently behaved like a local dictator, strutting about in a khaki uniform with red tie, leather leggings, and pistol. KSI enforcers intimidated workers, political leaders, and even American managers of local companies. When Echaús raided Binalbagan Central in early 1924, he did so with the assistance of KSI thugs. Mainawa-on tried to respond in kind to assaults upon its members but seemingly suffered more damage. Constabulary troopers spent much of their time confiscating weapons from the antagonists but faced difficulties in trying to control the situation, given the participation of planters and politicians in the melee.

Gradually the insular government won the upper hand. In July 1924 Governor-general Wood wrote to Montilla insisting that he resign from KSI, and the governor of Negros did distance himself from the organization; nevertheless, six months later provincial office holders still feared being seen by KSI members in the company of Montilla's enemy Rafael Alunan. The Bureau of Justice sent attorneys and auditors to check the books of both organizations and to ensure that no fraud occurred. Mainawa-on eventually closed down because of lack of funds, and KSI diminished in scope and size after Severino went to prison, ironically for adultery.

Violence and the backing of masoniclike organizations have been a part of Philippine politics since the nineteenth century; however, political historians may wish to look to the battles between KSI and Mainawa-on as early instances of a more intense level of rough-and-tumble electoral competition for which the Philippines has become so well known. Negrense liders have sometimes achieved notoriety for their employment of personal armies, and the KSI episode provides a very visible instance of that type of usage.[72] At the same time, KSI and Mainawa-on, while they did not primarily help duma'an and acsas, did highlight the worth of mutual-help societies, and such groups have operated in the province to this day.

Likewise, union activism produced but little improvement for sugar workers. Field hands occasionally walked away from plantations when conditions became too harsh, but genuine union organizing did not reach the province much before early 1930, by which time several small locals existed for cargadors, sawmill hands, pakyadors, and central workers. The only major strike action during the central era occurred from January 23 to February 28, 1931, when Federacion Obrera de Filipinas (FOF) sought to obtain union recognition on the docks and in the centrals of Negros. Founded in Iloilo in 1928 by newspaperman Jose Nava, FOF possessed the largest union membership (185,000) in the Visayas and exerted considerable control over shipping in the central Philippines. The strike on Negros failed, however, when the centrals refused to recognize the union and brought in scab labor from Panay and Negros. The Philippine Constabulary sided with the centrals, as did the provincial government under Governor Agustin Ramos. In the end only some of the strikers recovered their jobs, and centrals granted no concessions. Sugar output for the 1931–32 season reached its highest level to date.

A sidelight to the 1931 strike was that planters supported neither the centrals nor the strikers but sat on the sidelines, hoping to gain some leverage in their own pursuit of better participation. This action—or inaction—seemed typical of protest on Negros. Like the sporadic burnings of hacienda cane fields in the early 1930s by anonymous, disgruntled workers, dissent went unsupported, unanswered, and perhaps worse, unnoticed, ensuring failure for attempts to rectify the industry's economic inequities.[73]

Labor activism in central Luzon had its origins among the Manila work force in the late nineteenth century, but in its early years it had little success. In 1913, with the founding of Congreso Obrero de Filipinas (Philippine Labor Congress), union bosses such as Hermenegildo Cruz (later the director of labor), Crisanto Evangelista, and Jacinto Manahan introduced more effective management, developed a larger following, and won some concessions for their members. During and following World War I union activity widened, and a group of labor leaders attended their first worker conference outside the country, in Canton in 1924. With the encouragement and support of two Comintern agents, the American William Janequette (a.k.a. Harrison George) and the Indonesian Tan Malacca, Evangelista and Manahan in the mid-1920s steered the union movement in a leftist direction. In 1929 the Congreso Obrero split into right- and left-wing factions, and out of this rift sprang Kongreso Proletario de Filipinas (Katipunan ng mga Anakpawis ng Pilipinas) and Partido Komunista (1930) both under the leadership of radicals like Evangelista, Manahan, and Juan Feleo. Trade unionism remained firmly tied to the Manila and surrounding Tagalog area where Philippine industry concentrated; hence, its activities had little to do initially with sugar-growing tenants in Pampanga. Nevertheless, union leaders introduced to Philippine protest movements the idea of labor organization and a leftist and nationalist ideology, notions that traveled throughout central Luzon and beyond.[74]

The first tenant union, Pagkakaisa ng Magsasaka (Union of Peasants), later called Union de Aparceros de Filipinas, appeared in Bulacan Province in 1917. This association was but one of many that proliferated in central Luzon in the 1920s and that became constituents in 1924 of Katipunang

Pambansa ng mga Magbubukid sa Pilipinas (National Association of Peasants in the Philippines or KPMP). Manahan, Feleo, and other leaders of the left took an active role in this organizing, and such unions, along with other peasant protest movements like Tanggulan, Colorum, and Sakdal, attested to the growing dissatisfaction with conditions in the archipelago's paddy bowl.

Pampanga's rice casamac joined in the unrest as well. The first recorded incident, the burning of landholder rice stocks, took place in Candaba at the beginning of 1921, and during the following year the Bureau of Labor arbitrated seven more agricultural disputes in the province. In 1924 Governor Olimpio Guanzon tried unsuccessfully to create a system to resolve the growing number of conflicts that spread as far as Tarlac; meanwhile, peasants formed a five thousand–member organization called Anak Pawas (Sons of Sweat). Incidents of violence persisted throughout the decade and into the 1930s, especially in rice-growing sections of Santa Rita, Arayat, Mexico, San Luis, Candaba, and Masantol, but no town stayed free from unrest.[75]

While protest lapped the shores of central Luzon's sugarlandia, casamac who grew cane did not participate to any extent in the movement before the mid-1930s. In 1923 the *Manila Times* reported Jacinto Manahan's observations on the agrarian situation in Pampanga:

> The reason for Pampanga tenants' assuming a rather lukewarm attitude on the situation may be the fact that they get tolerably good treatment from their landlords. The province, besides, is not totally devoted to the production of rice, and the spread of the movement seems to be rapid only in those places where rice production is the principal occupation of the people. The people of the province of Pampanga are principally engaged in the raising of sugar cane, while in many of the lowland towns fishing is the chief source of the peoples' income.
>
> "The tenants' movement will certainly spread throughout the provinces of central Luzon," declared Jacinto Manahan, president of the National Confederation of Tenants and Farm Laborers, "but it will take time."[76]

The *Tribune* supported this commentary when in 1932 it reported on a Bureau of Labor survey that pointed to the fact that Pampanga's sugar tenants received better participation than did those in Batangas Province; however, rice tenants in Batangas fared better than their counterparts in central Luzon.

Evidence suggests that during most of the central era, even as relations between Pampanga's aparceros and landlords became strained, those who raised sugar on just part of their holding earned more than those who grew only rice. The difference had to do with dissimilar circumstances that resulted from improvements in both the rice and sugar markets. The Philippines, with its rapidly rising population and so much of its land devoted to cash crops, needed vastly increased amounts of rice, and the Central Luzon Plain proved the best place to produce those stocks. However, central Luzon, especially the longer-settled areas like Pampanga, was becoming more crowded, and its denizens consumed more of their own output. Density rose in the province by 30 percent between 1918 and 1939, from 349 per square mile to 456; meanwhile, agricultural hectarage expanded only 22 percent, from 100,400 hectares to 122,006. Rice land increased 26 percent, from 52,936 hectares to 66,453.[77]

To increase rice output in Pampanga (without interfering with sugar production), landowners needed to improve their yields, either through better farming methods or by further gouging the peasants. Since more scientific agriculture demanded heavy capital investments, landholders preferred first to tighten terms of aparcero contracts, charge higher interest rates on farm loans, remove inefficient tenants, agglomerate holdings, and demand more work from casamac. Some proprietors also resorted to outright cheating of tenants on the annual division of crops. Landlords tended to term these practices "making the tenant-landlord arrangement more businesslike," but casamac viewed the changes as unjust. Because of the increasing competition for holdings, however, tenants found themselves in a poor bargaining position and could not rectify the situation. Protest resulted.[78]

In the meantime, however, while the sugar market held, casamac growing cane maintained an acceptable standard of living. Income derived from a combination of sugar profits and some sales of rice, supplemented possibly with off-season work, kept sugar tenants from turning to the more radical organizations. Of those 149 cane growers questioned in the 1964 survey who might have joined such groups, only 17 did, while another 9 enrolled in the conservative, landlord-sponsored Katipunan Mipanampun (Mutual Protection Association or KM). This latter organization, founded by Representative Zoilo Hilario, an ally of Quezon and Sotero Baluyut, began in Pampanga and eventually spread throughout central Luzon. Writers of the era described KM as similar to KSI, with the same mutual-aid function and masoniclike structure. The group drew mainly from the towns, enlisting teachers, workers, local politicians, and casamac; it even had a women's auxiliary called the Amazons. A superpatriotic group, KM's members conducted flag-raising ceremonies, sponsored beauty contests, and supported economic protectionism; however, KM's chief function was to provide counterdemonstrations to those of the peasant unions. Lasting from roughly 1922 to 1924, KM represented the largest organization in the growing backlash against tenant radicalism.[79]

Only twice during the 1920s did sugar tenants briefly protest their treatment at the hands of landlords, and both complaints had to do with shifts in sugar prices. The rapid fall in price in 1922 and 1924 following the exceptional highs of the respective preceding years led tenants to believe they had been cheated, that they had received too little during the boom and had dropped back too far afterward. On these occasions they sought redress from landlords and, unsuccessfully, from Governor Olimpio Guanzon. As soon as prices stabilized, however, the protests ceased.[80]

Another factor favoring peace among sugar casamac was that they obtained some satisfaction from the government. During their two protests, aparceros complained that landlords provided them with incorrect mill data. In time the government passed a measure requiring landlords to furnish tenants with full documentation on the milling and disposing of sugar stocks. By contrast, rice farmers never succeeded in obtaining an effective law to protect them in their contracts with landlords. Sugar tenants thus appeared to have more clout than those who grew only rice.[81]

In an indirect way the sugar industry also contributed to unrest among rice tenants by forcing many of them off parcels of land and planting cane in their stead. Perhaps the most notorious case occurred in Dinalupihan, Bataan, where Pasumil acquired rights to farmland belonging to the Catholic Church. The central removed the rice tenants and in the process raised a storm among those evicted. Although the tenants lost, the area remained thereafter a hotbed of protest. Similar incidents on a smaller scale, involving landowners and tenants, happened elsewhere in Pampanga and Tarlac during these years of sugar prosperity.[82]

Two circumstances changed the relative passivity among sugar tenants: the coming of limitation and the rise of effective local leadership of the peasant movement. Beginning in 1933, talk of market restrictions, on top of already depressed sugar prices, began to alarm tenant farmers and to encourage landlords to harden the terms of sugar contracts. As the era of quotas dawned, close observers of the industry noted in the new situation a potential for unrest.[83] Meanwhile a new leader of Pampanga's tenants had recently emerged on the scene, in time to lead the next round of strikes against landlords and centrals.

One of the more pressing needs in the study of twentieth-century Philippine history is a good biography of Pedro Abad Santos, given his contributions, long unappreciated and misunderstood, to his country's intellectual and political development. Too often his reputation has been overshadowed by that of his younger brother, Supreme Court Chief Justice Jose Abad Santos, executed in 1942 for his refusal to collaborate with the Japanese military government.

The few scraps of source material on Pedro Abad Santos that have so far surfaced present a paradoxical view of him. Born in 1876 into a professional family of San Fernando, he grew up in the company of the local elite, enjoying such pastimes of the wealthy as tennis. Large sugar land holders including Alfredo Ganzon of Magalang and Roberto Toledo III of Floridablanca considered him a friend. Abad Santos attended the elite Manila school San Juan de Letran with schoolmates Manuel Quezon and Sergio Osmeña and completed his education at Ateneo de Manila and University of Santo Tomas. After passing the bar in 1907, he became a justice of the peace and provincial fiscal in the succeeding years. He and brother Jose briefly formed a law partnership in 1920–21, practiced in the capital area, and had as one of their clients the Manila Railroad Company. Despite his background, however, Pedro exhibited a genuine sympathy for and understanding of the plight of the poor and in later years spent much of his time in their company. Even so, he liked being referred to as "Don Pedro" or "Don Perico."

Abad Santos had a taste for public office, yet he chose to become a political outcast defending peasants in suits against landlords and founding Aguman ding Talapagobra ning Filipinas (Workers' Union of the Philippines) in 1929. Before then he served two terms in the Philippine Assembly from 1916 to 1923 and vied unsuccessfully against Sotero Baluyut for governor of Pampanga in 1927. He ran several times more for governor in the 1930s. Yet this same ambitious politico adopted a spartan personal lifestyle, electing to live in a nipa hut in the yard of his family house near the center of San Fernando, where he daily met with casamac seeking his legal help and moral support.[84]

There remains a core mystery as to why Abad Santos moved from his role as a conventional politician to spokesman for the peasants of his province. His siblings stayed within the fold: Antonio, a successful hacendero and businessman, served as president of San Fernando's municipal council; Irineo was successful in both farming and finance; Jose, a favorite of Quezon, worked his way up in the Department of Justice; while Quirino, a local justice of the peace, carried out provincial political chores for Quezon. Even Quirino did not understand why his eldest brother drifted so far to the left; however, he believed that Pedro's defeat at the hands of Baluyut affected this transformation. Other unsympathetic commentators also saw the move as one of revenge against the landowners and politicians who helped bring about his 1927 loss. Even supporter Casto Alejandrino felt that the landlords abandoned Abad Santos in the election because of his aid to tenants, and that this betrayal by his own class made his jump inevitable. The vengeance explanation scarcely accounts for Abad Santos's seventeen-year commitment, filled with great personal sacrifice and fraught with danger, to the cause of the aparcero. Deeper motivations surely lay behind his decision.

Present-day historian Antonio Tan sees in Abad Santos's record as a legislator evidence of a longstanding sympathy for the poor; however, the latter's opposition to a head tax and support for women's suffrage and legalization of divorce provide testimony only of a liberal attitude. Those stands indicate simply that Abad Santos possessed a social conscience, not that he might someday advocate dismantling the existing socioeconomic structure in favor of the casamac.

Luis Taruc and others explain the turn to the left as due to Abad Santos's association with communists and suggest that Evangelista and Manahan may have converted the lawyer from Pampanga. Local historian Mariano Henson hints that the visiting Tan Malacca affected Abad Santos's thinking. Conceivably, he might have learned something about Marxism from others, but that he altered his life because of their persuasion seems improbable. Testimony by relatives and associates makes one thing clear: Abad Santos possessed a keen intellect; indeed, he was, perhaps, the most original thinker the Left ever had, and he exerted a tremendous influence on those who came in contact with him, not the other way around.[85]

Ironically, for all his considerable intellectual prowess, Abad Santos left few written clues as to why he made his deep commitment to the cause of the poor. One needs to examine his actions for insight into his thoughts, and the events of his life reveal much about him. Furthermore, in some letters he wrote in the late 1930s to his friend the American Communist Sol Auerbach (a.k.a. James Allen), he demonstrated how far his thinking about social and political matters had progressed since his days in formal politics.

Above all, Abad Santos was a nationalist devoted to his country's independence. At the turn of the century he left a teaching job in Bacolor to become military secretary to General Maximino Hizon, one of the Revolution's diehard holdouts. For crimes committed Abad Santos faced a twenty-five-year sentence and stayed in prison until pardoned by President Theodore Roosevelt. Described at the time as being small in size and sickly, Abad Santos had already learned English and earned the respect of his prosecutors for his intellectual prowess. Despite his pardon, the patriot never wavered in his nationalism and in later years labored to have the exiled Hizon's remains brought back from Guam for reburial and to erect a statue in Pampanga to his former chief. In 1918 as a member of the Assembly, he urged the sending of the first Philippine independence mission to Washington and raised money toward that end. He himself joined the second mission in 1922.

Upon his return from Washington he withdrew from insular-level politics sometime in 1923 and repaired to Pampanga, which became his permanent base. Here he commenced defending peasants in their suits against landlords. One wonders if by this time he had become disillusioned with the duplicity of the Philippine leadership on the independence issue. At any rate, he now supported Osmeña rather than his friend Quezon, and during the debates over the Hare-Hawes-Cutting Act the two became involved in a bitter exchange when Quezon accused Abad Santos and his ally Honorio Ventura of cheating in earlier elections. Abad Santos answered the charge coolly, and cordiality between the two ceased.[86]

The weakening nationalist ardor of elected representatives in favor of more pragmatic economic goals clearly left Abad Santos disappointed and could account for his rejection of conventional politics and politicians; however, as both a nationalist and an inventive thinker, he still sought ways to gain his country's freedom and pondered the socio-political structure of an independent Philippines. From comments he made to Auerbach, it would appear that the protest swirling around him in Pampanga deeply affected his thought and that he became swept up in his late forties in the tide of unrest. He wrote in 1937:

> But in the Philippines we have no strong bourgeoisie. The bourgeois revolution has not been completed and left the feudal landlord system untouched. The ruling Filipino bourgeoisie is timid, ignorant and backward. It is timid because it is aware of its weakness. It is ignorant for even its intellectual leaders lack understanding of advanced political and economic thought. It is also backward for its outlook and methods are almost feudal. Therefore, I believe that in the Philippines an agrarian revolution will precede the proletarian revolution, as it has happened in China.[87]

Some have argued that he had little familiarity with theoretical Marxism, but as the above statement reveals, he knew the literature. Throughout his life he remained a voracious reader, and Auerbach and others supplied him with books. Nevertheless, Abad Santos fits the pattern of Asian leftists, including Ho Chi Minh and Mao Zedong, who sought to adapt communist theory to indigenous society. Like those contemporaries, he drew ideas from a variety of sources, perhaps the most important of which was local circumstances. He lived in the arena, not the ivory tower, and expressed himself in action rather than print.

A passage from another letter reveals the way Abad Santos operated. In considering the merits of shortening the commonwealth period in the face of a threatening Japan, he wrote: "All these things confuse me greatly. I intend to consult with fellow-workers in the labor movement, so that we may in common counsel find a way out for the right solution of our problems."[88] Abad Santos realized, as did Quezon, that the Philippine elite lacked strength, weakened as they were both by Quezon's machinations and by their economic dependency on America; however, the Capampangan sought not to lead in the same dictatorial manner but rather to build a new political edifice based on more democratic consultation. To make such a system work required enhancing the peasant's role in society. Abad Santos thus not only challenged Quezon, he also threatened the sugar industry with its rigid socioeconomic structure and its reliance on America's favors. Nestled too in Abad Santos's thought lay the principle of cooperative action, so natural to the Pampangan aparcero and small farmer.

After the courts declared the Communist party illegal in late 1931, Abad Santos formed the Socialist party the next year, using his peasant Aguman ding Maldang Talapagobra (League of Poor Workers; AMT) from Pampanga to provide a base of membership. He hoped thus to maintain an above-ground voice for the Left and an arm for carrying on the struggles in court. Peasants now boasted their own party, and the Philippine sugar industry faced an implacable political foe with a resourceful and dedicated spokesman. To the new organization Abad Santos attracted such talented younger cadre as labor organizer Casto Alejandrino from a nationalist landholding family in Arayat and the charismatic speaker Luis Taruc, originally from smallholder stock in San Luis. As the era of quotas dawned, the new party stood ready to challenge further planter exploitation.[89]

Independence promised retrenchment for the sugar industry, and its leaders started weighing new strategies for survival. Appraising the international market as inescapably grim, they contemplated expanding the domestic market by exciting the Filipino taste for their product. Free packets of sugar in workers' rations would create a craving, and ad campaigns could be designed to convince the poor to spend extra pesos for white sugar rather than save on the "less healthy" dark. Other sugarmen examined the prospect of crop diversification, of planting cotton, fruit trees, beans, mulberry bushes, and vegetables; meanwhile, the pages of *Sugar News* contained thoughts about gold-mining ventures and poultry raising. The era that commenced in bright optimism concluded in gloom.[90]

SIX

Quotas, 1935–1941

Mr. Manuel L. Quezon, acknowledged leader of the Filipino bourgeoisie, is again arriving home from one of his innumerable missions to the U.S. The political machine which [he] has built thru years of intrigue, misrepresentation, personal aggrandisement and enrichment is given a holiday to greet him. The leaders of finance and industry in whose hands he has been a willing tool, will be at the pier to pat his back. Thruout all the ballyho of "Mabuhay" and "Hurrah" he will remain a calm and engaging person with a holy feeling of having accomplished something for his country.

But which is HIS country? Is it Spain, the land of the Elizaldes, Sorianos, Ossorios . . .

Perhaps his country is the land of the Yulos and Alunans—the errand boys of the sugar interests.

Philippine Communist Party Handout (1935)

Following upon the first, harsh imposition of quotas in 1935 down to the invasion of the Philippines by Japan at the end of 1941, members of the Philippine sugar industry adjusted to a stagnant market. The quota system neither eliminated surpluses nor wholly protected prices; still, it probably staved off the demise of the export sugar industry. Filipinos sold their product above world prices and briefly experienced some prosperity. By 1941 sugarmen had learned to live with imposed restrictions and had adjusted their thinking, industrial structure, and activities to those limitations.

Quotas stunted production, and hacenderos found themselves more heavily regulated than ever before and having to depend more upon industry leaders to look after their interests vis-à-vis government. Profits became more inequitably distributed in favor of the upper crust of society, even as the pie ceased to enlarge; thus, limitations exacerbated tensions among the industry's participants, and the struggles grew in frequency and intensity. If sugar society achieved its modern shape during the era of centrals, that form solidified during the subsequent period of quotas. The Philippine sugar industry thus reached its maturity, no longer growing but

Table 15. Philippine Sugar Exports, 1934–41 (metric tons)

Year	*Export*	*Quota under U.S. Tariff Laws*	*Value of All Exports (%)*
1934	1,152,841	920,971	59
1935	516,233	833,123	35
1936	899,838	968,935	45
1937	871,045	984,581	38
1938	868,253	959,281	43
1939	874,728	955,143	32
1940	976,474	1,004,477	31
1941	775,651	996,161	n.a.

Sources: Roy A. Ballinger, *A History of Sugar Marketing*, Economic Research Service, Agricultural Economic Report, no. 197 (Washington, D.C.: U.S. Department of Agriculture, 1971), p. 40; Carlos Quirino, *History of the Philippine Sugar Industry* (Manila: Kalayaan, 1974), p. 58; *Sugar News* 16 (1935): 99, 456; 18 (1937): 433; 19 (1938): 45; 20 (1939): 404; *Tribune* (Manila), August 11, 1936, p. 2; December 8, 1938, p. 2; June 18, 1941, p. 12; Robert Huke, *Shadows on the Land: An Economic Geography of the Philippines* (Manila: Bookmark, 1963), p. 316.

Note: Because of existing laws and agreements, between 99 and 100 percent of all Philippine export sugar went to the U.S. market during these years.

rather facing a period of consolidation and declining vitality. Events of World War II and the postwar years scarcely altered before the mid-1970s patterns formed during the pre-1942 commonwealth period.

Sugar under Quotas

The age of quotas began in crisis. The Jones-Costigan Act decreed a retroactive limit on duty-free sugar shipped to the United States of just 920,971 tons for 1934, some 231,870 tons less than the amount actually sold; moreover, the Philippines still had 1934 sugar held in customs bond that could not enter the American market before January 1, 1935. Hence, Philippine sugarmen faced an effective 1935 quota of some 520,000 tons for sugar exported in that calendar year, less than half the total sent the preceding year (see table 15).

Whereas total centrifugal sugar production for the 1933–34 season reached a record 1,431,920 metric tons, that for the 1934–35 season came in at just 631,142 tons. Beginning as early as May 1934, Negrense hacenderos, in anticipation of the impending curtailment and because of a temporary credit squeeze, began laying off workers, and employment remained depressed until late in 1935. In early January 1935 sugar piled up in overcrowded warehouses while nervous millers and farmers awaited the government program to determine their individual quotas for the year. To lower their harvests, many planters destroyed standing cane; some diversified, raising livestock and other crops on a limited scale to support themselves. Anxiety rose highest among marginal producers, who feared that even a modest loss of output would move them below the survival level. The drop in production for 1935 represented a major blow to the well-being of workers and small farmers without an economic cushion. The consequences of crop reductions spilled over into related industries; thus, the government-owned Manila Railroad faced sharp revenue losses because of decreased sugar movement from central Luzon, and provincial and insular governments laid off employees in the face of declining tax revenues.[1]

Expressions of gloom haunted the local press as sugarmen anticipated the closing of the duty-free American market. Comparisons of the cost of producing and shipping Philippine, versus Cuban, sugar to U.S. refineries revealed that the former had almost no chance of ever competing on an even basis with its Caribbean rival. Furthermore, the state of the world sugar economy, of oversupply and underdemand, dictated long-term Filipino dependence on North American sales. This judgment seemed confirmed when attempts to improve local purchases of centrifugal and refined sugar came to naught. Instead, sugarmen found that avenue closed because shoppers continued to prefer cheaper muscovado sugars; what increase in consumption occurred, came about because planters sold cane not allowed to go to centrals to insular millers of crude sugar.

Bad news afflicted markets sporadically in the first half of 1935. Inauguration of the new quota system caused some temporary dislocations, and brief shortages in the availability of domestic Philippine sugar supplies created an anomalous situation whereby in the early months of that year local retail sugar sold at higher prices than the export product. In midyear rumors that the U.S. Supreme Court might strike down quota provisions of the Agricultural Adjustment Act caused the price of Philippine sugar to plummet (see figure 5). Enactment of Jones-Costigan had sent sugar prices back up to 1930 levels, but fears of its elimination caused momentary panic. Producers and buyers of insular sugar feared that in the event of such a judicial decision, Cuba would be allowed to flood the American market with its less expensive product, while the Philippines would still be bound by the duty-free limitations of the Tydings-McDuffie Act. Only when it appeared that the law would stand did sugar prices climb again.[2]

Not all initial consequences of the Jones-Costigan and Tydings-McDuffie acts proved harmful to the Philippine sugar industry. Assignment of quotas all the way down to the level of the individual farmer had proceeded effi-

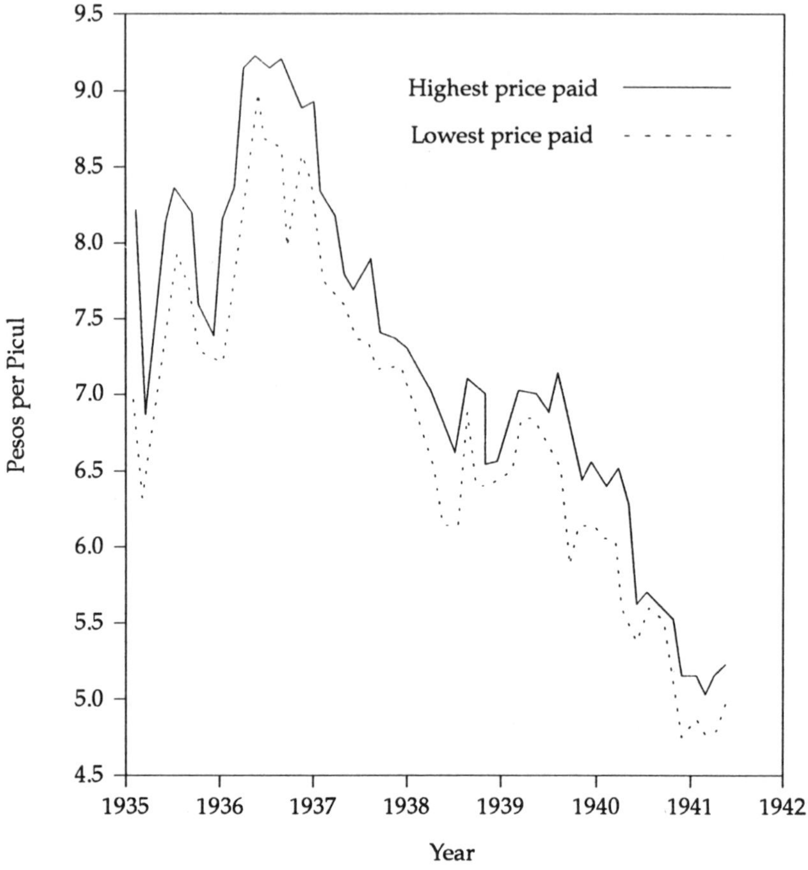

Figure 5. Sugar Prices on the Manila Market, 1935–41. *Sugar News* 16–22 (1935–41).

ciently and, by most accounts, equitably. Governor-general Frank Murphy, in charge of allocation of quotas, turned this complex project over to his assistant, E. D. Hester, and to the collector of insular customs, J. Weldon Jones, and they managed to keep the distribution free from political influence. By October 1935 each planter and miller had a firm allocation for the amount of sugar he or she could produce. A further advantage of market stabilization under the quota system flowed to planters when the New York Coffee and Sugar Exchange voted to allow trading in Philippine sugar futures, beginning in 1935. Planters and merchants could now sell their crop earlier, at times when they could realize a higher price for it. The government began releasing small quantities of domestic consumption ("B") and export ("A") sugar from warehouses as early as January 1935, and in March

Secretary of Agriculture Henry Wallace allowed mills to grind cane for the manufacture of twenty million gallons of alcohol for local and U.S. sale.[3]

A proviso of the Jones-Costigan Act allowed compensation to planters for cane burned during 1934–35. The payback money came from a processing tax on finished sugar (one-half cent per pound) imposed on U.S. refiners. Between January 1935 and July 1936 more than 17,000 Philippine planters received some $14,000,000 in payments at P2.40 per picul. To celebrate, Bacolod hacenderos held a "processing tax ball" accompanied by the usual beauty contests. These benefit payments to farmers, a typical New Deal program, ceased in the Philippines with the establishment of the commonwealth. Later in the 1930s the U.S. government revived the practice of returning sugar tax funds to the Philippines, but because of court decisions the money went to the commonwealth government for broader agricultural planning.

While the initial benefits program aided suffering farmers, distribution of funds did not proceed without problems, especially for tenant producers. Money went to planters and landowners of record at centrals; however, the law stated that all who actually grew cane on a reduced scale should receive a proportionate share of the payments. But casamac and inquilinos, primarily those from central Luzon who lacked documentary evidence of their production, had to depend on the largesse and goodwill of their richer partners to receive shares of the benefit payment, and some cheating took place.[4]

Economic distress associated with the 1935 constraints dissipated gradually during that year. Despite reduced operating hours, centrals still in debt to PNB yet managed small payments on their notes beginning as early as March. By December all mills resumed regular production schedules that continued into 1936, when market conditions improved to the point that even the Japanese purchased small quantities of Philippine sugar. Aside from 1935, sugar exports remained above the levels of the 1920s, and initially at least, prices rose, from a prequota low of P4.50 to P9.10 per picul in mid-1936. Most mills earned considerable profits, and by 1937 all the bank centrals save Binalbagan had redeemed their mortgages. The managers at both the San Carlos and Silay-Hawaiian centrals issued exuberant reports for 1936, and the general prosperity in sugarlandia led to an increase of P6,000,000 net profit over the preceding year for PNB. Subsequent seasons did not witness the same prosperity, but centrals still managed to pay dividends to investors until at least 1940. Philippine coconut oil and hemp quotas under Tydings-McDuffie subsequently underwent revision, but the sugar quota held firm.[5]

American officials decreed that both the Tydings-McDuffie and Jones-Costigan trade provisions, and those of the latter's successor, the Sugar Act of 1937, would continue to apply simultaneously. The Philippines was entitled to a quota of between 900,000 and 1,000,000 long tons based on its allotted share of U.S. annual consumption, but the independence act stipulated that only 800,000 long tons (812,846 metric) of raw "A" sugar and 50,000 (50,802 metric) tons of refined "AA" sugar could enter duty free. In practice insular sugarmen usually abided by the lower nondutiable figure, since with the tax added, they could not compete in terms of price with other suppliers (see table 15); thus, each year save 1940 they allowed their unfilled quota under U.S. tariff law to be divided among other offshore producers. The commonwealth government also set annual quotas for raw sugar for domestic consumption that varied between 70,000 and 150,000 short tons and a reserve supply ("C") of raw sugar of between 30,000 and 100,000 short tons to fill any shortfall in the export quota.[6]

Further legislation regarding sugar exports reaffirmed regulations already in place. In response to pressure from American refiners, the U.S. Congress refused to allow the Philippines to raise its quota of refined sugar or even to export a washed, purer grade of raw sugar called turbinado. In early 1937 Quezon and Roosevelt, in accordance with section thirteen of the Tydings-McDuffie Act, convened a conference of commonwealth and U.S. government representatives to adjust economic arrangements between the two states prior to and following Philippine independence in 1946. The Joint Preparatory Committee on Philippine Affairs recommended only minor alterations in sugar matters: for example, it urged postponement of the imposition of the first export tax (5 percent of the total U.S. duty) from November 15, 1940, to January 1, 1941. The Tydings-Kocialkowski Act of 1939 legalized that change. During April 1937, emissaries of the commonwealth participated with the American delegation in the London International Sugar Conference, called to regulate global production. As a signatory to the May 6 agreement, the Philippine government pledged not to export sugar, including muscovado, anywhere but to the United States so long as the Tydings-McDuffie quota lasted. The international agreement, designed to apply initially for five years, merely confirmed Philippine dependence upon the American market.[7]

While exports held constant, from 1936 on sugar prices followed a persistently downward course, hitting a low of P4.6 in April and May 1941. The market became so unfavorable that Spreckels and Company, formed in 1933 to purchase and export Philippine raw, ceased operations in late 1938, preferring to supply its parent U.S. West Coast refineries with greater quantities of Cuban sugar. The London agreement failed to reduce supplies sufficiently to reverse the slide, and prices dropped sharply during 1937 and the first half of 1938. Moreover, while other London signatories used the commencement of hostilities as an excuse to suspend their own quotas, the restriction on the Philippines to ship exclusively to the U.S. market remained in effect. Even on the eve of Pearl Harbor in 1941, when shippers appeared in Manila ready to purchase sugar for delivery to Russia via Vladivostok, the Philippines could not gain a release to fill those orders.[8]

The onset of world war did not push prices upward. In the East, Sino-Japanese conflict in Manchuria and northern China left India and Java without an important market for their product. When Hitler's armies crossed into Poland in September 1939, sugar futures in New York surged briefly, and Roosevelt suspended quotas; however, since various countries had stocked up in advance in anticipation of the war, local shortages failed to occur, and he reimposed quotas in December. In 1940 a combination of factors, including the expectation of higher prices and a rush to beat the first Tydings-McDuffie duty of 26 centavos per picul in January 1941, led Filipino producers to rush large quantities to market; however, the higher prices never materialized. By early 1941 sugar prices had sunk so low that exporters proved reluctant to ship, since they were not even earning the cost of production. When global stocks finally began to diminish and prices started to rise in late 1941, warfare made commercial vessels more expensive and scarce. The war-induced shortage of shipping only worsened conditions. Fifty kilos of ammonium sulfate, the preferred fertilizer, went from P7.50 to P9.00 between 1940 and 1941, while the price of a ten-pound bag of domestic granulated sugar fell from P6.15 to P5.80. George Fairchild devoted considerable effort that year in New York and Manila attempting to find transports; nevertheless, by early December the Philippines had not sent all its 1941 quota, and the invading Japanese found local warehouses stuffed with export sugar for 1942.[9]

Confronted by continuing world overproduction, rising freight rates, and the prospect of accelerating duties that would eventually make their sugar uncompetitive even in the U.S. market, Philippine sugarmen considered several remedies for their economic plight: lowering their production costs, limiting the number of producers, and diversifying their economic activities. Members of PSA suggested postponing the date of independence in order to maintain the privileged access for Philippine sugar. Others even spoke of nationalizing the industry in the event of dire emergency, but the first three plans, which all stressed cutting back on output and costs, received the most attention. And when planters and millers contemplated reducing expenses, they did not figure to do it by improving productivity—in those years sugar research by the industry largely ceased—rather, they thought to do so by cutting jobs and wages.[10]

While quotas became a fact of life, Manuel Quezon increased his control over the sugar industry and commenced charting its future. Recent scholarship has demonstrated how he gained near dictatorial power over the domestic political process at the insular, provincial, and local levels. He had rewarded some of his supporters by obtaining favors for them within the sugar industry, and as president of the commonwealth he sought to play an enhanced role in shaping the country's most economically vital activity. In a systematic way he strove to govern the sugar industry so as to encourage consolidation, to make it less politically influential, and to initiate internal changes that would weaken the potential for radicalism among poor sugar hands. Quezon had relied on sugar support in achieving victory over rivals Sergio Osmeña and Manuel Roxas during the political struggles over independence; now he employed sugarmen to act as his lieutenants in handling the industry.[11] To exert domination over sugar, lest its leaders oppose any of his plans or ambitions, he used a variety of mechanisms: supervision of the quota system, influence over PNB credit policy, and control over negotiations with the Americans on tariff relief and related matters.

The Philippine Sugar Administration, formed in late 1937, served as a major vehicle of Quezonian authority. Over its extensive staff he appointed two of his favorite henchmen, first Rafael Alunan and then in late 1938 Gil Montilla. Both had long careers in Negros politics, and the latter had served as speaker of the National Assembly when Quezon had needed a pliant friend in that position. As sugar administrators with cabinet rank they presided over an agency that not only set yearly domestic and reserve quotas, but settled numerous policy matters as well, including standardization of the size of sugar bags and regulation of muscovado sugar output that competed with centrifugal in the domestic market. Even more important, the administrator began to intervene in cases involving the reallocation of export quotas to planters and millers in the event of changes in land ownership and milling contracts. This latter authority, infrequently exercised before the Japanese occupation, offered the government great potential power over the lives and fortunes of many in the industry. With the first of the major milling contracts, at San Carlos, coming up for renegotiation in 1942, Quezon made it clear that the administration intended to play a part in redistributing industry profits more equitably. The Philippine Sugar Administration did not achieve absolute control over the industry; for example, it proved ineffective in preventing the dumping of sugar on the local market; nevertheless, sugarmen increasingly turned to this agency and to Quezon for decisions on policy matters.[12]

As senate president Quezon had in the 1920s and early 1930s exerted sway over PNB loan policy and had thus affected economic life in sugarlandia. In the later 1930s that influence only grew. Governor-general Frank Murphy in 1934 appointed a Quezon man, sugar corporation lawyer Jose Yulo, chairman of the board of directors of the bank, and Yulo stayed in that position until 1938 while simultaneously serving as the commonwealth's secretary of justice. Meanwhile, PNB greatly strengthened its financial position with record profits from sugar and with the recovery of its loans to the bank centrals. Quezon thus held direct access to the PNB's decision-making body, and he used his leverage and the bank's enlarged assets to control and protect the sugar industry. To provide relief for struggling hacenderos the bank gave mortgages on reserve sugar, supplied money at reduced interest rates, and even provided cash to tenants who could offer only their crops as security. At the same time, the bank sought to discourage planters from using their crop loans to invest in mining stocks and other outside ventures, as they apparently did in large numbers in 1937. The net effect of this overall policy was to keep many farmers in business despite slumping prices and to assure their political docility and allegiance to Manuel Luis Quezon.[13]

While Tydings-McDuffie and the Sugar Acts of 1934 and 1937 set the main parameters for political and economic relations between the commonwealth and the United States, protecting Philippine sugar interests still demanded considerable attention, and here again Quezon took command. Sundry problems required ongoing settlement, and he carried out the negotiations through such surrogates as Resident Commissioner Joaquin Miguel (Mike) Elizalde and Felipe Buencamino. Both sugarmen attended the London Conference, and the former, along with Jose Yulo, defended Philippine positions during deliberations of the Joint Preparatory Committee on Philippine Affairs. Over the course of seven years the commonwealth fought over recovery of the excise tax on sugar stipulated in the Sugar Act of 1937, postponement of imposition of the Tydings-McDuffie export tax, relief for the sugar industry because of the damage done by the shortage of wartime shipping, prohibition of the U.S. Army in the Philippines from buying cheaper Javanese sugar, and clarification of the definition of refined sugar under the quota system. The commonwealth did not always have its way in these matters; however, in directing the negotiations, Quezon clearly established himself as chief spokesman for, and defender of, the sugar industry. Before 1935 the PSA had served as the sugar industry's main voice in Washington; its role now diminished. Harry Hawes continued as the organization's lobbyist until the war, but the PSA overseas office shrank in both size and activity. Elizalde became the most important figure at the U.S. capital on behalf of Philippine sugar, for he defended the industry as a whole rather than, as did the PSA, chiefly the millers.[14]

The commonwealth government also strove to consolidate its sugar holdings at home. It purchased the Insular and Malabon Sugar Refineries and so gained control of about 85 percent of the country's refining capacity.

In addition, despite efforts by individual investors to buy the Binalbagan Central from PNB, Quezon elected to keep it and had the government purchase the outstanding private shares. Furthermore, the administration transformed the former Philippine Sugar Centrals Agency into the chief marketing agent for Binalbagan Estates Company. The government thus had a position in refining, in milling, in marketing, and through its ownership of the Manila Railroad Company, in transportation. In making its moves the government not only rationalized its own stake in the sugar industry, it also acquired further leverage to influence sugarmen.[15]

Sugar Society

Gauging precise changes in Philippine sugar society for so short a period as seven years represents a formidable task; however, events and actions in the period from 1935 through 1941 do indicate some ways in which people in the industry responded to the quota system. Limitations on production and declining prices after 1936 provided opportunities for the wealthy entrepreneur to expand his holdings, while they supplied incentives for others to bail out and to seek alternative investments. For smaller planters, mill workers, and farmhands, only the option to stay and fight for a share of dwindling industry profits remained.

With nearly stagnant sales, businessmen found it expedient to expand by acquiring the market share of others, and some consolidation occurred in the sugar industry. Four centrals changed hands in 1935 and early 1936: Bataan Sugar Company and Ormoc Sugar Company (Leyte) became the property of Gil Montilla's family, owners of Lopez Central in Sagay purchased Central Santos-Lopez in Iloilo Province, and control of Bacolod Central passed from the de la Ramas to the Lizares family. None of the first three acquisitions constituted more than a small fraction of the quota, but the latter mill ground a significant 4.41 percent, and coupled with the Lizareses' other centrals, Talisay and Danao (Negros Occidental), gave them almost 10 percent of the total Philippine export quota. By 1937 seven family groups or corporations dominated practically two-thirds of all sugar milling. Other attempts at takeover did not reach completion in the prewar period. Jose Yulo proposed purchasing Calamba Sugar Estate from the Ehrman-Spreckels conglomerate, both the Lopez family and Gil Montilla expressed interest in buying Binalbagan from the government, and the Ledesmas tried to obtain San Carlos. Although these bids proved unsuccessful, they confirm the rush toward agglomeration that pervaded the commonwealth years.[16]

Consolidation of mill ownership represented not only the enhancement of family holdings, but also an effort to put the industry on a more rational and efficient footing. Sugarmen emphasized making production more cost-efficient so that Philippine sugar could compete in future unprotected world markets, and the technical answer espoused by such experts as Carlos Locsin stressed better productivity through improved corporate organization. A younger scion of the Lizares family, Placido Mapa, an executive comfortable in English and trained in high finance, engineered the Bacolod acquisition. Mapa took over as manager from Rafael Alunan, who spoke mainly Spanish, always enjoyed provincial and national politics, and preferred to leave actual supervision at the central to others. The Lizareses added to their board of directors Cesar Ledesma, who had earned a solid reputation in sugar management. At other mills, too, rising young executives with technical expertise began to assume top management positions, individuals like Jose Tapia at Pasudeco. In 1937 Mapa succeeded Alunan as president of PSA, a move that severed the latter's major remaining tie to milling.[17]

Commenting on the Bacolod takeover, Nicholas Lizares noted that he purchased 23,000 shares from American sugarman Atherton Lee, who had earlier tried to buy the mill. Lizares also observed that his family had procured Danao from Spanish Friars.[18] The attempts to acquire San Carlos and Canlubang also fit the pattern of Filipinos looking to acquire foreign holdings, not just in sugar but in other industries as well. No doubt the approach of independence encouraged native entrepreneurs to invest in local industry and foreign sugarmen to consider divestment.

Not content to remain strictly in the sugar business, the Lizareses, like the Lopezes and others, continued to diversify their enterprises. To describe fully the flight of capital from the Philippine sugar industry into other investments in the archipelago would entail writing a lengthy business history of the commonwealth period; hence, only major trends appear here. Sugarmen put their money into gold, copper, iron, manganese, and chromite mining; urban, particularly Manila, commercial and residential real estate; film houses, Tagalog film making, newspaper publishing, and broadcasting; hotels and horse-racing tracks; all kinds of small manufacturing projects from stoves to fertilizer; food canning; commercial banking; financial services; and sea and air transportation. Negrenses increased their plantings of rice, and some of them experimented with new crops such as ramie, cotton, and rubber. To start raising the latter three, entrepreneurs from Negros and Pampanga started acquiring land in Mindanao, in such areas as Davao and the Koronadal Valley of southern Cotabato Province. In short, sugar money permeated virtually every area of insular business activity and provided sugarmen with considerable control over the commonwealth economy.

As the Philippines prepared for independence, the financial elite that occupied the board rooms of emerging companies included such sugar tycoons or former sugarmen as Juan Elizalde, Eugenio Lopez, Jorge Araneta,

Enrique Montilla, Jose de Leon, Benigno Toda y Toledo, and Alunan. While some families still operated as separate investing units, increasingly Negrenses and Capampangan participated in ventures as part of mixed groups involving individuals from diverse backgrounds. Americans including former Governor-general Francis Burton Harrison, General Douglas MacArthur, Binalbagan Central manager John Dumas, and John Stevenot, president of Philippine Long Distance Telephone; Philippine Chinese such as Alfonso Sycip; leading native politicians like Manuel Roxas, Claro M. Recto, Benigno Aquino, Sr., and Sotero Baluyut as well as Spanish mogul Jacobo Zobel all joined with sugarmen in different corporate enterprises.

With the market declining, room within the ranks of sugar's leadership shrank. To remain economically atop sugar society required considerable business acumen, for even within the industry, investors could now participate in a variety of ways. Sugarmen purchased and sold not only plantations, but also domestic, reserve, and export sugar; sugar futures; quotas; and shares in centrals. The wealthiest and most astute constructed a diversified portfolio of sugar and nonsugar investments. High finance entailed considerable risks—the de la Ramas, for instance, appear to have suffered severe reverses at this time—but remaining exclusively in sugar during a transitional period represented an even riskier proposition.[19]

Evidence abounded of the prosperity that lingered in sugarlandia, even as other indicators began to accumulate revealing that the wealth was becoming more unevenly distributed. Sugar barons behaved in the usual extravagant fashion: the University Club continued as the center of social activity for the Negrense "four hundred," while fancy-dress balls brightened the scene in more rural towns. Even though some of the wealthiest sugarmen removed to Manila, Bacolod persisted as the favorite playground of planters and millers with money. Amidst great pomp it became an incorporated city in 1938, and the government spent one million pesos to construct a spacious, well-appointed capitol. A new pier situated to the south promised to bring greater boat traffic to its door, and in 1936 the University of the Philippines began operating a campus in town.[20]

Pampanga bustled too. Townsfolk carried on a busy round of dances, receptions, and meetings, frequently under the auspices of such local social and political groups as Limbagan Club (San Fernando), Sociedad Pampangueña, Mountain Side Club (Magalang), Spider's Web, and Club Mekeni (Bacolor). The most renowned event of the season remained the Mancomunidad Pampangueña's annual ball, which drew distinguished guests from as far away as the Visayas. In 1941 a new college, St. Michael's, began offering classes in liberal arts and teacher training, and provincianos pointed proudly to the fact that Benvenido Gonzalez, a director at Pasudeco, became in 1939 the second Capampangan to serve as president of the University of the Philippines. The province had its own bar association, and to it belonged Diosdado Macapagal, 1936 insular bar topnotcher and rising young attorney whose local fame derived from his ability in poetic jousts with such other stars as author Amado Yuson.[21]

But the active social scene in sugarlandia belied the deteriorating economic conditions and tensions that now plagued hacendero life. Conditions remained so poor that between 1934 and 1938 automobile registrations in Negros Occidental dropped from 2,917 to 1,924; a number of big stores in Bacolod closed in 1940, and in that year *Makinaugalingon* started appearing only once instead of three times a week. The price of individual sugar quotas fell, and the value of sugar land dropped appreciably in both Luzon and Negros, as buyers preferred to invest in paddy fields. Between 1933 and 1941 rice production in Pampanga increased by 58 percent, in western Negros, by some 237 percent.[22]

Planters who depended exclusively or overwhelmingly on their farm income now confronted the reality of strictly limited production and falling prices, a situation that showed no promise of improvement in either the short or long run. Large hacenderos and landowners possessed sufficient cushion to ensure a good livelihood—at least until tariffs became too high—but the majority found themselves in more marginal, even desperate circumstances. All the big mills save Binalbagan continued to pay good dividends to shareholders during most of the commonwealth years, but planters who held only a minor fraction of the quota had to contemplate abandoning sugar production in favor of other food crops.

In August 1938 President Quezon ordered the just-created National Sugar Board to study the industry with the aim of making it more competitive. The board subsequently carried out a survey of conditions, the most thorough of its kind ever, made possible by new statistical information available through the Philippine Sugar Administration and through local studies conducted in each mill district. The report revealed much about the structure of sugar society under quotas: that a number of planters, particularly smaller ones, had left the industry; that the income disparity between big and lesser planters was enormous; and that mills did much better financially than did planters.

When the U.S. Sugar Administration prepared rosters of those with a fraction of the 1936 U.S. quota, they identified some 21,594 plantations with attached shares; however, three years later when the National Sugar Board conducted their survey, they listed only 18,823, a drop of 2,771. Presumably the loss came chiefly because many smaller owners and lessees sold or lost their quota and switched to another crop, usually rice or corn.

Farmers unloaded quotas separately and as part of land transfers, but the sales recorded in notarial registers did not ordinarily list the size of the allotment. Board statisticians, however, observed that the costs of production proved highest among the smallest planters, and they were most vulnerable under the new market conditions. The *Tribune* noted in 1937 that of the 389 planters in the Cadiz-Manapla area, 70 percent qualified as small planters, and many of those had given up raising sugar for want of funds. The progressive ownership at Victorias Milling Company began leasing modest (one hectare or so) plots of its plantations to encourage its own small farmers to raise rice. Large deals were still transacted—for instance, Emilio Lizares purchased lands and a 15,000-picul quota from Tabacalera—but the little farmer had more to gain by moving to another crop.[23]

The *Tribune* also reported as early as 1935:

> Secretary Torres declared that in Negros, as a result of the expiration of lease contracts between landowners and planters in sugar cane plantations, planters who merely cultivate the lands under lease agreement would be forced to quit and to look for new lands to develop. Mr. Torres said that the growing tendency among landowners in Negros is not to renew the lease but to cultivate the lands themselves. Landowners have been forced to work on their haciendas under new prevailing conditions, as a result of crop limitation and reduction in their income.[24]

Richer landlords and hacenderos consolidated their holdings and retrieved valuable quotas in the process. As a Department of Labor survey of 1936 noted:

> There seems to be no limit to the ambition of sugar planters to produce more and more. Whereas in the past a farmer who raised 10,000 piculs of sugar annually was a big hacendero, now he looks like a pigmy beside many a producer of 20,000 piculs, 30,000 piculs, 40,000 piculs, 50,000 piculs, 60,000 piculs, nay, 100,000 piculs and over annually.[25]

Other landowners chose to raise profits by charging lessees up to 50 percent more rent to continue farming.

Table 16, reproduced from the National Sugar Board's report, indicates just how quota size affected the lives of the individual hacenderos and the enormous disparity of wealth that existed within the industry. The board statisticians selected categories arbitrarily, and the data do not invite comparison with other periods; nevertheless, they do reveal the large number of people at the bottom of the socioeconomic pyramid and the small number

Table 16. Distribution of All Philippine Hacenderos by Quota Share and Income, 1938–39

Range of Quota (piculs)	*Number of Plantations*	*Percent of Total*	*Total Plantation Share of 55.23% (piculs)*[a]	*Average Share per Plantation (piculs)*	*Net Income per Plantation (pesos)*[b]
1–100	9,992	53.1	175,479	17.56	41.09
101–300	3,346	17.8	297,695	88.97	208.19
301–500	1,226	6.5	230,200	187.77	439.38
501–1,000	1,342	7.1	428,757	319.49	747.61
1,001–3,000	1,504	8.0	1,161,567	772.32	1,807.23
3,001–5,000	492	2.6	830,743	1,688.50	3,951.09
5,001–10,000	468	2.5	1,484,445	3,171.89	7,422.22
10,001+	453	2.4	4,300,996	9,494.47	22,217.06
Totals and averages	18,823	100	8,909,882	473.35	1,107.64

Source: *Report of the National Sugar Board to His Excellency the President of the Philippines*, August 2, 1939, Roxas Papers, National Library of the Philippines, Manila, p. 22.

[a]55.23% represents average planter's share at all Philippine centrals.

[b]Based on P2.34 per picul, which represents planter's profit after average planter's production cost.

at the top who qualified as sugar barons. The figures are confounded by the fact that some planters owned or leased more than one plantation, for the survey team counted 15,848 planters working the 18,823 plantations. Furthermore, lessees who constituted a majority of the hacendero population on Negros paid rent from their share. Finally, landowners in Pampanga divided their harvest with casamac, further confusing the income picture. Still, the table makes it clear how close to the edge the small sugar farmer lived. While annual wages in this period prove difficult to determine, one source estimated that Philippine factory workers earned a top annual wage of P240 per year and the average agricultural family earned P200. The vast majority of sugar planters, if they depended chiefly on their field income, earned the same or little more.[26]

To relieve their plight, planters in both Pampanga and Negros continued to agitate for a bigger share of participation in their milling contracts. Through their very vocal planters' groups, they argued that the mills showed fat profits while they struggled along at the survival level. Evidence seemed to support their claims. The National Sugar Board compiled statistics on returns on investment that showed centrals faring far better than planters (see table 17). Only at newer mills such as Tarlac and smaller ones

Table 17. Average Return on Investment, Planters and Centrals, Crop Year 1936–37

	Participation (%)		*Return on Investment (%)*	
Mill District	*Planter*	*Central*	*Planter*	*Central*
Pampanga/Tarlac				
Arayat	53.07	46.93	9.86	10.18
Bamban	50.00	50.00	10.20	9.81
Del Carmen	50.00	50.00	7.13	41.45
Mabalacat	55.00	45.00	10.78	8.44
Pasudeco	54.57	45.43	14.74	41.49
Tarlac	50.00	50.00	12.12	11.92
Negros Occidental				
Bacolod	59.44	40.56	12.43	14.26
Bearin	55.00	45.00	11.74	7.79
Binalbagan	60.00	40.00	14.55	23.73
Danao	55.00	45.00	13.71	8.78
Silay-Hawaiian	55.00	45.00	11.75	40.13
Isabela	60.00	40.00	13.64	20.32
La Carlota	59.25	40.75	15.56	14.44
Lopez	56.62	43.38	13.77	19.44
Ma-ao	60.00	40.00	12.29	19.07
Manapla	55.00	45.00	11.17	30.30
Palma	60.80	39.20	15.23	12.40
San Carlos	58.24	41.76	21.53	31.36
San Isidro	57.09	41.91	14.57	17.81
Talisay	55.00	45.00	9.60	32.32
Victorias	55.00	45.00	10.65	21.08

Source: *Report of the National Sugar Board to His Excellency the President of the Philippines*, August 2, 1939, Roxas Papers, National Library of the Philippines, Manila, pp. 16–17.

like Danao and Mabalacat did the rates equalize or favor the planters; and with the exception of La Carlota, at older, private plants the scale tipped heavily toward the mills. The rate of participation also bore some relation to the disparity in income, with six of the most profitable nine mills having a rate of from 50 to 55 percent.

Millers countered with the argument about the sanctity of contracts and further pointed out that, in Negros at least, planters suffered more because so many of them had to pay rent to landowners. Centralistas could not resist boasting that they paid higher wages and provided their workers with more benefits than did hacenderos. As far as their own profitability was concerned, millers reminded their antagonists that during the early years they took the risks in construction costs and paid no dividends to their stockholders. Finally, they pointed out that they profited more because their plants and operations employed modern technology. The National Sugar Board report confirmed this last contention, showing that millers did have lower production costs than planters and marketed their sugar better. Debate persisted between hacenderos and centralistas throughout the commonwealth period with only modest changes in contracts occurring. Talisay and Binalbagan raised their planters' share, and Pasudeco started giving higher rates when it renegotiated contracts as they came due. Otherwise central operators moved slowly in altering existing arrangements, fearing as they did the demise of the industry in 1946.[27]

In the struggles over participation, the planters' associations became powerful spokesmen for the hacenderos and inaugurated other programs as well. Planters' groups fought for the continuation of benefit payments after the original processing tax proceeds had been distributed. Through the strengthened Confederation of Sugar Cane Planters, they met and organized political action committees to affect legislation in the National Assembly and launched campaigns to increase domestic consumption and to encourage Philippine-American trade reciprocity. The Negros Sugar Planters' Federation sought to form an alliance with coconut and tobacco farmers to improve the overall marketing of Philippine products. In January 1939 hacenderos, under the leadership of Juan Ledesma, considered erecting their own plant to compete with the intransigent San Carlos Central.[28]

In Negros the tensions spilled over into the political arena as well. Two groups dominated politics in the sugar province during the commonwealth years: one led by Jose Yulo and Gil Montilla included leading centralistas such as Mapa and Lizares; the other, headed by Alunan, represented hacendero interests. Leading activist in the latter faction was young Alfredo Montelibano, first mayor of Bacolod City, then president of the Bacolod-Murcia Planters' Association, and in 1941 head of the Confederation of Sugar Cane Planters. In violence-marred campaigns the two groups battled over almost every office—mayoral, assemblymatic, senatorial, and gubernatorial. The real victor turned out to be Manuel Quezon, who used his arbitration to strengthen his hold over the industry leadership. Even Quezon, however, could not bring peace. He understood that tensions would subside only if centrals offered greater concessions, and he altered contracts at Binalbagan to encourage central generosity to planters and hacendero largesse toward farm workers. In neither instance did he succeed.[29]

The most dramatic event in the planter-miller struggle occurred in San Fernando, Pampanga, where on July 12, 1939, Gregorio and Carmelino Timbol gunned down Jose de Leon, Augusto Gonzalez, and constabulary captain Julian Olivas at the administrative offices of Pasudeco. The murder followed an argument over participation, which at the Pampanga central mostly remained at a low fifty-fifty. This incident and the subsequent trial created a sensation throughout the Philippines and prompted numerous editorials in local papers about the need to enhance planter shares of sugar profits. The two brothers belonged to a large, wealthy family from Angeles, although neither of them personally possessed a great fortune. Gregorio held a quota of a thousand piculs and at the time served as president of the Pasudeco Planters' Association. Both Timbols exhibited a violent streak: Carmelino was already facing indictment for shooting a tenant, and subsequently, Gregorio threatened to kill anyone who gave false testimony against him. Eventually, the two planters received death sentences, while their nephew Dalmacio Timbol earned a prison sentence of twelve years for complicity in the crime.

De Leon and Gonzalez, the two richest men in Pampanga and biggest Pasudeco shareholders, possessed fortunes at the time of their deaths of P2,500,000 and P1,300,000 to P1,500,000 respectively. Together they had made that central perhaps the most successful and progressively operated one in the archipelago (see table 17). Employees of the plant enjoyed excellent working conditions by contemporary standards including eight-hour work days, good housing, health facilities, and Christmas and off-season bonus programs. The company built at its own expense a schoolhouse, and de Leon personally contributed a chapel. Uniquely, management formed the Pasudeco Employees' Savings Fund that served workers and offered small mortgage loans. De Leon in particular earned a reputation as a generous boss and farseeing administrator.

Nevertheless, the Timbol brothers arrived at Pasudeco prepared to plead the case for higher participation. With the inauguration of quotas both had had to lease a farm to make ends meet. As sugar slipped through the P7 per picul barrier that July, they and other Pampangan farmers must have experienced a sense of desperation and frustration that only a better milling share could alleviate. Change, however, came too slowly.[30]

Confrontation

The imposition of quotas did not lead immediately to protest among farmhands and central workers in the sugar industry. Apparently the short-term jump in sugar prices in 1936 and early 1937, the ability of casamac to shift to rice cultivation, and receipt of some of the benefit payments warded off the worst effects of the limitations on export production. Not until late 1937 did the decline in prices and the inevitable layoffs start to take their toll. At that point unrest increased, and the climate in sugarlandia became decidedly more hostile. Kerkvliet tallied reported incidents of violence and came up with the findings in table 18. While these data refer to both sugar

Table 18. Incidents of Unrest by Province, 1935–41

	1935	*1936*	*1937*	*1938*	*1939*	*1940*	*1941*	*Total*
Pampanga	15	1	19	37	44	64	52	232
Tarlac	1	3	1	11	3	9	4	32
Negros Occidental	3	0	2	5	10	6	0	26

Source: Benedict J. Kerkvliet, *The Huk Rebellion: A Study of Peasant Revolt in the Philippines* (Berkeley and Los Angeles: University of California Press, 1977), pp. 40–41.

and rice peasants, they do indicate the overall trend in areas where sugar grew. Unrest in sugarlandia involved labor strikes against planters and centrals, burning of cane fields, rustling or ill treatment of cattle, and assault and murder. The background of radicalism among tenants in central Luzon meant that violence there commenced earlier and achieved a higher intensity than in Negros.[31]

Since the 1920s protest in rural Pampanga and southern Tarlac had been confined mainly to rice farmers, and rice strikes persisted unabated until the outbreak of war. Labor unions continued to operate as well, and in 1935 drivers and conductors of Pambusco, central Luzon's big transportation firm, carried out an unsuccessful strike for higher wages. An even larger strike, guided by Pedro Abad Santos and led by younger activists such as Luis Taruc, took place in 1938 at the government-owned Mount Arayat stone quarry; it succeeded in tying up the local courts for months.[32]

Within this climate of radicalism sugar tenants gradually moved toward more forceful protest. In early 1935 the government averted a major crisis when it intervened in a dispute between tenants and landlords over benefit payments from the processing tax. These payments from the American government, designed to ease the short export of the 1934–35 milling season, essentially accomplished that purpose. In Pampanga, however, many landholders attempted to keep all the money for themselves or give their tenants only a partial payment. Casamac, through their Socialist leaders, complained to authorities and threatened violence if they did not get their proper share. Public meetings and the sporadic burning of cane fields in Mabalacat, Santa Rita, and Angeles accompanied their formal protests, and even as those became more vehement, tenants and workers from other regions, including Negros, joined the movement for more equity. Through the intervention of Assembly Speaker Quintin Paredes, Labor Secretary Ramon Torres, and above all, Acting Governor-general Joseph Ralston Hayden, the planters reluctantly agreed to divide the proceeds. Enough money reached the casamac to dissipate tensions, but by no means did all farmhands receive a share. As late as 1941 the courts rendered verdicts on benefit payments, and they remained a source of labor complaint throughout the prewar era.[33]

Either as a consequence of the dispute over benefit payments or simply because of falling exports, more landlords in central Luzon and Negros started to shy away from traditional tenant and leasehold arrangements. The overall decline in the number of planters attests to this shift, and in Pampanga it stimulated greater protest. The old sugar casamac contract involved dividing the end product, centrifugal sugar or the cash from sales thereof, on a percentage basis. In the late 1930s landowners moved from this system of sharing toward paying their tenants money for the amount of cane delivered. With this piecework, casamac lost the sensation that they produced sugar for the market. The extent of this trend proves difficult to document, but by 1938 the *Tribune* reported casamac complaints, voiced by Socialist leaders, that they received only P1.50 to P1.70 per ton of cane and that if the wages did not rise, they preferred to return to the old samacan system. Possession of quotas, however, now provided the best income security, and hacenderos throughout sugarlandia tended to hoard them.

Planters employed other methods to reduce their tenants' portions of milled sugar. They gave illiterate casamac inaccurate mill reports and refused to share with them the bonuses paid by centrals for higher-purity sugar. Some of the bigger plantation operators switched to a straight wage system, thus removing the casamac further from any claim to the end product. Tenants and former tenants thus found themselves more dependent on seasonal employment and suffered a loss of income. An extensive study of wages in the sugar industry conducted in 1939 came to the following conclusions:

> 1. The scale of wages is much too low, being only one-half that set by law. These wages, based on time-work at some time and upon piece-work at another whenever the change is advantageous to the planter-employer, are further reduced in consequence thereof.
>
> Wages have been found to be more or less uniform although it has come to the knowledge of the investigator that some planters who are ready to conform with the minimum wage act are reluctant to do so because "the other planters are not willing to follow." . . .
>
> 2. Work is unsteady and, in the purely sugar-producing regions, where the farm worker finds very little or no opportunity to earn additional income, he is practically idle about four months of the year.

> 3. Working hours are long and prejudicial to the health of the worker. . . .
>
> 4. Lodging is practically the only convenience provided free to the laborer and his family by the plantation. . . .
>
> 5. The income of the entire family, in the strict sense of the word, amounts to P189.93 a year. . . .
>
> 6. The family spends almost the entire income for food and clothing of the lowest quality and quantity.[34]

Because of the growth in population, casamac could do little but compete for fewer, more onerous contracts. The Department of Labor survey in 1936 estimated 43,865 unemployed hands dwelt in Pampanga. Governor-general Frank Murphy as early as October 1934 expressed concern over unemployment in sugarlandia occasioned by the new limitations, but not until 1937 did the press regularly report on the problem.[35]

The same 1936 Department of Labor survey recommended that one way to alleviate unemployment and underemployment in farming areas was to open public lands to settlement, but for neither casamac nor plantation hands did resettlement provide a viable outlet. Capampangan always showed a reluctance to leave their close communities, save to move to nearby regions such as southern Tarlac, areas quite settled by the 1930s. Neither migrant work in Hawaii nor movement to distant, more hostile Philippine frontiers like Mindanao attracted casamac, who preferred to stay and contest for tenancies at home. Some Negrenses opted to move to less inhabited portions of their home province. The edges of northeastern Negros, the Canlaon Plateau in the island's central portion, and the Tablas Plateau in southern Cauayan as well as portions of neighboring Mindanao welcomed Negrense pioneers, but government red tape, rampant land grabbing, dangerous environments, and difficulty in obtaining a stake discouraged all but a few thousand settlers from homesteading. Most preferred to cling, when possible, to their traditional employment at diminished wages.[36]

Both in central Luzon and in Negros Occidental, among casamac, duma'an, sacadas, and central workers, the problem of survival became increasingly acute. To add to their misery, in those prewar years a series of natural disasters, including floods, typhoons, and in 1940 drought, afflicted the archipelago, leading several times to inflated rice prices. Sugar families thus faced hunger and malnutrition on a greater scale than usual at this time.[37]

In mid-1937 violence escalated in Pampanga's sugar areas, especially in the western towns, and landlords felt sufficiently threatened to form a protective association in March of that year. What began as tenant demonstrations and formal protests directed to Labor Secretary Torres became theft of sacks of sugar from landlord bodegas. In July casamac on the Toledo estate in Floridablanca struck for a 50 centavo raise, to P2 per ton, for cane delivered to Pasumil. The action spread from there to the nearby Toda properties and to the lands of Martin Gonzales in Lubao and by early 1938 reached well into Lubao and Guagua. Strikes subsequently expanded throughout northern Pampanga, to Arayat, Angeles, Mabalacat, and Magalang and up as far as Concepcion, Tarlac.

By now protests included the rampant burning of cane fields, which caused hacenderos significant financial losses. At harvest time planters frequently fired standing cane to remove the undergrowth and vermin; however, once the burning took place the cane immediately commenced losing sucrose content and had to be cut and ground quickly. When strikers set fields ablaze too early, the cane did not achieve its maximum sucrose content and lost additional value as it wasted in the fields awaiting harvesting and milling. Burning their cane was an easy way to intimidate landowners.[38]

Despite worsening economic conditions, Negros remained mostly calm during 1937 and 1938. More combined plantation operations and steeper costs of leaseholds translated into a tighter squeeze upon duma'an, whose wages declined as they faced greater job competition. Hacenderos at this time frequently employed pakyadors to do piecework. Investigators also noted the heavier use of the cantina system whereby duma'an and other workers had to pay higher prices for staples at plantation-operated stores. Through 1937 and 1938, however, even as central Luzon exploded and living conditions worsened, Negros remained quiet. The Federacion Obrera of Jose Nava conducted successful strikes at three small centrals in Kabankalan; all were essentially settled by arbitration; otherwise, little happened in the way of labor confrontation. Negrenses simply watched while Capampangan carried on the struggle during those middle years.[39]

Unrest in sugarlandia reached its prewar peak during 1939, 1940, and 1941. Sugar prices continued their slide and bottomed out at P4.60 on the Manila market in June 1941, a level at which few in the industry could profit. Peasants and workers most felt the effects of this drop and found their economic plight ever more desperate. The violence and frequency of their strikes produced a conservative backlash as landlords and government officials tried to suppress their protests.

Diverse and widespread strikes blanketed Pampanga as 1939 began. The killing of a migrant worker in Magalang on January 12 was just one of a growing number of hostile incidents between casamac and transient laborers. Meanwhile, cane and cane fields burned on various haciendas in

Magalang and San Fernando. The next day fifteen thousand sugar and rice tenants demanded the removal from the province of two unsympathetic judges. Shortly thereafter mill workers at Mount Arayat Central and Pasumil went on strike, and most corners of Pampanga harbored some form of protest as the province became the center of agrarian unrest in the archipelago. The protests of sugar workers overlapped with the vigorous strike actions of rice tenants on the Bahay Pare Estate of Roman Santos in Candaba. Provincial jails filled, even though officials sought to halt the spreading violence. In an attempt at coordinated action, Jose Nava launched a strike at Lopez Sugar Central in Negros, one his FOF lost to the management and its conservative Philippine Labor Union headed by Esteban Vasquez.[40]

In February President Quezon traveled to Pampanga to plead for restraint and to beg for time to allow the government to solve the various problems of the sugar industry. His request went unheeded. Casto Alejandrino won a court arbitration for workers at Mount Arayat Central in March, but the strike at Pasumil went on and became even more hostile. Murder, field burnings, and sabotage lasted throughout 1939, and at year's end newspapers reported sporadic cane fires in Negros for the first time.[41]

In mid-1939 Pampanga governor Sotero Baluyut, with the backing of politicians like Assemblyman Fausto Gonzalez Sioco and leading landlords, formed the Cawal ning Capayapan (Knights of Peace), an organization of nonradical peasants, field guards, and toughs, to intimidate strikers. In their blue and white uniforms, Cawals confronted and fought with dissidents in exchange for the tenancies of ousted casamac, crop bonuses, and public works jobs. Protests by Socialists about the Cawals failed to make the government curb the latter's activities, and battles proliferated between strikers and strikebreakers in the fields and factories as well as in the streets of the towns. Efforts by constabulary officers like Captain Olivas (subsequently murdered by the Timbols) failed to quell the violence.

The Cawals were created because of the frustration planters felt with government efforts to maintain order. Citizens complained that the local town police were too old, inefficient, and corrupt. The provincial and insular forces of law and order also could do little to protect sugarmen. As early as 1935 the commonwealth had started antiriot training at Fort Stotsenburg and stored antiriot gear there, and in 1938 authorities moved to increase the Pampanga state police force. However, that unit remained understaffed for want of funds. The Philippine Constabulary lacked the local knowledge to prevent the scattered hostilities that menaced sugarlandia. Cawals, on the other hand, received adequate compensation from private funds, even though they acted at the behest of Baluyut and town officials. Planters also took to defending their property themselves, and several—like Carmelino Timbol—shot dissatisfied tenants. Luis Taruc recalled going in the late 1930s to the edge of the Timbol property and confronting those armed planters and their retainers. Efforts at mediation between landowners and dissidents failed to produce more than temporary truces.[42]

By the beginning of 1940 a tentative agreement between tenants and landlords to divide crops sixty-five–thirty-five in favor of the former had largely fallen through, and the demonstrations, murder, and arson continued. A protracted six months' strike at Pasudeco produced an eventual victory for the strikers, who benefited from Socialist help. In Negros, especially the southern portions, workers carried on a similar set of actions, though on a lesser scale. Workers struck the haciendas of Secretary Jose Yulo there, as well as his large plantation in Floridablanca, Pampanga—where workers even threatened the plantation of the army chief, Major General Basilio Valdes. The violence continued through 1941, and discouraged planters in central Luzon talked of abandoning sugar farming. For the first time, too, credit began to dry up as worried lenders became reluctant to advance cash in such an unstable political climate. On the eve of the Japanese invasion, sugarlandia experienced poverty and confrontation on an alarming scale, with little hope of relief.[43]

The persistent, systematic protests in Pampanga contrasted sharply with the sporadic violence in Negros, and the reasons for the disparity of response lie in structural and historical differences between the two communities. Both areas suffered deeply because of diminished harvests and falling sugar prices, made worse in Negros because of that region's almost exclusive dependence on cane. Capampangan more readily changed crops than did Negrenses, although a small number of the latter, with the assistance of their hacenderos, did start to plant rice in the late 1930s. Nevertheless, duma'an probably experienced greater privation than did the casamac of Pampanga, and the hunger and poverty of those years appeared as intense as they are at present. Even so, duma'an, save for few in the southern end of the sugar region, hardly participated in the unrest of that era.

At least four factors contributed to the relative inaction of Negros farmhands. One was the isolation of workers on plantations, which made organized protest difficult and planter repression easy. In Pampanga, in contrast, casamac still resided in barrios where they freely communicated with one another. Intermarriage and kinship ties forged over generations facilitated joint endeavors unlikely in Negros. Casamac interviewed in 1970 provided evidence of community pressure at work to encourage participation in the protest movements. Fifty of them admitted to belonging to one or more of the radical organizations, chiefly the Socialists. Of that group, twenty-seven offered positive reasons for joining, mainly that they wanted to confront landlord cheating and that concerted action helped. Another sixteen claimed that they became Socialists because everyone else did and they felt obliged to enroll.

Second, planters could always replace disgruntled duma'an from the large pool of docile migrants from neighboring islands. Sacadas who came to Negros in the late 1930s did so to find relief from the grinding poverty of their home areas and gladly worked for the 20 to 50 pesos they received during the Negros harvest season. Their mere presence served to remind regular Negrense plantation laborers of the tenuousness of their own positions. In Pampanga landlords had difficulty employing such replacements, for the labor system depended on the highly skilled casamac to manage field preparation, planting, and weeding. Bringing in nonlocal cane cutters threatened the whole agricultural cycle. Outside workers could not readily integrate into tightly knit Pampangan rural communities, and they could be more readily identified and intimidated by casamac than by the duma'an of Negros.[44]

Third, its mixed rice- and sugar-growing communities seem to have made Pampanga more fertile ground for protest than Negros. Unrest originated among the subsistence-based rice farmers of central Luzon. The independent peasant possessed more freedom of action than did sugar workers who relied on salary and planter largesse for their well-being. Curiously, the interviews with Negrenses in 1970 indicate that the only concerted action came from a small group of rice tenants in the Binalbagan-Isabela area who had formerly been employed on sugar plantations. In the late 1930s they formed a federation of rice agsadors and successfully struck for a higher harvest share.[45]

Finally, farmhands on Negros lacked the kind of leadership tenants enjoyed in Pampanga. Local organizations like Kusug Sang Imol and Mainawa-on had long since become discredited or isolated from the Negrense work force. Neither Nava, a labor boss from Iloilo, nor conservative Bacolod newspaperman Esteban Vazquez nor Domingo Ponce of the Legionarios del Trabajo owned the ability, access, or drive to direct duma'an in major protest. Lack of a radical tradition undoubtedly contributed to this paucity of committed leadership. In contrast, the Socialist party of the Philippines (SPP), founded in 1932 by Pedro Abad Santos, met the needs of disaffected casamac. It advised tenants in their hostile struggles with landlords, provided legal defense for casamac in their court actions, organized strikes and peaceful demonstrations, lobbied for constructive insular legislation, and sought and used local political office on behalf of peasant needs and demands. The SPP thus became the strongest voice of peasant protest in central Luzon, for no other party, faction, or spokesperson so completely or successfully fought for and represented the sugar and rice casamac of the area.[46]

Pampanga had traditionally served as a base for dissidents who in some manner or other spoke for or symbolized the plight of the province's poor. By 1935, however, the Socialists monopolized that role. The occasional bandit found refuge on the slopes of Mount Arayat, and followers of messianic leaders dwelt in the province's lowlands; but casamac now overwhelmingly supported more secular leaders with a clear economic and political agenda. For various reasons other potential claimants to peasant allegiance, including the Katipunan Mipanampun, the Tanggulan, the Sakdals, and the Union Obrera (at Tarlac Central) all failed to secure extensive tenant followings.[47] Even other leftist groups, including the Communists, failed to take command of unrest in Pampanga's sugarlandia.

The Communist party of the Philippines (CPP) gained little following in Capampangan-speaking portions of central Luzon for several reasons. The party originated out of Manila's labor movement and appealed foremost to a Tagalog-speaking clientele. Its leaders, including the Lavas, Crisanto Evangelista, and Guillermo Capadocia, operated best in a more urban, industrial, labor-oriented setting and closely followed the Comintern line in its activities and stand on issues. For example, the CPP brief to the Joint Preparatory Committee on Philippine Affairs stressed three demands:

> 1. That immediate, complete and absolute independence of the Philippines be recognized, enabling thereby the Filipino people to constitute themselves into a democratic republic;
>
> 2. That complete severance of the present trade relationship between the United States and the Philippines be effected immediately, and in lieu thereof a new trade relationship based on equality recognized between friendly independent states be established; and
>
> 3. The complete withdrawal from the Philippines of all American armed forces together with military advisers be immediately effected.[48]

While Socialist leaders might agree with part of this platform, they concerned themselves far more with tenant-landlord issues and conducting strikes in central Luzon. The American Communist party sought to complete a merger between the CPP and SPP to improve the effectiveness of both groups, but the effort failed.

Following a series of meetings in late 1938 among CPP spokesman Crisanto Evangelista, U.S. Communist party representative Sol Auerbach, and Pedro Abad Santos, the two Philippine parties united to form the

Communist party of the Philippines with Evangelista as chairman and Abad Santos as vice-chairman. However, in Pampanga members continued to think of and refer to themselves as Socialists and drew their cadre from locals like Taruc, Casto Alejandrino, poet Lino Dizon, and Silvestre Liwanag. The two factions operated in separate orbits, each responding to its own leadership, addressing different agendas, having distinct constituencies, and professing alternate ideologies. Historian and former CPP member Alfredo Saulo noted:

> It is a fact that the CPP and SPP had certain differences which were not merely due to personal animosities and petty sectarianism among their middle rank cadres, as claimed by Jose Lava in his history of the CPP. These differences involved organizational problems, and even ideology, as evidenced by the fact that the socialists were generally lukewarm toward the communists because they believed the latter were "godless." The socialists also charged the communists with being "Moscow agents" and "not militant enough."
>
> The communists, on the other hand, accused the socialists of being anarchistic, too lazy to read Marxist literature, and prone to violence. Abad Santos, they added, often made press statements that deviated from the established political line of the CPP.[49]

Local Socialist cadre interacted with their Communist counterparts, figures like Juan Feleo in nearby Nueva Ecija; however, among the upper ranks, the two factions lived in uneasy partnership during the prewar years, and some of those personal antagonisms have persisted until today.[50]

Luis Taruc described Socialist organizing efforts in rural Pampanga as a learning experience. Cadre had to master the strategies of effective strikes, such as calling together tenants with a *tambuli* or carabao horn to picket fields. The leadership also had to discover how to enroll members in AMT, the mass action wing of the party. In addition, the party needed to enlist peasant wives and children to form auxiliaries to support strikers. Taruc admitted that he and others acquired skills in these matters by talking, working, and living with casamac. The knowledge gained, coupled with the skills mastered by actually participating in protests, the cadre passed on to a new generation of students at the Mass School of the Socialist party, in session during the commonwealth years.[51] Thus the Socialist leadership gradually strengthened its bonds with barrio folk and turned communal loyalty into concerted action.

The party also pursued formal political office as well. In 1937 Socialists Vivencio Cuyugan and Rufino Canda won mayoralties in San Fernando and

Mexico respectively, and party members captured majorities on the councils in both towns. Four years later they took eight mayoralties: Cuyugan in San Fernando, Casto Alejandrino in Arayat, Benigno Layug in Floridablanca, Francisco Sampang in Mexico, Agapito del Rosario (Abad Santos's nephew) in Angeles, Virgilio Ocampo in Mabalacat, Eliseo Galang in Candaba, and Patricio Yabut in San Simon. As a measure of the party's growing power and popularity, consider the race for provincial governor. Abad Santos received only 6,000 votes for governor in 1934; three years later he garnered 16,000, and in 1940 he won nearly 37,000. In that latter year he lost to Sotero Baluyut by just 6,000 votes.

Although the elected mayors did not come from peasant backgrounds—most were, like Cuyugan and Alejandrino, smaller landholders—they held a commitment to the party's ideals and outlook and used their offices on behalf of the casamac. For instance, Cuyugan strove to enfranchise more poor voters, and Agapito del Rosario worked to increase government credit to tenant farmers. Sampang in Mexico and Ocampo in Mabalacat suspended unsympathetic chiefs of police in their towns, and for the town fiesta in San Fernando in May 1941, Cuyugan appointed Luis Taruc head of the committee on programs and publicity!

Perhaps the most effective of the new Socialist mayors was Benigno Layug in Floridablanca. An Abad Santos lieutenant, Layug organized strikes among sugar tenants in late 1939 and several months afterward headed a movement to liquidate some one thousand outstanding casamac-planter accounts at Pasumil. Later he generated two thousand local signatures for a provincewide petition (initiated by Mayor Vivencio Cuyugan) requesting Quezon to disband the Cawals. He subsequently led a march of starving, jobless tenant families, hoping to have them reinstated on land from which they had been ejected. Selected as candidate for mayor in October 1940, Layug triumphed and entered office with a Socialist town council two months later. Among his first acts, he canceled an appropriation to expand the town hall and instead used the money to construct a dam. Through his intervention Pasumil agreed to hire only Capampangan during the 1941–42 season. He might have accomplished much more, but the Japanese occupation soon intervened. Despite efforts by conventional governors Angeles David and Baluyut, by late 1941 Pampanga had moved a considerable distance down the road toward a new political orientation.[52]

The overall direction of Socialist strategy came from Pedro Abad Santos, who did for his party what his contemporary Ho Chi Minh was doing for the Indochinese Communist party in northern Tonkin. Despite his advanced age (sixty-four in 1940) and physical frailty, Abad Santos, successor in a long line of leaders of peasants in central Luzon, worked energetically for the cause of the casamac. He served as party chief and daily discussed with tenants and cadre immediate actions and long-term plans. He determined when and where strikes should take place, how they should proceed, and when they should end. He also defended casamac in numerous court cases. As well, he served as the party's main spokesman, gave numerous speeches, and issued countless public statements and press comments forwarding the peasant viewpoint and challenging opposing arguments. Cadre and casamac universally acknowledged him, then and later, as the party's guiding light. To his small office in the family compound in San Fernando came foreign writers and Manila reporters, along with provincial and insular politicians—including, on occasion, Quezon—to discover the perspective of the archipelago's most influential, powerful, and articulate leftist figure.

One of the most original, incisive, and independent Filipino thinkers of his age, Abad Santos tailored his program to the needs of his constituents rather than to a single ideology, refusing to concern himself with Comintern orthodoxy. Against Communist dictum, he considered all members of AMT as party members. He also felt that the Philippines needed to maintain economic, political, and cultural ties with the United States, although that relationship would require more equity and mutuality of benefit than in the past. He understood that the nation's health depended on a more equitable sharing of wealth between rich and poor and thought a socialist model most aptly met that goal. However, Abad Santos explored many different courses in attempting to reach that end and took innovative actions.[53]

By entering the insular political arena, Abad Santos sought to advance tenant causes through traditional, nonviolent channels and to attract small businessmen and professionals to his socialist cause. In this endeavor, however, he achieved only mixed results. Despite Socialist victories in municipal contests, Abad Santos gained little, and may have lost some, prestige for himself and the party by joining the Popular Front in 1937. This latter party contained such traditional politicians as Honorio Ventura, Jose Alejandrino, Fausto Gonzalez Sioco, Emilio Aguinaldo, and Juan Sumulong, who united only in opposition to Manuel Quezon and in favor of landlord interests. The alliance produced only rancor and no electoral victories.[54]

Abad Santos and the Socialists even courted Quezon, because they viewed him as more liberal than other politicians. The commonwealth president realized, like Abad Santos, that his country's continued internal peace and order depended on a narrowing of the economic gap between rich and poor; to obtain that end, Quezon announced a program he called "social justice." While Abad Santos privately expressed doubts about Quezon's intentions to carry out such a program, publicly he backed the president. In 1935 the Socialist party refused to support Quezon's presidential opponent, Aguinaldo, and Quezon carried Pampanga with 65 percent of the vote. In subsequent years, whenever it seemed that Quezon might help the casamac, the party praised him; however, when he favored landlords, as when he supported unpopular sugar corporation lawyer Jose Yulo for the National Assembly, they criticized him. By mid-1940, however, as Quezon prepared to run for a second term, the disappointed Socialists refused to endorse him, and the breach seems to have become permanent.[55]

Quezon's commitment to social justice was at best equivocal. At least three in-depth studies—one by the Department of Labor (1936), another by the National Sugar Board (1939), and a third by the Institute of Pacific Relations (1939)—provided ample evidence of the harsh working conditions and low wages in the archipelago in general and in sugarlandia in particular. Even so, labor legislation concerning, for instance, the eight-hour workday, and tenancy laws like the Sugar Tenancy Act (Act No. 4113) proved either weak or unenforceable. The Department of Labor Report described the latter law as "absolutely inadequate" because it did not "define the status of the tenant when he becomes a tenant, nor the status of the landowner, nor his relation with the tenant. Compulsory use of written contract between the landowner and the tenant should also be highly considered."[56] Social justice provided a nice shibboleth for, and deflected criticism away from, the president, but it did not provide significant aid for the poor.

Quezon's program could not work for several reasons. First, influential agricultural members in the National Assembly did not support it. While Quezon could control the nominations and appointments of individuals and could perpetuate himself in office, he did not possess the power to coerce representatives of the sugar bloc on social legislation. Gopinath has written the following about the fate of portions of the social justice program:

> The laws, enacted to protect the interests of the farmhands, were also largely self defeating. . . . Act 4050, which governed the relationship between tenants and landlords in the rice regions, enumerated in clear terms the obligations of both tenant and landlord in the contract of labor. However, Section 29 of this act created a loophole for clever landowners. It provided that that law would take effect only in a municipality where the local council passed a resolution making it applicable in that municipality. Only then would the chief executive be able to promulgate its application in that municipality. The effect of this provision in practice rendered the law ineffective because the members of the municipal councils were themselves landlords or political proteges of landlords. In these circumstances, the law appeared to be dysfunctional.[57]

In similar ways landlords through their legislators vitiated other social justice measures.

Second, Quezon himself did not believe that government should stimulate social revolution but that it should only supply equal justice to all sides to prevent disorder. Hence, he promoted no law that helped the poor at the expense of the rich. Quezon undertook labor surveys, used the executive branch and the courts to try to arbitrate disputes between laborers and management and tenants and landowners, and sanctioned some nonviolent public demonstrations. He encouraged planters to follow the government example of paying higher salaries and offering better working conditions, as he did at the state-owned Binalbagan Central and Malabon Sugar Refinery. Finally, he reduced interest rates at PNB so that hacenderos could give better wages to their workers.[58]

But Quezon would not pass effective legislation on behalf of farmhands. In vetoing one such measure Quezon wrote:

> Act No. 4054 of the Philippine Legislature was intended to prevent the tenants from being exploited by the landowners through certain old practices . . . but it has never been the intention of the legislature in enacting these laws to deprive the landowner of his right of ownership which includes his right to cultivate the land and plant it with such crop as he may think necessary or convenient or profitable, or use the land for other purposes.

Further on Quezon added:

> I have been informed that some communist leaders and leaders of the so-called Socialist Party, which is nothing more or less than the Communist Party under another name, have been misleading the tenants into the belief that Commonwealth Act No. 608 was enacted for the purpose of permitting them to keep the land permanently so that they may cultivate it as they please, and that the owner of the land has lost his right to say what should be done with the land. . . . These preachings by communist leaders and others of their kind have been represented to the people as part of the social program of the government.

However, Quezon went on to quote Justice Jose Laurel by way of contradicting the communists.

> The promotion of social justice, however, is to be achieved not through a mistaken sympathy for any given group. . . . Social justice means the promotion of the welfare of all the people, the adoption by the government of measures calculated to in-

> sure economic stability of the component elements of society, through the maintenance of a proper economic and social equilibrium in the interrelations of the members of the community.[59]

In the end Quezon sent the Philippine Constabulary to Pampanga to enforce law and order, which concerned him far more than did social justice.

Third, Quezon did not support serious social change because he identified primarily with planter and miller interests. In addition to shares in Calamba Sugar Company, he owned several agricultural properties and fishponds in Pampanga, including a two hundred–hectare sugar estate in Arayat. There he and his wife Aurora enjoyed acting the role of benefactors to the local community and traditional patrons to their tenants. There too on February 16, 1941, at a ceremony inaugurating the Mount Arayat Hospital, Mrs. Quezon endured taunts by Mayor Casto Alejandrino. Despite attempts by the Quezons to portray themselves as model landlords, they did not escape the derision of the Socialists.[60]

Quezon and his associates and cabinet secretaries shared similar attitudes toward social justice and radicalism. Jose Laurel, Supreme Court judge and later Philippine president, provided Quezon with numerous anticommunist legal opinions. And when it briefly appeared that Quezon might not be allowed legally to run for a second term as president, he designated as his successor either Secretary of Justice Jose Yulo or Secretary of Interior Rafael Alunan. Even though his three successive appointees for secretary of labor were expected to arbitrate labor disputes, all revealed a bias against the disaffected poor. The first, Ramon Torres, came from the ranks of Negros Occidental planter politicians; the second, Jose Avelino, spoke openly against communism; and the third, Leon Guinto, suggested to his boss that the way to check communism in the Philippines was to call the social justice program "Quezonian communism" and to shift excess agricultural population to the remaining frontiers. Quezon chose in 1941 as his secretary of public works his chief political operative in Pampanga, former senator and governor Sotero Baluyut, bête noire of the Pampangan casamac dissidents.[61]

Quezon distrusted the poor and only reluctantly moved to acquire with government funds private estates like Bahay Pare and Buenavista for redistribution to peasants, lest it seem like a dole to the indolent. He shared the common belief of landowners, townsfolk, and millers that better markets and slight adjustments in the allocation of wealth within the sugar industry would solve the problems of poverty and unrest. He also believed with them that no need existed for strikes, especially politically motivated ones, because he thought such actions invariably led to illegal violence, as in Pampanga. Quezon believed that his social justice program, given time and adequate persuasion, would produce equity.[62]

While it may be true, as McCoy and Gopinath have argued, that Manuel Quezon became absolute master of the political process in the Philippines, by 1941 he may have lost to Pedro Abad Santos a more strategic battle for himself and subsequent presidents: the struggle for the "hearts and minds" of the nation's poor.[63] Despite his ofttimes expressed sympathy for workers and peasants, Quezon did little to help them. Among the problems of the commonwealth, including national defense, economic negotiations with the United States, governmental appointments, and maintaining control of the political apparatus, social justice seems to have occupied him little. In contrast, the Socialists in central Luzon at least had won some concessions on behalf of the poor and had earned a reputation for providing assistance when asked to do so. As Abad Santos said:

> We do not believe in social justice. . . . We don't invoke social justice; we believe that if the masses have to be saved it is by their own efforts; to organize, to unite, and their only weapon is—Strike. We believe that 10 years of Quezon's social justice preaching would not obtain for the workers what a single good strike will accomplish for them.[64]

The commonwealth era thus stands as an extremely crucial time in Philippine history, for during those years was established a key political and ideological dichotomy that has persisted to the present. Manuel Quezon created the model for presidential behavior that has guided all his successors. By remaining aloof from the serious demands of peasants and workers and relying on the support of landlord and corporate interests like the sugar bloc, he left the way open for leftist groups to court the poor and to learn how to organize among them. To these groups, then, to Abad Santos and his heirs in their various manifestations down to the current New People's Army, has gone the opportunity to become spokespersons for the archipelago's poor farmers. They have studied the needs of the country's majority and translated those needs into programs and courses of action. Members of leftist movements have made strategic errors and faced numerous setbacks in their clashes with the national government; however, the movement itself has never relinquished its lead in the struggle for the allegiance of the countryside.

Perhaps the most dramatic set of events that illustrate the dichotomy between a leftist group and the government took place in Lubao, at Hacienda Prado, an estate of 1,060 hectares with a quota of 28,000 piculs. The property belonged to Martin Gonzales, a successful hacendero whose tenants conducted a losing strike against him over the distribution of the processing tax. Upon his death, his heirs in 1937 leased the sugarlands, at P60,000 a year for three years, to Andres Goseco, whose troubles with 160 or so tenants began when he altered the terms of their leaseholds from the traditional crop sharing to the per ton basis for cut cane. The matter went before the Court of Industrial Relations, where Pedro Abad Santos defended the casamac. He won when Goseco agreed to abide by the old contract terms and the tenants were readmitted to their leaseholds. In January 1938 army intervention prevented a new clash after Goseco sought to employ Ilocano migrants in place of angry tenants who refused to cut cane for low wages. By early February fields on the estate had been fired five times, while tenants through their spokesman Abad Santos demanded higher pay or, preferably, a reversion to the traditional samacan contract. Again, too, they raised the issue of sharing the proceeds of the processing tax.

Over the next two years Goseco and the tenants of Prado remained in constant conflict, and the burnings went on unabated. Violence proliferated, and Goseco carried a gun to protect himself; some local Socialist leaders turned up dead. Casamac complaints at this time included Goseco's failure to advance money at the beginning of the planting/milling season, employment of imported cane cutters from Batangas Province, unfair distribution of the returns on 24,000 piculs of sugar, too low wages per ton for cane cut, and Goseco's tardy liquidation of his traditional tenants' annual sugar accounts. By the beginning of the 1940–41 milling season Goseco gave up his leasehold, driven out by the constant burning of his cane fields.

At this time the Prado casamac proposed to the owners through councillor-elect Roman Belleza that they rent the estate. The tenants would jointly manage the hacienda and divide among the owners, Pasumil, and themselves profits from the sale of the finished sugar. In short, they were creating a form of agricultural cooperative for the production and marketing of sugar. Cooperatives were scarcely a new idea in Pampanga—witness the Arayat Cooperative Marketing Association and the multiple ownership of Pasudeco. A joint government/private endeavor, the Floridablanca Farmers Financing Agency, a savings and loan institution for landlords and tenants, had recently started operation. The traditional communal ties among the Capampangan and the ability of their leaders made cooperatives work in Pampanga.

In December 1940 the Prado casamac, through their representative, Mayor Agapito del Rosario of Angeles, sought loans from PNB to allow them to manage the estate. The owners appeared willing to consider such an arrangement, because they feared losing the milling season and their quota if they did not. PNB, however, refused to provide the guarantee funds, and the owners, anticipating losses and poor performance on the part of the tenants, announced their intention of evicting the casamac and turning their leaseholds over to the Cawals. Tensions rose until Pedro Abad Santo stepped in and worked out a settlement whereby the tenants would act as managers, the owners would provide crop loans, and Pasumil would hold 20 percent of the milled sugar as a performance bond. By February 7, 1941, all parties had agreed to the contract.

Until the outbreak of the Pacific War the Prado scheme was so successful it became a model for other tenants, who sought to adopt it at their haciendas. However, local planters objected, no doubt realizing that such a system would change the socioeconomic face of agriculture as they knew it. Prado stood as the single most successful effort in the Socialist struggle to change conditions in sugarlandia. It flourished, despite government indifference and hacendero opposition, because Capampangan trusted one another. Never could such an arrangement have prospered among the disorganized, apathetic farm workers of Negros.[65]

Against the background of troubles in sugarlandia, the Philippine Commonwealth faced the increasing threat of Japanese invasion. As early as 1936 sugarmen started pledging funds to aid the government's underfinanced defense effort. However, even as late as 1940, when the first training began for units of the Seventh Military District of Negros and Bacolod had its first practice blackouts, the island demonstrated minimal preparedness for the coming onslaught. In Pampanga Pedro Abad Santos commented that Filipino peasants had little stake in the impending struggle and that they needed something for which to fight.

The blow came earlier than expected, in early December 1941. As the Basque planter Higinio de Uriarte, descendant of early nineteenth-century immigrants, abandoned his hacienda in La Carlota to join the guerrillas, the Socialists of Pampanga and Tarlac commenced their own preparations for war. Sugar casamac witnessed the infamous Bataan Death March, as the conquerers herded, abused, and executed defeated Filipino and American soldiers along the journey from Bataan to Capas, Tarlac.[66] Meanwhile, the Japanese took control of wharves laden with export sugar.

The final episode of the prewar history of the sugar industry involved Manuel Quezon, as he fled south from Corregidor to Australia. He lingered briefly in March 1942 in Bais, Negros Oriental, to conclude last-minute administrative business. There he spent frustrating hours communicating with officials in Negros Occidental and attempting to arrange payments to sugar central workers and sacadas who wished to return home at the end of the milling season. Planters and millers remained reluctant to pay those salaries without advances from PNB, and workers at Binalbagan Central were threatening to riot. Among his last actions Quezon ordered the manager at Binalbagan to obtain money from the bank and pay employees their salaries without bonuses. Despite the pending invasion of the island, Quezon commanded the Philippine Constabulary to proceed to the government-owned central to ensure that no riots occur.[67] For the next three years of Japanese occupation the sugar industry's serious problems of vanishing markets, increasing poverty, and labor unrest would remain on hold.

Epilogue

Across the sun-drenched square, the pale spinster
In her lily dress, Spanish veil and golden girdle
Traipses with a train of three tanned servant girls
Sweating in coarse clothes of heavy yellow

Jose Ma. Sison, *Prison and Beyond: Selected Poems, 1958–1983* (1984)

Three and a half years of Japanese occupation left the Philippine sugar industry in ruins. Almost all the archipelago's centrals became inoperable, either through wartime destruction or for want of spare parts. Elsewhere in Japan's new economic empire Java and Taiwan produced sugar in cheap abundance, and the military administration in the Philippines lacked the incentive and expertise to maintain insular production at prewar levels. Instead, the Japanese unsuccessfully sought to convert sugar fields to cotton and to manufacture molasses into alcohol for fuel. Sugar exports ceased, and local stocks eventually depleted to the point where the government had to introduce rationing. During the first postwar crop year of 1945–46, only five mills functioned, turning out just 11,000 tons of sugar.

Wartime disruptions dispersed Filipino sugar farmers, workers, and administrators, while American staff mostly languished in prison camps. In Pampanga and southern Tarlac, landlords fled to provincial towns or to Manila to weather the hard times and relinquished the countryside to peasants and to the newly formed guerrilla organization Hukbalahap (People's Anti-Japanese Army) with members drawn mainly from the ranks of the prewar AMT. The Huks, besides fighting the Japanese, provided local government, and in 1945 American troops returning to central Luzon found many municipal halls in Huk hands. In Negros some looting of haciendas and field burnings occurred at the beginning of the occupation, but eventually life settled down to a routine of surviving the hardships and scarcities created by war and ineffective Japanese governance. The majority of local planters waited out those harsh times in town centers, although a few stayed on their estates. Farmworkers temporarily planted corn and palay on sugar land, and returning hacenderos in 1945 faced a shortage of cane points when they went to put in their next crop.[1]

Despite the turmoil and damage to property, the industry's social order remained intact. Hacenderos and millers divided their allegiance between the old commonwealth government and the new occupation regime and thus assured themselves and their families of considerate treatment by the eventual winner. Those who resided near the plazas either cooperated with the Japanese in running the local government, passively acquiesced to their authority, or provided covert aid to the guerrilla opposition that held the rural areas. Among those who served the occupation were Negros governors Antonio Lizares and Vicente Gustilo, local director of the collaborationist Kalibapi political organization Oscar Ledesma, Bacolod mayor Alfredo Yulo, and president of the Federation of Planters' Associations Ildefonso Coscolluela. At the same time the Free Negros Government functioned in unoccupied territory, providing logistical support to civilians and military units and collecting intelligence for Allied forces. Governor Alfredo Montelibano headed the civilian branch, assisted by such deputies as Tranquilino Valderrama, Aurelio Locsin, Salvador Benedicto, and Miguel Gatuslao. Participants in his administration included propagandist Soledad Locsin and intelligence head Roberto Benedicto, a USAFFE (U.S. Army Forces in the Far East) officer who escaped Japanese confinement. When the war ended planters and millers resumed their traditional social roles.[2]

Members of sugar's top echelon likewise split their political loyalties. They, too, sought the survival of their class, as Nick Joaquin has suggested, by preventing any other group from assuming power during this period of instability. Under Japanese aegis Jose Yulo served as chief justice, Rafael Alunan as commissioner of agriculture and commerce, and Benigno Aquino successively as commissioner of interior, director general of the Kalibapi, and speaker of the assembly of the Second (Occupation) Republic. Meanwhile, Joaquin Elizalde continued to act as resident commissioner for the commonwealth government-in-exile in Washington. Some leading figures of the prewar sugar struggles did not outlast the occupation—an AMT strike force assassinated Pasudeco executive Jose Tapia in early 1942, and both Quezon and Pedro Abad Santos died of natural causes in 1944—but enough others, including Sotero Baluyut, survived to pick up their old roles once hostilities ceased.[3]

Post–World War II events in Philippine sugar history have seemed at times like little more than a replay of prewar scenarios. The major spark for post-1946 industry recovery came from a revised American trade policy that reversed the patterns of the Jones-Costigan and Tydings-McDuffie

Table 19. Post–World War II Philippine Sugar Industry Performance (metric tons)

Crop Year	*Number of Mills*	*Total Production*	*Total Export*	*Export to U.S.*	*U.S. Quota*
1945–46	5	11,715	—	—	—
1950–51	27	848,558	631,693	624,095	889,050
1955–56	25	1,105,449	934,071	873,583	889,050
1960–61	24	1,316,756	1,202,372	1,202,372	1,334,238
1965–66	26	1,401,980	1,054,729	1,054,729	1,091,334
1970–71	35	2,059,595	1,413,176	1,413,176	1,415,825
1975–76	38	2,924,567	1,466,200	961,100	none
1980–81	41	2,312,811	1,541,213	188,558[a]	none
1985–86	38	1,520,970	278,114	225,307[b]	200,000

Sources: *A Handbook of the Sugar and Other Industries in the Philippines, 1953* (Manila: Sugar News Press, 1953), p. 135; *Philippine Sugar Handbook, 1972 Edition* (Manila: Sugar News Press, 1972), pp. 66, 92–93; Yoshiko Nagano, "Philippine Sugar Industry in the Export-Oriented Economy—A Thorny Road to Modernization," paper submitted to the Third World Studies Program, University of the Philippines, August 10, 1978, p. 10; *Sugar News* 35 (1958): 89; Philippine Republic, Philippine Sugar Commission, *Philippine Sugar Commission Quarterly* 1 (October–December 1980): 9; Philippine Republic, Sugar Regulatory Administration, *Ten-Year Statistics on Philippine Sugar, CY 1980–81 to 1989–90* (Quezon City: Sugar Regulatory Administration, 1990), p. 1; *Asiaweek*, February 8, 1980, p. 49; Philippine Republic, National Economic and Development Authority, *Sugar Industry Study* (Manila: NEDA, 1985), pp. 210–11; letter from Yoshiko Nagano, Tokyo, to the author, April 16, 1989; International Sugar Organization, *Sugar Year Book, 1986* (London: International Sugar Organization, 1987), p. 187; Edgardo F. Yap, "The Philippine Sugarcane Industry Development (In Lieu of the Sugar Industry)," p. 3 (mimeo).

[a]Calendar year 1981.

[b]Calendar year 1986.

acts. Passed with the advice of High Commissioner Paul McNutt, PSA spokesman Harry Hawes, and Resident Commissioner Carlos P. Romulo, the Bell Trade Act of 1946 restored privileged Philippine access to the American market until 1954. Despite the protestations of some Filipino nationalists and a few Americans like former high commissioner Frances Sayre, the Philippines reverted to its old dependency on the American market. The price of this dependency was high, for the new nation had to offer economic and currency exchange concessions to the United States, including the stipulation that American entrepreneurs had the same access as their Filipino counterparts to the development of the archipelago's natural resources and to the operation of its public utilities—the notorious parity clause. However, the sugar industry benefited from the Bell Act, and, with further governmental and U.S. rehabilitation funds, revived.[4] Exports progressed first to, and then above, prewar levels (see table 19).

Other prewar economic patterns revived as well. The movement toward consolidation in the milling sector that began in the 1930s hastened after the war when only twenty-five of the prewar forty-six centrals were refurbished; furthermore, none of the smaller, less efficient factories went back into production. However, many of the same families and companies that controlled plants in the 1930s—the Elizaldes, Lopezes, Aranetas, Montillas, Roxases of Batangas, Ossorios, and Tabacalera among others—retained their domination following 1946. The trend toward Filipinization of milling also continued. Jose Yulo finally acquired Canlubang in 1948, the Lopezes bought Pasumil, the Cojuangcos purchased Central Azucarera de Tarlac, and the Ledesmas obtained San Carlos in 1957. Only Silay-Hawaiian, Central Bais (Negros Oriental), and Central San Pedro (Batangas) remained predominantly in foreign hands. PSA, rejuvenated under the leadership of Yulo, Manuel Elizalde, and Ernesto Escaler, reopened its Washington office to lobby for favored treatment for Philippine sugar.[5]

For planters and millers the issue of wartime collaboration faded rapidly in the face of renewed prosperity, and those who had supported the Japanese found themselves hastily and quietly rehabilitated. Jose Yulo, for example, went on to run, though unsuccessfully, for vice-president in 1953 and for president in 1957. By the early 1950s the leadership of the major planter organization, the National Federation of Sugar Planters, included individuals who had served both sides during the conflict: Oscar Ledesma as president, Alfredo Montelibano as first vice-president, and Ildefonso Coscolluela and Alfredo Yulo as members of the board. Candidates from the sugar bloc once more sought and filled offices at the provincial and national levels, and the industry and its future prosperity seemed assured.[6]

For workers in the industry old patterns resumed also, and duma'an and casamac again found themselves poverty-stricken. Neither field hands in Pampanga nor those in Negros possessed a champion with sufficient clout to improve their state against the opposition of hacenderos and centralistas. The Huk organization, reborn as the People's Liberation Army in the late 1940s and early 1950s, tragically failed to gain social and economic change in favor of the poor, primarily because of the government's armed suppression of the movement, with American military assistance. Taruc, Alejandrino, Liwanag, and others ended up serving long prison terms. The Huks may have lost, but ideas of equity and social justice, born in the barrios of central Luzon and forwarded by Abad Santos and his disciples, remained in the thoughts and aspirations of poor Capampangan. Old Huk cadre who survived the struggles and escaped imprisonment returned to their communities, where they kept alive the spirit of reform and economic justice.

The Huks never had any strong impact outside their central Luzon heartland, especially not in the sugarlands of the western Visayas. Huk leader Guillermo Capadocia was killed in his failed attempt to bring revolt to his destitute home province of Antique whence came so many of the Negros sacadas. Jose Nava joined the movement in 1949 but failed to convert the Panay peasants to the cause, and he died in prison in 1954.[7]

The duma'an of Negros remained nonmilitant and, as always, relied on planter largesse, even though the sugar elite and its political minions, in the absence of strong pressure, never volunteered meaningful social or economic concessions. The Philippine Congress passed the Sugar Act of 1952 in an effort to provide sugar workers with a share of the proceeds from the annual milling. However, lawyers for the putatively progressive Victorias Milling Company managed to tie up enforcement of the bill in the courts for many years, despite the efforts of a new union, the Federation of Free Farmers, and others to put it into effect.[8] Exploited Negros laborers thus realized no improvement in their working conditions, even as the industry experienced, beginning in 1956, its greatest prosperity since the 1920s.

The Laurel-Langley Act extended from 1956 to 1974 the privileged access of Philippine sugar to the American market; furthermore, the elimination of Cuba from that market in the early 1960s led to a gradual increase in the Philippine quota, from 889,000 metric tons in 1962 to a high of 1,451,402 in 1974.[9] Philippine hacenderos and millers responded to the improved commercial opportunities, as they had in the 1920s, by vastly expanding their production capacity. Cane hectarage rose from 206,672 in the 1959–60 crop season to 544,579 in 1975–76. Planters converted land devoted to other crops, including rice, to sugar, extended their cultivation onto hillsides, and even leveled mountaintops for additional fields. As a consequence of the farming of this more marginal land, overall productivity, already one of the lowest in the sugar world, fell some 14.9 percent, from 62.04 metric tons of cane per hectare to 52.8.[10]

Milling capacity expanded with the addition of nineteen centrals between 1964 and 1978. These new plants, built with Japanese, West German, British, and French equipment, were often financed through foreign loans guaranteed by the Philippine government. Many of these factories went up in nontraditional sugar areas, including the Bicol region of southern Luzon, the Cagayan Valley of northern Luzon, and Mindanao, and all required the conversion of surrounding agricultural property to cane fields.[11] The industry reached its production zenith during the 1975–76 season, when more land came under sugar cultivation and more sugar was produced than in any other year in the archipelago's history.

During this time evidence of sugar-induced prosperity appeared most visibly in the suburbs of Bacolod and Manila, where planters and millers resided in well-staffed, splendid dwellings, often with swimming pools and attractive gardens. New automobiles, foreign education for their children, and travel abroad continued as the sugarmen's favorite luxuries. A casual walk through downtown Bacolod at this time revealed that the city had spruced up its central plaza and that merchants in the local shops thrived on their commerce with hacenderos. In Pampanga the proliferation of housing subdivisions revealed improved economic conditions; however, much of the profit from sugar found its way into urban real estate in Metro Manila.[12]

In the late 1960s and early 1970s, even as hacenderos and millers enjoyed their improved lifestyle, writers rediscovered the plight of sugar workers, especially those in Negros. After a hiatus of some three decades, numerous articles and studies appeared exposing the deep poverty and malnutrition of those who labored in the cane fields. In many ways these works only updated the exposés of the 1930s. Motivated by the liberal ideas of Vatican II, contemporary Philippine Catholic clergy and laymen such as planter and prewar politician Jose Locsin played an important role in producing this new literature, which urged sugarmen to share more of the industry's profits with their laborers. The widening gap between rich and poor, no doubt, served as an immediate stimulus for these writers, as did such incidents as planters' brutal displacement of peasants from their marginal hillside farms in Cadiz.[13]

Ironically, the most highly publicized and cited essay, "The Sacadas of Sugarland," by Arsenio Jesena, S.J., concerned a group whose days were numbered. By the mid-1970s the labor force on Negros was becoming so large that planters did not have to seek harvest workers from other islands, since gangs of Negrenses now accomplished most of the cane cutting and loading formerly done by the visiting sacadas. Rapid population growth in the postwar years assured planters in Negros, as well as in Pampanga and southern Tarlac, of a more than abundant supply of year-round labor (see table 20). In both sugar regions there now existed an underclass of field hands who moved about in search of temporary employment. These workers enjoyed no economic security and sometimes competed with tenants and hacienda hands for the more permanent positions.[14]

Conditions for all participants in the sugar industry worsened considerably after 1975, and business has remained depressed since then. In 1974 the Laurel-Langley Act ended, and the Philippines lost its privileged niche in an American market that since World War II had granted its suppliers 1–4 cents a pound above the world price. The international market, plagued

Table 20. Population of Negros Occidental, Pampanga, and Southern Tarlac, 1939–80

	1939	*1960*	*1970*	*1980*	*Percentage Increase*
Negros Occidental	824,858	1,332,323	1,490,058	1,930,301	134
Pampanga	375,281	617,259	905,748	1,181,590	215
Southern Tarlac[a]	111,225	183,477	251,344	328,933	196

Sources: Philippine Commonwealth, Commission of the Census, *Census of the Philippines: 1939* (Manila: Bureau of Printing, 1940); Philippine Republic, Bureau of Census and Statistics, *Census of the Philippines: 1960* (Manila: Bureau of Census and Statistics, 1962–63); Philippine Republic, National Census and Statistics Office, *Nineteen-Seventy Census of Population and Housing* (Manila: National Census and Statistics Office, 1974); Philippine Republic, National Census and Statistics Office, *Nineteen-Eighty Census of Population: Final Report* (Manila: National Census and Statistics Office, 1980).

[a]Bamban, Capas, Concepcion, and Tarlac.

by oversupply, offered Filipinos no regular customers. In just the five years from 1975 to 1980 sugar's percentage of the nation's total exports dropped from 25 to 11 percent. International agreements among sugar exporters to regulate the market have failed noticeably, and only recently has the United States given the Philippines a quota, one too small to return health to the industry.[15]

Philippine sugarmen might have sustained a higher level of profitability after 1974, despite the loss of their prime market, for world sugar prices sometimes rose considerably above the Philippine production cost of 13 cents a pound; however, government interference further damaged the industry. Ferdinand Marcos employed the powers of his martial law regime to curb the political independence of the sugar bloc, a feat Manuel Quezon never entirely accomplished. Marcos immediately stripped away many of the assets of the family of his former vice-president and leading sugar baron Fernando Lopez and placed in solitary confinement Senator Benigno Aquino, Jr., from the prominent Tarlac sugar family. As time passed, Marcos, with the aid of his crony henchman Roberto Benedicto, extended his sway over the industry by controlling both the international marketing of Philippine sugar and the flow of agricultural credit.

In 1974 Marcos formed the Philippine Exchange Company (Philex) and later the National Sugar Trading Corporation (Nasutra), headed by Benedicto, which purchased all milled sugar, sold it abroad, and paid planters and centrals from those proceeds. These agencies, especially the latter, determined the rate of reimbursement, and sugarmen never knew exactly to whom and at what price their product had been sold. They not only resented the loss of control over these sales, they also realized that major discrepancies existed between the sale price and their reimbursement. Even worse, however, the government traders proved incompetent. For example, just as the U.S. quota ended in 1974, unusual circumstances forced the world price of raw sugar to an all-time peak of 65 cents a pound, but agency dealers chose to hold some of their export back and later had to sell it at a much reduced price. Sugar never again reached such a high, fluctuating between 23 cents in 1979 and 4 cents in 1984, settling at about 8 cents. While many of Nasutra's dealings were shrouded in mystery, hacenderos suspected that the agency never obtained the best prices and, through both speculation and peculation, hurt them badly.[16]

Complaints against Nasutra, however, remained muted, because the government held a lock on agricultural credit, both through the PNB and the newly formed Republic Planter's Bank, headed by the ubiquitous Benedicto. As the sugar industry came upon bad times beginning in the late 1970s, farm debt increased substantially; still, many planters in the 1980s, like those before them, lived lavishly and carried big loans that kept their farms in bondage to the banks. Those hacenderos who chose to contest Nasutra's hold over sugar marketing—many of whom belonged to the New Alliance of Sugar Producers—found few of their colleagues willing to join them for fear of foreclosure.[17]

A curious throwback to the 1920s has also appeared in the past decade, when many of the recently constructed mills went into receivership to PNB. Again bank centrals have become a government and industry problem; however, on this occasion the administration has taken the more drastic step of decommissioning several of them. Most older centrals have continued in operation, although in the mid-1980s Pasumil and Talisay had to close at least temporarily. Almost all planters have finally won their sixty-forty split, or better, but low prices of sugar have dimmed the glow of this victory. Hacenderos who wish to continue farming must discover ways to reduce their cost of production, as the millers have always suggested. Mechanization of field work to force down labor costs seems like an inevitable step in the quest for survival.[18]

External signs of worsening conditions in sugarlandia began to appear inexorably after 1975, and by 1982 the plaza of Bacolod and the buildings surrounding it looked dilapidated, while refugees from the countryside begged in the streets for money to feed their families. Judging from available studies, western Negros has fared worse financially than Pampanga and has become to the world press corps the paramount symbol of Philippine poverty and economic stagnation.[19]

Central Luzon has seemingly survived better for reasons geographical and historical. Since World War II and for the first time in the modern era, the population of Pampanga and southern Tarlac has grown faster than that of Negros, reflecting the former region's greater attachment to the Manila urban complex. Capampangan migrate or commute to the city and send remittances to their families; in addition, many work abroad, in Guam and the Middle East, for example. Evidence of the higher wages they earn overseas can be observed in the rising number of cinderblock houses they build in rural Pampanga upon their return. As the future prosperity of the Capampangan remains linked to access to a larger world, their reliance on the sugar industry declines.[20]

Because the more independent casamac have few bank loans and low production costs, they have been able to convert from sugar to rice farming and thus avoid the crisis of depressed sugar prices. Furthermore, under the land reform legislation of the martial law years, tenants could purchase from landlords only rice and corn land; hence, many tenants in central Luzon acquired ownership of parcels of rice land from their former owners. The region contains by far the greatest extent of any area in the Philippines converting from large to small, peasant holdings. Plantations still exist in the core of the old sugar area, but the overall expanse of sugarlands has been considerably reduced.[21]

Retirement of so many landlords from central Luzon has contributed to the success of the land reform. Since World War II, a considerable number of old landholders have preferred the comforts and safety of urban and suburban life, and the continuous presence of radicalism in rural central Luzon has also discouraged them from returning. Although the Huks were defeated in the early 1950s in their attempt to seize national power, they remained a force in the barrios and towns of Pampanga and Tarlac. Eventually, even their local political power waned, in part because of corrupt leadership in the late 1960s; however, in the 1970s a new generation of dissenters belonging to the New People's Army (NPA) replaced them.[22] Landowners found it more expedient to deal fairly with casamac than to face the threats and hostile acts of the rural rebels.

Without landlords, casamac have become more self-reliant. Perhaps the most advanced example of their independence can be found in western Pampanga, in the area near the old Hacienda Prado, where prewar tenants sought to grow sugar cooperatively. In Barrio Dampe, Floridablanca, a group of former casamac cultivate sugarland they bought with bank help and from which they successfully market cane to Pasumil cooperatively. Samahan Nayon Dampe (Dampe Cooperative) stands as a fitting memorial to Pedro Abad Santos and his efforts on behalf of the Pampangan peasantry.[23]

In a yet modest way Capampangan have begun introducing what they have learned about cooperative farming to the Negrenses. Two groups associated with a farming cooperative in San Simon, Pampanga, have started projects in Talisay and La Carlota to teach former sugar hands how to operate as competent smallholders. In Talisay the project is run through First Farmers Human Development Foundation with the encouragement and support of individuals such as Capampangan Edgardo Yap of the Philippine Sugar Association; the one in La Carlota started under the direction of Sister Milagros Dayrit of Asumpta Technical High School in San Simon.[24] Perhaps through these efforts the separate histories of Pampanga and western Negros will at last meet; however, how fruitful such projects prove remains to be seen.

Change comes far more slowly to western Negros, where the majority of duma'an continue under tight control and labor for paltry wages. Negrense sugar workers lack the skills to switch crops, and planters have offered them only limited opportunities to improve their lot. The NPA has begun making inroads into this province beset by ever-increasing poverty and violence; however, the NPA's greatest influence has come on the southern fringes of sugarlandia, in the Kabankalan area, and even further south, where radicalism traditionally prevailed. In addition to the NPA, a new movement of Christian Communities, encouraged by the liberal wing of the Philippine Catholic Church, has also formed among hill farmers; the Church operates a small central at Dacongcogon for their benefit. In the meantime, in the heartland of Negros the old sugar order holds sway. Armed planters continue to fend off NPA raiders, and the hacenderos threaten—no matter how much poverty surrounds them—to resist, with force if necessary, the efforts of the government to alter the old ways of doing things.[25]

Kabankalan sits on the the lower boundary of Negros sugar country, but the sugar farms there are mainly small and spread out on the undulating hill amid rice and corn fields. Farmers there do not at all fit the image of the wealthy Negrense hacendero; rather, they appear to suffer as much as do poor Negrense farmhands elsewhere. Because of the extensive poverty, caused in part by the marginality of the farmland, the area surrounding Kabankalan has become a center of unrest. Today the NPA and Christian Communities vie with one another for the allegiance of the inhabitants, and both groups oppose the heavy-handed actions of the Philippine Army.

The post-Marcos era has commenced in the Philippines, and Nasutra has gone the way of other martial law aberrations; however, world economic conditions have prevented significant recovery for the industry. The U.S. market, too, promises to remain a finite one for Philippine sugar, given pressure from America's own sugar producers, the demands of its other offshore suppliers, and the fact that its biggest food producers, including large bottlers Pepsi and Coca-Cola, now increasingly use corn sweetener in their products. Even if future Philippine sugarmen improve their productivity, they will have to depend for their livelihood on insular consumption and limited exports. The World Bank reports the industry's export earnings for the present as "stagnant," and there seems little prospect of revival.[26] However the sugar industry limps along hereafter, many thousands who toiled in the sugar fields will never again work there. More restricted production and mechanization will seriously reduce the labor force, and the poor conditions that have been a fact of life since 1975 will persist.

The successors of President Corazon Aquino, herself the heiress to an immense sugar fortune, now must decide what to do about sugar's future.[27] Perhaps the export industry has reached its old age and, for economic and social reasons, should give way to some substitute. The presence of so many poverty-stricken workers and a history of so much past misery and repression suggests that only some alternative endeavor will boost the Philippine economy and the well-being of millions of Filipinos.

Destination of Philippine Sugar Exports, 1840–1920 (*continued*)

Year	Europe (including Great Britain)[a]	%	Great Britain	%	Continental Europe (including Spain)	%	U.S.[b]	%	California and Pacific Ports	%	Australia	%	China, Japan, and Hong Kong[c]	%	Other	%
1893			100,155	38	4,414	2	62,084	23	0	0	0	0	79,310	30	19,925	7
1894			62,121	31	4,185	2	37,005	19	0	0	0	0	73,335	37	20,794	11
1895			93,693	40	4,073	2	41,245	18	0	0	203	0	76,089	32	19,327	8
1896			39,943	17	3,604	2	79,749	34	0	0	0	0	89,850	38	20,458	9
1897			47,792	23	1,804	1	15,467	8	0	0	0	0	130,998	64	9,277	5
1898			47,531	26	183	0	28,447	15	0	0	0	0	107,563	59	0	0
1899			18,256	19	2	0	22,460	24	0	0	0	0	53,831	57	0	0
1900			12,953	20	0	0	2,134	3	0	0	0	0	48,665	76	0	0
1901			27	0	0	0	2,007	4	0	0	0	0	51,079	96	0	0
1902			6,007	6	0	0	2,591	3	0	0	0	0	84,953	91	0	0
1903			0	0	0	0	34,349	38	0	0	0	0	56,650	62	0	0
1904			4,420	5	0	0	21,228	25	0	0	0	0	59,683	70	0	0
1905			508	0	0	0	43,619	41	0	0	0	0	62,552	59	0	0
1906			0	0	0	0	0	0	11,914	9	0	0	114,466	91	0	0
1907			11,850	10	0	0	8,838	7	2,034	2	0	0	101,215	82	0	0
1908			10,859	8	0	0	46,046	33	0	0	0	0	81,554	59	0	0
1909			0	0	0	0	45,565	37	6,730	5	0	0	72,420	58	0	0
1910			0	0	0	0	98,886	84	0	0	0	0	19,267	16	0	0
1911			4,753	2	0	0	188,395	90	0	0	0	0	16,557	8	0	0
1912			3,542	2	0	0	132,618	68	0	0	0	0	58,724	30	0	0
1913			0	0	0	0	30,628	20	0	0	0	0	124,366	80	0	0
1914			5,384	2	0	0	169,463	72	0	0	0	0	60,537	26	0	0
1915			20,361	10	0	0	82,869	39	0	0	0	0	106,981	51	0	0
1916			63,121	19	0	0	134,601	40	0	0	0	0	140,345	42	0	0
1917			3,987	2	0	0	64,858	31	0	0	0	0	138,356	67	0	0
1918			0	0	0	0	102,506	40	0	0	0	0	155,469	60	0	0
1919			4,832	4	314	0	32,161	24	0	0	0	0	98,669	73	85	0
1920			0	0	1	0	123,947	69	0	0	0	0	56,336	31	56	0

Sources: *Gúia de forasteros en las Islas Filipinas, para el año de 1842* (Manila: Sanchez, 1842), p. 216; Robert MacMicking, *Recollections of Manilla and the Philippines, During 1848, 1849, and 1850* (London: Richard Bentley, 1851), pp. 270, 272; Henry T. Ellis, *Hong Kong to Manilla and the Lakes of Luzon, in the Philippine Isles, in the Year 1856* (London: Smith, Elder, 1859), p. 288; Russell, Sturgis and Company, "Principal Articles of Export in 1854 and 1855," *Market Reports*, January 7, 1856 (Baker Library, Harvard University); John Bowering, *A Visit to the Philippine Islands (In 1858)* (Manila: Filipiniana Book Guild, 1963), p. 194; Manuel Azcarraga y Palermo, *La libertad de comercio in las Islas Filipinas* (Madrid: José Noguera, 1871), p. 246; Willett and Gray, *Weekly Statistical Sugar Trade Journal*, December 23, 1908, p. 447; Alexander R. Webb, "Sugar and Rice Culture in the Philippine Islands," *U.S. Consular Reports* 27 (1888): 244; Chamber of Commerce of the Philippine Islands, *Yearbook of the Philippine Islands, 1920* (Manila: Bureau of Printing, 1920), p. 154; Philippine Islands Bureau of Customs, *Annual Report of the Collector of Insular Customs, 1922* (Manila: Bureau of Printing, 1922), p. 261.

[a]Where no separate figures for Great Britain and Continental Europe (mainly Spain) exist.

[b]Figures from 1908 include small shipments to Canada as well.

[c]Figures from 1862 include both China and Japan and, apparently, Hong Kong.

APPENDIX C

Letter from Antonio Villanueva to the Director of Lands

Andres Bonifacio, La Carlota, Occ. Negros
October 27, 1919

Sir [Director of Lands],

In behalf of my own interest and the interest of my neighbors whose lots are shown as indicated with numbers of their respective applications and homestead entries, in the attached sketch, I have the honor to inform you of the following.

On October 6th of this year, a number of persons headed by Mr. Miguel Netumay of La Carlota, Occ. Negros, who afterwards we learned that he is an encargado of Mr. Samuel F. Ramos & Co., had come to our homes and told us that the lots we now occupy as indicated in the attached sketch are owned by the said Mr. Samuel F. Ramos & Co. In reply, we informed this encargado that the lots we occupy belong to the Government. Without minding what we said the next day (Oct. 7, 1919) this encargado with his men cleaned a site for a house to be erected there. This is an evidence of the conscienceless and aggressive determination to occupy our lots.

Later, we were informed that they will cultivate the land for sugar cane. Few days after, a good number of carabao were brought to the place in question. This shows further evidence of their interest to claim for our lots.

Now, that we are aware of the things taking place and not unmindful that we are being deceived, we wish to beg of you that without your mercy towards the poor and helpless but by no means right like us we will not be able to fight for our rights in order to get back our land for the reason that the claimants are the most prominent and well-to-do in this town. To inform you of the standing of the claimants, Mr. Samuel F. Ramos who is handling the claim is the Justice of the Peace in the Municipality of La Carlota, Dr. Vicente Locsin besides being the Physician of this district is one of the richest if not the richest man in the town of La Carlota, Occ. Negros and Mr. Angel Ledesma who has been elected Vice President of the Municipality of La Carlota, is a well-to-do gentleman, also.

The three above-mentioned gentlemen are listed as owners of lot No. 998 (Public land (River Bottom) according to 1916 list of lots found in the office of the Secretary of the municipality of La Carlota, Occ. Negros);

which, according to a title of transfer No. 1456 its inscription took place last September 11, 1919 and the Original Certificate on Sept. 8, 1919.

Mr. Marcelo Baldera who is said to have sold to these three gentlemen the above lot (No. 998) had only subscribed and sworn his declaration Tax No. 3894 and Certificate of same on the 21st day of March 1919, a period which is almost 5 years later than when the undersigned filed his Homestead Application No. 23024, H.E. No. 13117 (Filed May 2, 1914). Regarding a statement (Declaration Tax No. 3894 and Certificate) that taxes on lot No. 998, wherein our homestead lots are included, which commenced in the year 1915, I have the honor to state herewith that such taxes have only been paid last Sept. 24, 1919 at La Carlota, Occ. Negros under Provincial Treasurer Land Tax Receipt No. E-5197254. This shows that the land in question was Government's land (and we believe is still Government land) until they had paid fully the taxes. This is a proof that the Director of Lands was right to approve our applications because the time shows that the land was yet Government land at the time we applied for them.

We can not imagine what procedure they did in fixing the matter with the Provincial or Municipal Treasurer so that Mr. Marcelo Baldera could pay taxes of the year 1915 when the records found in the office of the Municipal Secretary of La Carlota, Occ. Negros show that the lot in question was Public Land since the year 1916.

As to the statement that Mr. Marcelo Baldera had acquired the lot in question through the rights of his ancestors, I declare herewith to the best of my knowledge and belief that none of his ancestors had ever cut down a single tree or had ever struck with the hoe the land we occupy.

Whether Mr. Marcelo Baldera had acquired right to register the lot No. 998, in question, through influence (which is probably the case) we can not tell because we did not have knowledge of the time he registered the land.

Sir, to inform you that we are poor and that we can be smashed, as most rich and influential people believe, I state herewith that my neighbors and I do not own even a spot of land here in the Philippines, except this land where we are now working.

As to their information that they would cultive the land for sugar cane, we do not care what crops they will plant in other portions of the lot (No. 998), provided that the claimants will not include the parts we occupy. We being poor who do not have capital like they have, do not propose to do more than to produce food stuffs that can help to maintain our living. They, being rich who have money to buy private lands at any time they want, if they have conscience and mercy on us, should leave us the portions we occupy and they can continue working on the portions that do not belong to us.

To mention the fact how hard it is in the life of a poor man to improve a piece of land, by planting bamboo, bananas and food crops, I wish you could imagine him, working either under sunshine or under rain; with iron bar to dig holes in the ground; with hoe to pulverize the soil oftentime bathed with sweat from head to heel.

The claimants informed that they would pay us the improvements we have made. They can say and do that but what about us? Where will then be our home sweet home? It is natural for human being, from childhood to manhood, that he loves more the things that he owns than those which are just loaned to him. In short I should say it will be more advantageous to have real Philippine Native Citizens . . . [as] owners than few rich influential land owners who usually keep the poor under miseries.

If we could only show you the bloody sweat that dropped from us on the land we now occupy, when we were at work, we [would] do so, but as we can not, we give you only an idea of the hardship that we endured in order to make improvements on the land we now dearly occupy. These rich people who are born with easy life naturally can not see nor figure the hardship we suffer. The only hardship they have (every body knows) is to break up their heads to fill up their ambitions or to look for ways, either thru influences or whatever means, by which they can increase their wealth.

There is a common saying here that "influence works wonder". We hope, however, that for our case, you would exert all our influence to save us from the threatening injustices and oppressions of the mighty. This is to say that the land we have been occupying since the Spanish time and lived faithfully therein will likely be taken by the mighty persons in a minute. We hope that these merciless rich people who are proud because they are influential and who think that they could easily rob the rights of the poor and non-influential ones be given a lesson by teaching them squarely by the power of the law which your office has in store for the poor. Negros in particular and the Philippines at large will never attain its highest development of prosperity if we the poor that make the mass or the greater part of the population will always be allowed to be oppressed by the rich and influence of richness and high offices.

To show how I had and have been faithfully observing the requirements of the Government, I enclose herewith papers showing collections made from me by the Municipal Treasurer of La Carlota, Occ. Negros.

O.R. No. 1024293 Ser. A, Initial payment of P10.00 Gen. Form 13 (A) and final payment of P10.00 O.R. No. 2047855 Ser. A for my homestead have been made in your office.

Since the policy of our Government is to distribute land equally as far as possible among her Citizens, I therefore hope that you will not tolerate that our land be taken from us by influential men who have no right at all to do so.

I wish to inform you that I have already received the Forms for Final Proofs on my land. I would be very glad to hear from you as soon as possible so that I can fill them out and submit for your consideration.

Equality among men is the safest foundation of Democracy.

Trusting for your immediate action on the matter, I beg to remain,

Very respectfully,

Antonio Villanueva

His thumb mark

The Director of Lands
Manila, P.I. . . .

Source: Quezon Papers, National Library of the Philippines, Manila.

APPENDIX D

Letter from G. Seaver to Archibald Harrison, Philippine National Bank

Bacolod, Occ. Negros
August 9, 1918

Archibald Harrison, Esq.
Secretary, Philippine National Bank
Manila, P.I.

Sir:

The inspection of the province of Negros Occidental covered a period of twenty-seven days, commencing July 12 and ending August 7, 1918, both dates inclusive. No Sundays or holidays were observed and the work continued every day, regardless of weather conditions. By starting very early and continuing until dark, we were able in the period mentioned to examine 230 mortgages in 16 municipalities, representing a money value of P3,461,370 and covering 49,695 hectares of land. Included in this work also, there were examined 127 crop loans granted for this year's crop, unpaid on last year's crop and delinquent since 1916, amounting to P2,209,311 approximately. The area covered by this inspection extends from Cauayan in the southern end of the province to Escalante near the northern extremity and from the coconut groves along the beach on the western boundary to the abaca and coffee plantations in the mountains near the eastern border, viz., Bacolod, Talisay, Silay, Victorias and Manapla, uninspected. All the properties not inspected lie in excellent agricultural district.

Your attention is invited to the following general conditions which the inspection disclosed should be remedied. Particular cases will be submitted to you separately and in more definite form.

EXCESSIVE AMOUNTS OF LOANS GRANTED

Great liberality seems to be the greatest characteristic of the Bank's attitude in Negros, both in the number of loans and the amount allowed on security offered. In the past, the amount of the loan seems to have been based upon a speculative selling price of the land, if a purchaser could be found, and not on the revenue derived from the crops raised thereon. From present indications, I believe the Bank will be the largest land-owner in the Island of Negros within five years, unless immediate steps are taken to curb the practice of granting loans on security with so little a margin above the loan value that a year or two of poor crops will depreciate it below the amount borrowed, especially if interest and amortization payments are not promptly collected.

Loans have been made for large amounts, for agricultural purposes, on mountain land 25 miles from the nearest market that has never been cultivated and, owing to its location and formation can never be cultivated. Many loans were found to be in excess of the assessed value of the land and, in other cases, the owner had declared the land at several times its value for the purpose of getting a larger loan from the Bank. In other cases, it was found that the Bank has granted loans for more than would be required to buy equally good land adjoining the property mortgaged and, in addition, a large crop loan is also granted. As might be expected, the mortgagor is in arrears in interest and amortization payments and, when payment is forced, the Bank will find itself with the land on its hands.

The practice of giving an increase in the loan to meet interest and amortization payments will lead to disaster if continued.

Several very striking examples have been found, demonstrating a great risk of loaning money on Spanish titles. In one case, there were found to be three Royal titles, covering the same tract of land. In another case, the Bank's mortgage is for 248 hectares under Royal title and the cadestral survey shows a fraction less than 137 hectares.

LOCAL AGRICULTURAL BANK INSPECTORS

Both Inspectors Grupe and Perez are old men, long passed the prime of life when it is possible for them to endure the exertion and fatigue incident to properly inspect agricultural property, except under the most favorable circumstances. The fact that both made a failure as hacenderos seems to be their greatest qualification for the position. Perez is too old and decrepit to walk and too fat to ride. Inquiries made on outlying property develop the fact that they approved several applications for loan without personal investigation and inspection.

Indications of dishonest methods by local inspectors are quite plentiful. Cases have been found wherein the inspector has collected money from the mortgagor to pay the cost of his inspection trip, etc. Several patrons of the Bank have told me that both inspectors expect a small gratuity for their service, especially if the matter is expedited. These matters were not investigated by me, as my instructions did not authorize me to investigate any officer or employee of the Bank. If the Bank's interests are to be protected, inspections must be more strict, rigid and frequent. The Bank will pay in bad loans, principal and interest lost many times the cost of proper inspection and supervision. As before stated, many mortgages have never been inspected and others have not been visited by the Bank's inspectors in years. Each property mortgaged should be inspected at least twice a year and a report by the inspector on prescribed form forwarded to the Agricultural Department of the Bank in Manila.

I recommend that in future all loans be passed by an Appraisement Board of three members, two of whom to be from the staff in Manila. Their duty will be to appraise the land on the basis of the revenue that will be derived, fixing the amount sufficiently low so that with all interest charges the land can be readily sold for more than enough to make the Bank safe.

FAILURE OF MORTGAGORS TO COMPLY WITH TERMS OF MORTGAGE

Of the 230 mortgages inspected, a great many have not complied with the terms under which the loan was granted and, as far as we can judge, had no intention of doing so at the time the money was obtained. Several of them frankly admitted it. Others claimed that they did not know what reasons were stated in the applications, the Bank's officials advised them to change the reasons given and suggested other purposes which the Bank's Directors favored and would, therefore, stand a better chance of being approved. In some cases, the money obtained from the Bank for agricultural purposes had been diverted into commercial or industrial investments, and instances were found where the money had been loaned out to other farmers at the rate of 25% per annum. Each of these will be the subject of a separate and later report. A majority had complied in part with the conditions under which the mortgage was granted, at least to such an extent that action against them is not recommended, unless after considering their cases, you direct otherwise.

PROTECTION TO CUSTOMERS

It appears that some men of influence in various communities, in one case, the Justice of the Peace, have induced owners to apply for a loan and acted as their agent in making out the papers; had the check forwarded in their care when the loan was approved; induced the owner to indorse it; cashed the check and deducted an amount they considered sufficient for their service, which, in one case reported, amounted to 50% of the loan. Recommend that in the future the applicants for loan be required to come to the Bank in person, that the papers be filled out without cost by the clerical force of the Bank, and that the money loaned be delivered only to the person mortgaging his property.

Respectfully submitted:

G. Seaver [Bank investigator]

Source: Quezon Papers, National Library of the Philippines, Manila.

APPENDIX E

Elected Provincial Officials Representing Western Negros and Pampanga, 1919–34

1919

Negros Occidental

Governor: Matias Hilado
Senator (8th District): Hermenegildo Villanueva
Rep. 1st Dist. (Northern): Lope P. Severino
Rep. 2nd Dist. (Central): Rafael Alunan
Rep. 3rd Dist. (Southern): Tito Silverio

Pampanga

Governor: Honorio Ventura
Senator (3rd District): Teodoro Sandiko
Rep. 1st Dist. (Northern): Pablo Angeles David
Rep. 2nd Dist. (Southern): Pedro Abad Santos
Rep. 2nd Dist. (Tarlac): Benigno Aquino, Sr.

1922

Negros Occidental

Governor: Gil Montilla
Senator: Espiridion Guanco
Rep. 1st Dist.: Serafin Hilado
Rep. 2nd Dist.: Vicente Jimenez Yanson
Rep. 3rd Dist.: Eliseo Limsiaco

Pampanga

Governor: Olimpio Guanzon
Senator: Santiago Lucero
Rep. 1st Dist.: Pedro Valdez Liongson
Rep. 2nd Dist.: Vicente Manapat
Rep. 2nd Dist. (Tarlac): Benigno Aquino, Sr.

1925

Negros Occidental

Governor: Jose C. Locsin
Senator: Hermenegildo Villanueva

Rep. 1st Dist.: Serafin Hilado
Rep. 2nd Dist.: Ramon Torres
Rep. 3rd Dist.: Isaac Lacson

Pampanga

Governor: Sotero Baluyut
Senator: Teodoro Sandiko
Rep. 1st Dist.: Pedro Valdez Liongson
Rep. 2nd Dist.: Ceferino Hilario
Rep. 2nd Dist. (Tarlac): Benigno Aquino, Sr.

1928

Negros Occidental

Governor: Agustin S. Ramos
Senator: Mariano Yulo Regalado
Rep. 1st Dist.: Jose C. Locsin
Rep. 2nd Dist.: Vicente Jimenez Yanson
Rep. 3rd Dist.: Emilio Montilla

Pampanga

Governor: Sotero Baluyut
Senator: Benigno Aquino, Sr.
Rep. 1st Dist.: Fabian de la Paz
Rep. 2nd Dist.: Macario Ocampo

1931

Negros Occidental

Governor: Isaac Lacson
Senator: Gil Montilla
Rep. 1st Dist.: Enrique B. Magalona
Rep. 2nd Dist.: Ramon Torres
Rep. 3rd Dist.: Emilio Yulo

Pampanga

Governor: Pablo Angeles David
Senator: Sotero Baluyut
Rep. 1st Dist.: Fabian de la Paz
Rep. 2nd Dist.: Zoilo Hilario

1934

Negros Occidental

Governor: Emilio Gaston

Senator: Isaac Lacson
Rep. 1st Dist.: Enrique B. Magalona
Rep. 2nd Dist.: Ramon Torres
Rep. 3rd Dist.: Agustin S. Ramos

Pampanga

Governor: Pablo Angeles David
Senator: Hermogenes Concepcion
Rep. 1st Dist.: Maximo Dimson
Rep. 2nd Dist.: Jose P. Fausto
Rep. 1st Dist. (Tarlac): Jose Cojuangco

Sources: *Makinaugalingon* [Native Ways]; *Manila Times; Tribune* (Manila); letter from Carl H. Landé, Lawrence, Kansas, to the author, January 23, 1991.

A Note on Sources

The published works and theses in these notes are available in major public and university libraries in the United States and the Philippines. It is necessary here only to identify and locate the collections that contain the unique materials cited on Philippine sugar and society.

Beyer Series. Collected research papers concerning Negros, Pampanga, and Tarlac by the students and colleagues of the late Professor H. Otley Beyer, Department of Anthropology, University of the Philippines. Formerly in Beyer's personal library in Manila, but now in Canberra, Australia.

Colgate-Rochester Divinity School, Rochester, N.Y. Baptist Mission Records, Negros and Iloilo provinces.

Harvard University, Baker Library, Graduate School of Business Administration. Papers of American merchants, particularly Jonathan Russell and Russell, Sturgis. Houghton Library. Personal diary of William Thomas Townsend, December 13, 1903–May 2, 1907.

Hawaiian Sugar Planters Association Archives, Honolulu. Papers referring mainly to San Carlos Milling Company and Hawaiian-Philippine (Silay) Milling Company.

Lilly Library, Bloomington, Ind. Paul V. McNutt Papers.

National Library of the Philippines, Manila. Historical Data Papers (local history compilations accomplished by local teachers and officials in the immediate post–World War II period); Manuel Luis Quezon Papers; Manuel Roxas Papers.

Newberry Library, Chicago. Ayer Collection Manuscripts.

Philippine National Archives, Manila. Materials referring to Pampanga, Negros Occidental, and Tarlac listed under the following headings: *Legajos de Varias Provincias; Protocolos* (1852–1902); *Notarios (1902–41); Radicaciones; Estadisticas; Memorias; Padrones; Elecciones.*

Philippine National Museum, Manila. Robert Fox, Field notes on Excavations of Balukbuk and Gubat sites, Porac, Pampanga, December 1959 to May 1960.

Public Record Office, London. Foreign Office Dispatches and letters of Vice-Consul and, later, Acting-Consul Nicholas Loney, Iloilo, Manila, and Madrid, 1857–67.

United States National Archives, Washington, D.C. Record Group 350, Records of the Bureau of Insular Affairs (includes manuscript reports of the governors of Pampanga and Negros Occidental, 1901–16); Department of State, Dispatches of the United States Consul in Manila, 1817–35; Record Group 395, Records of U.S. Army Overseas Operation and Commands (Philippines).

University of the Philippines Main Library, Quezon City. Luther Parker Collection.

Abbreviations

B&R	Emma Blair and James Alexander Robertson. *The Philippine Islands, 1493–1898.* 55 vols. Cleveland: A. H. Clark, 1903–9
BIA	Bureau of Insular Affairs, U.S. National Archives
BMR	Baptist Mission Records
BS	Beyer Series
Census: 1903	U.S. Bureau of the Census. *Census of the Philippine Islands: Taken under the Direction of the Philippine Commission in the Year 1903.* 4 vols. Washington, D.C.: Government Printing Office, 1905
Census: 1918	Philippine Islands, Census Office. *Census of the Philippine Islands: Taken under the Direction of the Philippine Legislature in the Year 1918.* 6 vols. Manila: Bureau of Printing, 1920
Census: 1939	Philippine Commonwealth, Commission of the Census. *Census of the Philippines: 1939.* 5 vols. in 8 wraps. Manila: Bureau of Printing, 1940
Census: 1960	Philippine Republic, Bureau of Census and Statistics. *Census of the Philippines: 1960.* Manila: Bureau of Census and Statistics, 1962–63
Census: 1970	Philippine Republic, National Census and Statistics Office. *Nineteen-Seventy Census of Population and Housing.* Manila: National Census and Statistics Office, 1974
Census: 1980	Philippine Republic, National Census and Statistics Office. *Nineteen-Eighty Census of Population: Final Report.* Manila: National Census and Statistics Office, 1980
HDP	Historical Data Papers
LI	*La Igualdad* (Bacolod), April 27, 1906–June 8, 1907
LL	*La Libertad* (Bacolod), July 4, 1899–July 22, 1900
LPC	Luther Parker Collection

M	*Makinaugalingon* [Native Ways] (Iloilo), May 1, 1913–October 24, 1940
MDB	*Manila Daily Bulletin*, January 1, 1920–March 31, 1920
MT	*Manila Times*, October 12, 1898–December 31, 1906
PAR	Philippine Islands, Department of Agriculture and Natural Resources. *Philippine Agricultural Review* 1–22 (1908–29)
PFP	*Philippines Free Press*, January 1, 1907–March 29, 1930
PN	*Philippine News* (San Francisco), December 13–19, 1973–April 7–13, 1979
PNA	Philippine National Archives
PRO	Public Record Office
QP	Quezon Papers
RF	*Revista de Filipinas*, July 1875–September 1877
RP	Roxas Papers
SN	*Sugar News* 1–35 (1919–58) (variously titled)
TT	*Tribune* (Manila), April 1, 1930–December 7, 1941
W&G	Willett and Gray. *Weekly Statistical Sugar Trade Journal* (New York) 22–44 (1898–1920)

Notes

CHAPTER 1. INTRODUCTION

1. John Leddy Phelan, *The Hispanization of the Philippines: Spanish Aims and Filipino Responses, 1565–1700* (Madison: University of Wisconsin Press, 1959), pp. vii–viii. On the role of economics see Daniel F. Doeppers, *Manila, 1900–1941: Social Change in a Late Colonial Metropolis* (Quezon City: Ateneo de Manila University Press, 1984), and Norman G. Owen, *Prosperity without Progress: Manila Hemp and Material Life in the Colonial Philippines* (Berkeley and Los Angeles: University of California Press, 1984).

2. William Lytle Shurz, *The Manila Galleon* (New York: E. P. Dutton, 1939), pp. 30–56.

3. Reviews of and references to studies on the history of sugar societies have appeared in the *World Sugar History Newsletter* edited by Bill Albert at the University of East Anglia. See also J. H. Galloway, *The Sugar Cane Industry: An Historical Geography from Its Origins to 1914* (Cambridge: Cambridge University Press, 1989).

4. Sidney W. Mintz, *Sweetness and Power: The Place of Sugar in Modern History* (New York: Viking, 1985), pp. 19–61; Wallace R. Aykroyd, *Sweet Malefactor: Sugar, Slavery and Human Society* (London: Heinemann, 1967), chaps. 2–6; Richard B. Sheridan, *Sugar and Slavery: An Economic History of the British West Indies, 1623–1775* (Baltimore: Johns Hopkins University Press, 1973); Richard S. Dunn, *Sugar and Slaves: The Rise of the Planter Class in the English West Indies, 1624–1713* (Chapel Hill: University of North Carolina Press, 1972); Robert Louis Stein, *The French Sugar Business in the Eighteenth Century* (Baton Rouge: Louisiana State University Press, 1988); Jan Breman, *Control of Land and Labour in Colonial Java: A Case Study of Agrarian Crisis and Reform in the Region of Cirebon During the First Decades of the 20th*

Century, Verhandelingen van het Koninklijk Instituut voor Taal-, Land- en Volkenkunde, 101 (Dordrecht, The Netherlands: Foris, 1983).

5. Noel Deerr, *The History of Sugar*, 2 vols. (London: Chapman and Hall, 1949–50); Alfred W. McCoy, "Rural Philippines: Technological Change in the Sugar Industry," in *The Philippines after Marcos*, ed. R. J. May and Francisco Nemenzo (London and Sydney: Croom Helm, 1985), pp. 182–87; Ruben R. Alcantara, *Sakada: Filipino Adaptation in Hawaii* (Lanham, Md.: University Press of America, 1981), pp. 81–82, 129.

6. Ellen Deborah Ellis, *An Introduction to the History of Sugar as a Commodity* (Philadelphia: John C. Winston, 1905), chap. 3; John Yudkin, *Sweet and Dangerous* (New York: Bantam, 1972); Jean Mayer, "The Bitter Truth about Sugar," *New York Times Magazine*, June 20, 1976, pp. 26–34; Ellen Ruppel Shell, "Sweetness and Health," *Atlantic Monthly*, August 1985, pp. 14–20; *University of California, Berkeley, Wellness Letter*, December 1989, pp. 4–5.

7. *Sugar '69* (Quezon City: National Federation of Sugarcane Planters, 1969), pp. 49–50; Alcantara, *Sakada*, pp. 1–96, *passim*; Rene Dumont, *Is Cuba Socialist?* (New York: Viking, 1974), pp. 68–69, 74, 142–43; Carmelo Mesa-Lago, *Cuba in the 1970s: Pragmatism and Institutionalization*, rev. ed. (Albuquerque: University of New Mexico Press, 1978), pp. 49–50; Medea Benjamin, Joseph Collins, and Michael Scott, *No Free Lunch: Food and Revolution in Cuba Today* (San Francisco: Institute of Food and Development Policy, 1984), pp. 120–31, 142–45. See also R. E. Elson, *Javanese Peasants and the Colonial Sugar Industry: Impact and Change in an East Java Residency, 1839–1940* (Singapore: Oxford University Press, 1984); Roger Plant, *Sugar and Modern Slavery: A Tale of Two Countries* (London: Zed Books, 1987); Alec Wilkinson, *Big Sugar: Seasons in the Cane Fields of Florida* (New York: Knopf, 1989); Bill Albert and Adrian Graves, eds., *Crisis and Change in the International Sugar Economy, 1860–1914* (Norwich and Edinburgh, UK: ISC Press, 1984) and idem, *The World Sugar Economy in War and Depression, 1914–1940* (London: Routledge, 1988).

8. Immanuel Wallerstein, *The Capitalist World-Economy* (Cambridge: Cambridge University Press, 1979), chaps. 1, 6. See also Doeppers, *Manila, 1900–1941*, p. 5. On the limitations of such an analysis, see McCoy's introduction in Alfred W. McCoy and Ed. C. de Jesus, eds., *Philippine Social History: Global Trade and Local Transformations* (Quezon City: Ateneo de Manila University Press, 1982), pp. 11–14.

9. Lucien M. Hanks, *Rice and Man: Agricultural Ecology in Southeast Asia* (Chicago: Aldine, 1972). A lesser example, for want of sufficient data, is Clifford Geertz, *Agricultural Involution: The Process of Ecological Change in Indonesia* (Berkeley and Los Angeles: University of California Press, 1966).

10. Julian H. Steward, *Theory of Culture Change: The Methodology of Multilinear Evolution* (Urbana: University of Illinois Press, 1955), p. 37.

11. Ibid.

12. Ibid., pp. 40–41.

13. For a model of comparative agricultural history, see Eric R. Wolf and Sidney W. Mintz, "Haciendas and Plantations in Middle America and the Antilles," *Social and Economic Studies* 6 (September 1957): 380–412.

14. Renato Constantino, *The Philippines: A Past Revisited* (Quezon City: Tala Publishing, 1974); Teodoro A. Agoncillo and Milagros C. Guerrero, *History of the Filipino People*, 5th ed. (Quezon City: R. P. Garcia, 1977).

15. *Bulletin Today* (Manila), June 13, 1982, p. 6.

16. Philippine Commonwealth, Department of Agriculture and Commerce, *Soil Survey of Pampanga Province, Philippines*, Soil Report 5 (Manila: Bureau of Printing, 1939); Philippine Republic, Bureau of Soils, *Soil Survey of Negros Occidental Province, Philippines*, Soil Report 14 (Manila: Bureau of Printing, 1951); Frederick L. Wernstedt, "Agricultural Regionalism on Negros Island, Philippines" (Ph.D. dissertation, University of California at Los Angeles, 1953); and Domingo C. Salita, "Land Use in the Province of Pampanga" (M.A. thesis, University of the Philippines, 1958).

17. *Philippine Sugar Handbook, 1972 Edition* (Manila: Sugar News Press, 1972), p. 106.

18. In the mid-1980s the Marcos government separated western Negros into two provinces, Negros del Norte with its capital at Cadiz City and Negros Occidental.

19. Rosanne Ruttan, *Women Workers on Hacienda Milagros: Wage Labor and Household Subsistence on a Philippine Sugarcane Plantation*, Publikatieserie Zuid- en Zuidoost-Asië, Anthropologisch-Sociologisch Centrum, no. 30 (Amsterdam: University of Amsterdam, 1982), pp. 17–18. See also Norman W. Schul, "A Philippine Sugar Cane Plantation: Land Tenure and Sugar Cane Production," *Economic Geography* 43 (April 1967): 157–69.

20. Violeta Lopez-Gonzaga, *Crisis in Sugarlandia: The Planters' Differential Perceptions and Responses and Their Impact on Sugarcane Workers' Households* (Bacolod: La Salle Social Research Center, 1964).

21. The more even rainfall in northern Negros contributes to its higher yields and a longer milling season; meanwhile San Carlos, which receives somewhat less rain than other districts and has a shorter milling season, is one of the only districts to make significant use of irrigation (Wernstedt, "Agricultural Regionalism," pp. 141, 169–77).

CHAPTER 2. FOUNDATIONS

1. Thomas R. McHale, "Early Technological Innovation in Sugar Cane Agriculture and Sugar Making Techniques in the Philippines (Abstract)," *Proceedings of the Ninth Pacific Science Congress* (Bangkok, 1963), 3:237; Sidney W. Mintz, *Sweetness and Power: The Place of Sugar in Modern History* (New York: Viking, 1985), p. 19; Thomas R. McHale and Mary C. McHale, eds., *Early American-Philippine Trade: The Journal of Nathaniel Bowditch in Manila, 1796*, Monograph Series, no. 2 (New Haven: Yale University Southeast Asia Studies, 1962), p. 31n; Cleve W. Hines, *Cane Production and Sugar Manufacture in the Philippine Islands*, Government of the Philippine Islands, Bureau of Agriculture, Bulletin 33 (Manila: Bureau of Printing, 1919), p. 13; Philippine Commercial Agencies, comp., *Economic Resources and Developments of the Philippine Islands* (Manila: Philippine Commercial Agencies, 1920), p. 49; *SN* 6 (1925): 465–68; Carlos Quirino, *History of the Philippine Sugar Industry* (Manila: Kalayaan, 1974), pp. 1–3. Linguistic evidence, including widespread use within the archipelago of the Malayo-Polynesian word *tubo*, or some variation thereof, for sugar cane supports this interpretation of the beginning and spread of sugar in the islands (*SN* 7 [1926]: 615–17). Sugar cane figures appear in the origin myths of at least two Philippine ethnic groups: the Bagobos and the Visayans (Noel Deerr, *The History of Sugar*, 2 vols. [London: Chapman and Hall, 1949–1950], 1:13; and Ma. Fe Hernaez Romero, *Negros Occidental Between Two Foreign Powers (1888–1909)* [Bacolod: Negros Occidental Historical Commission, 1974], p. 12).

2. Ch'en Ching-Ho, *The Chinese Community in the Sixteenth Century Philippines* (Tokyo: Centre for East Asian Cultural Studies, 1968), pp. 7–9; Wu Ching-Hong, *A Study of References to the Philippines in Chinese Sources from Earliest Times to the Ming Dynasty* (Quezon City: University of the Philippines, 1959), pp. 108–10; Fay-Cooper Cole, "The Wild Tribes of Davao District, Mindanao," *Field Museum of Natural History: Publication 170*, Anthropological Series 12 (1913), p. 85; Francisco Ignacio Alzina, S.J., "Historia de las islas e indios de Bisayas, parte mayor y mas importante de las Islas Filipina . . . año 1668," trans. Paul S. Lietz (ms. photocopy at the University of Chicago), bk. 1, pp. 391–99; Guido de Lavezaris and others, "Reply to Fray Martin de Rada," Manila, ca. June 1574, B&R, 3:270; letter from Andrés de Mirandaola to Felipe II, June 8, 1574, B&R, 3:56n.

3. Charles E. Nowell, ed., *Magellan's Voyage Around the World* (Evanston, Ill.: Northwestern University Press, 1962), p. 182; Juan Manuel de la Vega, "Expeditions to the Province of Tuy," Passi, July 3, 1609, B&R, 14:290; Guido de Lavezaris and others, "A Letter from the Royal Officials of the Filipinas Accompanied by a Memorandum of Necessary Things to Be Sent to the Colony," Cebu, May 28, 1565, B&R, 2:190; letter

from Guido de Lavezaris to Felipe II, Manila, July 17, 1574, B&R, 3:276; letter from Juan Pacheco Maldonado to Felipe II, Manila, ca. 1575, B&R, 3:299; Domingo de Salazar and others, "Relation of the Philippine Islands," Manila, June 25, 1588, B&R, 7:34; Domingo de Salazar, "The Chinese and the Parián at Manila," Manila, June 24, 1590, B&R, 7:221; Hernando Riquel and others, "News from the Western Islands," Mexico, January 15, 1574, B&R, 3:245; Andrew Van Hook, *Sugar: Its Production, Technology, and Uses* (New York: Ronald Press, 1949), pp. 126–36; and Ward Barrett, *The Sugar Hacienda of the Marqueses del Valle* (Minneapolis: University of Minnesota Press, 1970), pp. 3–4.

4. McHale, *Early Technological Innovation*, pp. 237–38; Alzina, "Historia de las islas," bk. 2, pp. 17–18; Juan de Medina, O.S.A., *Historia de la orden de S. Agustín de estas Islas Filipinas*, Manila, 1630, B&R, 23:213; Diego de Bobadilla, S.J., "Relation of the Filipinas Islands," Cádiz, 1640, B&R, 29:297; Anon., "Early Franciscan Missions," Manila, 1649, B&R, 35:320; Hernando de los Rios Coronel, "Memorial and Relation for His Majesty," Madrid, 1621, B&R, 19:285; Nicholas P. Cushner, *Landed Estates in the Colonial Philippines*, Monograph Series, no. 20 (New Haven: Yale University Southeast Asia Studies, 1976), p. 33.

5. *PAR* 21 (1928): 78–80; Juan Diez de la Calle, *Memorial, y noticias sacras, y reales del imperio de las Indias Occidentales, al mvy catolico . . . rey de las Españas . . . d. Felipe IV* (Madrid: n.p., 1646), p. 160v; Francisco Combes, S.J., *Historia de Mindanao y Joló* (Madrid: Imp. de la Viuda de Minuesa de los Ríos, 1897), p. 49; Philippine Commonwealth, Bureau of Plant Industry, *The Manufacture of Basi Sugarcane Wine Is One of the Other Products than Sugar Which Can Be Obtained from Sugar Cane* (Manila: Bureau of Printing, 1935); "Ordinances of Good Government," B&R, 50:220. In northern Luzon, *basi* made from fermented cane juice is still widely consumed.

6. Cushner, *Landed Estates*, pp. 43–44, 64; Dennis Morrow Roth, *The Friar Estates in the Philippines* (Albuquerque: University of New Mexico Press, 1977), p. 86.

7. Commercial grades of sugar were exported from the Philippines from the late seventeenth century on, and Chinese boatmen regularly traveled to Pampanga at that time, likely picking up sugar for the foreign dealers in Manila (Juan Francisco de San Antonio, O.F.M., *Chrónicas de las apostólica provincia de S. Gregorio de religiosos de n.s.p. San Francisco en las Islas Philipinas, China, Japón . . .*, 3 vols. (Sampaloc: Juan del Sotillo, 1738–44), 1:77; María Lourdes Díaz-Trechuelo Spinola, "The Role of the Chinese in the Philippine Economy," in *The Chinese in the Philippines, 1570–1770*, ed. Alfonso Felix, Jr. (Manila: Solidaridad Publishing House, 1966), pp. 187–93; Horacio de la Costa, S.J., *Asia and the Philippines* (Manila: Solidaridad Publishing House, 1967), pp. 115–16.

8. Juan Maldonado de Puga, "The Order of St. John of God," Granada, 1762, B&R, 47:167, 167n; Díaz-Trechuelo, "Role of the Chinese," pp. 204–8.

9. William Lytle Schurz, *The Manila Galleon* (New York: E. P. Dutton, 1939); Leslie E. Bauzon, *Deficit Government: Mexico and the Philippine Situado, 1606–1804* (Tokyo: Centre for East Asian Cultural Studies, 1981).

10. Serafin D. Quiason, *English "Country Trade" with the Philippines, 1644–1765* (Quezon City: University of the Philippines Press, 1966); idem, "The English 'Country Trade' with Manila Prior to 1708," *Philippine Economic Journal* 2 (1963): 201; Nicholas Norton Nicols, "Commerce of the Philippinas Islands and Advantages Which They Can Yield to His Majesty Carlos III," B&R, 47:257; Pierre Chaunu, *Les Philippines et le Pacifique des Ibériques (XVIe, XVIIe, XVIIIe siècles): Introduction Méthodologique et Indices d'Activité*, Ecole Pratique des Hautes Etudes, VIe Section, Centre de Recherches Historique, Ports—Routes—Trafics XI (Paris: S.E.V.P.E.N., 1960); Ruurdje Laarhoven Casiño and Elizabeth Pino Wittermans, "From Blockade to Trade: Early Dutch Relations with Manila, 1600–1750," paper presented at the Ninth Conference of the International Association of Historians of Asia, Manila, November 22, 1983, pp. 16–27.

11. Benito Legarda, Jr., "Foreign Trade, Economic Change and Entrepreneurship in the Nineteenth-Century Philippines" (Ph.D. dissertation, Harvard University, 1955), p. 188.

12. María Lourdes Díaz-Trechuelo Spinola, *La Real Compañía de Filipinas* (Sevilla: Escuela de Estudios Hispano-Americanos de Sevilla, 1965), p. 269; María Luisa Rodriguez Baena, *La Sociedad Economica de Amigos del Pais de Manila in el Siglo XVIII* (Sevilla: Escuela de Estudios Hispano-Americanos, 1966); Francisco Gutierrez Creps, *Memoria sobre el cultivo, beneficio y comercio del azúcar* (Manila: Celestino Miralles, 1878).

13. *Centenary of Wise and Company in the Philippines, 1826–1926* (n.p.: n.p., n.d.), p. 101; Legarda, "Foreign Trade," p. 229; Nicholas Tarling, "Some Aspects of British Trade in the Philippines in the Nineteenth Century," *Journal of History* (Manila) 11 (September-December 1963): 306–11; Peter Mathias, *The First Industrial Nation: An Economic History of Britain, 1700–1914* (London: Methuen, 1959), pp. 377–81; A. H. P. Edwards to Secretary of State John Forsyth, December 31, 1835, U.S. Consular Reports, Manila, U.S. National Archives.

14. McHale and McHale, *Early American-Philippine Trade*.

15. McHale, "Early Technological Innovation," p. 238; *SN* 4 (1923): 545, 6 (1925): 469–70; [Henry Piddington], *Remarks on the Philippine Islands and their Capital, Manila, 1819 to 1822: By an Englishman* (Calcutta: Baptist Mission Press, 1828), pp. 57–60; McHale and McHale, *Early American-Philippine Trade*, pp. 43–45; Legarda, "Foreign Trade,"

pp. 183–84; Tomás de Comyn, *Estado de las islas Filipinas en 1810: brevemente descrito* (Madrid: Imp. de Repullés, 1820), pp. 10–11; Jean Mallat de Bassilan, *Les Philippines: Histoire, géographie, moeurs, agriculture, industrie et commerce des colonies espagnoles dans l'Océanie*, 2 vols. (Paris: Arthus Bertrand, 1846), 1:133; Charles Wilkes, *Narrative of the United States Exploring Expedition: During the Years 1838, 1839, 1840, 1841, 1842*, 5 vols. (New York: G. P. Putnam, 1856), 5:289; Robert MacMicking, *Recollections of Manilla and the Philippines, During 1848, 1849, and 1850* (London: Richard Bentley, 1851), pp. 256–58; *Centenary of Wise and Company*, p. 88; Rafael Díaz Arenas, *Memoria sobre el comercio y navegacion de las Islas Filipinas* (Cádiz: Imp. de D. Domingo Féros, 1838), pp. 49–50; G. E. Nesom and Herbert S. Walker, *Handbook on the Sugar Industry of the Philippine Islands* (Manila: Bureau of Printing, 1912), pt. 1, p. 13.

16. Field notes of Robert Fox on Balukbuk and Gubat sites, Porac, Pampanga, December 1959 to May 1960, Philippine National Museum Excavations; John A. Larkin, *The Pampangans: Colonial Society in a Philippine Province* (Berkeley and Los Angeles: University of California Press, 1972), chaps. 2–3.

17. On Macapagal's career, see Nicholas P. Cushner, *Spain in the Philippines* (Rutland, Vt.: Charles E. Tuttle, 1970), p. 107.

18. Rafael Díaz Arenas, *Memorias históricas y estadísticas de Filipinas y particularmente de la grande isla de Luzon* (Manila: Imp. del Diario de Manila, 1850), chap. 5.

19. Juan de Plasencia, O.S.F., "Customs of the Pampangas in Their Lawsuits," B&R, 16:321–29.

20. Norman G. Owen, "The Principalia in Philippine History: Kabikolan, 1790–1878," *Philippine Studies* 22 (1974): 297–324.

21. José Basco y Vargas, "A Decree by Basco in 1784," B&R, 52: 291–301. On the need to control manpower in early Southeast Asian history see, e.g., Anthony Reid, "The Structure of Cities in Southeast Asia, Fifteenth to Seventeenth Centuries," *Journal of Southeast Asian Studies* 9 (September 1980): 243–50.

22. Nicholas P. Cushner and John A. Larkin, "Royal Land Grants in the Colonial Philippines (1571-1626): Implications for the Formation of a Social Elite," *Philippine Studies* 26 (1978): 102–11.

23. Spaniards introduced the idea of private ownership of land into the Philippines; however, it was the native elite who institutionalized the system throughout the archipelago (Cushner, *Landed Estates*, pp. 1–3).

24. Edgar Wickberg, "The Chinese Mestizo in Philippine History," *Journal of Southeast Asian History* 5 (March 1964): 62–100.

25. Yldefonso de Aragon, *Descripción geográfica y typográfica de la ysla de Luzon ó Nuevo Castilla con las particulares de las diez y seis provincias ó partidos que comprehende* (Manila: Imp. de D. Manuel

Memije, por D. Anastacio Gonzaga, 1819), pt. 4:3–38; Francisco Villacorta, O.E.S.A., *Administracion espiritual de las padres agustinos calzados de la provincia del Dulce Nombre de Jesus de las Islas Filipinas . . .* (Valladolid: Imp. de H. Roldan, 1833), pp. 72–82; *Illustración Filipina*, February 1, 1860, pp. 32–34; February 15, 1860, pp. 43–45.

26. Díaz-Trechuelo, *La Real Compañía*, p. 269; Díaz Arenas, *Memoria sobre el comercio*, p. 54; James A. LeRoy, *The Americans in the Philippines*, 2 vols. (Boston: Houghton Mifflin, 1914), 1:10.

27. Yldefonso de Aragon, *Estados de la población de Filipinas correspondiente a el año de 1818* (Manila: Imp. de D. Manuel Memije, por D. Anastacio Gonzaga, 1820), table 2; Mallat, *Les Philippines* 1:197.

28. Mariano A. Henson, *Mariano A. Henson's Pictorial and Historical Album of the City of Angeles, Pampanga* (Angeles: By the author, 1964); idem, *A Brief History of the Town of Angeles in the Province of Pampanga, Philippines* (San Fernando, Pampanga: Ing Katiwala Press, 1948), pp. 1–3; idem, *The Descendants of the Founder of Angeles, Pampanga, Don Angel Pantaleon de Miranda and of Don Severino Henson* (Angeles: By the author, 1966); idem, *The Hensons of Pampanga* (Angeles: By the author, 1948).

29. *Coleccion de documentos inéditos relativos al descubrimiento, conquista y organización de las antiguas posesiones españolas de ultramar*, vol. 2, *De las Islas Filipinas* (Madrid: Royal Academy of History, 1886), pp. 410–18.

30. Miguel de Loarca, "Relation of the Filipinas Islands," B&R, 5:47; Alzina, "Historia de las islas," bk. 3, chap. 5; Robustiano Echaúz, *Apuntes de la Isla de Negros* (Manila: Chofré y Cia, 1894), pp. 7–8, 94–101; Dean C. Worcester, *The Philippine Islands and Their People* (New York: Macmillan, 1899), pp. 265–69; Giovanni Francesco Gemelli Careri, *A Voyage to the Philippines* (Manila: Filipiniana Book Guild, 1963; original, 1699–1700), p. 55; HDP, San Carlos, pp. 13, 31; HDP, Hinigaran, p. 68; Mallat, *Les Philippines* 1:317–18; letter from Luther Parker to the Director of Education, Manila, January 13, 1913, BS, Visayas, 4:3–6; Timoteo S. Oración, "A Preliminary Report on Some Culture Aspects of the Bukidnons of Southeastern Negros Island, Philippines," *Unitas* 40 (1967): 156–81; idem, "The Magahats of Southern Negros, Philippines: Problems and Prospects," *Philippine Quarterly of Culture and Society* 2 (March-June, 1974): 21–29.

31. HDP, Hinigaran, p. 40.

32. San Antonio, *Chrónicas* 1:87; Juan de la Concepción, O.R.S.A., *Historia general de Philipinas*, 14 vols. (Manila and Sampaloc: Agustin de la Rosa y Balagtas and Hermano Balthasar Marino, 1789–92), 10:14–17, 13:149; Angel Martinez Cuesta, O.A.R., *Historia de la Isla de Negros, Filipinas, 1565–1898* (Madrid: Raycar, 1976), pp. 117–18, 127–28; Pedro Murillo Velarde, S.J., *Geographia historica de las Islas Philipinas, del*

Africa, y de sus islas adyacentes (Madrid: Gabriel Ramirez, 1752), p. 66; Manuel Buzeta, O.S.A., and Felipe Bravo, O.S.A., *Diccionario geográfico, estadístico, histórico de las Islas Filipinas*, 2 vols. (Madrid: José C. de la Peña, 1851), 2:558–59; Joaquín Martínez de Zúñiga, O.S.A., *Estadismo de las Islas Filipinas*, 2 vols. (Madrid: Imp. de la Viuda de M. Minuesa de los Ríos, 1893), 2:88; Félix Renouard de Sainte Croix, *Voyage commercial et politique aux Indes, aux Iles Philippines, à la Chine* . . . (Paris: Archives de Droit Français, 1810), 2:281; Joaquín Martínez de Zúñiga, O.S.A., *An Historical View of the Philippine Islands*, trans. John Maver (Manila: Filipiniana Book Guild, 1966; original 1803), p. 83; Anon., "Moro Raids Repulsed by Visayans" (pamphlet published in Manila, 1755), B&R, 48: 48–49; Chretien Louis Joseph de Guignes, "Observations on the Philippine Islands and the Isle de France," in *A General Collection of Best and Most Interesting Voyages and Travels in All Parts of the World*, ed. John Pinkerton, 17 vols. (London: Longman, Hurst, Rees, and Orme, 1812), 11:74.

33. Felipe Redondo y Sendino, *Breve reseña de lo que fue y de es la diócesis de Cebú en las Islas Filipinas* (Manila: Colegio de Sto. Tomás, 1886), pp. 139–44; Fernando Fulgosio, *Cronica de las Islas Filipinas* (Madrid: Rubio, Grilo y Vitturi, 1871), p. 84; Martinez Cuesta, *Historia*, pp. 12–15, 22–29, 53–64; Echaúz, *Apuntes*, pp. 13–14; letter of Governor Luis Villasis, Himamailan, Negros, April 20, 1840, Oficios de la Alcaldia m^{or} y Corregimiento de la Isla de Negros a la Superinted^{a} e Intend^{a} de la Hacienda, 1834–1858, Legajos de Varias Provincias, Negros, PNA; Modesto P. Sa-onoy, *A Brief History of the Church in Negros Occidental* (Bacolod: By the author, 1976), pp. 13–33.

34. *RF* 1:345–46; Mallat, *Les Philippines* 1:319–20; letters of Governor Luis Villasis, Himamailan, Negros, February 24, 1834, September 20, 1837, Oficios de la Alcaldia m^{or} y Corregimiento de la Isla de Negros a la Superintend^{a} e Intend^{a} de la Hacienda, 1834–1858, PNA; Zúñiga, *Estadismo* 2:88; Buzeta and Bravo, *Diccionario* 2:357–58.

35. Concepción, *Historia* 14:326–28; Echaúz, *Apuntes*, p. 9; Angel Martinez Cuesta, O.A.R., *History of Negros*, trans. Alfonso Felix, Jr. (Manila: Historical Conservation Society, 1980), pp. 124–25, 158; Francisco Varona, *Negros: historia anecdótica de su riqueza y de sus hombres* (Manila: General Printing Press, 1938), pp. 56–57. Montilla family tradition has it that Agustin was not really captured by Moros, that, indeed, he removed himself for some time because he had another family elsewhere (letter from Violeta Lopez-Gonzaga, Grand Rapids, Michigan, January 7, 1987, to the author). Nevertheless, Montilla's absence clearly raised the level of fear among the Christian denizens of Negros.

36. Mallat, *Les Philippines* 1:317–18; Martinez Cuesta, *History of Negros*, pp. 58, 110–12; HDP, Bacolod, Barrio Tangub, p. 34; Gemelli Careri, p. 55.

37. Echaúz, *Apuntes*, pp. 12–13.

38. Varona, *Negros*, pp. 80–81.

39. Letters from Governor Luis Villasis, September 20, 1836, and Governor José Saenz y Vizmanos, March 6, 1841, Himamaylan, Negros, Oficios de la Alcaldia m[or] y Corregimiento de la Isla de Negros a la Superintend[a] e Intend[a] de la Hacienda, 1834–1838, PNA; Gobierno Intendencia de Visayas, Expediente de Don Agustín Montilla, Isla de Negros, 1844, Legajos de Varias Provincias, Negros, PNA.

40. Romero, *Negros Occidental*, p. 22; Gobierno Intendencia de Visayas, Petition of the principales of Pulupandan, Isla de Negros, 1847, Legajos de Varias Provincias, Negros, PNA; Varona, *Negros*, pp. 49–54.

41. Varona, *Negros*, pp. 60–64; *A Britisher in the Philippines or the Letters of Nicholas Loney* (Manila: National Library, 1964), pp, 105–8. Montilla's 1844 petition to establish an agricultural settlement at Pulupandan indicated that, at that time, he had no intention of planting sugar.

42. *SN* 6 (1925):469; Echaúz, *Apuntes*, pp. 22–23; *Radicaciones de Estranjeros, Frances*, 1838–1898, Petition of Yves Germain Gaston for permanent residence in Negros, October 17, 1844, PNA; *A Gathering of the Descendants of Yves Leopold Germain Gaston, Hda. Sta. Rosalia, Manapla, Neg. Occ., Philippines* (souvenir program; n.p.: n.p., 1981), pp. 9–11; Romero, *Negros Occidental*, pp. 22, 32, 35; *Radicaciones de Españoles*, Petition of Don Manuel Saavedra on behalf of his brother José Saavedra for permission to live in Negros, July 28, 1849, PNA; Demy P. Sonza, *Sugar Is Sweet: The Story of Nicholas Loney* (Manila: National Historical Institute, 1977), p. 85n; Varona, *Negros*, pp. 141–42.

43. Yldefonso de Aragon, *Estados*, table 11; *Guía de forasteros en las Islas Filipinas, para el año 1847* (Manila: Colegio de Santo Tomás, 1847), pp. 338–39.

44. Martinez Cuesta, *History of Negros*, pp. 162–63.

CHAPTER 3. FRONTIERS

1. Noel Deerr, *The History of Sugar*, 2 vols. (London: Chapman and Hall, 1949–50), 2:532; *Sugar: Facts and Figures . . . 1952* (Washington, D.C.: United States Cuban Sugar Council, 1952), p. 44.

2. Antonio M. Regidor y Jurado and J. Warren Mason, *Commercial Progress in the Philippine Islands* (London: n.p., 1905), p. 39.

3. *Under Four Flags: The Story of Smith, Bell and Company in the Philippines* (Great Britain: n.p., n.d.), chaps. 3, 5; *SN* 9 (1928):649, 1 (1919):42; Benito Legarda, Jr., "Foreign Trade, Economic Change and Entrepreneurship in the Nineteenth-Century Philippines" (Ph.D. dissertation, Harvard University, 1955), pp. 345–46; Edgar Wickberg, *The Chi-*

nese in Philippine Life, 1850–1898 (New Haven: Yale University Press, 1965), pp. 84–88.

4. Wallace R. Aykroyd, *Sweet Malefactor: Sugar, Slavery and Human Society* (London: Heinemann, 1967), pp. 82–85, 106; Vladimir P. Timoshenko and Boris C. Swerling, *The World's Sugar: Progress and Policy* (Stanford: Stanford University Press, 1957), p. 17; *SN* 6 (1925):471; *A Britisher in the Philippines or the Letters of Nicholas Loney* (Manila: National Library, 1964), p. 71; Alfred S. Eichner, *The Emergence of Oligopoly: Sugar Refining as a Case Study* (Baltimore: Johns Hopkins University Press, 1969), pp. 38–42, 230–50; W&G, January 9, 1902, p. 8.

5. Bill Albert and Adrian Graves, eds., *Crisis and Change in the International Sugar Economy, 1860–1914* (Norwich and Edinburgh, UK: ISC Press, 1984); C. J. Robertson, *World Sugar Production and Consumption: An Economic-Geographical Survey* (London: John Bale, Sons, and Danielsson, 1934), pp. 2, 63–64; Jack T. Turner, *Marketing of Sugar*, Indiana University School of Business, Bureau of Business Research Study, no. 38 (Homewood, Ill.: Richard D. Irwin, 1955), p. 10; *Handbook of the Philippine Sugar Industry*, 2d ed. (Manila: Sugar News Press, 1929), pp. 39–42.

6. Deerr, *History of Sugar* 2:490–491, 531; Philippine Islands, Bureau of Customs, *Annual Report of the Insular Collector of Customs for the Fiscal Year Ended June 30, 1913* (Manila: Bureau of Printing, 1913), pp. 15–16. The 1887 consolidation of American eastern refineries into the Sugar Refineries Company allowed tycoon Henry O. Havemeyer to control raw sugar prices (Luzviminda Bartolome Francisco and Jonathan Shepard Fast, *Conspiracy for Empire; Big Business, Corruption and the Politics of Imperialism in America, 1876–1907* [Quezon City: Foundation for Nationalist Studies, 1985], p. 30).

7. John Foreman, *The Philippine Islands*, 3d ed. (New York: Charles Scribner's Sons, 1906), pp. 640–41; *MT*, October 1, 1900, p. 8; April 3, 1901, p. 4; W&G, February 9, 1905, p. 7; *PAR* 8 (1915): 152; John A. Larkin, *The Pampangans: Colonial Society in a Philippine Province* (Berkeley and Los Angeles: University of California Press, 1972), chap. 5; Alfred McCoy, "Ylo-ilo: Factional Conflict in a Colonial Economy, Iloilo Province, Philippines, 1937–1955" (Ph.D. dissertation, Yale University, 1977), pp. 92–102.

8. *PAR* 15 (1922): 205–8; *Prospectus of the San Carlos Milling Company, Limited* (Honolulu: n.p., 1912), p. 4; letter from J. D. Fauntleroy, Supervisor of Negros Occidental, to the President of the Provincial Board, Bacolod, August 25, 1903, BMR; *Census: 1903* 4:226–28. Rinderpest led to increased cattle rustling in Negros (Philippine Islands, Bureau of Constabulary, *Annual Report of the Director of Constabulary for the Fiscal Year 1909* [Manila: Bureau of Printing, 1909], p. 8).

9. Memo from Jose R. Luzuriaga to William H. Taft, Philippine Commission, Manila, February 1904, BIA, File 4122, incl. 7; John A. R. Newlands and Benjamin E. R. Newlands, *Sugar: A Handbook for Planters and Refiners* (London and New York: Spon, 1909), chap. 25.

10. Report of Jose R. Luzuriaga to the Philippine Commission (ca. 1904), BIA, File 4122, incl. 10; W&G, March 29, 1906, p. 6; April 19, 1906, p. 6; *Under Four Flags*, chap. 7; Charles Burke Elliott, *The Philippines to the End of the Commission Government: A Study in Tropical Democracy* (Indianapolis: Bobbs-Merrill, 1917), pp. 370–72; *PFP*, January 25, 1913, p. 6; *MT*, May 27, 1914, p. 1.

11. U.S. Congress, Senate, *Loss of Spanish Markets for Philippine Sugar and Tobacco by Reason of American Occupation*, S. Doc. 484, 60th Cong., 1st. sess., 1908, pp. 1–10; Bonifacio S. Salamanca, *The Filipino Reaction to American Rule, 1901–1913* (Hamden, Conn.: Shoe String Press, 1968), pp. 121–39; *SN* 9 (1928): 651. Congress gave the Philippines tariff concessions only after the U.S. treaty with Spain expired, for it allowed the latter free entry into the American market via the Philippines.

12. Cleve W. Hines, *Cane Production and Sugar Manufacture in the Philippine Islands*, Government of the Philippine Islands, Bureau of Agriculture, Bulletin 33 (Manila: Bureau of Printing, 1919), pp. 105–202; Deerr, *History of Sugar* 2:559–77; Eichner, *Oligopoly*, pp. 31–36; G. H. Jenkins, *Introduction to Cane Sugar Technology* (Amsterdam: Elsevier, 1966), pp. 5–6, 283, 286–87, 325; V. E. Baikow, *Manufacture and Refining of Raw Cane Sugar* (Amsterdam: Elsevier, 1967), pp. 4–6. The cost, for example, of the machinery and railway for the first central constructed at San Carlos, Negros Occidental, in 1910 came to $700,000 (*Prospectus of the San Carlos Milling Company*, p. 2).

13. Francisco Gutierrez Creps, *Memoria sobre el cultivo, beneficio y comercio del azúcar* (Manila: Celestino Miralles, 1878), pp. 60–74; Paul de la Gironière, *Aventures d'un gentilhomme breton aux Iles Philippines* (Paris: Firmin Didot Frères, Fils et Cie, 1857), pp. 432–33; Rafael Díaz Arenas, *Memoria sobre el comercio y navegacion de las Islas Filipinas* (Cádiz: Imp. de D. Domingo Féros, 1838), pp. 49–50; Jean Mallat de Bassilan, *Les Philippines: Histoire, géographie, moeurs, agriculture, industrie et commerce des colonies espagnoles dans l'Océanie*, 2 vols. (Paris: Arthus Bertrand, 1846), 1:132–33; *A Gathering of the Descendants of Yves Leopold Germain Gaston, Hda. Sta. Rosalia, Manapla, Neg. Occ., Philippines* (souvenir program; n.p.: n.p., 1981), pp. 9–11; Henry T. Ellis, *Hong Kong to Manilla and the Lakes of Luzon, in the Philippine Isles, in the Year 1856* (London: Smith, Elder, 1859), p. 96; G. E. Nesom and Herbert S. Walker, *Handbook on the Sugar Industry of the Philippine Islands* (Manila: Bureau of Printing, 1912), pt. 1, p. 14; letter of the Luzon Sugar Refining Co. [Smith, Bell and Company, Agents] to the Philippine Commission, Manila, May 27, 1907, BIA, File C-1275, incl. 4.

14. Chamber of Commerce of the Philippine Islands, *Yearbook of the Philippine Islands* (Manila: Bureau of Printing, 1920), p. 156; Philippine Commercial Agencies, comp., *Economic Resources and Development in the Philippine Islands* (Manila: Philippine Commercial Agencies, 1920), pp. 52–53; *PAR* 3 (1910): 731, 6 (1913): 76; *SN* 1 (1919): 13. Carlos Ledesma confirmed the lack of planter interest in farming (interview, Makati, Metro Manila, March 12, 1986).

15. M. J. Lannoy, *Iles Philippines* (Brussels: Delevingne et Callewaert, 1849), p. 127; Ramon González Fernández and Federico Moreno y Jeréz, *Anuario filipino para 1877* (Manila: Est. tip. de Plana, 1877), p. 46; Roy A. Ballinger, *A History of Sugar Marketing*, Economic Research Service, Agricultural Economic Report, no. 197 (Washington, D.C.: U.S. Department of Agriculture, 1971), pp. 9–15; Deerr, *History of Sugar* 2:441–43.

16. *RF* 2 (May 1877), 225, 230–32; Alexander R. Webb, "The Sugar Industry of the Philippines," *U.S. Consular Reports* 31 (1889): 375–76; idem, "Sugar and Rice Culture in the Philippine Islands," *U.S. Consular Reports* 27 (1888): 242. On the classification of Philippine sugar see *SN* 1 (1919): 18; 1 (1920): 13–15. Manila shipped 19,104 metric tons of pilon sugar to Asian ports in 1906; 19,458 in 1907; 37,734 in 1908; and 20,861 in 1909 (W&G, December 13, 1906, p. 6; February 13, 1908, p. 59; March 4, 1909, p. 86; March 3, 1910, p. 87).

17. *SN* 4 (1923): 7–15; Philippine Commercial Agencies, *Economic Resources*, p. 54; Philippine Islands, Bureau of Science, *Press Bulletin No. 73* (Manila: Bureau of Printing, 1917), p. 3; Carlos Quirino, *History of the Philippine Sugar Industry* (Manila: Kalayaan, 1974), pp. 61–62. The local Pampangan cottage industry of making clay pilones died out at this time as well (HDP, San Fernando). See also *SN* 7 (1926): 286; *PAR* 10 (1917): 97; *Philippine Sugar Handbook, 1972 Edition* (Manila: Sugar News Press, 1972), p. 20; *MT*, November 6, 1919, p. 8; March 13, 1920, p. 8; March 24, 1920, p. 6; *PFP*, September 27, 1919, p. 9. The shortage of wartime shipping curtailed the ability of exporters to reach markets other than those in Asia (letter from Alfred D. Cooper, Agent for San Carlos Milling Company, to Governor-general Francis Burton Harrison, Manila, July 2, 1918, QP; *MDB*, March 1, 1918, pp. 1, 4; Philippine Islands, Bureau of Commerce and Industry, *Statistical Bulletin No. 3, of the Philippine Islands, 1920* (Manila: Bureau of Printing, 1921), p. 218; letter from George Fairchild, Manila, to George M. Rolph, Sugar Equalization Board, Washington, D.C., ca. September 1918, BIA, File 4122, incl. 165).

18. John R. Hanson, III, *Trade in Transition: Exports from the Third World, 1840–1900* (New York: Academic Press, 1980), pp. 119, 124–25; Creps, *Memoria*, p. 78. After more than three decades of relative stability, from 1870 to 1902 the peso fell in relation to the dollar from 1.0435 to .4152 (*Census: 1903* 4:563n).

19. Each large Philippine central during the 1923–24 milling season required, on average, more than 5,000 hectares of cane to meet its production needs (*SN* 6 [1925]: 529). Richard John Gilbert, "The Introduction of American Capital into the Sugar Industry of the Philippines and Its Impact on the Pre-Existing Patterns of Land" (M.A. thesis, University of Hawaii at Manoa, 1967), pp. 30–31, 43, 47–49; Mark Aaron Glago, "American Private Capital in the Philippines, 1898–1941" (M.A. thesis, University of Hawaii at Manoa, 1966), pp. 16–18; W. Cameron Forbes, *The Philippine Islands*, 2 vols. (Boston and New York: Houghton Mifflin, 1928), 2:58–60; Elliott, *Tropical Democracy*, p. 358; Dean C. Worcester, *The Philippines Past and Present*, ed. Ralston Hayden (New York: Macmillan, 1930), pp. 590–96.

20. *Prospectus of the San Carlos Milling Company*, p. 1.

21. Letter from George Fairchild, Manila, to Manuel Luis Quezon, Washington, D.C., May 23, 1917; letter from Charles Willis, New York, to Manuel Luis Quezon, New York, June 15, 1917; letter from George Ross, Pacific Commercial Company, New York, to Manuel Luis Quezon, Manila, March 17, 1918, QP.

22. Glago, "American Private Capital," pp. 18, 25–26, 30–31; Quirino, *Philippine Sugar Industry*, pp. 49–66; Yoshiko Nagano-kano, *The Structure of the Philippine Sugar Industry at the End of the American Colonial Period and After 1974*, Third World Studies Center, Commodity Series, no. 3 (Quezon City: Third World Studies Center, University of the Philippines, 1981), pp. 9–10.

23. Nagano, *Structure*, pp. 7–11; letter from George Fairchild to Governor-general Francis Burton Harrison, Manila, October 9, 1919; letter from General Venancio Concepcion, President of PNB, to the Board of Directors of PNB, June 21, 1920, QP; *PFP*, March 22, 1913, p. 8; April 26, 1913, p. 8; *M*, September 15, 1917, p. 4.

24. *MT*, February 11, 1919, p. 1; May 25, 1919, p. 2; September 9, 1919, p. 3; August 20, 1968, p. 13; letter from Ernest J. Westerhouse, General Manager of the Manila Railroad Company, to Speaker of the House Sergio Osmeña, Manila, August 2, 1918, QP; *First Report of the Hawaiian-Philippine Co., Philippine Islands, Fiscal Years Ended September 30, 1921 and September 30, 1922* (Honolulu: Hawaiian-Philippine Co.), p. 16; *PFP*, March 8, 1919, p. 19; April 19, 1919, p. 27; *MDB*, August 25, 1921, p. 19; *Compilation of Committee Reports for the Fourth Annual Convention of the Philippine Sugar Association, Manila, P.I., September Sixth to Tenth, 1926* (Manila: Philippine Sugar Association, 1926), p. 2.

25. On the worldwide frontier phenomenon see William H. McNeill, *The Great Frontier: Freedom and Hierarchy in Modern Times* (Princeton: Princeton University Press, 1983); and Walter Prescott Webb, *The Great Frontier* (Austin: University of Texas Press, 1951), chaps. 1–6. See also

John A. Larkin, "Philippine History Reconsidered: A Socioeconomic Perspective," *American Historical Review* 87 (June 1982): 612–24.

26. HDP, Hinigaran, pp. 2, 87, 117; HDP, San Carlos, pp. 17–18; HDP, Pontevedra, pp. 1–2, 4; HDP, Saravia, pp. 2, 26, 37–38; McCoy, "Ylo-ilo," p. 81; *RF* 2 (1875): 146; letter from Acting Consul Nicholas Loney, Manila, to Foreign Secretary Lord Edward Stanley, London, January 31, 1867, PRO, F.O. 72/1155; *A Britisher*, p. 109; letter from A. A. Forshee, Bacolod, to T. S. Barbour, Boston, February 9, 1909, BMR.

27. Robustiano Echaúz, *Apuntes de la Isla de Negros* (Manila: Chofré y Cia, 1894), pp. 15–17; Angel Martinez Cuesta, O.A.R., *History of Negros*, trans. Alfonso Felix, Jr. (Manila: Historical Conservation Society, 1980), p. 222; Francisco Varona, *Negros: historia anecdótica de su riqueza y sus hombres* (Manila: General Printing Press, 1938), p. 27; Loney to Farren, July 10, 1861, p. 25; Marcelino Simonena, O.A.R., *Father Fernando Cuenca of St. Joseph, Augustinian Recollect*, trans. Ma. Soledad L. Locsin (Bacolod: Negros Occidental Historical Commission, 1974), pp. 14–16, 21–28; Rafael Díaz Arenas, *Memorias históricas y estadísticas de Filipinas y particularmente de la grande isla de Luzon* (Manila: Imp. del Diario de Manila, 1850), cuaderno 17, no. 6.

28. Alfred W. McCoy, "A Queen Dies Slowly: The Rise and Decline of Iloilo City," in *Philippine Social History: Global Trade and Local Transformations*, ed. Alfred W. McCoy and Ed. C. de Jesus (Quezon City: Ateneo de Manila University Press, 1982), pp. 303–7; Wickberg, *The Chinese*, p. 77; John T. Omohundro, *Chinese Merchant Families in Iloilo: Commerce and Kin in a Central Philippine City* (Quezon City and Athens, Ohio: Ateneo de Manila University Press and Ohio University Press, 1981), p. 16; Varona, *Negros*, pp. 27–31; *Proclamation and Inauguration of the City of Cadiz* (Cadiz, Negros Occidental: n.p., 1966), p. 34; *Saravia Centennial Anniversary and Inauguration of the New Town Hall* (Saravia, Negros Occidental: n.p., 1959), p. 1.

29. McCoy, "Queen," pp. 308–9; Demy P. Sonza, *Sugar Is Sweet: The Story of Nicholas Loney* (Manila: National Historical Institute, 1977), pp. viii, 138; *A Britisher*, pp. 66–67. Annual sugar exports from Iloilo rose from 759 metric tons in 1855 to 141,614 in 1920 (McCoy, "Ylo-ilo," p. 26).

30. Martinez Cuesta, *History of Negros*, pp. 231–32; HDP, San Carlos, pp. 31, 41, 53–54, 57; W&G, December 23, 1908, p. 448; *M*, May 15, 1918, p. 3; July 31, 1918, p. 3. In 1918, 6.5 percent of land in Negros Occidental devoted to agriculture was still classified as public lands, meaning, presumably, land recently homesteaded (*Census: 1918* 3:218–19).

31. Information on property ownership comes in large part from notarial registers in the Philippine National Archives, Manila. Until 1902, they were called *protocolos*, thereafter *notarios*. They contain lists and descriptions of notarized documents including a wide variety of contracts relating to real estate and agricultural matters. The books I consulted do

not constitute even a third of those available for the period, but they do appear to be representative of the whole. The numbers of the books used, which do not refer to dates, are *Protocolos,* 1723–49, 1806–10, 1815–19; *Notarios,* 7545, 7548, 7550, 7551, 7552, 7555, 7562, 7564, 7585, 7586, 8170–72, 8179, 8195, 8855, 8857, 10320, 15580, 15631.

Of those names on the list of gobernadorcillos of Hinigaran in the period 1806 to 1844, only two, Mongcal and Grijaldo, appear on the 1896 list of Negros sugarland owners or in the *protocolos;* see HDP, Hinigaran, p. 3; *Estadisticas,* Negros Occidental, 1896, PNA; *Protocolo,* 1874, Negros Occidental, PNA. On Valderrama and Juan Araneta, see Modesto P. Sa-onoy, *Valderrama* (Bacolod: Negros Historical Commission, 1979), chaps. 1, 2; *SN* 13 (1932): 698–99; "Negros News" by W. O. Valentine, ca. 1923, W. O. Valentine file, BMR; Varona, *Negros,* p. 75; *Protocolos,* 1808, 1818, Negros Occidental, PNA.

32. *Estadisticas,* Negros Occidental, 1896, PNA; *Census: 1918* 2:380; *Census: 1939,* 1, pt. 3, pp. 7–8; Martinez Cuesta, *History of Negros,* pp. 255, 376; Simonena, *Father Fernando,* p. 7; *M,* July 31, 1915, p. 3; "History of Silay" (Silay: n.p., ca. 1959), p. 1. (mimeo); *Protocolos,* 1738, 1739, 1746, Negros Occidental, PNA.

The Clavaria Law of 1849 stipulated that all native Filipinos had to have last names, and for those who did not, mostly the poor, a list of names was supplied from an alphabetical roster of some sixty thousand Spanish names. Towns were supplied sections of the list, and people in a given locality tended to be assigned surnames beginning with the same letter. In numerous barrios in Negros, this phenomenon of a common first letter occurs, heuristic evidence of a common place of origin on a neighboring island. See, for example, HDP, Pontevedra, p. 9. See also McCoy, "Queen," pp. 317–22; McCoy, "Ylo-ilo," p. 72; Loney to Farren, July 10, 1861, p. 10; John R. White, *Bullets and Bolos* (New York: Century, 1928), pp. 55–56.

33. *Protocolos, Notarios,* Negros Occidental, PNA; White, *Bullets,* pp. 40–41, 44; Webb, "Sugar Industry," p. 375; *SN* 12 (1931): 283–84; 14 (1933): 92–93, 622–24; HDP, San Carlos, p. 23; Simonena, *Father Fernando,* p. 23; Rámon Martínez Vigil, O.P., *Elementos de geografía descriptiva particularmente de las Islas Filipinas* (Manila: El Colegio de Sto. Tomás, 1895), p. 89; *Radicaciones de Estranjeros, Aleman,* January 29, 1857, PNA; Martinez Cuesta, *History of Negros,* p. 255; Manuel Azcarraga y Palermo, *La Libertad de comercio en las Islas Filipinas* (Madrid: José Noguera, 1871), pp. 168–69; Sonza, *Sugar Is Sweet,* chap. 18; letter from Nicholas Loney, Madrid, to James Murray, Foreign Office, London, December 31, 1862, p. 3, PRO, F.O. 72/1042; *SN* 12 (1931): 283–84; 14 (1933): 92–93; *PFP,* September 18, 1909, p. 6; July 25, 1914, p. 5.

34. Oscar Lopez, ed., *The Lopez Family: Its Origins and Genealogy*, 4 vols. (Manila: Eugenio Lopez Foundation, 1982), provides information on 2,676 heirs of Basilio and Maria Sabina Jaranilla Jalandoni through seven generations. See also McCoy, "Ylo-ilo," pp. 65–72.

35. Annual Report of the Governor of Negros Occidental, 1901, BIA, sec. vii; HDP, Hinigaran, p. 83; Martinez Cuesta, *History of Negros*, pp. 261–62; White, *Bullets*, p. 180.

36. The usual equivalents were as follows: One ganta of rice or corn seedlings plants 20 ares of land. Five gantas of rice or corn seedlings plant 1 hectare of land. One cavan of rice or corn seedlings plants 5 hectares of land. One lacsa equals 10,000 cane points, and 2 lacsas and a fraction plant 1 hectare, the exact amount dependent on the quality of the land; the better the land, the more points could be planted. As late as 1886, farmers in Negros were complaining about the lack of a land registration system (Miguel Pérez et al., "Crónica semihistoria de Filipinas y en especial de las Islas Visayas desde 1877 a 1887" [ms., Newberry Library], p. 3).

37. Martinez Cuesta, *History of Negros*, pp. 378–87; *Notarios*, 7562, 7564, Negros Occidental, PNA; *M*, December 15, 1917, p. 3; letter from G. Seaver, Field Investigator, Manila, to Archibald Harrison, Secretary of the PNB, August 15, 1918, QP. On colonial land laws see Vicente J. Francisco, *The Cadastral Act, Public Land Act, and Laws on Mortgages* (Manila: East Publishing, 1938).

38. Martinez Cuesta, *History of Negros*, p. 387; Karl J. Pelzer, *Pioneer Settlement in the Asiatic Tropics* (New York: American Geographical Society, 1948), pp. 108–10; "The Torrens Title System of Registration in the Philippines," June 25, 1915, BIA, File 1762, incl. 47-a; Vicente Mills, *Planned Surveys*, Philippine Commonwealth, Department of Agriculture and Commerce, Technical Bulletin, no. 8 (Manila: Bureau of Printing, 1937), pp. 138–41; *MT*, March 28, 1920, p. 13; *M*, May 6, 1915, p. 2; May 20, 1915, p. 3; *Notarios*, Negros Occidental, PNA.

39. McCoy, "Queen," pp. 320–22; Martinez Cuesta, *History of Negros*, p. 297; White, *Bullets*, pp. 156–57; HDP, Victorias, p. 51; *M*, July 10, 1920, p. 1; July 21, 1920, p. 4. In Negros in 1970, the biggest scandal was the use of bulldozers by the mayor of Cadiz to drive swidden farmers off upland portions of that municipality so he could plant sugar.

40. Echaúz, *Apuntes*, pp. 94–101; *PFP*, August 14, 1920, p. 38; Philippine Islands, Bureau of Constabulary, *Annual Report . . . 1913*, p. 4; letter concerning the Dacongcogon Settlement Farm School, from Secundino M. Amantoy, Kabankalan, September 18, 1982, to the author; Niall O'Brien, *Seeds of Injustice: Reflections on the Murder Frame-up of the Negros Nine in the Philippines* (Dublin: O'Brien Press, 1985).

41. *RF* 2 (1875): 146; *Estadisticas*, Negros Occidental, 1896, PNA;

Protocolos, Negros Occidental, PNA; Varona, *Negros*, p. 155. Newspapers listing haciendas for sale included *El Eco de Panay* (Iloilo), March 8, 1887, p. 4; *LI*, April 6, 1907, p. 2; *M*, June 19, 1920, p. 2. The twelve families with the largest land holdings in 1896 were Yulo, 3,453 hectares; Lacson, 1,883 hectares; de la Rama, 1,663 hectares; Lopez, 1,440 hectares; Locsin, 1,258 hectares; Benedicto, 1,139 hectares; Montilla, 1,116 hectares; de Luzuriaga, 1,113 hectares; Ledesma, 1,067 hectares; Ardosa, 1,028 hectares; Gonzaga, 939 hectares; and de Canete, 900 hectares.

42. Varona, *Negros*, pp. 69–72, 110–13, 125–26, 134–35; Felix B. Regalado and Quintin B. Franco, *History of Panay* (Jaro, Iloilo City: Central Philippine University, 1973), pp. 474–76.

43. Loney to Farren, April 12, 1857, pp. 64–65; Varona, *Negros*, pp. 84, 147–49; Nesom and Walker, *Handbook*, pt. 1, p. 14; McCoy, "Queen," p. 310; Legarda, "Foreign Trade," pp. 466–74; Pérez et al., "Crónica," p. 3; *A Gathering*, pp. 13–14, 34; *M*, June 5, 1913, p. 2; December 27, 1913, p. 4; May 11, 1915, p. 3; May 8, 1918, p. 3; *LI*, June 11, 1906, p. 1; *Protocolos, Notarios*, Negros Occidental, PNA. Even the PNB, on occasion, gave anticipatory crop loans to bad risks. On the wide range of creditors of Russell, Sturgis, see E. H. Green vs. Estate of Jonathan Russell, ms. 1247, Baker Library, Harvard University.

44. *M*, August 12, 1915, p. 2.

45. Jaime Escobar y Lozano, *El indicador del viajero en las Islas Filipinas* (Manila: Chofré, 1885), p. 137; John Foreman, *The Philippine Islands* (London: Sampson Low, Marston, 1892), pp. 474–75; Henry Savage Landor, *The Gems of the East*, 2 vols. (London: Macmillan, 1904), 2:272; William Thomas Townsend, Personal Diary, December 13, 1903–May 2, 1907, Houghton Library, Harvard University; *LL*, October 3, 1899, p. 3; April 7, 1900, p. 3; *LI*, May 1906–April 1907; Philippine Islands, Bureau of Education, *Local Geographical and Historical Notes: Province of Occidental Negros* (Manila: Bureau of Printing, 1915), pp. 3–4; Annual Report of the Governor of Negros Occidental, 1916, BIA, pp. 7, 11; *M*, October 1917–October 1920; Varona, *Negros*, pp. 76–77; White, *Bullets*, p. 118; Manuscript Report of the Taft Commission, Trip to Negros Occidental, 1901, BIA, p. 38; *SN* 1 (1919): frontispiece; Felicidad A. Jugo, "Classes of Society in Occidental Negros," BS, p. 1; Echaúz, *Apuntes*, pp. 30–31.

46. *A Gathering*, pp. 15–16; Varona, *Negros*, pp. 149–50, 156–58; Francisco Sádaba del Carmen, O.R.S.A., *Catálogo de los religiosos agustinos recoletos de la Provincia de San Nicolás de Tolentino de Filipinas . . .* (Madrid: Imp. del Asilo de Huérfanos del Sagrada Corazón de Jesús, 1906), pp. 862–63, 865; Cavada, *Historia* 2:327; Melecio B. Lamayo, "Social and Economic Condition of My Town," BS, pp. 1–4; Doreen Fernandez, *The Iloilo Zarzuela: 1903–1930* (Quezon City: Ateneo de Manila University Press, 1978), p. xii; *El Eco de Panay*, March 8, 1887, p. 3; *MT*, September

11, 1901, pp. 2–3, 6; *M*, 1913–1920; White, *Bullets*, p. 27; HDP, Bacolod, p. 10; *PFP*, July 18, 1914, p. 5; June 12, 1920, p. 36; John Arnold, ed., *The Philippines: The Land of Palm and Pine* (Manila: Bureau of Printing, 1912), p. 143.

47. "Relacion de las Haciendas en la jurisdiccion de este pueblo [Eustaquio Lopez] con los nombres de los propietarios y de los encargados y numero de jornaleros que trabajan en cada una de ellos," Record Group 395, 2620 Division of Visayas, U.S. National Archives. See also Edith Steinmetz, Report, Bacolod, 1907, BMR; Echaúz, *Apuntes*, p. 43; Foreman, *Philippine Islands* (1892), p. 442; Pérez et al., "Crónica," p. 1. The Annual Report of the Governor, Negros Occidental, 1908, BIA, p. 7, notes a drop in the number of sugar plantations, from 678 in 1905 to 326 in the current year, a result of harsh economic conditions.

48. *PFP*, February 3, 1912, p. 30. In 1903, of 2,013 farms 10 hectares or larger (not specifying crop, but probably including the bulk of the sugar farms), 160 were operated by cash tenants and 241 by share tenants. In 1918, the figures were 3,322 farms, 275 cash tenants and 430 share tenants. In both years almost all the other farms were owner operated or managed by salaried workers (*Census: 1903* 4:273; *Census: 1918* 3:107). See also *M*, October 18, 1917, p. 1; January 12, 1918, p. 2; Loney to Farren, July 10, 1861, pp. 9, 14–15; Memoria, Negros Occidental, 1890, PNA, pp. 18–19; Echaúz, *Apuntes*, pp. 43–45; Foreman, *Philippine Islands* (1892), p. 315; *Protocolo*, 1817, *Notarios*, 7550–52, 7555, 7564, 7585–86, 8171–72, 8195, 10320, 10362, Negros Occidental, PNA.

49. *Renacimiento Filipino*, September 14, 1911, pp. 328–30; Echaúz, *Apuntes*, chap. 9; Webb, "Sugar Industry," pp. 375–76.

50. Tomas Concepcion, "Native Marriage Customs in Occidental Negros [ca. 1918]," BS, p. 7; *M*, November 4, 1916, p. 3; Romualdo M. Araneta, "Social Classes and Beliefs of the People in Bago, Occ. Negros," BS, pp. 1–4; mission letter of Archibald A. Forshee, Bacolod, March 11, 1903, BMR.

51. Echaúz, *Apuntes*, pp. 160–63.

52. *Renacimiento Filipino*, November 7, 1911, pp. 580–81; Echaúz, *Apuntes*, pp. 61–63, 160–63; Foreman, *Philippine Islands* (1892), p. 317; *M*, October 3, 1920, p. 3; the tax list shows 805 Chinese in Negros in 1894, about 90 percent of whom worked as "jornaleros," perhaps in sugar mills (Gobierno Politico Militar de la Provincia de Negros Occidental, "Empadronamiento general de los Chinos de esta provincia . . . fecha 16 de Marzo ultimo," PNA).

53. "Relacion de las haciendas enclavadas en la jurisdiccion de este pueblo . . . [Silay]," December 12, 1900; "Relacion de los Hacenderos dentro de la jurisdiccion de este pueblo [Guimbalaon] y el numero total de sus operarios," January 17, 1901, Record Group 395, 2620 Division of the Visayas, U.S. National Archives; Edith Steinmetz, "A Short Trip in the

Philippines," Bacolod, 1908, BMR; *Renacimiento Filipino*, September 14, 1911, p. 329; November 7, 1911, p. 580; Yves Henry, *Technical and Financial Conditions of the Production of Sugar in the Philippines*, trans. Irwin McNiece (Manila: Philippine Sugar Association, 1929), pp. 53–54; Landor, *Gems* 2:274; *MT*, December 12, 1919, p. 2; letter from Stephen Hise, Bacolod, to F. P. Haggard, Boston, April 21, 1902, BMR; *Protocolos*, 1817, 1818, Negros Occidental, PNA.

54. *Notario*, 7564, Negros Occidental, PNA; José Felipe del Pan, *Las Islas Filipinas, progresos en 70 años* (Manila: Imp. de la Oceania Española, 1878), p. 379; *M*, December 27, 1913, p. 1; November 13, 1920, pp. 1–2; Foreman, *Philippine Islands* (1892), p. 449; *SN* 1 (1920): 3–4; *PFP*, February 6, 1915, p. 7; Gobierno P. M. del Distrito de Isla de Negros, "Novedades, Varias Provincias," April 30, 1875 [Bacolod], Legajos de Negros, PNA.

55. White, *Bullets*, pp. 160–61; U.S. War Department, U.S. Philippine Commission, *Annual Report of the Philippine Commission, 1903* (Washington, D.C.: Government Printing Office, 1904), pt. 3, p. 122; Martinez Cuesta, *History of Negros*, p. 200; Philippine Islands, Constabulary, *Annual Report . . . 1911* (Manila: Bureau of Printing, 1911), p. 6.

56. *Protocolos*, 1807, 1817, 1818, Negros Occidental, PNA; Martinez Cuesta, *History of Negros*, p. 232; *M*, 1913–20, passim; White, *Bullets*, pp. 52–53, 110–14, 117–18; U.S. War Department, U.S. Philippine Commission, *Annual Report . . . 1905*, pt. 3, p. 88; Emilio Tarrosa, "The Life of the People of Negros Occidental in the Last Half of the Nineteenth Century as Told by the Traditions," BS, pp. 10–11; Memoria 1890, Negros Occidental, PNA; Annual Report of the Governor of Negros Occidental, 1906, BIA, p. 6; Díaz Arenas, *Memorias*, "Suplemento y Adiciones", BIA, File 1184, incls. 14, 28. Information on appointed and elected officials in Negros can be found in *Elecciones*, Negros, PNA, various *guias*, and most twentieth-century Philippine newspapers.

57. Ignacio Villamor, *Criminality in the Philippine Islands, 1903–1908* (Manila: Bureau of Printing, 1909), p. 75.

58. Memoria 1890, Negros Occidental, PNA; Pérez et al., "Crónica," pp. 3–4; *PFP*, October 3, 1908, p. 3; June 18, 1910, p. 12; March 30, 1918, pp. 18, 20–21; *SN* 1 (1919): 26–27; 1 (1920): 3–4; 2 (1921): 486–87. Gilbert ("American Capital," p. 16) asserts that competition from a rising number of hemp and coconut plantations caused a shortage of migrant labor in Negros in the 1890s.

59. Letterbook, 1900, Record Group 395, 4340 Manapla Detachment, U.S. National Archives; Annual Report of the Governor of Negros Occidental, 1903, BIA, p. 13; Annual Report of the Governor of Negros Occidental, 1910, BIA, p. 4.

60. *MT*, August 28, 1919, p. 5; Circular 21, Philippine Constabulary, BIA, File 1184, incl. 132; the Insular Lumber Company, BIA File 11457;

Negros-Philippine Lumber Company, BIA, File 27419. Extensive information exists on public and private education on Negros; see, for example: Evergisto Bazaco, O.P., *History of Education in the Philippines,* 2d ed. (Manila: University of Santo Tomas Press, 1953), pp. 305–11; *Guía oficial de Filipinas, 1889,* 2 vols. (Manila: M. Pérez, 1888), 2:274; *LI,* May 9, 1906–July 26, 1906; *M,* April 24, 1918, p. 4; June 2, 1918, p. 4.

61. Tarrosa, "The Life," p. 10.

62. *Capagmasusian Qñg Aldo Pañgasilang Ning Magalang* [The Souvenir Program on the Founding Day of Magalang, December 13, 1863–December 13, 1954] (Magalang, Pampanga: n.p., 1954), pp. 19–33. See also Larkin, *Pampangans,* chaps. 4–8.

63. "Datos historicos de este municipio de Mexico, provincia de la Pampanga, Islas Filipinas," LPC, pp. 3–4; Macario G. Naval, "Pottery and Pilon-Making in Santo Tomas, Pampanga," BS; Philippine Islands, Bureau of Education, *Local Geographical and Historical Notes: Province of Pampanga* (Manila: Bureau of Printing, 1915), pp. 4–6.

64. *Tarlac Province: 100th Year Anniversary, December 25–30, 1974,* souvenir program (n.p.: n.p., 1974); *Census: 1903* 2:203–4; *Census: 1918* 2:249–251; *Protocolos, Notarios,* Pampanga, PNA. Nineteenth-century Capampangan pioneers into southern Tarlac included Braulio Aquino and Pablo Quiambao, great-grandfathers of Senator Benigno Aquino, Jr. (Nick Joaquin, *The Aquinos of Tarlac: An Essay on History as Three Generations* [Mandaluyong, Metro Manila: Cacho Hermanos, 1983], pp. 26–30).

65. Yldefonso de Aragon, *Descripción geográfica y topográfica de la ysla de Luzon ó Nueva Castilla con las particulares de las diez y seis provincias ó partidos que comprehende* (Manila: Imp. de D. Manuel Memije, por D. Anastacio Gonzaga, 1819), pt. 4, pp. 2–17; Alfred Marche, *Luçon et Palaouan: Six Années de Voyages aux Philippines* (Paris: Librairie Hachette et Cie, 1887), pp. 180–81; "Gobierno Municipal de Floridablanca, Provincia de la Pampanga, I.F.," LPC, p. 2; Cavada, *Historia,* 1:162; *Census: 1903* 4:235.

66. González Fernández and Moreno, *Anuario . . . 1877,* advertisement section, Almacen Santo Cristo, n.p.; *Notario* 10818, entry for January 15, 1915, Pampanga, PNA; interviews with three former workers at Joven's factory, Bacolor, August 11, 1964.

67. Provincia de la Pampanga, Padron, 1887–88, Serie 1a, Españoles, PNA; Terrenos de la Pampanga, Expedientes Nos. 31, 39, 40, 42, PNA; Mariano A. Henson, *A Brief History of the Town of Angeles in the Province of Pampanga, Philippines* (San Fernando, Pampanga: Ing Katiwala Press, 1948), p. 10n; Edith Moses, *Unofficial Letters of an Official's Wife* (New York: D. Appleton, 1908), p. 62. Pardo de Tavara owned the farm in Floridablanca from 1901 until 1908 and also held a big agricultural property in Tarlac, Tarlac, until July 1920 (Larkin, *Pampangans,* p. 191n; *Notario* 21068, entry of July 16, 1920, Pampanga, PNA). His active in-

volvement in extending spurs of the Manila-Dagupan Railroad toward both Floridablanca and Magalang hints that he may have profited handsomely from his ownership of these properties of more than 100 hectares each.

68. Information on the commercial agricultural activities in Pampanga comes from the notarial registers in the Philippine National Archives. See Larkin, *Pampangans*, pp. 72–73n, 211n, 279n; John A. Larkin, "The Causes of an Involuted Society: A Theoretical Approach to Rural Southeast Asian History," *Journal of Asian Studies* 30 (1971): 793.

69. Rural Credit Associations, BIA, File 26692, incls. 26-a, 47; *LI*, May 25, 1906–October 26, 1906; *PFP*, March 20, 1909, p. 12; February 13, 1915, p. 1; November 21, 1914, p. 30; *M*, May 4, 1918, p. 2.

70. Marshall S. McLennan, *The Central Luzon Plain: Land and Society on the Inland Frontier* (Quezon City: Alemar-Phoenix, 1980), pp. 94–95; letter concerning the application of Don Roberto Toledo y Gil to reside in Pampanga, October 16, 1854, *Radicaciones de Españoles*, PNA; "Gobierno Municipal de Floridablanca . . . ," pp. 1–4; *SN* 1 (1920), frontispiece to no. 15; *PFP*, October 24, 1908, p. 4; Nesom and Walker, *Handbook*, pt. 1, p. 19.

71. Manuel Buzeta, O.S.A., and Felipe Bravo, O.S.A., *Diccionario geográfico, estadístico, histórico de las Islas Filipinas*, 2 vols. (Madrid: José C. de la Peña, 1851), 1:190; Frederic H. Sawyer, *The Inhabitants of the Philippines* (London: Sampson Low, Marston, 1900), pp. 239–40; Foreman, *Philippine Islands* (1906), pp. 273–74; "A Report on Economic Conditions, Pampanga Province, San Fernando, Mexico, Minalin, Guagua, Lubao and Arayat. Prepared by the Class in Economics and Mrs. Lois Stewart Osborn, [of Pampanga High School]," San Fernando, ca. 1915. (typewritten), BIA, File 363, incl. 296, Exhibit L.

72. Letter from Agricultural Supervisor N. P. Creager, Bacolor, to Chief of the Bureau of Agriculture F. Lamson, Manila, August 14, 1903, BIA, File 2403, incl. 27; *PFP*, July 1, 1911, pp. 18, 20, 29; *MT* October 12, 1919, p. 4; letter from Director of the Bureau of Labor Faustino Aguilar, Manila, to Senate President Manuel Quezon, August 2, 1918, QP; Philippine Islands, Bureau of Labor, *Labor: Bulletin of the Bureau of Labor* (Manila: Bureau of Printing, 1920), 2, no. 5, p. 10; no. 6, p. 28.

73. Will of Jose Mariano Panlilio executed in 1852; will of Vicente Lim-Ongco executed in 1854; *Protocolo*, 1847, Pampanga, PNA. On the business dealings of Jose Puig, see *Protocolos*, 1920, 1921, 1923, 1929, 1931, 1932, 1933 for the years 1890–94, Pampanga, PNA. Though a Spaniard, Puig remained a farmer in Pampanga after the coming of the American regime; see U.S. War Department, U.S. Philippine Commission, *Annual Report . . . 1907*, Appendix, 810. On Pamintuan see *Notario* 21090, entry of November 19, 1918, Pampanga, PNA. On the other magnates see Larkin, *Pampangans*, p. 212n; *Notario* 12225, entry of July 29, 1919, Pampanga, PNA.

74. Jose Rizal, *The Lost Eden* (*Noli me Tangere*), trans. Leon Ma. Guerrero (Bloomington: Indiana University Press, 1961), p. 28; Soledad Borromeo-Buehler, "The *Inquilinos* of Cavite: A Social Class in Nineteenth-Century Philippines," *Journal of Southeast Asian Studies* 16 (March 1985): 80–81; will of Don Florentino Dayrit executed September 2, 1897, *Protocolo* 1944, Pampanga, PNA.

75. U.S. War Department, U.S. Philippine Commission, *Annual Report . . . 1907*, Appendix, 800, 810–12; U.S. War Department, U.S. Philippine Commission, *Annual Reports of the War Department for the Fiscal Year Ended June 30, 1901. Report of the Philippine Commission* (Washington: Government Printing Office, 1901), pt. 2, p. 16; Forbes, *Philippine Islands*, 1:300.

76. "A Report on Economic Conditions."

77. Larkin, *Pampangans*, pp. 97, 118n, 185–200, 263–69; *MT*, July 27, 1964, p. 19.

78. Buzeta and Bravo, *Diccionario*; Bazaco, *Education*, pp. 230, 305–10; Mills, *Planned Surveys*, pp. 148–51, 272–73.

79. José Fernández Giner, *Filipinas: Notas de viaje y de estancia* (Madrid: Administración, 1889), pp. 76–88; *PFP*, July 11, 1914, p. 26. The practice of using intermarriage, even first cousin marriage, to ensure continued family ownership of property is widely employed in the Philippines among both Christians and Muslims; see, for example, Thomas M. Kiefer, *The Tausug: Violence and Law in a Philippine Moslem Society* (New York: Holt, Rinehart and Winston, 1972), p. 40.

80. John A. Larkin, "The Capampangan Zarzuela: Theater for a Provincial Elite," in *Southeast Asia Transitions: Approaches through Social History*, ed. Ruth T. McVey (New Haven: Yale University Press, 1978), 158–90; Ramon C. Aquino, *A Chance to Die: A Biography of Jose Abad Santos, Late Chief Justice of the Philippines* (Quezon City: Alemar-Phoenix, 1967), pp. 8–10; *Guía de forasteros en Filipinas, para el año de 1865* (Manila: Los Amigos del Pais, 1865), p. 88.

81. Memoria de Pampanga, 1890, PNA; *PAR* 15 (Summer 1927): 93–94; *MDB*, April 21, 1920, p. 6; *MT*, April 25, 1920, p. 6.

82. In addition to signing contracts with Toledo and Gonzalez (2,500 hectares), Pasumil also acquired contractual rights to the cane of the Dinalupihan estate of neighboring Bataan Province, and these three holdings provided a strong base of lands upon which the Canlubang interests could construct their central; see *MDB*, December 1, 1919, p. 5; November 12, 1920, p. 4; June 13, 1921, p. 2; *SN* 1 (1920), frontispiece to no. 16.

83. *SN* 32 (1956): 1–3; *Notarios* 12229, 21069, 21209, 23602, Pampanga, PNA.

84. *Notarios*, Pampanga, PNA.

85. Some farmers in Magalang tried to convert their tenants into wage laborers at this time (interview with planter Alfredo Ganzon, Angeles,

June 21, 1964). The notion of using tenants in depressed periods was confirmed in the March 12, 1986, interview with Mr. Carlos Ledesma.

86. The imbalance in favor of sugar reached a crisis between 1918 and 1920, when natural calamities and the World War I–induced shortage of ship bottoms led to a scarcity of imported grain that caused extensive starvation and rioting in sugar-prosperous Negros and Pampanga (*M*, March 6, 1918–January 14, 1920; *MT*, January 2, 1919–May 18, 1920; "Synopsis of Constabulary Reports of Food Shortage and Help Afforded by Constabulary," Memorandum to the Chief of Constabulary, Manila, September 20, 1919, QP).

87. Willem Wolters, "A Comparison Between the Taxation Systems in the Philippines Under Spanish Rule and Indonesia Under Dutch Rule During the 19th Century," *Asian Studies* 21 (April, August, December 1983): 79–106; Frank H. Golay, "The Search for Revenues," in *Reappraising an Empire: New Perspectives on Philippine-American History*, ed. Peter W. Stanley (Cambridge: Harvard University Press, 1984), pp. 231–60; *PAR* 1 (1908): 432–37.

88. The following quotation reveals in a noneconomic context the difficulty Negrense planters had in organizing:

> Nearly every haciendero (in Negros) is possessed of rifles and shotguns, ranging in number from one to ten or a dozen. They are not to be relied upon as an adjunct to the constabulary or municipal police, for each haciendero looks out for his own first and the public welfare afterwards. There is no such thing, as we have in the States, of the people of a locality arming themselves to resist the raids of outlaws or to form a posse to go to the assistance of their neighbors or to aid municipal police or the constabulary.
>
> (U.S. War Department, U.S. Philippine Commission, *Sixth Annual Report of the Philippine Commission, 1906* [Washington: Government Printing Office, 1906], pt. 3, p. 88)

CHAPTER 4. SUGARLANDIA

1. Dennis Morrow Roth, "Philippine Forests and Forestry, 1565–1920," in *Global Deforestation and the Nineteenth-Century World Economy*, ed. Richard Tucker and J. F. Richards (Durham, N.C.: Duke University Press, 1983), p. 33.

2. *SN* 14 (1933): 341–43.

3. *M*, September 11, 1920, p. 1.

4. Memorandum from Secretary of Agriculture, Island of Negros, Juan Araneta, Ma-ao, to The Military Governor of Negros, November 30, 1900, U.S. War Department, Record Group 395, Department of Visayas, 3rd District, 2620, U.S. National Archives; John R. White, *Bullets and Bolos* (New York: Century, 1928), pp. 44–46.

5. *PFP*, May 20, 1911, p. 5. Liongson's attitude toward his agricultural enterprise contrasts sharply with that of eighteenth-century Virginia's tobacco planters, who took enormous pride in the quality of their own crops and measured each other's social status by that quality. This difference in attitude may in part reflect the difference in the stringent requirements for growing tobacco, as opposed to the more lax techniques possible for raising sugar; see T. H. Breen, *Tobacco Culture: The Mentality of the Great Tidewater Planters on the Eve of Revolution* (Princeton: Princeton University Press, 1985), chap. 2.

6. White, *Bullets*, pp. 49–50.

7. *PFP*, February 26, 1910, p. 1.

8. José María Mourin, "Recuerdos de una expedicion á la Pampanga en Diciembre de 1876" (ms., Newberry Library), pp. 19–20, 50–52. See also Ferdinand Alençon, *Luçon et Mindanao* (Paris: Michel Lévy Frères, 1870), pp. 58–79.

9. John Foreman, *The Philippine Islands* (London: Sampson Low, Marston, 1892), pp. 447–48.

10. Gilda Cordero-Fernando, ed., *The Culinary Culture of the Philippines* (Manila: Bancom, 1976), pp. 14–15.

11. White, *Bullets*, p. 30.

12. Edith Moses, *Unofficial Letters of an Official's Wife* (New York: D. Appleton, 1908), pp. 65–66. White (*Bullets*, p. 118) observed this same change over generations, although he attributes it—wrongly, I think—to reversion to traditional ways in old age.

13. *PFP*, June 26, 1915, p. 10. See also *LI*, June 11, 1906–December 20, 1906.

14. Francisco Varona, *Negros: historia anecdótica de su riqueza y de sus hombres* (Manila: General Printing Press, 1938), pp. 138–39.

15. *PFP*, June 24, 1916, p. 8; May 12, 1917, p. 21.

16. Miguel Pérez et al., "Crónica semihistoria de Filipinas y en especial de las Islas Visayas desde 1877 a 1887" (ms., Newberry Library), pp. 1–2.

17. *PFP*, July 12, 1913, p. 20. See also Annual Report of the Governor of Negros Occidental, 1906, BIA, pp. 1–2; Annual Report of the Governor of Negros Occidental, 1909, BIA, pp. 1–4; letter from Charles Cox, Coast and Geodetic Survey, near Iloilo, April 21, 1907, to his father, Pittsfield, Ill. (sent to the BIA by the latter), File C1242, incl. 55; W&G, December 23, 1908, p. 447.

18. *M*, February 26, 1916, p. 2.

19. Ibid., June 16, 1920, p. 3.

20. Letter from La Camara de Comercio Filipino, Manila, April 22, 1912, to Resident Commissioners Benito Legarda and Manuel Luis Quezon, Washington, D.C., QP; *MDB*, November 23, 1914; August 1, 1921, p. 4; *PFP*, June 7, 1913, p. 20; June 21, 1913, p. 23; August 3, 1918, p. 27; *M*, May 30, 1913, p. 2; *PAR* 2 (1909): 662.

21. *PFP*, December 4, 1915, p. 13. See also *MT*, April 23, 1919, p. 7; *PFP*, January 13, 1917, p. 1; May 9, 1925, p. 42.

22. Daniel F. Doeppers, *Manila, 1900–1941: Social Change in a Late Colonial Metropolis* (Quezon City: Ateneo de Manila University Press, 1984), pp. 56–58.

23. *MT*, February 24, 1920, p. 9.

24. *M*, May 11, 1918, p. 2.

25. *PFP*, October 10, 1908, p. 15.

26. *LI*, July 26, 1906, p. 2.

27. U.S. War Department, U.S. Philippine Commission, *Annual Report of the Philippine Commission, 1900–1901* (Washington, D.C.: Government Printing Office, 1901), pt. 2, p. 80.

28. Manuscript Report of the Taft Commission, Trip to Negros Occidental, 1901, BIA, p. 39.

29. Ibid., p. 38; *MT*, May 22, 1900, p. 1; Manuel Gatbonton, *Ing Candawe* (n.p.: n.p., 1933), p. 52; brief sketch of Aniceto Lacson in Philippine who's who, ca. 1905, in author's possession.

30. Alfred W. McCoy, "'Muy Noble y Muy Leal': Revolution and Counterrevolution in the Western Visayas, Philippines, 1896–1907" (unpublished paper); Ma. Fe Hernaez Romero, *Negros Occidental Between Two Foreign Powers (1888–1909)* (Bacolod: Negros Occidental Historical Commission, 1974); Milagros C. Guerrero, "Luzon at War: Contradictions in Philippine Society, 1898–1902" (Ph.D. dissertation, University of Michigan, 1977); John A. Larkin, *The Pampangans: Colonial Society in a Philippine Province* (Berkeley and Los Angeles: University of California Press, 1972), chap. 5.

31. "Expediente sobre propuesta para que se conceda el dictado de 'Muy Leal' a la provincia de la Pampanga, 15 Octobre 1897," Legajo de Pampanga, PNA.

32. C. R. Fuentes, *Apuntes documentados de la revolución en toda la Isla de Negros* (Iloilo: El Centinela, 1919), p. 128. See also letter from General E. S. Otis, Military Governor, Manila, to Adjutant General, U.S. Army, July 23, 1899, BIA, File 979, incl. 13; instructions from Apolinario Mabini, Malolos, to Commissioner to Negros Zoilo Mauricio, March 23, 1899, in *The Philippine Insurrection Against the United States*, ed. John R. M. Taylor (Pasay City, Philippines: Eugenio Lopez Foundation, 1971), 5:624.

33. Letter from Aniceto Lacson, Bacolod, May 27, 1899, to President William McKinley, BIA, File 979, incl. 5, p. 2.

34. Richard John Gilbert, "The Introduction of American Capital into the Sugar Industry of the Philippines and Its Impact on the Pre-Existing Patterns of Land" (M.A. thesis, University of Hawaii at Manoa, 1967), pp. 52–53.

35. Petition to Civil Governor Taft from sugar planters in Panay and Negros, Iloilo, September 11, 1901, BIA, File C1242; *MT*, September 24, 1901, p. 8; December 29, 1901, p. 1; Mrs. Campbell Dauncey, *An Englishwoman in the Philippines* (London: John Murray, 1906), p. 330; *LI*, September 11, 1906, pp. 1–2; October 4, 1906, p. 3; October 26, 1906, p. 3; *PFP*, October 24, 1908, p. 3.

36. Annual Report of the Governor of Negros Occidental, 1906, BIA, n.p.

37. Petition of the "Comite de Intereses Filipinos," Pampanga Province, to President Taft, August 12, 1905; letter from Captain H. A. Hutchings, Senior Inspector of Constabulary, Pampanga, to Adjutant, First Constabulary District, Manila, August 19, 1905, BIA, File 13206, incl. 1.

38. *PFP*, April 3, 1909, p. 12; April 10, 1909, p. 12; April 17, 1909, p. 12.

39. Annual Report of the Governor of Pampanga, 1909, BIA, p. 4.

40. Annual Report of the Governor of Negros Occidental, 1909, BIA, pp. 11–12.

41. Petition from the Agricultural Association of Pampanga, Bacolor, October 13, 1915, to the Philippine Resident Commissioners, Washington, D.C., QP.

42. *PFP*, April 8, 1916, p. 5.

43. A classic example of misunderstanding the life of the poor was Jose Rizal's 1890 essay "On the Indolence of Filipinos" (reprinted in *La Solidaridad*, trans. Guadalupe Fores-Ganzon [Quezon City: University of the Philippines Press, 1973], 2:465–607). Instead of denying as untrue the notion that the Filipino farmer was indolent, he attributed such indolence to the debilitating effects of weather and colonialism.

In the context of Pampanga, a gross misstatement of the peasant outlook appears in perhaps the most famous Capampangan zarzuela *Alang Dios!* (There Is No God!) by Juan Crisostomo Soto. At the beginning of Act II, after a few lines about workers' idleness and the good pay they receive, a chorus of laborers sings:

> We of the masses
> Through sweat, tears, and sacrifices
> Allow the rich the chance
> To live in abundant peace.
> Happy are those
> Whom wealth has favored.
> Happier still the poor
> Whom wealth has yet to spoil.
>
> (Juan S. Aguas, *Juan Crisostomo Soto and Pampangan Drama* [Quezon City: University of the Philippines Press, 1963], pp. 97–98)

44. Because of the political tensions still rampant in Pampanga at this time, I chose not to record the names of the interviewees and not to ask questions that might have exposed them to risk. The interview data will ultimately be deposited in the archives of the University of the Philippines at Diliman.
45. Interview of landowner, age 71, in Angeles, July 18, 1964.
46. Interview of landowner, age 81, in Guagua, July 16, 1964.
47. Interview of landowner, age 69, in San Fernando, June 28, 1964.
48. Interview of tenant, age 84, in Porac, July 20, 1964.
49. Interview of tenant, age 89, in Guagua, July 22, 1964.
50. Interview of tenant, age 75, in Angeles, July 15, 1964.
51. Interview of tenant, age 73, in San Fernando, July 8, 1964.
52. Interview of tenant, age 78, in Mexico, August 6, 1964.
53. Interview of tenant, age 78, in Mexico, August 11, 1964. On a case of abuse involving the death of a tenant, see *MT*, March 15, 1902, p. 1.
54. Interview of tenant, age 76, in San Fernando, June 23, 1964.
55. Interview of tenant, age 100, in Angeles, July 13, 1964.
56. Interview of landowner, age 78, in Guagua, July 22, 1964.
57. Interview of landowner, age 72, in Angeles, July 17, 1964.
58. Interview of landowner, age 76, in Guagua, July 21, 1964.
59. Interview of tenant, age 95, in San Fernando, June 26, 1964.
60. Interview of tenant, age 74, in Magalang, July 27, 1964.
61. Interview of tenant, age 85, in San Fernando, July 2, 1964.
62. Interview of tenant, age 75, in Guagua, July 22, 1964.
63. Interview of landowner, age 82, in Angeles, July 17, 1964.
64. Interview of landowner, age 81, in Guagua, July 16, 1964.
65. Interview of landowner, age 74, in San Fernando, July 1, 1964.
66. Interview of tenant, age 74, in San Fernando, June 26, 1964.
67. Interview of tenant, age 70, in Porac, July 21, 1964.
68. At that time I also collected data from casamac in Pampanga; however, for this chapter, use of the 1964 interviews appeared preferable.
69. Interview of duma'an, age 80, in Murcia, July 4, 1970.
70. Interview of duma'an, age 80, in Hinigaran, June 11, 1970.
71. Interview of duma'an, age 80, in Isabela, June 25, 1970.
72. Interview of duma'an, age 80, in Himamaylan, June 12, 1970.
73. Interview of duma'an, age 115 (?), in Binalbagan, June 10, 1970.
74. Interview of duma'an, age 70, in Pulupandan, June 15, 1970.
75. Interview of duma'an, age 90, in Pulupandan, June 15, 1970.
76. Interview of duma'an, age 70, in La Carlota, June 8, 1970.
77. Interview of duma'an, age 70, in La Carlota, June 4, 1970.
78. Reynaldo Clemeña Ileto, *Pasyon and Revolution: Popular Movements in the Philippines, 1840–1910* (Quezon City: Ateneo de Manila University Press, 1979), chap. 6; David R. Sturtevant, *Popular Uprisings in the Philippines, 1840–1940* (Ithaca, N.Y.: Cornell University Press,

1976), pp. 134–37; Ignacio Villamor, *Criminality in the Philippine Islands, 1903–1908* (Manila: Bureau of Printing, 1909), pp. 51–53; Philippine Islands, Bureau of Constabulary, *Annual Reports of the Director of Constabulary, 1905–1910* (Manila: Bureau of Printing, 1906–11); "Historia del pueblo de San Luis, de la provincia de la Pampanga, Islas Filipinas," LPC, p. 20; *PFP*, April 23, 1910, p. 21; July 30, 1910, pp. 4, 10, 23.

79. Letters from Governor Francisco Liongson, San Fernando, to the Executive Secretary, Manila, October 21, 22, 24, 1913; letter from Liongson to House Speaker Sergio Osmeña, Manila, October 25, 1913, QP; interview with Victor Larin, age 101, in Barrio Barit, Candaba, August 8, 1970; interview with Isidoro Bondoc, age 83, Barrio San Isidro, San Luis, August 8, 1970; interview with Zacarias Carlos, age 88, Barrio Barit, Candaba, August 8, 1970. Over the years a schism had developed in Santa Iglesia, the faction of Larin believing that Apong Ipe still spoke to the faithful, that of Bondoc asserting that he did not.

80. John Bancroft Devins, *An Observer in the Philippines, or Life in Our New Possessions* (Boston: American Tract Society, 1905), p. 83; U.S. War Department, U.S. Philippine Commission, *Fifth Annual Report of the Philippine Commission, 1904* (Washington, D.C.: Government Printing Office, 1904), 1:578; Ileto, *Pasyon and Revolution*, p. 307; Guerrero, "Luzon at War," pp. 179–80, 183–84; Jose P. Santos, *Ang Tatlong Napabantog na "Tulisan" sa Pilipinas* [Three Famous "Bandits" in the Philippines] (Gerona, Tarlac: n.p., 1936), p. 18.

81. Alfred W. McCoy, "*Baylan:* Animist Religion and Philippine Peasant Ideology," in *Moral Order and the Question of Change: Essays on Southeast Asian Thought*, ed. David K. Wyatt and Alexander Woodside, Monograph Series, no. 24 (New Haven: Yale University Southeast Asian Studies, 1982), pp. 342–80; Evelyn Tan Cullamar, *Babaylanism in Negros: 1896–1907* (Quezon City: New Day, 1986), chaps. 3–6; Romero, *Negros Occidental*, pp. 168–87. Various sources give as Isio's name, Dionisio Magbuela, Dionisio Papa y Barlueia, and Dionisio Siguela. He signed his documents simply Dionisio Papa.

82. General James Smith, Report, July 31, 1899, in U.S. War Department, *Annual Reports of the War Department for the Fiscal Year Ended June 30, 1899* (Washington, D.C.: Government Printing Office, 1899), p. 345.

83. Taylor, *Philippine Insurrection* 5:625.

84. On Isio's later activities in Negros, see *LL*, August 8, 1899–August 5, 1900; *MT*, April 22, 1899–November 2, 1902; *LI*, February 14, 1907–April 20, 1907; *PFP*, February 10, 1907–September 28, 1907; Manuscript Report of the Taft Commission, p. 39; Annual Reports of the Governor of Negros Occidental, 1902–8, BIA; White, *Bullets*, pp. 41–109; Cullamar, *Babaylanism*, pp. 59–66.

85. Taylor, *Philippine Insurrection* 2:415; Cullamar, *Babaylanism*, Appendix H.

86. Annual Report of the Governor of Negros Occidental, 1902, BIA, sec. 9.

87. *LL*, January 4, 1900, p. 3. On other planter efforts to suppress the social revolution, see *MT*, July 25, 1899, p. 2; May 10, 1900, p. 1; *LL*, January 16, 1900, p. 3; February 1, 1900, p. 3.

88. Philippine Islands, Bureau of Constabulary, *Annual Report of the Director of Constabulary, 1905–1906* (Manila: Bureau of Printing, 1906), pp. 4–5.

89. Ibid., *1909–1910* (Manila: Bureau of Printing, 1910), pp. 5–6. See also Sturtevant, *Uprisings*, p. 137.

90. Santos, "*Tulisan*," pp. 17–18; Ileto, *Pasyon and Revolution*, p. 301.

91. McCoy, "'Muy Noble'," p. 25.

92. White, *Bullets*, pp. 64–66. Articles in *La Libertad* during 1900 indicate that haciendas remained the main targets of the babaylanes. See also Manuscript Report of the Taft Commission, p. 39.

93. Interview of carter, age 69, in Angeles, July 14, 1964.

94. Interview of farmer overseer (katiwala), age 69, in Porac, July 17, 1964.

95. Ileto, *Pasyon and Revolution*, p. 295. In their interviews both Victor Larin and Isidoro Bondoc spoke about the market at San Luis.

96. On everyday forms of resistance by the poor see Benedict J. Tria Kerkvliet, *Everyday Politics in the Philippines: Class and Status Relations in a Central Luzon Village* (Berkeley and Los Angeles: University of California Press, 1990), chap. 5; James C. Scott, *Weapons of the Weak: Everyday Forms of Peasant Resistance* (New Haven: Yale University Press, 1985).

97. George Beckford, *Persistent Poverty: Underdevelopment in Plantation Economies of the Third World*, rev. ed. (London: Zed Books, 1983), p. 206.

CHAPTER 5. CENTRALS

1. Noel Deerr, *The History of Sugar*, 2 vols. (London: Chapman and Hall, 1949–50), 1:131, 490–91; *SN* 4 (1923): 157–58, 413; 7 (1926): 286; *PFP*, December 26, 1925, p. 25.

2. *MT*, March 9, 1919–June 21, 1920; *MDB*, March 4, 1920, p. 5; *PFP*, July 12, 1919, p. 16; June 11, 1921, pp. 8, 11; July 9, 1921, p. 9; *SN* 1 (September 1919): 10–11, 17–23; 7 (1926): 205–6, 244–49, 409–10; 9 (1928): 72; *PAR* 18 (1925): 191; 19 (1926): 89.

3. Norman G. Owen, "Philippine Economic Development and American Policy: A Reappraisal," in *Compadre Colonialism: Studies on the*

Philippines under American Rule, ed. Norman G. Owen, Michigan Papers on South and Southeast Asia, no. 3 (Ann Arbor: Center for South and Southeast Asian Studies, 1971), p. 110; *MDB*, January 1920; U.S. Congress, House, *Annual Report of the Governor General, Philippine Islands, 1923*, H. Doc. 485, 68th Cong., 2d sess., 1924, p. 149; *SN* 10 (1929): 159; 13 (1932): 81.

4. BIA 2403-71A; Philippine Islands, Department of Agriculture and Commerce, *Philippine Statistical Review* 2 (1935): 71.

5. Letter from George H. Fairchild, Manila, to Manuel Quezon, Manila, May 2, 1929, QP; *SN* 11 (1930): 305; *PFP*, March 30, 1912, pp. 2–3.

6. Information on Silay-Hawaiian comes from that company's annual reports for 1922 to 1934 located in the Hawaiian Sugar Planters Association Library in Honolulu.

7. Guilford L. Spencer and George P. Meade, *Cane Sugar Handbook: A Manual for Cane Sugar Manufacturers and Their Chemists*, 8th ed. (New York: John Wiley and Sons, 1945), pp. 48–49.

8. Cesar Gamboa, "Hacienda Administration and Methods of Cultivation on Occidental Negros," in *Cane* (Provincial Carnival Association publication for the provincial carnival held in Bacolod, April 7 to 17, 1928); *SN* 5 (1924): 463–65; *PFP*, October 20, 1923, p. 8; *SN* 13 (1927): 490; 14 (1933): 96–97.

9. Yves Henry, *Technical and Financial Conditions of the Production of Sugar in the Philippines*, trans. Irwin McNiece (Manila: Philippine Sugar Association, 1929), p. 73; *SN* 4 (1923): 437–38; 6 (1925): 349, 361; *PFP*, January 31, 1920, p. 9; November 25, 1922, p. 9; *PAR* 14 (1921): 418–20; 16 (1923): 22–29; 18 (1925): 107–123; Philippine Islands, Department of Agriculture and Natural Resources, *Philippine Journal of Agriculture* 2 (1931): 163–177; letter from Jose Camus, Department of Agriculture and Natural Resources, Manila, to General Secretary, Institut International D'Agriculture, Rome, July 8, 1930, BIA, File 3287, incl. 12; *A Handbook of the Sugar and Other Industries in the Philippines, 1953* (Manila: Sugar News Press, 1953), p. 16.

10. "Five crop data, 1920, 1921, 1922, 1923, 1924—Central del Carmen," Pampanga Sugar Mills, Del Carmen, n.d. (ca. 1925) (ms., Hawaiian Sugar Planters Association Library), tables 8, 9; Henry, *Technical and Financial Conditions*, p. 46; Alden Cutshall, "Trends of Philippine Sugar Production," *Economic Geography* 14 (April 1938): 155; *SN* 4 (1923): 663–72; 6 (1925): 69–70, 387–89; United States Tariff Commission, *Sugar: Report to the President of the United States*, Report, no. 73, 2d series (Washington, D.C.: Government Printing Office, 1934), pp. 194–95.

11. Cutshall, "Trends," p. 156; *SN* 7 (1926): 7; Rafael Mateo Piguing, "The Philippine Sugar Industry" (Ph.D. dissertation, Michigan State Col-

lege of Agriculture, 1935), 118; *PFP*, June 3, 1922, p. 9; September 17, 1927, 2–3, 8; *M*, July 6, 1926, p. 4.

12. Peter W. Stanley, *A Nation in the Making: The Philippines and the United States, 1899–1921* (Cambridge: Harvard University Press, 1974), pp. 35–48; Supervising Contract between Isabela Central and PNB, August 20, 1921, QP; *MT*, September 22, 1919, p. 1; *PFP*, April 23, 1921, p. 13; March 27, 1926, p. 26; *MDB*, August 25, 1921, p. 20; *M*, June 29, 1921, p. 1; letters from Venancio Concepcion, Manila, to Manuel Quezon, August 15, 1929, and November 16, 1931; letter from Venancio Concepcion, Manila, to Wenceslao Trinidad, San Fernando, Pampanga, January 31, 1929; reply from Trinidad to Concepcion, February 2, 1929, QP. Concepcion spent two and a half years in jail and after several attempts to return to the sugar business failed, spent his last years dependent on the generosity of his friends in politics and in the sugar industry.

13. Annual Report on the Operations and Conditions of the Philippine National Bank for the Year 1925, pp. 3–6; Report from the Administrator General, PNB, to Governor-general Leonard Wood, July 10, 1922, pp. 2–4; letter from Governor-general Leonard Wood, Manila, to the President of the PNB, April 19, 1923; report from Emilio Montilla, President, Isabela Sugar Co., Isabela, N.O., to Governor-general Leonard Wood, February 13, 1923; letter from H. I. Shoemaker, General Manager, Isabela Sugar Co., to PNB President Wenceslao Trinidad, March 26, 1923; letter from E. W. Kopeke, Bacolod-Murcia Sugar Central, to D. M. Semple, Manager, Philippine Sugar Centrals Agency, Manila, July 12, 1923; report of Arthur Fischer and Wenceslao Trinidad to the Board of Directors, PNB, April 24, 1923, QP.

14. Report from Insular Auditor Ben F. Wright to Governor-general Wood, ca. July 1, 1925; letter from Rafael Corpus, President, PNB, to Manuel Quezon, Member, Board of Control, PNB, July 16, 1926; letter from Manuel Quezon, Senate President, to Governor-general Leonard Wood, April 22, 1925, QP; *PFP*, June 27, 1925–June 2, 1928; *SN* 6 (1925): 372; 15 (1934): 89; *M*, July 17, 1925, p. 1; August 18, 1925, p. 4; September 15, 1925, p. 1; *TT*, June 22, 1930–January 12, 1934.

15. Echaús still owed PNB P2,500,000 in 1930. The saga of Binalbagan Central is told in a wide variety of sources including *M*, June 24, 1915–March 7, 1930; *MDB*, January 3, 1920, p. 1; March 11, 1920, p. 5; *PFP*, June 25, 1921–August 14, 1926; *SN* 1–15 (1920–1934); and Isideria J. Ignacio, "A Study of the Cultural Contributions of the Three Sugar Centrals (Bacolod-Murcia Milling Company, Binalbagan-Isabela Sugar Company, and Victorias Milling Company) in Negros Occidental with the View to Propose Plans for Their Improvement" (M.A. thesis, Silliman University, 1954), pp. 21–22. In addition, Manuel Quezon, as president of the Philippine Senate and member of the PNB Board of Control, had a continuing interest in Binalbagan, and his papers contain many reports and

letters concerning the case. See, for example, Report of Gil Montilla, Governor of Negros Occidental, regarding the troubles at Binalbagan Central, February 1, 1924: "Resolution of the Board of Directors, Binalbagan Estate, Inc.," April 7, 1924; letter from Rafael Alunan, President and Manager of Bacolod-Murcia Milling Co., Bacolod, to Francisco Enage, President Pro-tem Philippine Senate, Manila, July 24, 1924; letter from Enrique Echaús, President, The Visayan General Supply Co., Manila, to the Members of the Board of Control, February 9, 1925; letter from Ben F. Wright, Insular Auditor, Manila, to Rafael Corpus, President PNB, Manila, October 27, 1925, QP.

16. *SN* 11 (1930): 409–10; *TT*, June 22, 1930, p. 7; *M*, November 19, 1926, p. 1.

17. *Boston Transcript*, December 13, 1920; *PFP*, March 17, 1923, p. 33; April 28, 1923, p. 9; *SN* 4 (1923): 85; "Extract from the Report of the Philippine National Bank," October 20, 1922; letter from Paredes and Buencamino, Attorneys, Manila, to the Board of Directors, PNB, May 10, 1923; letters from J. B. Hardon, Hayden, Stone and Company, Manila, to Governor-general Leonard Wood, Manila, December 15, 1925, and January 12, 1926, QP; *M*, July 31, 1925–September 16, 1927.

18. *PFP*, September 23, 1928, pp. 6, 8.

19. BIA, File 16979, File 27078, File 27685, incls. 1–12; File 21387, subject card, p. 27, incl. 14; File 24689, incls. 8, 11, 48, 78; File 23908, incl. 1; *MT*, June 1, 1901–July 11, 1920; *PFP*, January 6, 1912–July 5, 1924; *SN* 1 (1919): 13; 9 (1928): 206–7; *MDB*, June 23, 1921, p. 4; January 7, 1922, pp. 1, 3; *TT*, February 14, 1932, p. 7; letters between John Switzer and Manuel Quezon, Manila, New York, and San Mateo (California), January 7, 1918; July 23, 1931; September 2, 1931; January 1, 1934, QP.

20. Lewis E. Gleeck, *The Manila Americans (1901–1964)* (Manila: Carmelo and Bauermann, 1977), pp. 187–88; BIA, File 24689, incls. 8, 13, 55; File 16979, incl. 15; File 3037, incl. 38; File 25996; File 10523, incl. 29; *MT*, July 24, 1919, p. 1; July 27, 1919, p. 7; August 9, 1920, p. 4; letter from George Fairchild, Manila, to Governor-general Francis Burton Harrison, New York, April 16, 1919, QP.

21. *Philippine Sugar Handbook, 1972 Edition* (Manila: Sugar News Press, 1972), p. 8; BIA, File 28206; *SN* 10 (1929): 170; 13 (1932): 764–66; 14 (1933): 101–2; *PFP*, October 6, 1923, p. 9; September 21, 1929, p. 30; *TT*, May 17, 1930, p. 1; October 29, 1932, p. 1.

22. Ignacio, "Cultural Contributions," p. 18; *MT*, July 13, 1920, p. 8; August 6, 1920, p. 6; *PFP*, January 12, 1924, p. 30; *M*, December 14, 1920, p. 3; *Handbook of the Philippine Sugar Industry*, 2d ed. (Manila: Sugar News Press, 1929), pp. 236–41; letter from Chief of the Bureau of Insular Affairs F. L. Parker, Washington, to Philippine Trade Commissioner Frank McIntyre, Washington, January 20, 1931, BIA, File 28206, incl. 8A; *SN* 9 (1928): 8–15; 11 (1930): 360–62; *TT*, July 13, 1930, p. 19; pamphlet on

behalf of the Confederacion de Asociaciones y Plantadores de Caña Dulce, Inc., Manapla, N.O., to the visiting Members of the Congressional Mission, December 20, 1934, QP.

23. Roy A. Ballinger, *A History of Sugar Marketing*, Economic Research Service, Agricultural Economic Report, no. 197 (Washington, D.C.: U.S. Department of Agriculture, 1971), p. 32; Luis E. Aguilar, *Cuba 1933: Prologue to Revolution* (Ithaca, N.Y.: Cornell University Press, 1972), pp. 41–42; Robert F. Smith, *The United States and Cuba: Business and Diplomacy, 1917–1960* (New Haven: College and University Press, 1960), pp. 29–30; Theodore Friend, "The Philippine Sugar Industry and the Politics of Independence, 1929–1935," *Journal of Asian Studies* 22 (February 1963); idem, *Between Two Empires: The Ordeal of the Philippines, 1929–1946* (New Haven: Yale University Press, 1965), pp. 82–83; Garel A. Grunder and William E. Livezey, *The Philippines and the United States* (Norman: University of Oklahoma Press, 1951), pp. 216–17; *SN* 3–15 (1922–34); *PFP*, January 12, 1923, pp. 26–27; February 6, 1927, pp. 34, 39; letter from John Switzer, New York, to Manuel Quezon, Washington, July 24, 1931, QP.

24. Michael Onorato, *A Brief Review of American Interest in Philippine Development and Other Essays* (Berkeley: McCutchan, 1968), pp. 113–22; Bernadita Reyes Churchill, *The Philippine Independence Missions to the United States, 1919–1934* (Manila: National Historical Institute, 1983), pp. 87–116; John Switzer, *A Square Deal for the Philippine Islands: A Series of Articles by John Switzer, Based Upon His Testimony Before the House Ways and Means Committee of the House of Representatives, February 25th, 1929* (New York: Philippine-American Chamber of Commerce, 1929).

25. *SN* 13 (1932): 269; 14 (1933): 202. See also cablegram from Jose Yulo, Manila, to Rafael Alunan, Washington, January 3, 1933, QP; *TT*, August 23, 1931, p. 5.

26. Statement of Amando Avanceña, The Mixed Mission, April 23, 1933, QP. See also *PFP*, January 25, 1930, p. 60; *TT*, March 8, 1932, pp. 1, 3.

27. Letter from Manuel Quezon, on shipboard to Hong Kong, to John Switzer, New York, October 18, 1931, QP. See also letter from Manuel Quezon, San Mateo, California, to Camilo Osias, Resident Commissioner, Washington, September 10, 1931; cablegram from Manuel Quezon, Manila, to Sergio Osmeña and Manuel Roxas, Washington, January 2, 1933, QP.

28. Ernesto D. Bohol, ed., *Full Text of Hawes-Cutting-Hare Bill, Commented by Prominent Filipino Leaders and Foreigners* (Manila: Loyal Press, 1934).

29. *PFP*, March 16, 1929, p. 28; *TT*, April 19, 1933, p. 1; October 13, 1933, p. 1; April 26, 1934, p. 3; Minutes of the Executive Committee of

the Philippine Sugar Association, February 12, 1934, QP; Harry B. Hawes, *Philippine Uncertainty: An American Problem* (New York: Century, 1932).

30. *SN* 13 (1932): 650–54; 14 (1933): 78, 195, 370–72; Friend, *Between Two Empires,* pp. 117–18. Benigno Aquino, Sr., is usually just associated with Central Tarlac; however, his first wife, Maria, was the sister of his friend Manuel Urquico, prominent Central Luzon businessman and a founder of, major investor in, and member of the board of Pasudeco (Nick Joaquin, *The Aquinos of Tarlac: An Essay on History as Three Generations* [Mandaluyong, Metro Manila: Cacho Hermanos, 1983], pp. 101–3).

31. Jack T. Turner, *Marketing of Sugar,* Indiana University School of Business, Bureau of Business Research Study, no. 38 (Homewood, Ill.: Richard D. Irwin, 1955), pp. 73–75; radiograms from Frank Parker, BIA, Washington, to Governor-general Frank Murphy, Manila, June 21, 22, 23, 1933, BIA, File 5483, incl. 27; *TT,* April 5, 1933, p. 3; *SN* 15 (1934): 205–8, 302, 355; radiogram from Creed Cox, BIA, Washington, to Governor-general Frank Murphy, Manila, September 26, 1933; Minutes of the Meeting of the Board of Trustees of the Philippine Sugar Association, Manila, September 29, 1933; Transcript of Testimony of Hon. Harry B. Hawes Representing the Philippine Sugar Association in the Hearings on the Proposed Marketing Agreement Under the Agricultural Adjustment Act, August 10 and 11, 1933; Report of Hon. Rafael Alunan to the Board of Trustees of the Philippine Sugar Association, July 22, 1933, QP; *American-Philippine Trade Relations: A Memorandum for Hon. Thomas Walker Page, Chairman for Reciprocity Information, In Connection with Proposed Trade Agreement with Cuba. Submitted by Harry B. Hawes, U.S. Representative, Philippine Sugar Association* (Washington: n.p., 1934). The bill was named after its main sponsors, Congressman Marvin Jones of Texas and Senator Edward Costigan of Colorado.

32. *SN* 15 (1934): 274–75, 350–51, 354–55; *TT,* May 26, 1934, pp. 1–2; June 23, 1934, p. 1; June 24, 1934, p. 1; Memorandum to the Trustees of the Philippine Sugar Association, April 3, 1934; Memorandum on the Allocation of the Sugar Quota from Amando Avanceña to Manuel Quezon, June 2, 1934; Memorandum from Manuel Quezon to Governor-general Frank Murphy, June 16, 1934; Memorandum on Crop Loans from PNB President Rafael Corpus, 1934, QP; *M,* June 19, 1934, p. 4.

33. Joshua Bernhardt, *The Sugar Industry and the Federal Government: A Thirty Year Record (1917–47)* (Washington, D.C.: Sugar Statistics Service, 1948), pp. 172–73, 187–88; *TT,* May 20, 1934–December 22, 1934; Minutes of the Executive Committee of the Philippine Sugar Association, Manila, June 4, 1934, QP; *SN* 15 (1934): 375–76.

34. *SN* 9 (1928): 4; 11 (1930): 668; 13 (1932): 392, 469–70; *M,* November 16, 1926, p. 1; April 22, 1932, p. 3; *PFP,* November 11, 1922, pp. 20–21; October 18, 1924, p. 2; *TT,* October 31, 1936, p. 3.

35. *PFP*, March 31, 1923, p. 6; *SN* 10 (1928): 429, 508–9; *TT*, May 10, 1931, p. 13; Ignacio, "Cultural Contributions," pp. 25–26; telegram from Jorge Vargas, Manila, to Rafael Alunan, Washington, May 29, 1929; letter from Wenceslao Trinidad, President PSA, to Manuel Quezon, Manila, March 2, 1932; letter from Earl B. Schwulst, Vice-president, PNB, Baguio, to Governor-general Dwight Davis, Baguio, April 20, 1931, QP.

36. *TT*, August 22, 1930, p. 1; April 10, 1931, p. 1; February 3, 1933, pp. 11–16; September 2, 1934, p. 1; *M*, February 12, 1926–February 17, 1933; *SN* 1–15 (1920–34); *PFP*, February 2, 1924, pp. 12–13; October 1, 1927, p. 28.

37. Quezon's correspondence, as well as local newspapers and yearbooks, carried constant information about political figures. See, for example, letter from Manuel Quezon, Manila, to Macario Arnedo, Apalit, Pampanga, May 29, 1934, QP; *Cornejo's Commonwealth Directory of the Philippines*, 2 vols. (Manila: Cornejo, 1939), 2:1592–93; *Saravia Centennial Anniversary and Inauguration of the New Town Hall* (souvenir program) (Saravia, Negros Occidental: n.p., 1959), pp. 1–2; Faustino P. Gutierrez, *Ninu't Ninu qñg Capampañgan* [Who's Who in Pampanga] (Manila: Catimawan, 1934), p. 4; *TT*, September 23, 1931, pp. 9–11. Magalona chaired the crucial assembly labor and immigration committee (*SN* 14 [1933]: 470).

38. *SN* 5–15 (1924–34); *TT*, May 27, 1930, p. 1; *PFP*, January 12, 1924, p. 9; Minutes of the Executive Committee, PSA, February 10, 1934, p. 2; May 7, 1934, p. 2; Circular no. 170, February 27, 1934; Circular no. 185, April 27, 1934, for the Trustees of PSA; letter from Pedro Vazquez, Acting President of Binalbagan Estate, Binalbagan, to Manuel Quezon, Manila, January 20, 1923, QP; "Estimated Amount of Taxes which the Philippine Sugar Industry Directly and Indirectly Pays Annually," in *Documents and Papers on the Philippine Sugar Industry* (1933), in the Hawaiian Sugar Planters Association Library, Honolulu; Baldomero T. Olivera, *Jose Yulo: The Selfless Statesman* (Mandaluyong, Metro Manila: U.P.-Jorge B. Vargas Filipiniana Research Center, 1981), chaps. 4–9; *M*, May 24, 1931, p. 1.

Born in Bago, Negros Occidental, Yulo, a brother-in-law of Juan Araneta, worked in Manila and held sugar lands in Floridablanca. Ventura's government career ended when he clashed with Quezon over support for the Hare-Hawes-Cutting Bill, a bitter dispute that divided Pampanga's politicians and sealed the alliance between Quezon and Sotero Baluyut (press statement maligning Ventura by Manuel Quezon, QP; *TT*, May 12–November 21, 1933, passim).

39. *PFP*, January 25, 1913, p. 6; July 23, 1932, p. 57; *SN* 7 (1926): 82. One of the big misusers of PNB loans was Ricardo Nolan, an attorney from Bacolod (see Appendix D), who also happened to be a very vocal supporter of the initial idea of the government supplying loans to farmers.

40. Isobelo T. Crisostomo, *Cory: Profile of a President* (Quezon City: J. Kriz, 1986), pp. 6–8; list of (Pampangan) sugar-cane planters, 1920–35 owning from 500 to more than 1,000 hectares of land and milling upwards of 1 million to 6 million pounds of sugar, given to the author by Mariano A. Henson; *PFP*, November 3, 1928, p. 30; March 23, 1929, p. 19; *SN* 11 (1930): 753; 13 (1932): 443–44; 14 (1933): 33; Court of First Instance, Province of Pampanga, Registration of Title on Behalf of Manuel Quezon, June 23, 1927, QP; Benedict J. Tria Kerkvliet, *The Huk Rebellion: A Study of Peasant Revolt in the Philippines* (Berkeley and Los Angeles: University of California Press, 1977), p. 55.

41. Thomas R. McHale, "The Sugar Industry of the Philippines in the 1970s," paper presented at the PDCP-UPIEDR Lecture Series, Manila, January 20, 1970, pp. 65–66.

42. Negrenses faced the anomalous situation in 1931 of having local muscovado sugar selling at a higher price than centrifugal (*M*, December 8, 1931, p. 4). Information on leaseholding comes from ninety-four contracts contained in the notarial registers for Negros used in this chapter. PNA *Notarios* consulted had the following numbers: 39424, 39426, 39428, 39441, 39477, 39535, 39543, 39563, 39569, 39581, 39589, 39782, 39785, 39835, 39836, 39863, 39928, 39929, 39930, 39931, 39932, 40123, 41024. Registers for Pampanga used elsewhere were numbered 12230, 21099, 21100, 21105, 21106, 21107, 21108, 21140, 21220, 21221, 21222, 21223, 23463, 23590, 35135, 35144, 35146, 35148, 35150, 35184, 35186, 35188, 35192, 35226, 35236, 35262, 35590.

43. *M*, August 6, 1930, p. 2. Among those in Negros who answered an information questionnaire, 220 had been either straight duma'an (160) or a combination of duma'an and rice acsas (60); in contrast, only 22 sugar acsas and 15 who had been both duma'an and sugar acsas appeared in the survey. Furthermore, references to sugar acsas in the literature showed up only occasionally.

44. Richard John Gilbert, "The Introduction of American Capital into the Sugar Industry of the Philippines and Its Impact on the Pre-Existing Patterns of Land" (M.A. thesis, University of Hawaii at Manoa, 1967), p. 82; *PFP*, September 11, 1926, p. 36; *SN* 2 (1920): 486; 6 (1925): 641; 7 (1926): 38; *M*, April 6, 1926, p. 3; BIA, File 26782, incl. 5-B.

45. John T. Omohundro, *Chinese Merchant Families in Iloilo: Commerce and Kin in a Central Philippine City* (Quezon City and Athens, Ohio: Ateneo de Manila University Press and Ohio University Press, 1981), pp. 18–19; *SN* 7 (1926): 747–48; 15 (1934): 103; *M*, May 21, 1926, p. 4; *PFP*, September 9, 1922, p. 9; August 28, 1926, p. 28; July 29, 1932, p. 29; Annual Report of Stockholders by the Board of Directors of the Philippine National Bank, for the year ending 1925, QP; *Notarios*, Negros Occidental, Pampanga, PNA. Three smaller banks giving agricultural credit

were Bank of the Philippine Islands, Luzon Surety Company, and People's Bank and Trust Company.

46. Letter from PNB President Rafael Corpus, Manila, to Manuel Quezon, Manila, March 30, 1926, QP.

47. *PFP*, September 17, 1927, p. 61.

48. *Notarios*, Pampanga, PNA; *SN* 14 (1933): 94; 15 (1934): 740–41; *TT*, September 17, 1930, p. 12; *MDB*, May 19, 1922, p. 1; interview with Mariano A. Henson, Angeles, June 5, 1964.

The cooperative system at Arayat contrasts with the one in operation at Binalbagan at about the same time. There the hacenderos simply authorized the Binalbagan, Isabela Planters Association to sell stocks of sugar for them at the best price possible with no provisions for any financing (individual contracts registered as Document 39785, *Notarios*, Negros Occidental, PNA).

49. *PFP*, June 12, 1926, p. 28; September 18, 1926, pp. 2, 26; January 1, 1927, pp. 54–55; *TT*, August 27, 1930, p. 1; letter from Paleriano Cuenco, Talisay, to Manuel Quezon, Manila, February 4, 1925; letter from Jose Ramos, President of the Bacolod-Murcia Planters Association, Manila, to the Board of Directors, PNB, Manila, August 2, 1929, QP; *M*, July 8, 1932, p. 1; *SN* 14 (1933): 155; 15 (1934): 610.

50. Letter from W. B. Charles, Bacolod, to James H. Franklin, A.B.F.M.S., New York, January 3, 1922, BMR. *Census: 1939*, 1, pt. 3, Negros Occidental, pp. 33–38.

51. *PFP*, January 24, 1925, p. 2.

52. *SN* 15 (1934): 177; *PFP*, April 7, 1928, p. 32. *Notarios*, Negros Occidental, PNA, detailed the loans of planters, including car loans and second mortgages. Even the truly wealthy could end up in overwhelming debt. At the time of his death, Mariano Lacson Ledesma owed about P800,000 to PNB and Bachrach Motor Company, a debt his family found virtually impossible to pay (Memorandum to PNB from Rafael Lacson, March 5, 1930, QP). As a comparison, Negros Occidental, with an expanse of 3,125 square miles, possessed 242.1 miles of first-class roads for its 1,195 autos in 1930; meanwhile, Pampanga, with an area of only 823 square miles, had 126.4 miles of first-class roads for its 729 automobiles (BIA, File 2146, incl. 99).

53. The Pampanga Carnival Supplement published as part of the April 22, 1933, issue of the *Tribune* illustrates many points about culture in Pampanga. See also *PFP*, June 26, 1920, p. 22; October 3, 1925, p. 10; January 9, 1926, pp. 12–13; *TT*, August 23, 1933, p. 8; *SN* 6 (1925), no. 6, frontispiece; *Nineteen Thirty-five Directory and Souvenir: Agricultural, Commercial, Industrial, and Professional Guidebook for the Provinces of Pampanga and Tarlac and the Cities of Manila and Baguio* (Manila: Mariano E. Samia, 1935–36), 1:16–36.

54. *SN* 10 (1929): 128–29.

55. Interview with Ramon Ramos, Bacolod, May 27, 1970.

56. Aside from the agricultural debt, no other sugar subject attracted more attention in local periodicals than labor shortages. See, for example, *SN* 1 (1920): 9; 11 (1930): 231; *PFP*, May 5, 1923, p. 11; September 21, 1929, p. 41; *M*, April 15, 1932, p. 2; *TT*, February 5, 1933, p. 12; October 20, 1933, p. 11.

57. The description of sacada life derives from in-depth interviews I conducted in Bugasong, Tibiao, and Culasi, Antique, during late June 1970 with a group of migrant workers over sixty who traveled to Negros during the central era. See also *Compilation of Committee Reports for the Fifth Annual Convention of the Philippine Sugar Association, Manila, P.I., September Twelfth to Seventeenth, 1927*, pp. 150–51; *TT*, October 4, 1931, p. 13; December 17, 1932, pp. 46–47; BIA, File 2121, incl. 15; Rafael Alunan, Plaintiff, vs Baltazar Necesito, Pio V. Autojay, and Federico Javier [contratistas], Defendants, Court of First Instance, Philippines, 22d Judicial District, Bacolod, QP; *SN* 7 (1926): 136–43, 747; 8 (1927): 981.

A duma'an from Saravia, sixty-two-year-old Leopoldo Gumayao, indicated that in the early 1920s, although he owned rice land in Capiz, Panay, he earned more going to labor for wages on Negros; however, several sacadas noted that work in Negros was much harder than in Antique. It appears that wages for sacadas went down from P0.90 to P0.60 per day after 1930, but the evidence is by no means solid, given the way contratistas kept the books for sacadas. In general, those sacadas who eventually went on their own to Negros fared much better than those who worked for a contratista (*M*, August 22, 1924, p. 4; March 11, 1932, p. 2; July 1, 1932, p. 4).

58. *SN* 10 (1929): 127–29. In general, *Sugar News* extolled the workers' benefits, while *Makinaugalingon* pointed out the numerous serious industrial accidents.

59. *SN* 5 (1924): 697. Information on sugar tenant farming in Pampanga comes mainly from an information questionnaire given to 195 casamac in 1970 in Pampanga and from Higinio D. Mendoza, "The Small Sugar Planters in Pampanga" (1928), BS; Philippine Islands, Bureau of Labor, *The Activities of the Bureau of Labor* (Manila: Bureau of Printing, 1930), pp. 119–20. See also *PAR* 18 (1925): 318; *SN* 6 (1925): 20–25; 8 (1927): 830.

60. *Census: 1939*, 1, pt. 3, Negros Occidental, pp. 4–5; pt. 4, Pampanga, p. 5, Tarlac, pp. 3–4. Total Philippine population grew from 10,314,310 in 1918 to 16,000,303 in 1939.

61. Alfred W. McCoy, "A Queen Dies Slowly: The Rise and Decline of Iloilo City," in *Philippine Social History: Global Trade and Local Transformations*, ed. Alfred W. McCoy and Ed. C. de Jesus (Quezon City: Ateneo de Manila University Press, 1982), pp. 326–46; *PFP*, March 31, 1923, pp. 4–6; May 3, 1924, pp. 4–5; August 14, 1926, p. 50; *M*, February

2, 1923–July 10, 1934; *SN* 15 (1934): 103; *TT*, May 21, 1933, p. 4; letter from W. B. Charles, Cadiz, to J. H. Franklin, A.B.F.M.S., New York, May 7, 1926; open letter from Harry W. Munger, Iloilo City, to Friends in the United States, January 10, 1934, BMR.

62. *TT*, May 24, 1930, p. 1; July 25, 1931, p. 3; *M*, December 29, 1921–January 30, 1934; *PFP*, June 23, 1923, p. 48; November 28, 1925, p. 57; December 3, 1927, p. 7; letters from May Coggins, Bacolod, to Miss McVeigh, A.B.F.M.S., New York, January 11, 1925, and February 12, 1925; letter from W. B. Charles to his home congregation, July 31, 1923, BMR; Doreen G. Fernandez, *The Iloilo Zarzuela; 1903–1930* (Quezon City: Ateneo de Manila University Press, 1978), pp. 141–63.

63. Evangelina Hilario-Lacson, *Kapampangan Writing: A Selected Compendium and Critique* (Manila: National Historical Institute, 1984), p. 55. See also Sol H. Gwekoh, *Diosdado Macapagal: Triumph over Poverty* (Manila: G and G Enterprises, 1962), pp. 20–21; *PFP*, March 25, 1922, p. 9; December 29, 1928, p. 17; *TT*, August 27, 1930–January 22, 1933; BIA, File 11764, incl. 4; *Nineteen Thirty-five Directory*, pp. 16–26.

64. *M*, August 17, 1921–June 19, 1934; *PFP*, November 17, 1923, p. 9; *TT*, May 24, 1931, p. 2; August 7, 1932, p. 12; August 26, 1932, p. 11.

65. *M*, 1920–1934; *PFP*, September 17, 1921, p. 11; December 17, 1932, 56–57; *MDB*, September 8, 1922, p. 2; Philippine Islands, Bureau of Commerce and Industry, *Commercial Handbook of the Philippine Islands, 1924* (Manila: Bureau of Printing, 1924), p. 168.

66. The participation dispute was reported in the pages of the *Tribune* (April 19, 1930–February 28, 1934), *Makinaugalingon* (February 9, 1931–April 26, 1932), *Sugar News* (vols. 11, 14, 15), and the Quezon papers. See, in particular, letter from Governor Agustin Ramos, Bacolod, to the Chief of the Executive Bureau, Manila, April 5, 1929; letter from Manuel Quezon, Manila, to Governor-general Dwight Davis, Manila, July 10, 1930; letter from Placido Mapa, Talisay-Silay Milling Co., Talisay, to Manuel Quezon, Manila, December 28, 1932; letter from Jose Escaler, President of the Agricultural Association of Pampanga, San Fernando, to Manuel Quezon, Manila, December 26, 1921, QP; *TT*, February 25, 1934, p. 8; interview with Pasudeco employee Leoncio Nucum, San Fernando, Pampanga, July 19, 1970; *SN* 11 (1930): 419–20; 14 (1933): 628–32.

67. *PFP*, March 1, 1924, pp. 2, 7; April 5, 1924, pp. 2, 7, 15; August 6, 1927, p. 28; *TT*, August 14, 1931, p. 2; Manuel Gatbonton, *Ing Candawe* (n.p.: n.p., 1933), p. 72.

68. Philippine newspapers covered Intrencherado in many articles from November 1925 to as late as the mid-1930s. Particularly useful sources included comments by former adherents Valentin Cemira, Geronimo Ragasa, Feliciano Tabligan, and Cornelio Mendoza. See also David R. Sturtevant, *Popular Uprisings in the Philippines, 1840–1940* (Ithaca,

N.Y.: Cornell University Press, 1976), chap. 8; *M*, June 21, 1927, p. 2; July 5, 1927, p. 4; *PFP*, May 21, 1927, pp. 2, 25, 27, 36–37, 40.

69. The Brender story appeared in issues of *Makinaugalingon* from July 24 to October 19, 1928. See also Alfred W. McCoy, "*Baylan*: Animist Religion and Philippine Peasant Ideology," in *Moral Order and the Question of Change: Essays on Southeast Asian Thought*, ed. David K. Wyatt and Alexander Woodside, Monograph Series, no. 24 (New Haven: Yale University Southeast Asian Studies, 1982); *PFP*, July 7, 1928, p. 28; August 18, 1928, p. 28; July 27, 1929, p. 28; *M*, April 3, 1925.

70. McCoy, "Queen," pp. 338–39; Serafin E. Macaraig, *Social Problems* (Manila: Educational Supply Company, 1929), pp. 407–8; *M*, August 4, 1922–January 8, 1926; *PFP*, October 14, 1922–May 19, 1933. Because Quezon became involved, numerous letters in his files refer to the two as well; see, in particular, letter from Angel Marin, Delegate General, KSI, Bacolod, to Manuel Quezon, Manila, October 21, 1923; letter from Rafael Alunan, Bacolod, to Manuel Quezon, Manila, December 13, 1924; letter from Representative Hermenegildo Villanueva, Bacolod, to Manuel Quezon, Manila, January 18, 1925, QP. Further information came from interview questionnaires for twenty-eight members of KSI, ten members of Mainawa-on, and three members of a smaller mutual aid society, Magbinuligay (Togetherness). Marin eventually pleaded guilty to libeling Judge Eduardo Gutierrez-David. Mainawa-on listed among its sponsors Representative Manuel Roxas, later Speaker of the House of Representatives.

71. During the era, *Makinaugalingon* and *Sugar News*, in various issues, noted at least six other mutual aid groups operating in Negros. In 1982, while visiting Kabankalan, I became acquainted with the Half Century Club, Inc., an organization that supplied P1,000 to the relatives of deceased members.

72. On the current state of private armies on Negros, see *Newsweek*, August 10, 1987, p. 44.

73. *M*, January 6, 1931–May 6, 1931; *TT*, January 9, 1931–February 28, 1931; *SN* 12 (1931): 75, 139–40. On other labor actions see McCoy, "Queen," pp. 333–44; *TT*, January 20, 1932, p. 1; *M*, November 16, 1923, p. 1; March 10, 1930, p. 1; February 23, 1931, p. 1; *PFP*, June 4, 1927, p. 28. One of the few positive results of the strike from labor's point of view was the replacement in the next governor's election of the hostile Ramos by the more neutral, rather ineffective Isaac Lacson.

74. William H. Mayfield, "The Development of Organized Labor in the Philippines" (M.A. thesis, University of the Philippines, 1956), pp. 8–10, 20–21; "The Peasant War in the Philippines," *Philippine Social Sciences and Humanities Review* 23 (June-December 1958): 379; Dante C. Simbulan, "The Socialist Movement in the Philippines" (M.A. thesis, University of the Philippines, 1961), pp. 22–28; Kenneth K. Kurihara,

Labor in the Philippines (Palo Alto, Calif.: American Council, Institute of Pacific Relations, 1945), pp. 60–63; cable from Manuel Quezon and Sergio Osmeña, Manila, to Secretary of War Henry Stimson, Washington, July 20, 1930, QP. On Tan Malacca's sojourn to the Philippines see *PFP*, August 20, 1927–September 24, 1927.

75. Kerkvliet, *Huk Rebellion*, pp. 35–51; Conrado S. Sabelino, "A Study of the Legal (or Parliamentary) Struggle of the Communist Movement in the Philippines" (M.A. thesis, University of the Philippines, 1958), pp. 18–19; Serafin E. Macaraig, *An Introduction to Sociology*, ed. Marcelo Tangco (Manila: University of the Philippines, 1948), pp. 253–55; Harlan R. Crippen, "Philippine Agrarian Unrest: Historical Backgrounds," *Science and Society* 10 (Fall 1946): 345; interview with Judge Wenceslao Ortega, Baliwag, Bulacan, June 21, 1970; interview with Ramon Permato, Baliwag, Bulacan, June 21, 1970; interview with Casto Alejandrino, Camp Crame, Quezon City, May 11, 1970; Gatbonton, *Ing Candawe*, p. 29; Philippine Islands, Bureau of Labor, *Quarterly Labor Bulletin* 4 (1922), nos. 15–16, 18–19; Katherine Mayo, *The Isles of Fear: The Truth about the Philippines* (New York: Harcourt, Brace, 1924), pp. 42–46; *PFP*, September 8, 1923, p. 9; March 15, 1924, p. 6; *TT*, June 19, 1931, pp. 1, 14; August 10, 1933, p. 14; June 10, 1934, p. 11; *Philippines Herald*, June 8, 1932.

76. *MT*, April 23, 1923, p. 4. See also *TT*, November 8, 1932, p. 2; interview with Peregrino Taruc, Camp Crame, Quezon City, June 19, 1970; interview with Ernesto V. Santos, Philippine Sugar Institute, Quezon City, June 8, 1970; *SN* 6 (1925): 182.

77. In comparison, Negros Occidental's density rose from 127 per square mile to 264, some 120 percent; however, agricultural hectarage also went up, from 110,256 to 219,436, or about 100 percent, at the same time (*Census: 1918* 1:219, 231; 3:336; *Census: 1939, Real Property*, pp. 398, 446).

78. Philippine Islands, Bureau of Labor, *Labor: Bulletin of the Bureau of Labor* 8 (March 1927): 83; Kerkvliet, *Huk Rebellion*, pp. 40–41; tenant interviews, 1964, 1970.

79. *PFP*, December 23, 1922, pp. 46, 54, 56; November 3, 1923, p. 40; November 8, 1924, pp. 44–45; interview with Pedro Rueda, Del Carmen, San Fernando, Pampanga, July 31, 1970; interview with Pedro Pelayo, Angeles, June 14, 1964; interview with Sotero Garcia, Angeles, June 21, 1964; *TT*, January 6, 1933, p. 9; August 29, 1933, pp. 1, 11; Gatbonton, *Ing Candawe*, pp. 67–68; cable from Serviliano Ibanez, Secretary General of KM, San Fernando, to Manuel Quezon, Manila, December 23, 1923, QP. Two other small antitenant associations were Sapni ning Lahi (Companions of the Race) in Magalang and Batung Maputi (White Stone) (Fausto F. Gonzalez Sioco, "The Cause of Communism in the Philippines," *Living*

Age 360 [1941]: 548–49; interview with Gregorio Briones, Angeles, November 3, 1970; interview with Gonzalo Pangilinan, Arayat, July 11, 1970).

80. Mayo, p. 43; HDP, Barrio Baliti, San Fernando, pp. 30–31.

81. *TT*, January 17, 1933–June 23, 1934; interview with Jose Santos Cuyugan, San Fernando, Pampanga, July 17, 1970.

82. *PFP*, November 5, 1927, p. 28; December 17, 1927, pp. 10–13, 60–61; October 27, 1928, p. 28; *SN* 8 (1927): 938–40; *TT*, April 24, 1930, p. 1; Macaraig, *Social Problems*, pp. 252–53.

83. *TT*, February 12, 1933, p. 13; June 2, 1933, p. 8; interview with Casto Alejandrino, Camp Crame, Quezon City, May 18, 1970.

84. Interview with Quirino Abad Santos, San Fernando, Pampanga, August 2, 1970; Ramon C. Aquino, *A Chance to Die: A Biography of Jose Abad Santos, Late Chief Justice of the Philippines* (Quezon City: Alemar-Phoenix, 1967), pp. 3–13, 33; Gutierrez, *Ninu't Ninu*, p. 36; interview with Roberto Toledo, III, Floridablanca, August 15, 1970; interview with Alfredo Ganzon, Angeles, June 5, 1964; Florence Horn, *Orphans of the Pacific, the Philippines* (New York: Reynal and Hitchcock, 1941), pp. 112–13; *PFP*, June 19, 1909, p. 12; *MT*, April 8, 1919, p. 2; June 7, 1919, p. 7; *TT*, August 5, 1932, p. 13; August 19, 1932, p. 8; Simbulan, "Socialist Movement," pp. 138–39; Directory of the Philippine Columbian Association, Pasay City, 1920; letters between Pedro Abad Santos, San Fernando, Pampanga, and Doctor Eliseo Santos, Manila, October 26, 1923; November 1, 1923, QP; *Protocolos* 1930, 1938, *Notarios* 4911, 5924, 6142, 7094, 10818, 10838, 23596, 23598, 23601, Pampanga, PNA.

85. Minutes of the Extraordinary Session of the Municipal Council of San Fernando, Pampanga, January 24, 1918, Municipal President Antonio Abad Santos presiding; miscellaneous correspondence concerning Quirino Abad Santos, August 20, 1922–December 10, 1932, QP; interview with Casto Alejandrino, Camp Crame, Quezon City, April 12, 1970; interview with Luis Taruc, Ateneo de Manila, Quezon City, June 16, 1970; interview with former representative Emilio Cortes, Manila, August 3, 1970; Antonio S. Tan, *The Ideology of Pedro Abad Santos' Socialist Party* (Quezon City: Asian Center, University of the Philippines, 1984), p. 3; Mariano A. Henson, *Pampanga and Its Towns (A.D. 1300–1965)*, 4th ed. (Angeles: By the Author, 1965), p. 77. I borrow the term "conventional politician," with its meaning of nonradical representative of entrenched interests, from Renato Constantino: see his *The Making of a Filipino: A Story of Philippine Colonial Politics* (Quezon City: Malaya Books, 1969), pt. 1.

86. BIA, File 7252, incls. 1–26; *PFP*, January 18, 1919, p. 9; *MT*, December 28, 1919, p. 1; Churchill, *Independence Missions*, p. 429; List of Members of the Independence Commission, August 26, 1919; letter from Pedro Abad Santos, San Fernando, Pampanga, to Manuel Quezon, Manila, July 22, 1933, QP; *Ing Catala* [The Press] (San Fernando, Pam-

panga), July 5, 1930; *TT*, July 25, 1933, pp. 1, 8; September 26, 1933, p. 11.

87. James S. Allen, *The Radical Left on the Eve of War: A Political Memoir* (Quezon City: Foundation for Nationalist Studies, 1985), p. 74.

88. Ibid., p. 81.

89. Simbulan, "Socialist Movement," pp. 28–35, 142–43; "The Huks in Retrospect: A Failed Bid for Power," *Solidarity* 102 (1985): 64–74; *SN* 8 (1927): 500; 10 (1929): 365; Uldarico S. Baclagon, *Lessons from the Huk Campaigns in the Philippines* (Manila: M. Colcol, 1956), pp. 255–60, 262–64.

90. *SN* 11–15 (1930–34); *PFP*, September 21, 1930, p. 43; *M*, April 13, 1934, p. 2; *TT*, August 25, 1931–July 1, 1934; *Annual Reports of the Philippine Sugar Association* (Manila: n.p., 1932), p. 15.

CHAPTER 6. QUOTAS

1. *TT*, May 4, 1934–May 28, 1935; *SN* 15 (1934): 527; 16 (1935): 480; 18 (1937): 116–17; *M*, July 27, 1934, p. 1; August 14, 1934, p. 1.

2. *TT*, January 6, 1935–March 12, 1937; *SN* 15 (1934): 459–63; 16 (1935): 383–84, 413, 551–52; 17 (1936): 143–44, 421–23.

3. Interview with E. D. Hester, Army and Navy Club, Manila, August 3, 1982; *TT*, December 8, 1934–March 29, 1935; *SN* 16 (1935): 63–65; 17 (1936): 325–29, 381–84; 19 (1938): 155–57; Philippine Islands, Office of the Governor-General, *Executive Orders Relative to Sugar Allocation: Issued by the Governor-General During the Year 1935*, 4 vols. (Manila: Bureau of Printing, 1936).

4. *SN* 16 (1935): 52; *TT*, May 10, 1934–January 30, 1938; John E. Dalton, *Sugar: A Case Study of Government Control* (New York: Macmillan, 1937), pp. 233–36; cable from Jorge Vargas, Manila, to Manuel Quezon, Washington, 1935; letter from Captain Bonner Fellers, Office of the President of the Philippines, Shoreham Hotel, Washington, to Creed Cox, Bureau of Insular Affairs, Washington, April 21, 1937, QP.

5. *TT*, March 6, 1935–August 8, 1937; *SN* 18 (1937): 96; 19 (1938): 56; *Report of the National Sugar Board to His Excellency the President of the Philippines*, August 2, 1939, pp. 19–21, RP; Marcial P. Lichauco, *Roxas* (Manila: Kiko, 1952), p. 114; Garel A. Grunder and William E. Livezey, *The Philippines and the United States* (Norman: University of Oklahoma Press, 1951), pp. 230–32.

6. *SN* 16–20 (1935–39); *TT*, April 19, 1936–August 13, 1940; *A Handbook of the Sugar and Other Industries in the Philippines, 1961* (Manila: Sugar News Press, 1961), p. 162; Jack T. Turner, *Marketing of Sugar*, Indiana University School of Business, Bureau of Business Research Study, no. 38 (Homewood, Ill.: Richard D. Irwin), pp. 83–88.

7. Telegram from Manuel Quezon, Manila, to Felipe Buencamino, London, April 4, 1937; telegram from Vice-president Sergio Osmeña, Washington, to President Manuel Quezon, Manila, May 26, 1939, QP; *TT*, March 5, 1939, p. 2; June 3, 1939, p. 3; Joseph Ralston Hayden, *The Philippines: A Study in National Development* (New York: Macmillan, 1942), pp. 791–96; letter from High Commissioner Paul V. McNutt, Manila, to President Franklin D. Roosevelt, Washington, June 30, 1938; letter from President Roosevelt, Washington, to High Commissioner McNutt, Manila, September 29, 1938; letter from Francis B. Sayre, Chairman, Interdepartmental Committee on Philippine Affairs, Department of State, Washington, to President Roosevelt, October 28, 1938, Box 1938, McNutt Mss., Lilly Library, Bloomington, Ind.; *International Agreement Regarding the Regulation of Production and Marketing of Sugar, London, May 6, 1937* (London: His Majesty's Stationary Office, 1937).

8. *TT*, December 29, 1938, p. 3; April 10, 1941, pp. 1, 4; November 28, 1941, p. 1; *SN* 14 (1933): 398; 15 (1934): 104; 18 (1937): 32; telegram from Joaquin M. Elizalde, Washington, to President Manuel Quezon, Manila, September 15, 1941; communication to U.S. High Commissioner Francis B. Sayre, Manila, from President Manuel Quezon, Manila, November 28, 1941, QP.

9. *TT*, September 2, 1939–December 6, 1941; *SN* 19 (1938): 327; 22 (1941): 62, 83, 313; Philippine Commonwealth, Bureau of Census and Statistics, *Journal of Philippine Statistics* 1 (1941): 59, 70. George Fairchild had extensive correspondence in 1941 with Quezon on shipping for Philippine sugar.

10. *SN* 19 (1938): 90–93, 127–29, 324–27; 20 (1939): 275–76; 21 (1940): 352; *TT*, June 11, 1937–October 2, 1940; Thomas R. McHale, "The Sugar Industry of the Philippines in the 1970s," paper presented at the PDCP-UPIEDR Lecture Series, Manila, January 20, 1970, p. 75.

11. "The actual nature of the government of the Commonwealth of the Philippines. An attempt to answer the question, is there a dictatorship in the Philippines?" Memorandum from Justice George A. Malcolm, Manila, to High Commissioner Paul McNutt, Manila, July 6, 1937, Box 1937, McNutt Mss., Lilly Library; Aruna Gopinath, *Manuel L. Quezon: The Tutelary Democrat* (Quezon City: New Day, 1987), chap. 2; Alfred W. McCoy, "Quezon's Commonwealth: The Emergence of Philippine Authoritarianism," in *Philippine Colonial Democracy*, ed. Ruby R. Paredes, Monograph Series, no. 32 (New Haven: Yale University Southeast Asian Studies, 1988). On Quezon's role in the sugar industry see letter from Governor Pablo Angeles David, San Fernando, Pampanga, to Manuel Quezon, Manila, May 27, 1937; letter from Manuel H. Javelona, Justice of the Peace, Bago, N.O., to Manuel Quezon, Manila, August 9, 1935; letter from Santiago H. Granada, Isabela, N.O. to PSA President Rafael Alunan, Manila, July 16, 1935, QP.

12. *Handbook 1961*, p. 16; *TT*, September 17, 1937–October 28, 1939; *SN* 19 (1938): 520; 20 (1939): 184–85; Gopinath, *Quezon*, p. 86; letter from Jose Yulo, President of the National Assembly, Manila, to Resident Commissioner Joaquin Elizalde, Washington, January 10, 1939; cable from Manuel Quezon, Manila, to Sergio Osmeña, Washington, January 18, 1939, QP.

13. Baldomero T. Olivera, *Jose Yulo: The Selfless Statesman* (Mandaluyong, Metro Manila: U.P.-Jorge B. Vargas Filipiniana Research Center, 1981), p. 34; *TT*, August 25, 1934–October 8, 1940; *SN* 21 (1940): 413; 22 (1941): 117.

14. Harry B. Hawes, "In the Matter of the Classification of Philippine Sugar as a 'Non-Essential' Commodity," testimony before the United States Maritime Commission, July 29, 1941 (Washington, D.C.: n.p., 1941).

15. *TT*, April 15, 1936–July 25, 1940; *M*, May 20, 1936, p. 3; November 22, 1939, p. 1; *SN* 21 (1940): 321; letters from Attorney Jose Ma. Lacson, Manila, to Manuel Quezon, Malacañan Palace, September 21, 1938, and April 17, 1939; letter from Presidential Secretary Jorge Vargas, Manila, to Enrique Montilla, Manager of Isabela Sugar Co., Manila, October 14, 1941, QP.

16. The seven largest milling interests were Ehrman-Spreckels (10.62 percent of the total U.S. quota), Ossorio (10.03 percent), Elizalde (9.94 percent), Lizares (9.88 percent), Tabacalera (9.76 percent), Montilla (8.58 percent), and Pasudeco (6.78 percent) (Yoshiko Nagano, "The Oligopolistic Structure of the Philippine Sugar Industry during the Great Depression," in *The World Sugar Economy in War and Depression, 1914–1940*, ed. Bill Albert and Adrian Graves [London: Routledge, 1988], pp. 174–75). See also *TT*, January 8, 1935–January 5,1941; *SN* 17 (1936): 32, 124; letter from M. Cuaderno, PNB, to Manuel Quezon, Manila, July 29, 1936, QP. Financier Vicente Madrigal acquired Canlubang just before the outbreak of war.

17. "Memorandum for His Excellency the President on: The Philippine Sugar Problem," RP; Francisco Varona, *Negros: historia anecdótica de su riqueza y de sus hombres* (Manila: General Printing Press, 1938), pp. 370–80; *SN* 17 (1936): 452; 18 (1937); 2, 327–28; 19 (1938): 416–17; *TT*, March 31, 1934–November 20, 1938; Florence Horn, *Orphans of the Pacific, the Philippines* (New York: Reynal and Hitchcock, 1941), pp. 137, 214, 247.

18. *TT*, February 16, 1936, p. 11.

19. Stephen A. Resnick, "A Socio-Economic Interpretation of the Decline of Rural Industry Under Export Expansion: A Comparison Among Burma, Philippines and Thailand, 1870–1938," Center Discussion Paper, no. 74, presented at the Economic Growth Center, Yale University, September 17, 1969, pp. 60–61; *SN* 16–22 (1935–41); *TT*, August 6, 1935–

October 30, 1941; *M*, April 28, 1937, p. 1; July 15, 1939, p. 1; February 10, 1940, p. 1; Modesto P. Sa-onoy, *Valderrama* (Bacolod: Negros Occidental Historical Commission, 1979), pp. 30–41; Karl J. Pelzer, *Pioneer Settlement in the Asiatic Tropics* (New York: American Geographical Society, 1948), pp. 135–41. Notarial registers for Negros Occidental had the following numbers: 39471, 39479, 39590, 39606, 39660, 39763, 39782, 39785, 39929, 40028, 40030, 40031, 40033, 40034, 40035. Notarial registers in Pampanga were mostly identified by notary but also included numbered registers 35188, 35190, 35192, 35262.

20. *TT*, May 12, 1935–December 31, 1940; Horn, *Orphans*, pp. 242–43; *M*, June 13, 1936–September 7, 1940; HDP, Bacolod, pp. 2, 13, 21; *SN* 17 (1936): 32, 489; letter from H. W. Munger, Fabrica, Negros Occidental, to Randolph Howard, New York, April 26, 1935; letter from H. W. Munger, Fabrica, Negros Occidental, to J. W. Decker, New York, August 16, 1941, BMR.

21. *TT*, February 27, 1934–June 9, 1941; Sol H. Gwekoh, *Diosdado Macapagal: Triumph over Poverty* (Manila: G and G Enterprises, 1962), chap. 2.

22. Philippine Islands, Department of Agriculture and Commerce, *Philippine Statistical Review* 2 (1935): 40–41, 69; Philippine Commonwealth, Department of Agriculture and Commerce, *Bulletin of Philippine Statistics* 6 (1940): 281–82; *Journal of Philippine Statistics* 1 (1941): 7–8, 59, 70; *TT*, July 8, 1939, p. 3; *SN* 21 (1940): 315; *M*, October 5, 1940, p. 2; October 24, 1940, p. 1.

23. *SN* 16 (1935): 621; 17 (1936): 339, 510; 18 (1937): 152; 22 (1941): 238; *Report of the National Sugar Board*, p. 22; Document 39590, *Notarios*, Negros Occidental, PNA; *TT*, May 18, 1937, p. 16; Horn, *Orphans*, p. 243; *M*, July 18, 1936, p. 1; April 20, 1940, p. 4.

24. *TT*, May 7, 1935, p. 1.

25. Philippine Commonwealth, Department of Labor, "Fact-finding Survey Report, 1936," typewritten (Manila: Division of Labor Statistics, Department of Labor, 1936), p. 202.

26. Kenneth K. Kurihara, *Labor in the Philippines* (Palo Alto, Calif.: American Council, Institute of Pacific Relations, 1945), p. 39; information from thirty-three 1970 questionnaire interviews with Negrense rice agsadors, most of whom had converted from sugar to rice farming in the late 1930s.

27. *SN* 18 (1937): 191–93; 19 (1938): 387; 20 (1939): 445; *TT*, October 18, 1939, pp. 1, 13; January 12, 1940, pp. 1, 13.

28. Cable from Amando Avanceña, President of the Confederation of Sugar Planters' Associations, Bacolod, to Secretary of War George Dern, Washington, September 23, 1935, QP; *SN* 16 (1935): 407–8; 18 (1937): 295; 19 (1938): 515–16; *TT*, January 22, 1935–July 14, 1940; *Honolulu Advertiser*, January 28, 1939.

29. Letter from Enrique C. Locsin, Bacolod, to Hon. Manuel Roxas, Manila, February 10, 1939, RP; letter from Manuel Quezon to Jose Yulo, Manila, February 24, 1941, QP; *TT*, January 13, 1937–September 2, 1941; *M*, May 22, 1940, p. 1; June 1, 1940, p. 1.

30. *Notarios*, Pampanga, PNA; *TT*, July 8, 1939–March 18, 1941; *M*, May 4, 1940, p. 1; interview with Luis Taruc, Ateneo de Manila University, Quezon City, June 17, 1970.

31. Information concerning events in the section on confrontation comes chiefly from the pages of the *Tribune* issues January 1935–December 1941.

32. Interviews with Casto Alejandrino, Camp Crame, Quezon City, April 5 and 12, 1970; Luis Taruc, *Born of the People* (New York: International, 1953), pp. 40–45, 84; *TT*, June 22, 1935–March 29, 1938.

33. *SN* 16 (1935): 296; *M*, August 22, 1936, p. 1; July 27, 1940, p. 3; interview with Luis Taruc, Ateneo de Manila University, Quezon City, June 16, 1970; HDP, Barrio Baliti, San Fernando, p. 31; "Fact-finding Survey," p. 246.

34. I. T. Runes, *General Standards of Living and Wages of Workers in the Philippine Sugar Industry* (Manila: Philippine Council, Institute of Pacific Relations, 1939), pp. 29–30.

35. *TT*, October 4, 1934, p. 3; "Fact-finding Survey," p. 239; *M*, June 7, 1939, p. 3; "Annual Report of the Governor of Negros Occidental, August 28, 1939," p. 12, QP; interview with Antonio Angeles, Bacolor, July 28, 1970; interview with Eugenio Tabong, Lubao, August 13, 1970.

36. "Fact-finding Survey," p. 26; Pelzer, *Pioneer Settlement*, pp. 110–14; Varona, *Negros*, pp. 391–94; Benedict J. Kerkvliet, *The Huk Rebellion: A Study of Peasant Revolt in the Philippines* (Berkeley and Los Angeles: University of California Press, 1977), pp. 35–36; Frederick L. Wernstedt, "Agricultural Regionalism on Negros Island, Philippines" (Ph.D. dissertation, University of California at Los Angeles, 1953), p. 212; *M*, December 23, 1939, p. 1; *Notarios*, 39660, 39763, 40028, 40030, Negros Occidental, PNA; letter from Santiago Diego, Isabela, Negros Occidental, to Secretary of Finance Manuel Roxas, Manila, June 18, 1940, RP.

37. Letter from Governor Pablo Angeles David, San Fernando, Pampanga, to Manuel Quezon, Manila, October 11, 1935, QP, p. 239; Kerkvliet, *Huk Rebellion*, p. 37; "Fact-finding Survey," pp. 13–14.

38. *SN* 7 (1926): 284–85.

39. *M*, December 2, 1936, p. 3; March 13, 1937, p. 1; April 10, 1937, p. 5; May 6, 1939, p. 2; *SN* 19 (1938): 516; "Fact-finding Survey," p. 198.

40. *SN* 20 (1939): 109, 254; interview with Eugenio Pangilinan, Angeles, July 24, 1970; interview with Juan Dalusung, Angeles, July 21, 1970; Kerkvliet, *Huk Rebellion*, p. 43. Both Judge Hermogenes Reyes and Judge Jose M. Paredes actually passed favorably on tenant cases (*TT*, March 18, 1938, p. 16; February 6, 1941, p. 1; Gerardo Castro vs. Fausto de los Reyes,

Civil Case no. 6887, Court of First Instance, Third Judicial District, January 24, 1941, QP).

41. Interview with Casto Alejandrino, Camp Crame, Quezon City, May 11, 1970; Philippine Commonwealth, President, 1935–1944 (Quezon), *Speech of His Excellency, Manuel L. Quezon, President of the Philippines on New Deal for the Laboring Classes in the Philippines (Delivered before a mass gathering of farm laborers and tenants at San Fernando, Pampanga, February 14, 1939).*

42. Interview with Luis Taruc, Ateneo de Manila University, Quezon City, June 17, 1970; *SN* 22 (1941): 231; Harlan R. Crippen, "Philippine Agrarian Unrest: Historical Backgrounds," *Science and Society* 10 (Fall 1946): 352–53.

43. *M*, January 3, 1940–March 16, 1940; *SN* 21 (1940): 107, 368, 551–52.

44. Interviews with four former sacadas and one cabo, Bugasong and Culasi, Antique, June 26–29, 1970.

45. Interviews with five former rice agsadors, Binalbagan and Isabela, June 10–25, 1970.

46. Alfred W. McCoy, "A Queen Dies Slowly: The Rise and Decline of Iloilo," in *Philippine Social History: Global Trade and Local Transformations*, ed. Alfred W. McCoy and Ed. C. de Jesus (Sidney: Allen and Unwin, 1982), pp. 338–44.

47. "Fact-finding Survey," pp. 84–97.

48. U.S. Department of State, *Joint Preparatory Committee on Philippine Affairs: Report of May 20, 1938*, Publication 1216, Conference Series 36, 3 vols. in 4 wraps (Washington, D.C.: Government Printing Office, 1938), 3:888.

49. Alfredo B. Saulo, *Communism in the Philippines: An Introduction* (Quezon City: Ateneo de Manila University, 1969), p. 34.

50. James S. Allen, *The Radical Left on the Eve of War: A Political Memoir* (Quezon City: Foundation for Nationalist Studies, 1985), pp. 47–49; "The Huks in Retrospect: A Failed Bid for Power," *Solidarity* 102 (1985): 99–103; interview with Luis Taruc, Ateneo de Manila University, Quezon City, June 16, 1970; Kerkvliet, *Huk Rebellion*, pp. 51–53.

51. Taruc, *Born of the People*, pp. 33–46; *PN*, April 8–14, 1978, p. 2; Uldarico S. Baclagon, *Lessons from the Huk Campaign in the Philippines* (Manila: M. Colcol, 1960), pp. 270–71.

52. Letter from Mayor Agapito del Rosario, Angeles, to Manuel Quezon, Manila, July 30, 1941, QP; interview with Tiago Santiago, Floridablanca, August 14, 1970.

53. Antonio S. Tan, *The Ideology of Pedro Abad Santos' Socialist Party* (Quezon City: Asian Center, University of the Philippines, 1984); David R. Sturtevant, *Popular Uprisings in the Philippines, 1840–1940* (Ithaca, N.Y.: Cornell University Press, 1976), pp. 249–51; *M*, July 19,

1939, p. 1; Horn, *Orphans*, pp. 112–113; William J. Duiker, *The Communist Road to Power in Vietnam* (Boulder, Colo.: Westview, 1981), pp. 26–28.

54. Catherine Porter, *Crisis in the Philippines* (New York: Knopf, 1942), pp. 50–53; Dapen Liang, *Philippine Parties and Politics: A Historical Study of National Experience in Democracy* (San Francisco: Gladstone, 1970), pp. 227–34; Dante C. Simbulan, "The Socialist Movement in the Philippines" (M.A. thesis, University of the Philippines, 1961), pp. 35–37.

55. Allen, *Radical Left*, pp. 76–80; Tan, *Ideology*, pp. 26–28; Horn, *Orphans*, p. 87; *Philippine Statistical Review* 2 (1935): 220.

56. "Fact-finding Survey," p. 54.

57. Gopinath, *Quezon*, p. 93.

58. *SN* 18 (1937): 135; 19 (1938): 390; 20 (1939): 251–52, 259, 425–29; *M*, July 12, 1939, p. 2; July 15, 1939, p. 2.

59. Veto Message of Manuel Quezon to the Members of the National Assembly, June 21, 1941, QP.

60. Letter from Jose A. de Jesus, Private Secretary to President Quezon, Manila, to Governor Sotero Baluyut, San Fernando, March 25, 1940; letter from Jose A. de Jesus, Private Secretary to President Quezon, Manila, to District Engineer Arturo Nitorreda, San Fernando, January 27, 1941; letter from Angel Morales, Municipal President, Lubao, to Mrs. Aurora Quezon, Manila, March 19, 1937; letter from Division Superintendent of Schools Venancio Trinidad, San Fernando, to Mrs. Aurora Quezon, Manila, October 24, 1939; Memorandum from Antonio K. Abad, Manila, to Mrs. Aurora Quezon, Manila, February 20, 1941; Extract of the Minutes of the Ordinary Session Celebrated by the Municipal Council of Arayat, Pampanga, April 15, 1939, QP; Kerkvliet, *Huk Rebellion*, pp. 55–58; Michael P. Onorato, "Some Views on the Quezon Manuscript Collection in Manila," *Philippine Studies Newsletter* 16 (March 1988): 13.

61. Confidential Memorandum from Justice Jose P. Laurel, Baguio, to Manuel Quezon, Baguio, May 31, 1941; Memorandum from Secretary of Labor Leon Guinto, Manila, to Manuel Quezon, Manila, May 23, 1941; cablegram from Governor Sotero Baluyut, San Fernando, to Manuel Quezon, January 1, 1938, QP; *TT*, February 21, 1939, p. 2; April 9, 1939, p. 32; June 19, 1941, p. 16; *M*, October 24, 1940, p. 1; Sturtevant, *Uprisings*, pp. 249–51.

62. Conference between His Excellency, the President, and Mr. Wilkins of the *Bulletin*, February 9, 1939, QP; *SN* 18 (1937): 345–48; 21 (1940): 44–45.

63. McCoy, "Quezon's Commonwealth," p. 123; Gopinath, *Quezon*, chap. 2.

64. *TT*, February 6, 1938, magazine section, p. 42.

65. *SN* 18 (1937): 336, 400; 20 (1939): 536–37; *TT*, January 14, 1941, p. 12; February 7, 1941, p. 9; February 12, 1941, p. 8; interview with Pablo Gonzales, Prado, Lubao, August 18, 1970; interview with Mateo Vitug, San Isidro, Lubao, August 13, 1970.

66. *TT*, February 18, 1941, p. 2; interview with Federico Villaforte, Pulupandan, June 15, 1970; Uldarico S. Baclagon, *They Chose to Fight: The Story of the Resistance Movement on Negros and Siquijor Islands* (Quezon City: Capitol, 1962), pp. 2–3; Higinio de Uriarte, *A Basque among the Guerrillas of Negros* (Bacolod City: Civismo Weekly, 1962), pp. 18–22; *PN*, April 7–13, 1979, p. 4.

67. Correspondence of Manuel Quezon, Bais, Negros Oriental, February 26, 1942 to March 13, 1942, QP; Manuel Luis Quezon, *The Good Fight* (New York: Appleton-Century, 1946), p. 288.

EPILOGUE

1. Thomas R. McHale, "The Sugar Industry of the Philippines in the 1970s," paper presented at the PDCP-UPIEDR Lecture Series, Manila, January 20, 1970, pp. 80–86; Teodoro A. Agoncillo, *The Fateful Years: Japan's Adventure in the Philippines, 1941–1945*, 2 vols. (Quezon City: R. P. Garcia, 1965), 2: 524–31; Benedict J. Kerkvliet, *The Huk Rebellion: A Study of Peasant Revolt in the Philippines* (Berkeley and Los Angeles: University of California Press, 1977), chap. 3; Higinio de Uriarte, *A Basque among the Guerrillas of Negros* (Bacolod: Civismo Weekly, 1962), chap. 2.

2. Minutes of the Meeting of Sugar Planters Held at the Cosmos Building, Bacolod City, on May 24, 1943, at 10 A.M., QP; Uldarico S. Baclagon, *They Chose to Fight: The Story of the Resistance Movement in Negros and Siquijor Islands* (Quezon City: Capitol, 1962), chaps. 9–10; Uriarte, *Basque*, chaps. 16–20; Donn V. Hart, "Guerrilla Warfare and the Filipino Resistance on Negros Island in the Bisayas, 1942–1945," *Journal of Southeast Asian History* 5 (March 1964); Hawaiian Philippine Company, Map of Portions of the Silay-Saravia Cadastre, Negros Occidental, Philippines, Showing the Status of Property within the Company's District—Revised February 4, 1949 (Honolulu).

3. Alfred W. McCoy, " 'Politics by Other Means': World War II in the Western Visayas, Philippines," in *Southeast Asia Under Japanese Occupation*, ed. Alfred W. McCoy, Monograph Series, no. 22 (New Haven: Yale University Southeast Asian Studies, 1980), pp. 191–206; Philippine Republic (Japanese Occupation), Department of Interior, *Speech Delivered by the Commissioner of the Interior, Honorable Benigno S. Aquino, Before the Officers of the USAFFE in Camp Stotsenburg, Pampanga on July 31, 1942*; Baldomero T. Olivera, *Jose Yulo: The Selfless Statesman* (Mandaluyong, Metro Manila: U.P.-Jorge B. Vargas Filipini-

ana Research Center, 1981), chaps. 19–25; Nick Joaquin, *The Aquinos of Tarlac: An Essay on History as Three Generations* (Mandaluyong, Metro Manila: Cacho Hermanos, 1983), chap. 6; Luis Taruc, *Born of the People* (New York: International, 1953), p. 58; *PN*, January 16–22, 1975, p. 11; William Alexander Sutherland, *Not by Might: The Epic of the Philippines* (Las Cruces, N.M.; Southwest, 1953), p. 94.

4. Erich H. Jacoby, *Agrarian Unrest in Southeast Asia*, 2nd ed. (London: Asia Publishing House, 1961), pp. 227–32; Shirley Jenkins, *American Economic Policy Toward the Philippines* (Stanford: Stanford University Press, 1954), chaps. 4–7.

5. McHale, "Sugar Industry," pp. 87–95; Carlos Quirino, *History of the Philippine Sugar Industry* (Manila: Kalayaan, 1974), pp. 58–69, 135–36; Yoshiko Nagano, "Philippine Sugar Industry in the Export-Oriented Economy—A Thorny Road to Modernization," paper submitted to the Third World Studies Program, University of the Philippines, August 10, 1978, pp. 13–17; Olivera, *Jose Yulo*, pp. 166–68.

6. Quirino, *History*, pp. 137–45; Olivera, *Jose Yulo*, chap. 31.

7. Kerkvliet, *Huk Rebellion*, chaps. 5–7; Taruc, *Born of the People*, pp. 212–77; Alfred W. McCoy, "A Queen Dies Slowly: The Rise and Decline of Iloilo," in *Philippine Social History: Global Trade and Local Transformations*, ed. Alfred W. McCoy and Ed. C. de Jesus (Sidney: Allen and Unwin, 1982), p. 345; *PN*, November 13–19, 1976, p. 13.

8. Antonio Ledesma, Gerry Bulatao, Nini Abarquez, Felix Pasquin, and Rufino Suplido, eds., *Liberation in Sugarland: Readings on Social Problems in the Sugar Industry* (Manila: KIBAPIL, 1971), pp. 55–65.

9. Nagano, "Thorny Road," p. 10; Gary Hawes, *The Philippine State and the Marcos Regime: The Politics of Export* (Ithaca, N.Y.: Cornell University Press, 1987), p. 91.

10. Rosalinda Pineda-Ofreneo, "The Philippine Sugar Crisis in an International Setting," *Journal of Contemporary Asia* 15 (1985): 465; Hawes, *Marcos Regime*, p. 176; interview with Hacendero Allan Gamboa, Bacolod, August 11, 1973; Norman W. Schul, "Changing Land Use in a Western Negros Sugar Cane District," paper given at the First Annual Conference of the Philippine Studies Association, Western Michigan University, May 25–June 1, 1980, pp. 12–13.

11. Nagano, "Thorny Road," pp. 17–18.

12. Howard M. Leichter, *Political Regime and Public Policy in the Philippines: A Comparison of Bacolod and Iloilo Cities*, Special Report, no. 11 (DeKalb, Ill.: Northern Illinois University Center for Southeast Asian Studies, 1975), pp. 45–49; interview with Father Henares and Brother Armand, La Salle High School, Bacolod, July 28, 1973; interview with Brother Daniel Ortiz, La Salle College, Bacolod, August 11, 1973; *Far Eastern Economic Review*, June 24, 1974, p. 70; *PN*, December 13–19, 1973–September 10–16, 1977; Maria Vida P. Ventura-Dacumos, "Study

of Elites in a Modernizing Community: Three Approaches in the Study of Community Power Structure" (M.A. thesis, University of the Philippines, 1970).

13. Ledesma et al., *Liberation*, pp. 71–78, 81–87. See also Frank Lynch, S.J., *A Bittersweet Taste of Sugar: A Preliminary Report on the Sugar Industry in Negros Occidental* (Quezon City: Ateneo de Manila University Press, 1970); *The Sugar Workers of Negros* (n.p.: Association of Major Religious Superiors in the Philippines, 1975); Dennis Shoesmith, ed., *The Politics of Sugar: Studies of the Sugar Industry in the Philippines*, People Monograph, no. 1 (Frankton, Australia: Asian Bureau Australia, 1977); *Pahayag* (Honolulu), March–April 1977, pp. 9–11; Filomeno V. Aguilar, Jr., *The Making of Cane Sugar: Poverty, Crisis and Change in Negros Occidental*, La Salle Monograph Series, no. 2 (Bacolod: La Salle Social Research Center, 1984).

14. *Action Now* 1, no. 44 (October 18, 1969). See also Violeta Lopez-Gonzaga, *The Sacadas of Negros: A Poverty Profile*, Research Notes Series, no. 1 (Bacolod: La Salle Social Research Center, 1984), p. 10; idem, *The Sugarcane Workers in Transition: The Nature and Context of Labor Circulation in Negros Occidental* (Bacolod: La Salle Social Research Center, 1985), pp. 2–3; interview with Alan Gamboa, Bacolod, August 11, 1973; Yoshiko Nagano, *Share Tenancy and Landless Rural Workers: Reflections on the Feudalism and Capitalism Debate*, The Philippines in the Third World Papers Series, no. 40 (Quezon City: Third World Studies Center, University of the Philippines, 1984), pp. 18–33. Scott Guggenheim, at the Third World Studies Center, University of the Philippines, on August 12, 1982, noted that sacadas from Negros Occidental now cut cane in and around Tuguegarao, Cagayan, in northern Luzon.

15. *Philippine Sugar Handbook, 1972 Edition* (Manila: Sugar News Press, 1972), p. 80 foldout; Yoshiko Nagano, "Philippine Sugar Economy in Crisis: Views from the Center and the Periphery," *Philippine Journal of Industrial Relations* 8 (1986): 106–9; Ponciano Intal, Cristina David, and Gerald Nelson, "Philippine Economic Policies and Agricultural Development: A Review and an Agenda for the Future," paper given at the Seminar on Economic Development in the Philippines: Analysis and Perspectives, School of Economics, University of the Philippines, December 5–6, 1985, p. 26; David Reinah, "Philippine Sugar Industry Market Considerations and United States Policy," in *Rebuilding a Nation: Philippine Challenges and American Policy*, ed. Carl H. Landé (Washington, D.C.: Washington Institute Press, 1987), pp. 144–51; Pineda-Ofreneo, "Sugar Crisis," pp. 466–68.

16. Emmanuel S. de Dios, ed., *An Analysis of the Philippine Economic Crisis: A Workshop Report* (Quezon City: University of the Philippines Press, 1984), pp. 42–49; *Fortune*, February 1977, pp. 106–14; Charles C. McDougald, *The Marcos File: Was He a Philippine Hero or a Corrupt*

Tyrant? (San Francisco: San Francisco Publishers, 1987), pp. 233–38; Hawes, pp. 94–99; *Philippine Times* (Chicago), December 10, 1979, p. 5; *Buffalo News*, February 5, 1984, p. 1; *Far Eastern Economic Review*, October 3, 1980, p. 37; April 18, 1985, pp. 60–63; Pineda-Ofreneo, "Sugar Crisis," pp. 461–63; Reinah, "Market Considerations," pp. 141, 143–45, 152; interview with Father Edgar Saginsin, La Carlota, August 11, 1973; interview with Carlos Ledesma, Makati, March 12, 1986; George C. Abbott, *Sugar* (London: Routledge, 1990).

17. Interview with Attorney Johnny Hagad, Offices of Hilado and Hilado, Bacolod, November 5, 1982; interview with Joe Dureza, Bacolod, November 4, 1982; Violeta Lopez-Gonzaga, *Crisis in Sugarlandia: The Planters' Differential Perceptions and Responses and Their Impact on Sugarcane Workers' Households* (Bacolod: La Salle Social Research Center, 1986), chap. 3. One planter described Benedicto's credit stranglehold through the RPB as having the hacenderos "by the eggs" (interview with Juvy Dianongco, Kabankalan, November 6, 1982).

18. Nagano, "Crisis," pp. 111–13; *Philippine Sugar Handbook, 1972 Edition*, p. 18; "A Preliminary Study on the Sugar Centrals in Mindanao," *Mindanao Focus* 3 (January 1986): 4–24; Alfred W. McCoy, "Rural Philippines: Technological Change in the Sugar Industry," in *The Philippines after Marcos*, ed. R. J. May and Francisco Nemenzo (London and Sydney: Croom Helm, 1985), pp. 175–90.

19. Violeta Lopez-Gonzaga, *Crisis and Poverty in Sugarlandia: The Case of Bacolod*, Monograph Series, no. 3 (Bacolod: La Salle Social Research Center, 1985), chap. 2; *PN*, February 5–11, 1977, p. 2.

20. Realidad Santico-Rolda, "The Capampangan Changing Life Styles: A Case Study," in *Seven Probes in Rural South East Asia: Socio-Economic and Anthropological*, ed. Barend Jan Terwiel (Gaya, Bihar: Centre for South East Asian Studies, 1979), pp. 51–63; *PN*, January 15–21, 1977–August 5–11, 1978; *Bulletin Today*, July 18, 1982, p. 2; *Asiaweek*, December 3, 1982, p. 47.

21. Conrado F. Estrella, *Philippine Report: Agrarian Reform in the New Society* (Manila: By the Author, 1974), pp. 129–93; interview with Gerry Rodriguez, General Manager of Pasudeco, San Fernando, March 11, 1986.

22. *PN*, March 14–20, 1974–May 20–26, 1978; "Preparing for Revolution in the Philippines: The United Front in the Philippines," *Southeast Asia Chronicle* 62 (May-June, 1978): 14–16; *New York Times*, November 23, 1965, p. 14; Richard J. Kessler, *Rebellion and Repression in the Philippines* (New Haven: Yale University Press, 1989).

23. Interviews with Gerry Rodriguez, March 11, 1986; Alfredo Arrastia, Pasudeco, March 11, 1986; interview with Gloria and Dan Deegan, members of Samahan Ngayon Dampe, Floridablanca, April 3, 1992; *PN*, November 28–December 4, 1974, p. 12.

24. Interview with Edgardo Yap, Executive Vice-president, Philippine Sugar Association, Makati, March 12, 1986; interview with Sister Milagros Dayrit, on flight between Bacolod and Manila, March 14, 1986; *New York Times*, October 18, 1987, p. 20.

25. *PN*, July 29–August 4, 1978, p. 3; *Philippine Daily Inquirer*, March 8, 1986, p. 16; *Ang Pahayagang Malaya* (Manila), March 15, 1986, p. 12; *Wall Street Journal*, April 3, 1986, pp. 1, 10; *Asiaweek*, April 12, 1986, p. 26; *Star* (Kuala Lumpur), June 27, 1987, p. 13; *New Straits Times* (Kuala Lumpur), June 29, 1987; "The Negros Enigma," *Diliman Review* 34 (1988), no. 4, 14–20; John A. Larkin, "Father Gore Faces Murder, Gun Charges," *National Catholic Reporter*, March 4, 1983, p. 6; Alfred W. McCoy, *Priests on Trial* (Ringwood, Victoria: Penguin Australia, 1984); Niall O'Brien, *Seeds of Injustice: Reflections on the Murder Frame-up of the Negros Nine in the Philippines* (Dublin: O'Brien Press, 1985).

26. Pineda-Ofreneo, "Sugar Crisis," p. 455; *Asiaweek*, January 28, 1988, p. 62; World Bank, *Annual Report, 1988* (Washington, D.C.: World Bank, 1988), p. 91.

27. Yoshiko Nagano, "Agrarian Reform under Aquino: A Macro-View from Negros," *Solidarity* 120 (October-December 1988): 83–90.

Index

Compositor:	Braun-Brumfield, Inc.
Text:	10/13 Aldus
Display:	Aldus
Printer:	Braun-Brumfield, Inc.
Binder:	Braun-Brumfield, Inc.